I TATTI STUDIES IN
ITALIAN RENAISSANCE HISTORY

Published in collaboration with I Tatti
The Harvard University Center for Italian Renaissance Studies
Florence, Italy

GENERAL EDITOR
Kate Lowe

ABORTION IN
EARLY MODERN ITALY

JOHN CHRISTOPOULOS

Harvard University Press

Cambridge, Massachusetts

London, England

2021

First printing

Library of Congress Cataloging-in-Publication Data

Names: Christopoulos, John, 1983- author.
Title: Abortion in early modern Italy / John Christopoulos.
Other titles: I Tatti studies in Italian Renaissance history.
Description: Cambridge, Massachusetts : Harvard University Press, 2021. |
    Series: I Tatti studies in Italian Renaissance history | Includes
    bibliographical references and index.
Identifiers: LCCN 2020017721 | ISBN 9780674248090 (cloth)
Subjects: LCSH: Abortion—Italy—History—16th century. |
    Abortion—Italy—History—17th century. | Abortion—Moral and ethical
    aspects—Italy—History. | Abortion—Religious aspects—History. |
    Abortion—Law and legislation—Italy—History.
Classification: LCC HQ767.5.I8 C57 2021 | DDC 362.1988/80094509031—dc23
LC record available at https://lccn.loc.gov/2020017721

For Avery and Sam

CONTENTS

Introduction

The Meanings of Abortion

*I*n sixteenth- and seventeenth-century Italy, women procured abortions and had them forced upon them. Single and married women, both elite and non-elite, had abortions when they believed enduring pregnancy and childbirth to be harmful: abortions were had to conceal sexual relations, avert social and material hardship that could accompany children, and alleviate potentially dangerous health issues. A variety of healers provided services and sold products to these ends. Sometimes abortion was procured intentionally through medicines and physical traumas; sometimes it was an accident, caused by unintended interventions, labors, violence, illness, or health-related complications. Sometimes abortion worked and recovery was swift; other times it didn't work and women continued their pregnancy to term; sometimes it resulted in physical harm and death, not unlike childbirth. In some circumstances, abortion was considered a sin and a crime; in others it was not. Sometimes abortion resulted in scandal, prosecution, and punishment; often it was responded to with sympathy and support—it was forgivable, acceptable, deemed necessary, and relatively unproblematic. More often than not abortion was ignored, something individuals, communities, and authorities turned a blind eye to. Despite increasingly heated rhetoric and new legislation seeking to change its meanings and regulate its practice, abortion remained widely sought, accessible, and generally tolerated. In early modern Italy, abortion was a fact of life.

These statements might surprise those who come to this book assuming that, at this time and place, abortions could not be had and therefore were not had, except by the very desperate, willing to risk life and limb. Early modern Italy was, after all, the headquarters of the Catholic Church and in the midst of an intense program of moral and social reform, commonly referred to as the Counter- or Catholic Reformation. Because the Catholic Church maintains a strict prohibition on abortion today, it is easy to assume it always has. The current *Catechism of the Catholic Church* makes such a historical argument: "Since the first century the Church has affirmed the moral evil of every procured abortion. This teaching has not changed and remains unchangeable."[1]

Indeed, current-day expectations regarding abortion in the premodern past are likely shaped by assumptions about the power of authorities and institutions, such as the Catholic Church, and the extent to which they could condition the behaviors and mentalities of their subjects. To support such an assumption, one need only read the famous and infamous declaration of Pope Sixtus V: issued in 1588, Sixtus's bull *Against those who Procure, Counsel and Consent in any way to Abortion* unconditionally prohibited induced abortion, which he defined as the "untimely death and killing" "of a soul created in the image of God" and of "children . . . before they could receive from nature their portion of light"—an "abhorrent and evil act." Sixtus declared that those procuring, administering, or assisting in abortion were automatically excommunicated from the faith and to be prosecuted by ecclesiastical and secular tribunals as "true murderers who have actually and really committed homicide."[2] For over four hundred years, theologians, scholars, and general commentators interested in the history of abortion have looked to Sixtus's bull as the foundations of modern Catholic policy on the subject.

However, people in the sixteenth century did not always believe or do what their leaders desired; nor were leaders consistent in the absolutism of their positions. Only three years after the abortion bull, the new pope Gregory XIV issued a moderation softening Sixtus's stance, which was deemed too radical and unimplementable. And the historical record is full of individuals—women and men, lay and clerical, ordinary and elite—who did not agree with the definition of abortion as an unequivocally "abhorrent and evil act." In the historical record, we find individuals who terminated their own and other women's pregnancies and refused to accept excommunication or found it irrelevant. We find communities accepting, helping, and ignoring individuals who sought and had abortions. We find authorities refusing to prosecute procurers and practitioners, or punish them as "true murderers." We will meet many of these individuals in the pages of this book.

How might we try to explain the gap between prescriptions (and popular lore) and practices surrounding abortion in the early modern past? As always, if we take the official statements of authorities as our only guides, we would believe the worlds they desired and tried to create—through legislation, other statements of "shoulds" and "musts," and threats of draconian discipline—actually existed. In doing so, we would erase the presence, agencies, and moralities of myriad individuals who made up the world, individuals who believed and acted differently. In short, we would ignore reality. When we expand our source base and adjust our methodology with the aim of recovering the thoughts, practices, and experiences of as many individuals as possible, especially women, we discover a society that is, not unlike our own, far more complicated. We see that early modern Italy was not an absolute and timeless antiabortion culture, that exemplary "Catholic Italian" and "traditional family" society some today might wish to conjure for political ends. Rather, Italians at all levels of society held many views on abortion, and their responses to its practice varied. Diverse actors were involved in the conversation, and a diverse set of ideas and concerns were being discussed and debated. Following a variety of actors—from poor rural and urban working women to aristocratic matrons, from university educated physicians and apothecaries to midwives and barbers, and from parish priests and confessors to judges and popes—reveals that sixteenth- and seventeenth-century Italians were ambivalent about abortion. By ambivalent I mean having mixed feelings, being pushed and pulled in different directions by powerful compulsions that were often at odds with each other. This book tries to understand that ambivalence. It resists the impulse to homogenize early modern society and its institutions by investigating the variety of meanings Italians gave to abortion. It asks how and why meanings were created, reproduced, modified, and challenged in theoretical discussions, statements of doctrine, policy and law, ecclesiastical and civic politics, medical practices, and everyday life. Above all, it strives to foreground women's perspectives on this topic. Then as now, there was no one response to abortion. Early modern Italians' attitudes toward and experiences of abortion were as intricate and complicated as our own.

The Politics of Reproduction

As far as we know, human beings have practiced the intentional termination of pregnancy throughout history, often putting themselves at odds with official systems of morality, religion, law and prevailing systems of gender relations. Today, abortion can dominate political discourse and news headlines around the world. The urgency of our current moment and the deep emotions felt about the subject on all sides can overwhelm and often foreclose dialogue across ethical and political lines. A historical study of abortion in another time and place allows us to step back and observe from a distance how a society both similar to and different from our own engaged the matter.[3] Many of the issues framing abortion debates today were also discussed by sixteenth- and seventeenth-century Italians, and those before them: Why do women have abortions? What control do they have over the process? How do women experience abortion and what is at stake for them? What role do men play in the abortions? What role do political, religious, legal, and medical authorities and institutions have in matters pertaining to sexual relations, reproduction, and women's bodies? What moral, social, and legal status is afforded the embryo and fetus? These questions are recognizable, but societies and cultures past and present have interpreted and answered them differently. No society, culture, religion, or state is monolithic, and these questions have elicited a vast array of viewpoints shaped by myriad factors. However, all viewpoints must be assessed against the backdrop of what appears to be a persistent demand for abortion, abundant evidence of its practice, and ongoing power struggles over women's bodies, health and reproductive rights.

Early modern Italians were thinking about and reworking the meanings of abortion as they experienced profound social and cultural change. The population of the peninsula grew consistently following the Italian Wars (1494–1559), until it was decimated by the plagues of 1629–1631 and 1656–1657. Population pressures during the late 1500s coincided with steady economic decline, inclement weather, and poor harvests, resulting in scarce resources and high-priced staples. For many, this meant the expectation and experience of hunger, malnutrition, and death. Work-related mobility increased as stable employment became harder to come by. People on the move—often male agricultural laborers and soldiers, from countryside to countryside or to growing and increasingly crowded cities—meant fragmented families, a phenomenon exacerbated by outbreaks of war and plague. Poverty seemed constantly on the rise, with women and children suffering most acutely and more visibly. Although charitable institutions multiplied, they could never meet the needs of all who required aid. Mortality rates for children appear to have been high, especially in the first year of life, due to adverse and unhygienic living conditions, malnutrition, and disease. Year by year, orphanages saw more and more abandoned children. The general situation was perceived as a major, debilitating problem affecting the moral, social, and economic health of communities, cities, and states.[4] These historical factors triggered growing feelings of precariousness and insecurity and precipitated "crisis talk" about all sorts of things, including morality, gender, and class relations. They also shaped meanings of abortion.

Against this backdrop, Italian states and the Catholic Church were engaged in entwined processes of moral, social, and institutional reform. The Catholic Church was involved in multifaceted campaigns against the threats, real and perceived, of Protestantism and other faiths in Europe, the Mediterranean, and emerging European overseas colonies. Ecclesiastical authorities were hard at work establishing Catholic doctrine, standardizing devotional practices, and reforming ecclesiastical structures. Centralizing territorial states were also committed to parallel programs of reform. Although their interests, commitments, and methods often differed, the Church and states were united in the effort to produce orthodox, pious, and disciplined subjects and societies through ideological management and institutional oversight.

Beliefs and behaviors deemed theologically problematic, immoral, and socially destabilizing were to be weeded out and replaced with newly defined ways of thinking and behaving—historians have referred to these processes linking the Church and state in programs of moral and social discipline as *confessionalization*. While ecclesiastical and secular authorities were the most visible architects of this reform, lay people— elite and common, male and female—were often equally if not more important drivers, demanding and negotiating changes in social and spiritual life, while ignoring, resisting, and even rejecting top-down impositions. Although commitments vacillated, strategies diverged, interests often conflicted, and results varied from place to place and authority to authority, in the hundred years following the closing of the Council of Trent (1563), the Church and states, communities, and individuals imagined and attempted programs that sought to make society more godly and ordered.[5]

The politics of the body, gender, and sexuality were central to the reform process. Sex outside of marriage had long been considered a root of moral decay and catalyst for social disorder. In the sixteenth and seventeenth centuries, secular and ecclesiastical authorities propagated traditional Christian positions on sexual morality and produced new precepts for the management of sexual relationships, including marital ones.[6] In sermons, the confessional, and works of devotion, women and men learned that sex was only for married couples and for the sole purpose of procreation. They learned from direct moral and religious education, published legislation, and widespread public discourse and also from experiences in secular and ecclesiastical tribunals (including the Inquisition) that fornication, rape, adultery, concubinage, clerical sexuality, bigamy, incest, sodomy, same-sex sexuality, bestiality, and other non-marital and non-reproductive sexual practices were sins and could be punishable crimes.[7] Italians also learned that intentionally induced abortion could be a gravely sinful practice: it angered God and put one's body, soul, and community in jeopardy.

Ecclesiastical authorities took the lead in trying to change mentalities toward abortion, and civic authorities followed suit. Much of the moral rhetoric on abortion produced in the sixteenth and seventeenth century assumed (or pretended) women and men did not know what it really meant—that individuals who procured or assisted in

Fig I.1 A righteous man chopping down the tree of sin. Abortion, the central branch, joins heresy, homicide, the "nefarious sin" (i.e., sodomy), adultery, incest, and other sins and crimes that a godly society is to purge.

Giacinto Manara, *Notti Malinconiche nelle quali con occasione di assistere a Condannati a morte* (Bologna: Giovanni Battista Ferroni, 1658), frontispiece. Courtesy of Special Collections, John M. Kelly Library, University of Toronto, St. Michael's College.

abortions or who tolerated the practice did so because they did not know or fully grasp its spiritual consequences—and a deluge of didactic literature and legislation sought to change that. During this heightened period of reform, the Church produced powerful and enduring discourses about abortion, sexuality, and women's bodies and disseminated them through various institutions and media. However, the messages broadcast were mixed and often contradictory. The Church did not speak with one clear or consistent voice on this matter, and neither did the state. Authorities generally agreed that abortion required regulation but debated and disagreed over what regulation meant and how to do it.

For moralists, the value of the fetus and the salvation of its soul determined the meaning of abortion.[8] A woman's womb was to be thought of and treated as the site of divine presence. God was thought to be literally at work inside a woman's body, fashioning blood and seed into a fetus and investing it with an immortal soul. Intervening in pregnancy and terminating a fetus was deemed "against nature" (*contra natura*), a contravention of God's plan and a rejection of a divine gift. Procurers of abortion and those who assisted them were, in the words of an outspoken Dominican friar, "horrendous monsters and enemies of the human race."[9] Intentionally terminating pregnancy was a sin and a crime, and both the individual who procured it, the healer who administered or facilitated it, and the society that allowed it would incur God's wrath. Authorities proposed direct and sustained religious education, created new and unprecedented legislation, and threatened increasingly harsh punishment in order to change attitudes and practices.

But there were important distinctions. At the doctrinal level, most pertinent was the gestational stage of the unborn at the time of abortion. Abortion early in pregnancy was judged less grave than it was later in gestation. Early modern Europeans understood pregnancy as a process whereby a conception developed into a human being in stages. The first stage that mattered was "formation": the level of physical development during which a conception formed essential organs and articulated limbs and assumed the recognizable form of a human being. The timing of formation was thought to depend on the fetus's sex: according to Aristotle and the Hippocratic-Galenic medical tradition, male

fetuses were formed by approximately forty days after conception; female fetuses, believed to be constitutionally colder and moister, required more time to solidify and take shape and were thought to be
formed at about eighty days. The second stage, and the most critical
from the theological perspective, was "animation" or "ensoulment": the
moment when God infused a fetus with an immortal human soul, believed to occur once it was fully formed. While acknowledging that the
exact timing for the infusion of the soul could not be known with certainty, theologians and philosophers mapped animation onto formation, and canon law officially held that animation occurred at forty
days from conception in male fetuses and eighty for female fetuses.

The "paradigm of animation" had been deeply engrained in Christian thinking since the time of Augustine and framed attitudes toward
abortion. Throughout the middle ages and into the early modern period, the orthodox and official position of the Catholic Church was
that abortion induced after animation was the destruction of a human
soul that could be baptized and enter the kingdom of heaven. (Where
that lost soul went was a matter of intense and anguished debate.) This
was considered a form of homicide. Before a conception was animated,
it was not considered a human being, so abortion preanimation was
sinful but not homicide.[10]

Delayed animation meant ambiguity. Theologians, philosophers,
and canonists conceded that, while inside a woman's body, there was no
way to know with certainty whether the conceived was male or female
and, before an obvious point, animated or not. Dating animation was
difficult because the moment of conception was always uncertain.
While the canonical position held that male fetuses were animated at
forty days from conception and female fetuses at eighty, common wisdom held first movement to be the best indicator of pregnancy and of
the transition from coagulated seeds to a fetus with a soul (a process
referred to in English as "quickening"). However, for many, a woman's
sensation of motion was too uncertain and subjective to determine
such an important matter: it put too much authority in women's embodied experience—they might miss a fetus's first movement or lie
about it. Moreover, medical authors thought that a fetus's movements
might only be discernable after about three months. This uncertainty
created a space for the practice of abortion: the earlier in pregnancy

abortion was had, the less grave its spiritual consequences. During the sixteenth century, some authorities became increasingly uncomfortable with this flexibility.

The most novel and dramatic attempt to change meanings and practices surrounding abortion was Sixtus V's aforementioned 1588 papal bull, the first ever papal law on abortion in the history of the Church. Sixtus's major introduction was to eliminate the distinction between a pre- and postanimated fetus and declare that all abortions were murder, punishable by automatic excommunication and handed over to secular authorities for capital punishment. Traditionally, bishops had spiritual jurisdiction over cases of abortion and often deputized their confessors to handle them in the secrecy of the confessional. Sixtus thought these clerics too lenient and revoked their authority over abortion, reserving its absolution to the papacy alone: to save their souls and their lives, individuals who had or participated in abortions had to seek forgiveness directly from the pope. This departure from centuries-old theoretical understandings, established doctrine, canonical tradition, and ecclesiastical practices was deemed radical and caused controversy within the Church. Clerics and theologians disagreed with Sixtus's definition of abortion and his proposed methods of regulating its practice. They also challenged his claims to exclusive authority over its absolution. Sixtus's bull was also resisted and ignored by secular authorities and ordinary women and men. Less than three years after its issuance, it was moderated by Sixtus's second successor, Gregory XIV, on grounds it was too radical, politically controversial, and practically unenforceable. In 1591, Pope Gregory XIV reinstated the canonical status quo, reaffirming the distinction between abortion pre-and postanimation and reestablishing bishops' jurisdiction to handle individual cases within their diocese. In the seventeenth century, the Church continued efforts to reform attitudes toward abortion through pastoral instruction combined with threats of punishment meant to get laity and clergy to internalize the message that abortion was a grave sin, but debate and disagreement continued around the central issues.

While ecclesiastical authorities were debating the meanings of abortion and how best to change attitudes toward its practice, civic, legal, and medical authorities were to apply themselves to its regulation. The theologically rooted belief that abortion was a form of homicide, combined with pervasive anxieties linking undisciplined sexuality and pregnancy outside of marriage with disorder, motivated civic authorities to criminalize its practice through legislation. Nonetheless, tribunals rarely investigated cases of abortion. When they did, judges did not enforce their states' abortion laws, as these were often imprecise and, as argued in Chapter 3, interpreted as symbolic statements meant to uphold moral norms rather than commitments to actively change practices.

Like their medieval predecessors, early modern civil jurists accepted the canonical distinction between pre- and postanimation abortion but debated whether the latter was equivalent to the crime of killing a human being and whether it should be prosecuted accordingly.[11] Most answered in the negative. The most influential jurists of the sixteenth and seventeenth centuries did not equate an animate fetus with a born child or abortion with homicide. For civil jurists (and perhaps the general population), "viability"—the stage at which a fetus was thought capable of living outside of a woman's body—mattered more than animation. In the sixteenth and seventeenth centuries, viability was legally set at the seventh month of gestation, before which a fetus was thought to lack the functions necessary for life and was therefore not ready for life outside the womb. Before the seventh month of gestation, a fetus was not legally considered a human being because it could not live in the world as a human being, and it was not treated as such in practice. In the civil arena, only the live birth of a fetus judged to be at least seven months gestated could influence the flow of inheritance. In the criminal arena, it was only the intentional termination of a viable fetus that could be treated as homicide. But here too was ambiguity; fetuses developed at different rates, and the boundary between a six- and an eight-month fetus was hazy.

Practically, jurists were also skeptical as to whether judges could discover—with the certainty needed for conviction—the causes of terminated pregnancies and fetal death. Even with the help of expert medical practitioners, judges struggled to distinguish the signs of spontaneous abortion (what English speakers refer to as "miscarriage") from procured abortion or of late miscarriage / stillbirth from neonaticide. Without a confession, intentionality was often impossible to determine. Jurists generally agreed that abortion was often too contentious and uncertain to be decided in a courtroom, especially when the life of the suspect could hang in the balance. In theory and in practice, jurists followed the so-called rule of lenity, also known as the principle of *in dubio pro reo*: when evidence of abortion was too ambiguous and there was no confession, the accused was to receive the more lenient penalty or none at all. Many jurists openly opposed the death penalty for abortion altogether; disciplinary and charitable labor, fines, lashings and exile were deemed more appropriate; some explicitly stated that cases of abortion were better handled in the confessional than in a courtroom.

By and large, the Church and states had to rely on medical institutions and ultimately individual practitioners to regulate the practice of abortion. As part of broader efforts to centralize medical authority and regulate the marketplace, in the sixteenth and seventeenth centuries, civic health boards increasingly legislated on abortion and threatened disciplinary measures against healers participating in it. Medical authorities officially reinforced the theological stance that abortion was sinful and tried to restrict the traffic of purgative herbs—such as savin, aristolochia, and rue—that could be used to terminate pregnancy by threatening fines and corporal punishment.[12] But many healers—from university-educated physicians to midwives, barbers, and herbalists—made a living selling products and services that could be used for abortion and did not share the Church's official stance on the practice. The demand was great and there were many suppliers. Moreover, individuals could procure abortions secretly, with or without the participation of a healer. As we will see in Chapter 1, there were diverse ways to do so, with methods and products so widely known and easily accessible that policing was impossible. Strictly regulating the practice was beyond the capability of any medical institution.

Medical regulation was also difficult because of the uncertainties surrounding generation, pregnancy, and its termination. While early modern medical practitioners embarked on intense and unprecedented study of women's anatomy, physiology, illnesses, and therapy to better understand and intervene in women's health, maximize fertility, and minimize risks in pregnancy and childbirth, they conceded that the female body continued to confound. One could not know with certainty whether a woman was pregnant, especially early in term. Signs suggesting pregnancy were also symptoms of womb-related illnesses. The cessation of menstruation, a growing belly, and the sensation of motion within it, accompanied by lactation in later months, were all indicators of pregnancy and signs of obstructed fluids and malign growths, which, if left untreated, threatened a woman's fertility and her life. The therapies used to heal women of these disorders encouraged menstruation and contractions to empty the womb of pathological obstructions and were the same therapies used to accelerate and facilitate childbirth, help expel afterbirth or a dead fetus, or terminate one in development.

The ambiguities of women's bodies created anxiety surrounding women's health and healing, but also offered opportunities for regulating reproduction. Women, too, could mistake the signs of pregnancy for those of illness, and vice versa. Interventions meant to heal could unknowingly or unintentionally terminate pregnancy: restoring menstruation could be just that or it could be and often was an early term abortion. Women and men crafted illness narratives about menstrual retention or dropsy of the womb in order to procure products to induce abortion. Medical practitioners were told to beware of such illness narratives and to scrutinize the tellers, but warnings were difficult to heed and easy to ignore. When questioned after the fact, women, men, and their healers used discourses of ambiguity to exonerate themselves from wrongdoing. Accountability and guilt were difficult to establish in cases of alleged abortion as the burden of proving cause and intention was often insurmountable. The ambiguity of their own bodies could put some women at risk, but for those seeking to terminate pregnancy, it was also a vital resource.

Even with the papal incursions at the end of the sixteenth century, the medical, theological, legal, and perhaps socially accepted consensus until the end of the seventeenth century was that the danger and spiritual gravity of abortion grew with the gestational age of the fetus, only becoming homicide after a live birth. Authorities therefore struggled with the resulting conflict: abortion had to be discouraged because it was officially sinful, but the earlier in the pregnancy, the less grave and dangerous, and the easier it was to tolerate.

But who had abortions and why? While authorities were discussing and disseminating ideas about the souls of fetuses and the monstrousness of procurers of abortion, and while they issued legislation and attempted regulation, they also had to contend with the broader social dynamics that compelled women to seek and have abortions, that drove men to force it on women, that motivated healers to participate in its practice and onlookers to help or look away. Medical, theological, and legal attitudes toward abortion were intrinsically tied to and cannot be separated from social issues. Authorities who tried to regulate abortion had to confront gender and class inequalities that shaped sexual relationships, the social politics of reproduction, and women's lives.

Discovering who had abortions and understanding their reasons is challenging. We have few sources in which individuals admit, in their own words and free from coercion, to procuring abortion and openly discuss their motivations. As such, we cannot recover a history of abortion in the way ethnographers and oral historians might. Nevertheless, an abundance of available documentation allows us to study what early modern Italians wrote and said about abortion and their experiences of it, and to contextualize these perceptions within broader social, medical, religious, and legal developments. Based on available evidence, a few claims can be made. First, there was no specific "kind" of woman who had an abortion. Women from all walks of life procured abortions at various stages in pregnancy for many reasons, and these depended on a variety of factors, including her life circumstances, where she fit in society, what the pregnancy meant to her, and how she imagined her future. Sometimes women had no say in the matter: abortions were forced upon them by more powerful others, including the men responsible for the pregnancy, parents, and other familiars. Women had and were forced to have abortions to alleviate social, material, and physical hardships that pregnancy and children could bring or exacerbate. This included pregnancies generated from problematic relationships or relationships that became problematic because of a pregnancy. Women also had abortions for health reasons, where the termination of pregnancy was thought to be therapeutic or a consequence of medical interventions deemed necessary. Motivations and causes were not mutually exclusive.

Aside from these general observations, what we can recover more concretely from a variety of primary sources are some of the ways abortion was represented and, in particular, how it was gendered and classed. Two main discursive framings can be discerned regarding the kinds of women who were characterized as procuring abortions or for whom abortions were procured. In much moralizing literature, abortion was represented as a practice of promiscuous and opportunistic single women seeking to evade the consequences of their actions. The assumption that women were by nature lusty, irresponsible, and physically and intellectually weak ran deep in early modern Italian and broader European and Christian world views. It was claimed that women had an inordinate and dangerous appetite for sex and were unable to foresee and deal with its consequences, a discourse used to justify patriarchy. A further assumption was that women had abortions when they were pregnant from extra-marital sex and were unable to marry their lovers. Sexually irresponsible women who found themselves pregnant were assumed to acquire materials and knowledge from other sinful women; midwives were assumed to be expert in the arts of abortion, as were prostitutes and pimps, because this knowledge was thought necessary to their livelihoods. In this framing, women were depicted as autonomous sexual agents and abortion as a way of concealing sexual transgression: it was women's weaknesses and immorality that were responsible for the problem of abortion.

A second competing and contradictory framing represented abortion as a practice of vulnerable and victimized women. Moving from moralistic works of prescription to descriptive sources like trial records, which contain women's own voices on this subject, reveals that abortion was often depicted as a practice of young, abandoned, widowed, and poor women, for whom pregnancy threatened life and limb; women who were coerced into sexual relationships with false promises of marriage or economic support; and women who were sexually exploited or subjected to sexual violence. Moreover, many sources depict abortion as something men forced upon women they impregnated. In this framing, women were represented as victims and abortion as a desperate and dangerous intervention they felt compelled to undertake or that was forced upon them, often against their will.

In sum, commentators imagined and perhaps wished for only two possibilities: women had abortions because they were sinful or because they were victims. Abortion was a practice of sexually promiscuous or perpetually imperiled beings. While they carried fundamentally different moral, social, and legal implications, both framings applied stereotypically gendered interpretations to the practice, along with

essentialist understandings of women's "nature." Such framings rested
on the assumptions that abortion was a problem stemming from undisciplined sexuality, both women's and men's, that the female body
was its cause and, therefore, also the cause of broader moral and social
turpitude. The regulation of sexuality and women's bodies became in-
tegral parts of reform schemes put in place to create moral and social
order.

In theory, female confinement provided a convenient solution for
dealing with the connected problems of non-marital sex and social disorder, out-of-wedlock pregnancy and female poverty. Keeping single
women indoors, the logic went, lessened the chances of sexual misad-
ventures and assault, and pregnancy outside of marriage, thus elimi-
nating motivations for abortion and infanticide, and alleviating the
unending stream of abandoned children flooding orphanages and
draining resources. While elite single women might be kept in monas-
teries until they married or were permanently enclosed in them as nuns,
poor and laboring single women from fragmented families could seek a
place within charitable institutions run by religious orders and lay con-
fraternities to safeguard women's bodies and souls. There was a persistent fear that women turned to prostitution when they could not sustain themselves by other means. The stated mission of many of the
women's shelters that proliferated in the sixteenth and seventeenth centuries was to prevent vulnerable young women from entering—or being
forced into—this life of sin and hardship and to rehabilitate those who
had. Conservatories throughout Italy fed the bodies of "poor little virgins" and tried to preserve "the innocence of those bodies from wicked
men," as well as from older women who might coerce them into a life of
prostitution.[13] Other shelters focused on older women who had already
succumbed and those who had experienced various hardships that put
them at high risk of succumbing to prostitution: shelters for women
who wanted to renounce the trade or had suffered in abusive marriages
were established throughout the peninsula. Some of these institutions
were meant to provide temporary shelter, others more permanent; some
provided girls and women with gifted or earned dowries to marry; some
offered repose from hardship in exchange for labor; some prepared
women to enter domestic service and sometimes convents, where they
might take orders and become brides of Christ.[14]

While the stated purpose of these institutions was to protect vulnerable women from the dangers of society, it was also clear they were meant to protect society by emptying it of them. Enclosures protected men from seductive and desperate female bodies, and honorable women from being corrupted through exposure to the sights and sounds of prostitution or coerced into entering this life of sin. Although no custodial institution was ever hermetically sealed, and even the strictest ones remained porous, a woman seeking the aid of such shelters had to cut ties to her community, friends, and family (including her children) and submit to institutional supervision, for her own good and that of society at large. The drive to help and protect poor, vulnerable, and exploited women was inseparable from religious and secular ideals regarding sexual morality and anxieties over women's bodies, gender relations, and social order.

Of course, the vast majority of single women did not live in shelters, nor did society really intend them to. Many households depended on their young women's productive bodies too much to give them to conservatories, and others could not afford the monthly fees they charged for room and board. Some women patronized these institutions for a brief period, others never considered it, and some were turned away and denied support. Nevertheless, while institutional interest in and repressive effects on women's lives should not be overestimated, the discourse that linked single womanhood and poverty with sexual exploitation, pregnancy, abortion, infanticide, and physical and spiritual ruin was powerful. Pervasive rhetoric and personal experiences taught that the world could be a dangerous place for non-elite single women, young and old. Predatory and violent men lurked in the streets, markets, piazzas, even the churches of bustling cities and small towns and targeted single women.[15] Women took risks as they crossed, fraternized, and flirted with these men, and especially when they engaged in non-marital sex. Their world was portrayed, perceived, and often experienced as full of perils. For many women, pregnancy could make an already difficult life disastrous—and abortion a practical solution to at least some of life's hardships.

Although rhetoric on sexual morality and abortion was heavily directed toward women, it was widely and openly acknowledged that men's sexual misconducts often lay at the heart of the issue. In practice, communities and secular and ecclesiastical authorities sought to regulate the practice of abortion by disciplining the desires and behaviors of men, lay and clerical, elite and common, single and married.[16] Abortion was often gendered, both indirectly and directly, as a man's crime. Indirectly, men's sexual misconducts and abuses created situations where women felt compelled to have abortions. Directly, men asked, coerced, and physically forced the women they impregnated to have abortions. In early modern Italy, men were often the primary agents and beneficiaries of abortion, and often the ones held responsible for its practice.

Italian cities were full of bachelors and men living apart from their wives and families, and their sexual behaviors were matters of communal and institutional concern. In the sixteenth and seventeenth centuries, men generally married in their late twenties or thirties. Some never married, others did not remarry after their wives died. Elite families often restricted marriage to the firstborn son in order to consolidate family assets. In this scheme, a preferred strategy was to place non-inheriting sons into the Church, where they could climb the ecclesiastical hierarchy to lucrative and powerful positions. The Church was also a promising career path for non-elite men: seminaries often reserved spots for the sons of the poor, and families could count on many short- and long-term benefits of sons in the clergy. Clerics of various sorts represented a substantial portion of the overall male population, one that was, especially following the Council of Trent, unconditionally prohibited from engaging in sexual relations. War, migratory labor, and transpeninsular and transnational commerce put scores of men on the move, many of whom never returned home, resulting in dislocated and fragmented families. All these factors shaped demography and social, gender, and sexual relations in important ways. Extended and permanent bachelorhood, widespread clerical ordination, and men living apart from their wives and communities did not mean abstinence. Men formed short- and long-term intimate and sexual relationships, and bartered for and forced sex upon a variety of women. Male migration also meant the women left behind were exposed to sexual opportunities with other men—some desired and consensual, others coerced and forced. Widespread non-marital sex resulted in a high incidence of pregnancy and the practice of abortion or, when this failed or was not attempted, in increasing numbers of illegitimate children, many of whom were given to orphanages. It could also lead to infanticide.

While communities and authorities were genuinely concerned with the problems undisciplined male sexuality posed to social order and morality, they also knew solutions were difficult to formulate and enforce. Enclosing single men was never an option. In a paradigmatic case of inconsistency between moral ideals and reality, transactional sex with "dishonorable" women was viewed as the preferred way for men to satisfy sexual desires outside of marriage. Although prostitutes were both blamed for the ills of the times and seen as pitiable and requiring saving, they had long been morally justified as the sexual outlet safeguarding respectable women from male lust and offering men an alternative to sodomy. "Authorities allow certain evils so that other worse evils are not committed," wrote the Jesuit Domenico Ottonelli. Paraphrasing Augustine, he explained that "prostitutes allow for the removal of occasions of adultery, incest, abominable sacrilege, and other even worse sins." In this sense, sex workers were thought to perform a crucial social role: "Remove the prostitute from the human community, and you will see everything go to ruin with lust."[17] The cardinal, jurist, and statesmen Giovanni Battista De Luca unabashedly stated that prostitution should be tolerated "especially in this city of Rome, since here there is an ecclesiastical Curia, with a great number of bachelors, and of young and wealthy nobles."[18] For many men, prostitutes were a relatively "low-cost" option for sexual and affective relationships. For authorities and society at large, they helped balance the sexual ecology and social order, while earning a living and contributing to the economy and their communities.[19]

Nevertheless, the availability of women engaged in sex work, which was substantial in most cities and seemed to grow during hard times, did not stop men from having sexual relations with women they were not supposed to. Men seduced virgins into sexual relations with false promises of marriage or compensation. Men violently raped. They seduced and coerced married women into adultery. The walls of custodial institutions did not necessarily keep men away from women "protected" inside. Women in shelters were sometimes targeted by men living and working nearby and were vulnerable to clerics charged with their physical and spiritual care inside conservatory walls. Confessors solicited and abused women in the confessional during the sacrament of pen-ance—considered heresy and prosecutable by the Inquisition. Men preyed on their servants, kin, and close relatives inside their very homes. While generally hidden, incest (in close grades of consanguinity) appears not to have been uncommon.[20] Domestic seclusion and institutional enclosures intended to separate and protect single women from predatory men could create opportunities for intimacy and abuse. More than women's immoderate lust, individuals, communities, and institutions identified men's undisciplined desires as the driver of non-marital sex, the primary cause of pregnancy outside of marriage and, therefore, of abortion.

In these framings, men were generally portrayed as sexual agents and predators, women as essentially vulnerable and perpetually victimized; and all forms of non-marital sex were presented as illicit. While this reflects how some may have felt, such representations must be approached critically as discourses and investigated as to how accurately they represent individual experiences and communal responses. While the oppressive patriarchal structures, imbalances of power, coercion, and different types of violence that shaped sexual relations and women's lives should not be underemphasized, neither should we assume that early modern Italy was a culture where women could not make sexual and reproductive choices (though they were often profoundly constrained) and all men were violent rapists (though many were and force was a regular and, within limits, expected feature of sexual relations).[21] Sexual relationships and reproductive decisions were intricately negotiated (though always in the context of asymmetrical power), and sources offering glimpses into them conceal as much as they might reveal.

At the core of a social history of sexuality, reproduction, and abortion lies an important epistemological problem: How do we discover what people did, why they did it, and what they felt about it? Much of our knowledge of early modern Italian non-marital sexual relationships comes from trial records where witnesses describe behaviors and relationships after they became problematic and were brought to the attention of authorities. In retelling the story of a relationship, individuals, whose testimonies were recorded verbatim (or at least were supposed to be) by court scribes, rarely meditated on the good but focused on and fashioned the bad as it served their interests—women and men downplayed their agency and emphasized their victimhood. Nevertheless, trial records reveal that women and men pursued a range of sexual opportunities and nurtured intimate relationships outside of marriage. Although by definition sinful and sometimes officially criminal, pre-marital sex, fornication, concubinage, and even adultery were common and often unproblematic. Women and men entered fleeting sexual and long-term "marriage-like" relationships for practical material reasons and also out of desire and affection—motivations often overlapped.[22] Many couples did not marry: some were constrained by age, rank, disapproval of family, or law; others simply found the prospect unattractive for reasons we cannot know. Often, such relationships were stable, accepted, even validated by communities and authorities. Pregnancy, however, was often the critical factor destabilizing nonmarital relationships and making them problematic in the eyes of kin, neighbors, and onlookers.

Of course, pregnancy outside of marriage was always riskier and came with higher costs—social, material, physical, and emotional—for women than for men. Pregnancy was energy and resource draining, and childbirth often dangerous. A newborn required milk and attention, further draining energy and making earning a living difficult. For a young woman who was supposed to be a virgin, pregnancy and children out of wedlock could diminish her chances of marriage and bring dishonor to her family, unless she was able to secure adequate compensation from her impregnator. A pregnant unwed servant might be dismissed, either because her pregnancy brought dishonor to the house she served or because she might be physically unable to keep up with her chores or return to work promptly following childbirth.[23] Conservatories and shelters threw out women who became pregnant while under their charge. While some women might profit from childbirth by becoming wet nurses for families or orphanages, many understood pregnancy in these circumstances to be a hardship. For a woman in a sexual relationship with a priest or a close relative, pregnancy could bring scorn and scandal and often the attention of authorities. For a married woman, pregnancy from an adulterous relationship could mean separation and violence. Dishonored men threatened to murder their daughters, sisters, and wives when they were found pregnant out of wedlock, and some did.[24] Some women contemplated and may have committed suicide to evade the consequences of exposure. Moralists warned it was a slippery slope from non-marital sex to ruin. While discourses linking single womanhood, sexual sin, pregnancy, and poverty were used to shape gender and class relations, the situations described were also observable realities. Pregnancy outside of marriage threatened a woman's relationships with family and neighbors, her livelihood, and potentially her very survival. There was a relationship between non-marital sex, pregnancy, and long-term suffering. Women, their friends, and their families knew the risks and tried to reduce and mitigate them. Launching a suit against her impregnator was possible but always an uphill battle and came with considerable risks; sometimes the man had vanished. A woman who found herself pregnant outside of marriage and could not secure the support of a partner might try to procure an abortion. Many did, sometimes helped by kin, friends, and strangers. Some women suffered complications and a few died; others succeeded and managed the side effects with minimal physical or social harm. For some women, abortion didn't work; they continued their pregnancy to term and managed the consequences of childbirth as best they could.

Non-marital sex and pregnancy could also come at significant cost to men, though never as high as the cost to women. For the transient and itinerant—migrant laborers, soldiers, itinerant clerics, merchants, those who were mobile and perhaps marginal in the communities they found themselves in—evading the consequences of sexual intercourse could be as easy as skipping town. For men with roots, kin, assets, and reputations in their local communities, pregnancy could expose a clandestine sexual relationship or an instance of sexual violence kept secret, and lead to turmoil. A man who impregnated a woman who was supposed to be a virgin (without delivering adequate compensation), another man's wife, a widow, a nun, his domestic servant, or a relative risked shaming himself, dishonoring his family, earning the scorn of his neighbors, and facing retribution by the woman's kin. Men were brought to court and sued for raping a virgin and for breach of promise to marry following sexual intercourse and defloration. The aggrieved usually sought compensation, but the law might also sentence such a man to corporal punishment and exile.[25] A cleric who impregnated a parishioner could be chastised by the community he served and become a source of scandal for the reforming Church—he risked losing his clerical status and source of income, and, as a lay person, he could be transferred to a secular court for criminal prosecution. Of course, men could and did deny liability. They deployed standard defenses: marriage was never promised; she was not a virgin; sex was consensual; she was a prostitute and was compensated; she had multiple sexual partners; someone else was responsible for the pregnancy; she was making a false accusation for financial gain. While clearly self-serving, such claims could work because contemporaries believed that these things occasionally happened, that poor women and their families used sex and pregnancy as a resource to extort men, and perhaps sometimes they did.[26] But these claims did not always work, especially when neighbors knew about the sexual relationship or witnessed the sexual assault, and communal opinion held the woman to be trustworthy and the man not. Men who behaved in such ways might be deemed "infamous" and "notorious," labels that could wreak havoc on their own and their kin's social and economic relationships. Violence might erupt against the offender and develop into a vendetta between families. Men, therefore, also knew the consequences of pregnancy outside of marriage and sought abortions to evade them. They turned to male healers (physicians, apothecaries, and surgeons) for materials and often supplemented these with violence, putting women in terrible danger and sometimes causing their death. Abortion was often something men did to women.

In sum, there were many circumstances and motivations related to sexuality and reproduction that led women and men to contemplate and procure abortions, and for communities to facilitate or ignore it. According to civic and ecclesiastical authorities, the better solution was to conceal pregnancy and childbirth and deliver the newborn to a foundling home, which by the seventeenth century were part of welfare programs in every major Italian city. Abandonment was acceptable and encouraged. Both women and men (including married couples) deposited their newborns in orphanages, some permanently, some hoping to reclaim them when they could. For individuals who feared reprimand or public censure, abandonment could be accomplished in secret: under cover of darkness, anonymous individuals placed newborns on the exposed portion of turntables built into the outside walls of foundling homes and spun the wheel to move the infant into shelter, where personnel would tend to it.[27] Others paid brokers to transport their newborns to orphanages in bigger cities. However, for some, this strategy was not as easy as its ubiquity might suggest. It meant a woman had to carry a fetus for nine months and give birth. If concealment was a priority, every passing month increased the chance of exposure. Women might try to conceal pregnancy locally for as long as possible and then travel to a nearby city to give birth in anonymity and place the newborn in a foundling home there. But this required organization, help, and money.[28] It was especially difficult for rural women to travel—their absence from local life was sure to be noticed. For many single women in trying circumstances, and for the men with whom they were pregnant, finding solutions could be a matter of survival. If a woman could not make it to a foundling home, she might deliver in secrecy and possibly resort to infanticide.

The history of abortion has often been entangled with that of neonaticide / infanticide, a practice that preoccupied moralists, authorities, and society much more than abortion.[29] Scholars have assumed abortion and infanticide were practiced by similar kinds of individuals for similar reasons: when abortion did not terminate an unwanted pregnancy, those in desperate need resorted to infanticide, defined as the delivery of an infant that was viable, capable of surviving outside a woman's body, and whose death resulted from neglect, exposure, or physical violence. Infanticide has a more abundant early modern archival record and has, therefore, received more focused attention from historians, with recent studies suggesting it may have been more common in early modern Italy than previously assumed.[30] Nevertheless, not everyone who contemplated or failed at abortion contemplated or attempted infanticide. Infanticide was a more difficult decision for many to make and execute. While married people may have been able to explain an infant's death in various ways, neighbors might wonder and confessors might ask questions. For single women, infanticide meant carrying a pregnancy to full term, delivering a child, and organizing its death by exposure or violence. The chances of being found out were great, as many trial records show.

While abortion and infanticide could be understood as part of a continuum of dealing with threatening pregnancies, there are important reasons to disentangle them and study abortion in its own right.

First, law and theology distinguished between the practices. "Truly separate are abortion and the killing of a child already well born," wrote Martin de Azpilcueta (Doctor Navarrus), a leading sixteenth-century theologian, canonist, and consultant for the Sacred Apostolic Penitentiary in Rome. He distinguished abortion from infanticide by the "gravity," "method," and "reason" they were committed. Gravity pertained to the loss of the aborted or killed being. Infanticide was unequivocally homicide and a mortal sin; the death of a newborn by exposure or violence was the murder of a human being, baptized or not. In the sixteenth and seventeenth centuries, most Italians did not use the formal Latin-derived term *infanticide* but spoke of murder, killing a newborn or child, and homicide. Whether or not a judge sentenced an individual who committed infanticide to death, the crime was considered homicide. Abortion, on the other hand, was not unequivocally viewed as such. Even after the fetus was thought to have acquired a soul and had taken on human form, it did not share the moral, social, and legal value of a born child. The termination of a fetus inside a woman's body was therefore different from the termination of a born child's life, though its loss could cause deep sorrow. Infanticide and abortion were also distinguished by method. The former was committed by direct violence, which included neglect, exposure, abandonment, and force directly on a human being. Methods of terminating pregnancy were less direct and more uncertain: the consumption of herbs and drugs intended to induce contractions and encourage purgation, surgery in the form phlebotomy, and blunt-force trauma to a woman's body. Regarding motivation, infanticide was seen as willful murder in order to rid oneself of the social or economic burdens of an actual child, whereas abortion, according to Azpilcueta, was likelier for the "concealment of an offence," by which he meant non-marital sexual intercourse.[31]

Theoretically then, infanticide and abortion were distinct. In practice, however, judges, medical practitioners, individuals, and communities sometimes struggled to distinguish between abortions later in pregnancy, stillbirth (where the fetus was well formed and potentially viable), and neonaticide (the killing of a newborn immediately after its birth). Often, clear boundaries between these could not be drawn, but abortion was more common, a socially, spiritually, and legally, if not physically, safer option. Studying it in its own right and investigating its varied meanings reveal ideas, practices, and facets of early modern Italian society and culture that would otherwise remain obscured.

For instance, abortion was not always procured for reasons entirely related to sexuality. Pregnancy could be terminated for health reasons or as a consequence of health-related interventions. So-called therapeutic abortion was much discussed in medical, theological, and legal literature and, though controversial, was accepted and practiced. It was understood that pregnancy could turn even minor illnesses fatal; pregnancy-related illness could also threaten a woman's future fertility. Induced abortion or medical therapies that could lead to abortion were, in certain cases, accepted forms of therapeutic intervention. In this context, married and elite women sometimes emerge in the historical record: a famous example includes the pregnant Duchess of Florence Eleonora di Toledo who, in 1551, was prescribed and consumed strong purgative medicines to treat a particularly dangerous blockage of fluids, anticipating the medicine might terminate her pregnancy, which was judged to be in its sixth month. (The case is further discussed in Chapter 1.) In these situations, a woman's health, future fertility, and the preservation of her life were valued above the potential loss of a fetus, even one that was formed and animated. Authorities tried to regulate this practice by legislating that only a physician, and not a lower-status healer or the woman herself, was to make this decision by weighing the threat to a woman's health against medical complications she might suffer and the value of the fetus. In practice, many healers lower in the medical hierarchy were consulted, and women likely made these decisions for themselves.

Abortion was also experienced and responded to in the context of gender-based violence. The termination of pregnancy caused by or related to injuries stemming from assault or some form of trauma inflicted on a pregnant woman was considered a sin and a crime that society and courts took seriously. Causing a woman to miscarry by means of violence was a criminal offence for which the assaulted woman, her husband, or kin could demand reparations, generally in the form of compensation for the harm and danger to the pregnant woman's life and the loss of a potential offspring. If the woman died, the assailant could be charged with homicide.[32] Criminal courts often investigated cases of abortion by assault and called on medical practitioners to examine abused women's bodies and aborted fetuses and to determine causes. Abortion by assault was commonly, although not exclusively, ascribed to men, often husbands. In most cases, the termination of pregnancy may not have been the intended aim of an assault—violence against women was common and domestic violence acceptable within certain limits—but sometimes violence was intentionally inflicted to terminate pregnancy. Though probably effective, abortion by means of violence was regarded as very dangerous, and sometimes (perhaps often) resulted in the woman's death.

Individuals, communities, and institutions took all these factors, contexts, and circumstances into account when they were confronted by or had to evaluate individuals who sought or had abortions. Often the response was understanding rather than the pursuit of punishment. Behaviors officially condemned by the Church and states could be evaluated differently on the ground. Prescriptions against the intentional termination of pregnancy were often ignored, flexibly interpreted, opposed, or rejected at a local level, not only by laity but also by clergy and civic authorities. Only rarely were procurers of abortion brought into the disciplinary apparatus of the Church and states, and, generally, it was the nature of the sexual relationship and personalities involved that mattered more to a community than the abortion itself. Abortion was denounced to the authorities for investigation as a symptom of a social problem that could not be mediated privately or locally.

Tribunals primarily investigated cases of abortion in the context of scandal. Early modern Italians feared the consequences of scandal and generally tried to suppress them, leaving abortion more likely to be ignored and hushed up than brought to public attention. However, abortion in the context of a problematic sexual relationship could be strategically exposed to stoke scandal and invite institutional attention in order to further one's interests.

Broadly speaking, the noun *scandal* was used to describe the mix of indignation, public controversy and disorder that occurred when a community learned and circulated information about a transgression, usually related to sexuality. It was a widely held maxim that sexual wrongdoing that could bring dishonor, shame, and even prosecution should be kept secret and hidden from public knowledge for the benefit of all involved, and for society more broadly. Abortion was often sought, facilitated, and accepted to conceal sexual transgressions and prevent the reproductive and social harm these might have for women, men and their kin, and that could throw communities into disarray. Institutions, too, encouraged secrecy and preferred such extra-legal solutions, and Church and civil law incentivized it. The Church had long taught that broadcasting sins encouraged others to sin, and civic authorities feared the disorder that could ensue. As we will see in Chapters 2 and 3, authorities—from jurists and judges to bishops and popes—held that penalties for certain sexual sins and crimes, including abortion, should, in certain circumstances, be mitigated if they were committed to prevent scandal. They also discouraged individuals from bringing these cases to light in order to prevent the resentment and turmoil that might result from investigation. Secrecy was deemed a priority when it came to the sexual misdeeds of elites and especially of the clergy who were supposed to be moral exemplars and representatives of the ecclesiastical establishment. Fearing the consequences to its corporate reputation, authority, and legitimacy, the Church sought to keep priests' transgressions secret, often to the detriment of the individuals they abused.[33] At all social levels, personal interest and the threat of disorder justified the flexing of prescriptions and laws to suppress scandal. Abortion was one example of many such cases.

But in some circumstances abortion did come to light, bringing scandal and prosecution. Individuals and communities were unwilling to countenance abortion when it was procured by someone who was disliked, had a history of misdeeds and antagonistic relationships, or was labeled *infamous*. Because abortion was officially considered a sin and crime, one that authorities increasingly claimed to take seriously, it offered the opportunity to launch a suit against a transgressor. Abortion was often ancillary and sometimes even used as a pretense to air other interpersonal and often unrelated grievances in court. Here too, the targets of discipline were often men who procured abortions to evade the consequences of illicit sexual relationships, and not the women who had them. Witnesses denounced and often embellished the deeds of troublesome, abusive and predatory men and charged them with threatening the moral health and social order of their communities. This sometimes included elites and priests who abused their privilege and earned public scorn. Institutions risked further scandal and harm to their legitimacy if they did not take these cases seriously. The Church in particular risked the charge of corruption, the specter of anticlericalism and possibly heretical challenges to the faith if it did not at least give the appearance of following through on its Tridentine promise to discipline priests who abused their charges. In these cases, the women who had abortions were not depicted as promiscuous sinners, but were objectified and valued as the victims and evidence of men's misdeeds.

Cases of abortion that made it to court and into the historical record must therefore be read primarily through the lens of local social relations and micropolitics, and not as examples of the top-down disciplining of sexuality, women's bodies, and reproduction. The fact that individuals denounced and institutions investigated only a small minority of people for abortion and only in specific circumstances, while ignoring, tolerating, and accepting its practice by others, raises important questions about what histories of abortion we can reconstruct from available historical sources. We know all sources are inherently biased. Moralists and legislators targeted already vulnerable and marginalized individuals as the agents of sin and crime. Communities generally identified outsiders, those lacking the protection and oversight of kin, and occasionally clerics and elites who abused their privilege and power, as violators of social and moral order—and it is these individuals who tribunals primarily investigated. Those who were liked, deemed honorable contributors to their societies, and who had abortions for reasons that did not disturb the moral sensibilities of their communities, were helped or ignored. Married couples are a case in point.

Primary sources are relatively silent on the practice of abortion by and for married women except in instances of adultery or for therapeutic purposes. Moralists did not explicitly include married women or men among the usual suspects they sought to chastise and reform; jurists almost never discussed the practice of abortion in a marital context. I have not found a case of any tribunal investigating abortion procured to terminate a pregnancy that resulted from marital sex. This silence, of course, does not mean married people did not have abortions. Rather, it speaks to privilege. Married women and men enjoyed greater privacy and were less exposed to stinging moralizing and prying eyes. Neighbors and onlookers were uninterested in denouncing married couples for their birth control practices, and authorities could not and did not want to inquire too closely into marital life, as it would violate understandings of decorum and honor. I think we can, however, assume abortions were contemplated, attempted, and had in the context of family-limitation strategies, that both married women and their husbands desired and sought abortions, and that this would have been tolerated. Practices officially prohibited to single women and men might have been acceptable for married couples raising children and contributing to their communities. This privilege was extended to unmarried women and men of good standing. The toleration of abortion was conditional on the social positioning of its procurer.

In the end, the absence from the historical record of what we might call "ordinary" abortion means our knowledge of its meanings comes primarily from "extraordinary" abortion—cases usually revolving around transgressive sexuality and abuse that caused disorder and scandal and led to prosecution.[34] That these recorded cases almost certainly represent a fraction of the practice, however, does not mean their historical value and importance are not great. In fact, these cases reveal, in poignant detail, that even when men were the targets of discipline, the prosecution of abortion centered on and exacerbated the hardships of women, in particular those who were already in some way vulnerable. In criminal and ecclesiastical trials, women's experiences of abortion and sexual abuse—frequently linked to poverty—were broadcast to the community and then exposed before authorities in order to discipline men. Women were often forced to undergo violent and degrading physical examinations of their bodies by court appointed medical practitioners. Even when there was no risk of punishment to themselves, women were tortured to exact confessions to shaming sexual relationships, sexual violence, and abortions that proved men's misdeeds. The alleged good that came from disciplining a bad guy, it was thought, outweighed the harm that official investigation would have on his victim. Carefully recorded, archived, and preserved for posterity, the documentation generated by judicial investigation allows researchers to recover a history of abortion, but one that depends on and emphasizes women's pain. I hope that my recreation of parts of some women's lives from sources highlighting trauma to their bodies and selves has not rendered them hapless one-dimensional subjects.[35] While each woman's route towards abortion was unique, and we do not know how their lives played out after the authorities stopped inquiring into them, the sexual violence and imbalanced power relations that court records bring to light were experiences many women shared and features of early modern Italian society.

Despite increasingly heated rhetoric and new legislation seeking to create new meanings about abortion and to regulate its practice, in the sixteenth and seventeenth centuries, it remained widely sought, accessible, and generally, if uncomfortably, tolerated, because it benefited individuals and society and contributed to social order. Abortion was treated as a problem only when it benefited the wrong people. Early modern Italians were aware of the inconsistencies of their prescriptions and practices surrounding abortion, and they were more or less okay that.

The Language of Abortion

Language around abortion always carries important ideological and political valences that influence perceptions and shape experiences. Sixteenth- and seventeenth-century Italians used many terms to talk about terminated pregnancy. They had meanings on two levels: first, the denotational, or literal-definitional, level; second, the connotational level—the ideas, feelings, and broader sociocultural and political meanings these words evoked. While most people rarely reflect on the literal meanings of idioms used, heard, or read, they still frame our thought processes.[36]

Derived from the Latin *abortus / aborsus,* the formal Italian noun was *aborto* and verb *abortire,* although speakers and writers mostly used colloquial and idiomatic words. These included the nouns *disgravi-danza / sgravidanza,* the verbs *disgravidare / sgravidare* and *dispreg-nare / spregnare,* where the prefix *dis-* or *s-* before the word "pregnant" (*gravida, pregna*) indicated its opposite—as a noun, "pregnancy loss," as a verb "to abort," or literally "to reverse pregnancy" or "unpregnate." Pregnancy terminated before the delivery of a fully formed and viable infant was euphemistically described as a *parto acerbo,* an unripe or immature delivery or its product. The word *parto* itself denoted both the birthing process (delivering or bringing forth) and the infant who was being born.[37] The dictionary of the Accademia della Crusca specified that the word *acerbo* was generally used for describing fruit and that this included the "fruit" growing and ripening in the womb.[38]

Italians also used an evocative array of words to talk about abortion that semantically had nothing to do with pregnancy. In his *Vocabulary of Latin Words in Italian,* the polymath Girolamo Ruscelli wrote that the Latin noun *abortio / abortionis* is generally translated as "lo sconciarsi, il partorir avanti il tempo, il disperdersi."[39] *Il partorir avanti il tempo* was a definition: delivery before the proper time or prematurely. *Il sconciarsi* and *il disperdersi,* two of the most common terms used for abortion during the sixteenth and seventeenth centuries, were analogies whose applicability to pregnancy termination was not semantically obvious but required a conceptual and phenomenological association. In its verb form, *sconciare* meant "to corrupt," "to ruin," "to spoil," "to disorder," "to trouble," "to molest," "to mar." As a noun, *il sconciarsi, la sconciatura, lo sconcio,* meant something "disordered," "spoiled," "foul," "ugly," "crude," "ill handled," a "molestation," a "mishap or ill luck."[40] It was a synonym of the noun *guasto*: "waste," "a corruption," something "rotten," "rancid," or "ruined."[41] Similarly, the noun *disperdimento* and the verbs *disperdere / sperdere* (modifications of *perdere,* to lose) meant "to bring to perdition," "to disperse," "to ruin," "to lose" (here the prefix *dis-* served as an intensifier rather than a reversal or negation).[42] The verbs *disertare* and *dolersi* were used as idioms for abortion as well. *Disertare* was a synonym of *guastare* and carried connotations of waste and destruction. *Dolersi* (the reflexive of *dolere*) meant to feel pain, to be pained, to hurt, to ache, to suffer, to be sorrowful.[43] Unlike the words *disgravidare* and *dispregnare,* which were unambiguous, *sconciare, disperdere, disertare,* and *dolersi* were not lexically related to pregnancy or semantically to its termination but were used analogically for the imagery they evoked. These terms carried extra information that framed the event, practice, and product of terminated pregnancy as something more than what they literally denoted, that is, the expulsion of a fetus in formation or one that had died in the womb. The common use of these terms indicates a perceived association or correspondence between terminated pregnancy and waste, destruction, loss, and pain. By the sixteenth century, these terms were conventional synonyms of *aborto,* and this was often their primary meaning. On some level, words such as *sconciare* may have deanthropomorphized the aborted by emphasizing the passing of waste, a failure of the fruit in the womb to mature into a human being, rather than termination of one (more on this point below).

Vocabulary about abortion was also somewhat regional. In their edition of the *Decameron,* Luigi Groto and Girolamo Ruscelli commented on Boccaccio's use of *spregnare* to refer to an induced abortion. In the story of the simpleton Calandrino, who is fooled into believing he is pregnant and instructed to have an abortion (*Dec.* 9.3), Dr. Simone can make Calandrino "abort [*spregnare*] without any pain." Groto and Ruscelli felt the need to explain the Tuscan term to a wider Italian audience: "*Spregnare,* which is also said *sgravidare,* and which in the Kingdom [of Naples] they say *dolersi,* and those in Rome *sconciarsi,* and the Latins *aborti,* that is, bringing forth the fetus prematurely."[44] While regional specificity should not be assumed—*sconciarsi* appears to have been used throughout the peninsula—using a regionally specific word in a publication intended for a wide audience could hurt clarity. For example, in the 1569 Italian edition of Martin de Azpilcueta's best-selling *Manual for Confessors and Penitents,* originally written in Catalan, the book's translator, Cola di Guglinisi, opted for the word *dolersi* over *aborto* or other synonyms: a woman sins mortally "if she has procured to *dolersi.*" However, in the 1584 edition of the same translation published by the same press (Gabriel Giolito) *dolersi* was changed to *sconciarsi*: a woman sins mortally "if she has procured to *sconciarsi.*"[45] The editor, it seems, thought that *sconciarsi* was more understandable or in more common usage throughout the peninsula. In a competing translation of Azpilcueta's book (also published in 1584, by the Venetian printer Giorgio Angelieri), Camillo Camilli (who translated the text from Latin, not the original Spanish, into Italian) chose the term *disperdersi.* However, in a 1591 compendium of Azpilcueta's *Manual,* Camilli also opted for *sonciarsi.*[46]

Authors and speakers recognized that the variety of Italian words for abortion could make communicating about it difficult, so they sometimes used multiple synonyms in the same sentence. In his *Oration against the Courtesans* (1575), Sperone Speroni moralized that prostitutes sin against God and nature when they terminate their pregnancies: "Being pregnant, they use all art and great risk to *isconciarsi e disgravidare,*" "to abort and to terminate their pregnancy."[47] The same formulation was used about a century later by the Jesuit historian Daniello Bartoli in his discussion of Japanese reproductive practices: "The art of *sconciarsi e disgravidare* is widely spread throughout Japan and is much in use by women."[48] In the vernacular edition of Bartolomeo Fumi's popular Latin manual for confessors, the Florentine translators titled his section on abortion "Dell'Aborso, o disperdere, o sconciarsi."[49] Redundancies were meant to ensure clarity.

Clarity was important because *aborto* and its idioms are polysemic. A polyseme is a word that can have multiple meanings, often though not always semantically related. Three distinct meanings of *aborto* relating to pregnancy are relevant here.

The first is *aborto* as an event and bodily experience. Dictionaries primarily defined *aborto* as an expulsion of a fetus before it was fully formed or viable or the expulsion of a fetus that had died in the womb. Idiomatic language included the nouns *il sconcio, la sconciatura, la sgravidanza, lo disperdimento*. Lexicographers defined these words as "imperfect delivery," when a pregnant woman delivers "out of time," and to "cast [the fetus] untimely." Abortion here was a dynamic and violent process of expelling a fetus before it was ready for life outside a woman's body or ejecting one that had died.

The second meaning is *aborto* as practice: interventions done postcoitus by or to a woman to induce the expulsion of a fetus that is not yet viable or that is dead or interventions intended to cause fetal death. Unlike contemporary English, which uses the term *miscarriage* to distinguish between spontaneous and procured abortion, Italian speakers and authors generally, though not always, qualified the term with the adverb "procured" (*procurato*) or the verbs "to make" (*fare*) or "to commit" (*commitere*) before or after *aborto* and its idioms. In 1594, responding to allegations that he administered or forced a woman to have an abortion, the priest Antino de Benedictis vehemently declared, "It is not true that . . . I have procured abortion [*procurato aborto*]."[50] Similarly, in a 1613 trial, witnesses testified that a suspect sought out surgeons and apothecaries "to have [someone] commit the said abortion [*per far commettere il detto aborto*]."[51] The verbs "to procure," "to commit," and "to make" indicated intervention, agency, and intention and distinguished this from miscarriage.

The third meaning was *aborto* as object: the being expelled from the womb before it was "complete" or "perfect," meaning before it was fully formed and able to live outside a woman's body. The more precise and formal terms were *feto abortivo,* "aborted fetus," or *l'abortivo,* "the aborted." The colloquialisms *la sconciatura, lo sconcio,* and *la sperditura* also commonly identified the aborted fetus, but these terms were more imprecise as they could mean both the aborted object and abortion as event.[52]

The myriad meanings of *aborto* and its colloquial synonyms suggests that the word could have an unclear referent and lead to ambiguity. This is certainly the case for a twenty-first-century reader of primary sources from the early modern period, but it could also have been the case for contemporary speakers and readers. An extra cognitive step was needed to understand the precise meaning and the implications the author / speaker intended to communicate. Syntax and context provide the means to disambiguate. Consider the following examples from different genres of sixteenth- and seventeenth-century primary sources.

In his bawdy dialogue *Six Days* (1534–1536), Pietro Aretino had his protagonist, the savvy prostitute Nanna, admit that she tricked one of her clients into thinking she was pregnant with his heir—something the man desired—so that he might take care of her. To avoid being caught in the deception, Nanna tricked him again by faking an abortion: "I let myself drop to the floor, doing it with real abandon. I pretended as though I were aborting [*fingendo di essermi sconcia*]." By *sconcia,* Nanna clearly meant experiencing the pains of miscarriage. Niccolò Machiavelli used the same word in his *Mandrake Root* (1524) but to convey a different meaning. The fixer Ligurio tries to convince the greedy priest fra Timoteo to procure an abortifacient potion for a young woman from a good family who finds herself four months pregnant in a convent. Ligurio promises fra Timoteo a large sum of money if he would "give the girl a potion that will make her abort [*per farla sconciare*]." In this context, *sconciare* clearly meant a procured abortion, as indicated by the active voice and the use of the verb *fare.* Ligurio's request is met with momentary moral trepidation—fra Timoteo hesitates because this abortion would be a sin. Both Aretino and Machiavelli used the term *sconciare* instead of *aborto* because it was a more popular term and also because of the imagery of waste and ruin, both physical and perhaps moral, it brought to mind. Following her fainting, Nanna has her servant bring a basin of water containing a lamb fetus, which, Nanna said, "you would have sworn was a *sconciatura*," clearly intending to mean an aborted human fetus. When her suitor saw it, "he was in despair because [he believed] the baby had died without being properly baptized."[53] Similarly, Machiavelli's Ligurio convinces the apprehensive fra Timoteo to provide the abortion by arguing that it would have only good consequences and that the only "offence" would be toward the "piece of unborn flesh [*un pezzo di carne non nata*], without feelings, which could be lost [*sperdere*] all the same in a thousand ways."[54] Both authors used these terms (*sconcia, sconciare, sconciatura, pezzo di carne, sperdere*) to comically underscore the ambiguity of generation, of the products of the womb, and of women's bodies, as well as the moral ambiguity of abortion.

Lexical variety and semantic ambiguity surrounding *aborto* are also found in the poem "Nella sconciatura della Signora Veronica Spinola" ("On Veronica Spinola's Abortion"), by the celebrated baroque poet Giovan Battista Marino. The poem was an expression of sympathy and an attempt to console the noblewoman Veronica Spinola-Doria following a miscarriage.

> Perche disperso, e morto
> Habbia con parto acerbo, & imperfetto
> Il tuo nobil concetto,
> Spinola bella, intempestivo aborto,
> Turbar non devi il bel giglio sereno,
> Nè sciorre al pianto il freno.
> A le bellezze eccelse, e singolari
> Forme simili, o pari
> Nel mondo haver non lice.
> In Cielo un Sole, in terra una Fenice.[55]

(Although, beautiful Spinola, an untimely abortion [*intempestivo aborto*] / Has dissipated and killed / With an immature and imperfect birth [*parto acerbo*] / Your noble conception / You do not have to trouble your serene brow / Nor give free rein to your weeping. / In the world, it is not per-

mitted / To have forms that are similar or equal / To exceptional and singular beauties / In the sky, just one Sun, on
the Earth just one phoenix.)

In this short poem Marino used three different words or phrases to
refer to a terminated pregnancy: *sconciatura* in the title, *parto acerbo*, and
intempestivo aborto. Each could refer to either the event or the expelled
being. The content of the third and fourth verses allows the reader to
disambiguate: it is the "noble conception" that experiences an "untimely abortion" and "immature birth." The word *sconciatura* in the title
however remains ambiguous: it could be rendered into English as either
"On Veronica Spinola's (Spontaneous) Abortion" or "On the Conception that Veronica Spinola Aborted." By highlighting the "noble conception" in the poem, Marino, it seems, intended the title to refer to the
latter, which was the object of Veronica's weeping and troubled brow.
One wonders, however, whether he selected the word *sconciatura* over
aborto for a specific reason. Marino did not refer to the aborted as a
fetus or a baby but as a *concetto*—a word that also had various meanings.
John Florio distinguished the noun *concetto*, "a conceit or apprehension
of the minde," from the verb *concepere* and the nouns *conceputto* / *concetto*, "to conceive with childe." The dictionary of the Accademia della
Crusca defined *concetto* as "an imagined thing, invented by our intel-
lect" and *concepire* as "the retention of a man's seed in the uterus of a
woman to form the fetus."[56] Marino appears to have selected this term
to highlight the ambiguity of that which was aborted: Was it a fetus in
formation or was it a concept, a projection of a future child that Veronica carried in her womb and imagined in her mind? Perhaps he was
attempting to console her by deemphasizing the humanness of that
which was aborted. The "untimely abortion" and "immature and imperfect birth" did not dissipate and kill a fetus or a baby but rather a
conception, something that was to remain an abstraction, a conceit. It
is unclear whether Veronica found Marino's attempt to console her
through word play and compliments about her "exceptional and singular" beauty comforting or cruel.

The precarious nature, presence, and imagined future of an
aborted fetus are also themes of a sonnet by Bartolomeo Dotti titled
"Per un aborto conservato in un'ampolla d'acque artificiali dal signor

Giacopo Grandis fisico anatomico eccellentissimo" ("On the Abortion Conserved in an Ampoule of Artificial Water by Signor Giacopo Grandis, Most Excellent Physician and Anatomist").

> Questo, Giacopo mio, Sconcio funesto,
> Cui diè morto Natale il sen Materno,
> Se maturo nascea, moria ben presto,
> E Voi d'intempestivo il feste eterno.
>
> Non so, se dolce latte, o pianto mesto
> Gli sia di quel Cristal l'umore interno;
> So ben che l'Alvo suo fu come questo;
> Poiché Utero da Vetro io non discerno.
>
> Vive quasi per Voi, chi per sé langue.
> Embrione morì, scheletro nacque,
> Fatto parto immortal d'Aborto e sangue.
>
> Huomo, impara. Insegnarti al *Grandi* piacque,
> Che sia Ventre di Donna, e Maschio Sangue
> Più fral del Vetro, e men Vital de l'Acque.

(This woeful abortion, my Giacopo, which produced a dead birth from a mother's womb, if it had been born mature, would soon have died; so you turned it from untimely into eternal.

I don't know if the internal humor of that crystal is sweet milk or sad weeping; but I well know that its uterus was like this; because I do not distinguish between a uterus and a glass.

One who wastes away lives through you, as it were. It died an embryo, it was born a skeleton, it was made an immortal birth from an abortion and blood.

Learn, man. It was Grandi's wish to teach you what a woman's womb is and how male blood is frailer than glass and less vital [i.e., essential for life] than water.)

Dotti's sonnet is unambiguously about a fetus conserved in a glass ampoule. The opening line refers to that fetus as a *sconcio funesto*, a "woeful abortion." Not only was this fetus dead and wasted in the womb, but if it had matured, been born, and lived, it eventually would have died (as all humans do) and wasted away. The anatomist Giacopo (Iacopo) Grandi, however, was able to cheat death and the natural process of ruination through art and science: "One who wastes away lives through you, as it were." The object in the glass ampoule "died an embryo" and was "born a skeleton," but the abortion that brought its life to an end also brought it to the attention of Grandi, who made it immortal through artificial water. The poem ends by commanding the reader to learn from Grandi and his creation: by studying the preserved aborted fetus one learns "what a woman's womb is," for according to Dotti it is no different than the ampoule. By studying the arrested and immortal specimen, one also contemplates the fragility of life (both fetal and human): "male blood," the essential ingredient in generation, is no match for artifice.[57]

Italians formally distinguished between the products of human procreation: *conceputto / concetto* (conception), "the retention of a man's seed in the uterus of a woman to form the fetus"; *embrione* (embryo), "the conceived [being] in the uterus before it has the required features and necessary form," or "perfect shape"; and *feto* (fetus), a term used to mean "the creature in a mother's belly" after it acquires recognizable human shape but before it has developed sufficiently for life outside of a woman's body.[58] Most speakers used the term *creatura* (creature) to speak about a being in the womb regardless of its gestational age, as well as one that had been expelled. The word literally meant a "created thing or being," but in this context it meant a product of human procreation. *Creatura* was also used to talk about a newborn or an infant before baptism, upon which it would receive a new soul and name and officially become a member of the Christian community. That a fetus in the womb, an aborted fetus, and a newborn child could all be called *creatura* could lead to confusion. While the formal term for an expulsion of an unformed fetus was *embrione,* most speakers colloquially referred to it as a *pezzo di carne,* a piece of flesh, as Machiavelli did in the *Mandrake Root.* Individuals could also refer to a fetus in the maternal body and one that had been aborted as a *bambino* (baby). Used in common parlance without careful thought to semantics, for rhetorical effect or strategically in court, *concetto, pezzo di carne, embrione, feto, creatura,* and *bambino* were terms that either invested or divested the object in or delivered from a woman's womb with personhood.

While all the meanings of *aborto* had important social, religious, legal, and medical implications, scholars and authorities carefully discussed when a product of procreation could be legally designated as an *aborto,* a fetus expelled into the world dead or prematurely, or as having been "born" *(nato)* and therefore considered an infant and a human being, even if it died shortly thereafter. The foremost medical forensics expert of the early modern period, Paolo Zacchia, gave this question of language and ontology special consideration in his monumental treatise *On Medical Legal Questions:* "Precisely which sort of delivery deserves the name of 'abortion'?" In a lengthy and technical discussion, Zacchia concluded that a fetus is considered to be aborted, and therefore is an "abortion," when it is delivered dead or when it is delivered by an unnatural or violent cause before being *vitalis,* a term that literally meant "alive" but that is, in this context, best translated into contemporary English as "viable"—the term that medical associations and the law currently use to describe a fetus that is able to "survive independently of the maternal environment."[59] Even though anatomists in his own time were carefully investigating fetal development, Zacchia and his contemporaries looked to Hippocrates as the authority on this matter, putting viability at around seven months from conception. Before the seventh month, a fetus might appear fully formed, but it is considered immature and not able to sustain life outside a woman's body, Zacchia explained, because it lacks the operations or functions essential for life. Zacchia noted that the ability to suckle milk and expel urine and feces, which he maintained could not happen before the seventh month, were necessary for the "actions of life." Physiological development and the causes of the expulsion and death of the fetus determined whether an abortion had occurred and whether a being was called an *aborto.* A fetus delivered "alive," in the sense of breathing and moving, but that "cannot in any way survive except due to a miracle," Zacchia argued, was considered an *aborto,* as was a fetus at any stage of development that had died inside a woman's body. A fetus that had gestated for more than seven months, that was sufficiently developed, that could suckle milk and expel waste, and that was therefore able to survive outside of its mother's body was not considered an *aborto,* even if it died shortly after delivery. Such a being was referred to as an *infans,* an infant or baby.[60]

Discussion of definitions and categories by Zacchia and other jurists were not merely academic: whether or not a being was legally considered "born" and therefore a "child" or "aborted" and therefore an "aborted fetus" mattered a great deal to civic, criminal, and ecclesiastical courts and to broader society. Criminal trials often centered on whether a being that a woman delivered was evidence of induced abortion, abortion caused by violence, or neonaticide. For civil jurists, the legal flow of inheritance sometimes rested on the gestational age and status of an expelled or delivered fetus. The consensus was that a "born child" could legally be considered a player who influenced the transmission of inheritance while an "aborted fetus" could not. This usually mattered in cases when the mother died in childbirth and the father or other paternal kin lay claim to her dowry or in cases where the father died before the child was born and the mother or maternal kin lay claim to his assets. In both cases, the born, living, and viable child was needed to inherit the assets and to pass them along to kin should it die. Zacchia argued that a woman who "brought forth a living fetus after the [end of the] sixth month, or even better after the seventh month had begun" should be entitled to the legal privileges of giving birth to a child and being legally regarded a mother. However, "a woman who has given birth before [the beginning of] the seventh month, or who has brought forth a dead child even at the right time, should not be said to have given birth, but should rather be said to have [had] an abortion."[61] Naturally, the boundary between fetus and infant, abortion and childbirth was hazy. Zacchia discussed the ambiguity of fetuses delivered after the sixth and before the ninth month and admitted that determining the precise moment when a fetus became viable was very difficult and often could not be known with certainty. Nevertheless, he and his contemporaries were occasionally called upon by courts and litigants to make such determinations.[62]

This excursus into the words that sixteenth- and seventeenth-century Italians used to talk about reproduction, pregnancy, and abortion reinforces the fact that language matters and should never be taken for granted in any historical endeavour, but in particular this one. Throughout this book, seemingly familiar, arcane, ambiguous, jarring, and offensive words from primary sources will be quoted. My aim is to examine the ideologies that underlie this historical language and how these ideologies shaped experience and social praxis. When I am not making a point about language, I generally use modern and clinical words. I use the term *abortion* to refer to induced abortion, here defined as postcoital interventions that were intended to expel what early modern Italians called a *conceptus, embrione, pezzo di carne, creatura,* and *bambino.* I use the modern English terms *miscarriage* and *stillbirth* to refer to the spontaneous or non-induced termination of pregnancy at different stages. I fully acknowledge that all language surrounding reproduction, pregnancy, and its termination is political and cannot be free of bias.

Sources and Chapters

This book explores the meanings of abortion from the perspectives of three discursive frames through which sixteenth- and seventeenth-century Italians perceived, experienced, and responded to its practice: medicine, religion, and law. I weave together distinct disciplinary approaches, including social, cultural, medical, religious, and legal history and move between macro- and microhistorical analyses. I use diverse, seemingly unrelated, and previously unexamined sources to uncover multiple perspectives, including court documents and especially witness testimonies recorded verbatim in trials investigated by criminal, ecclesiastical, and medical tribunals; theological treatises and popular works of devotion; secular and ecclesiastical legislation, codes of law, and jurisprudence; works of medical theory, pharmacology, surgery, and midwifery and books of medical recipes; personal letters; and works of fiction. Taken together, these sources bring to the fore some of the attitudes sixteenth- and seventeenth-century Italians had toward abortion. At the same time, abortion offers a fascinating lens through which to explore developments in medical ideas and practices, theology and ecclesiastical politics, criminal jurisprudence and legal institutions, as well as interpersonal and communal relations, sexual and gender politics, and women's lives.

Chapter 1 looks at medical ideas and practices. Women and men turned to a variety of healers for materials and interventions to terminate pregnancies. Although health boards tried to regulate the practice, a variety of healers participated in abortions in different ways: they assessed women's bodies and diagnosed pregnancy; prescribed and administered medicines, and performed surgeries for its termination; and evaluated and tended to women's bodies and aborted fetuses postfactum. Sometimes healers knowingly and intentionally administered abortions; sometimes they did so unwittingly, or so they might claim. While anatomists and academic physicians were actively researching women's bodies and their illnesses in order to comprehend, manage, and intervene in fertility, reproduction, and pregnancy, the female body remained opaque and unpredictable. Pregnancy, especially within its first few months, was always uncertain and its symptoms difficult to distinguish from those of illnesses. Widely available purgative medicines and surgeries used to heal women of womb-related illnesses could cause abortion. These factors created situations where the causes and intentionality of abortion could be unclear, both for medical practitioners and women themselves. Women and men desiring abortions could manipulate these ambiguities for their own ends; medical practitioners could fall back on them to exculpate themselves from wrongdoing. The uncertainties of the female body and the availability of purgative medicines stymied attempts to strictly regulate the practice.

Chapter 2 explores the evolution of religious thinking on abortion and ecclesiastical responses to its practice. The post-Tridentine Church wrestled with how to define, regulate, and change mentalities toward a practice that was officially regarded a sin but one that was widely practiced and socially tolerated. Ecclesiastical authorities proposed direct and sustained religious education and the threat of increasingly harsh punishment. However, there was discord in the Church over what abortion actually meant and how it ought to be handled. Popes, cardinals, bishops, theologians, canonists, ecclesiastical judges, confessors, and the laity debated and often disagreed on the spiritual meanings of abortion and whether and how its procurers should be disciplined. While Catholic religious discourse on abortion moved in a more rigid direction throughout the early modern period, ecclesiastical authorities acknowledged that its practice was tied to broader social issues, beyond simple solutions, and they generally took into account circumstances and factors that persuaded an individual to have or participate in an abortion. More often than not, procurers received absolution with penance. This included clerics who sought abortions for or forced them upon women they had impregnated. In the sixteenth and seventeenth centuries, neither clergy nor laity was willing to accept that abortion was unequivocally a mortal sin that irredeemably damned their souls.

Chapter 3 examines secular law on abortion and how criminal tribunals investigated it. Civic authorities throughout Italy identified abortion as a crime and tried to regulate its practice by issuing laws threatening severe penalties. However, these laws were often imprecise and varied over time and from place to place. Jurists discussed and debated what abortion meant, how it should be legally categorized, investigated, and punished, and the numerous factors judges ought to consider before issuing sentences. By and large, most jurists were reluctant to grant the fetus legal personhood and opposed the death penalty altogether. Criminal tribunals rarely investigated cases of procured abortion. When they did, the accused often went unpunished due to evidentiary uncertainties. Those who were deemed guilty of some wrongdoing were sentenced to fines, disciplinary labor, corporal punishment, or exile depending on the particulars of the case. Trial records reveal that, in most cases, women represented themselves and were treated as victims of men's abuses rather than purposeful agents of abortion. The law recognized women as the "weaker sex," and judges sometimes used this principle to mitigate their criminal responsibility; it was often clear their impregnators caused, demanded, orchestrated, and benefited from the abortion or put women into situations where they had little choice. The ambiguities surrounding abortion and the social realities that motivated its practice led judges to prioritize honor and social order over the rigorous enforcement of laws.

In between these chapters, the reader will find three stories of abortion drawn from trial records. While every chapter of this book uses trial records from various tribunals, in combination with other sources, to elucidate medical, religious, and legal aspects of abortion, here I focus on the details of the cases and proceed microhistorically. Their telling narrows the optics of the study and reduces the scale to show how three women at the turn of the seventeenth century—Rosana Ansaloni from Rome, Femia de Andreozza from Trevignano, and Maria de Vecchis from Sezze—encountered abortion within the messiness of their lives. I try to reconstruct the conditions and factors that led them to have abortions; to illuminate what abortion meant in the context of their sexual relationships, families, neighborhoods, and communities; and to see how local political configurations conditioned their options and with what consequences. Each story is a lens through which to observe how social, sexual, and affective relationships, familial and communal moral economies, and institutional politics intertwined with and ran up against medical, religious, and legal attitudes on abortion, themes that are explored in the chapters that precede and follow each story. Rosana's, Femia's, and Maria's stories recalibrate prescriptive and professional framings by exposing, in vivid and poignant detail, the various and overlapping dangers many women faced and how they dealt with them. Through their stories, we can begin to understand what abortion could mean for flesh-and-blood individuals caught in trying circumstances and what was at stake for families, communities, institutions, and broader society.

CHAPTER ONE

Abortion and Women's Bodies

*I*N LATE 1605, don Lauro Sarrio, a priest from Monte San Giovanni (a small hilltop town in the Lazio countryside), needed a physician and apothecary. It was an emergency. He traveled to the larger town of Alatri (approximately twenty kilometers northwest). A stranger in this town, Lauro found a fellow priest, Prospero di Cassandra, and asked for a physician. When they arrived at the doctor Giuliano Amato's house, he was in bed with a severe case of gout. Lauro explained that his sister back in Monte San Giovanni was in a bad state. She had been in labor for eight days and could not give birth. It was feared the fetus was dead in her womb, putting her in extreme danger. He implored the physician for a remedy to help her deliver. Doctor Giuliano wrote a prescription for a beverage consisting of borage, cinnamon, cassia, and a decoction of pennyroyal. "If the fetus was alive, this recipe would help the said woman give birth," the physician told Lauro; "if the fetus was dead it would help her expel it."[1] Lauro took the prescription to the town apothecary Teofilo Mari, who mixed the ingredients. Lauro paid the apothecary (1 testone) and, in haste, returned to Monte San Giovanni hoping the medicine would work.

Marsilia Tomasi was the woman who would consume the beverage. But there was more to this story than Lauro had told the physician and apothecary. Marsilia was not his sister but his cousin through marriage. The two had had a sexual relationship for some time. The danger, fear, and urgency Lauro expressed to the physician and apothecary in Alatri were all real, but not caused by a medical issue. Lauro feared he and Marsilia, who was married to one of his relatives, would get in trouble for their sexual transgressions. He therefore hatched a plan to get materials to terminate her pregnancy. Marsilia drank the purgative and their confidant-relative, Isabetta, supplemented it by jumping on Marsilia's back and pushing on her kidneys. The drink and blows worked, and Marsilia aborted two approximately seven-months-developed fetuses. They were buried along an old road leading to the town mill. The governor of Frosinone heard about the affair and, along with the vicar of Veroli, who had jurisdiction over the priest, began an investigation. Marsilia admitted to all the allegations and claimed Lauro orchestrated the abortion; Lauro denied everything and suggested Marsilia was pregnant by her now deceased husband or the man she had just recently married and that she had miscarried or procured an abortion on her own.

An investigation into the lives of Marsilia Tommasi and the priest Lauro Sarrio illuminates important elements that motivated individuals to seek abortion, as well as the various politics—sexual, gender, familial, religious, and legal—that shaped its experience. We shall explore these entangled elements throughout this book. This chapter focuses on medicine as practice and discourse. By medical discourse I mean ways of understanding, speaking about, and engaging with the physical body as it relates to health and illness, diagnosis, therapy, and care. This includes the words and deeds of various health practitioners and medical institutions, as well as those of lay-medical parties (that is, people who were the focus of, interacted with, and shaped the thought and practice of medical practitioners but who were not themselves medical practitioners). Although it was not the only system of knowledge and language ideology for thinking about women's bodies, pregnancy, and abortion, medicine provided a prominent frame for their understanding.

Italians lived in some of the most medically sophisticated cities and states in early modern Europe, and were remarkably health literate.

Abortion was a feature of the medical landscape. Healers at all levels of the medical establishment provided women and men with materials and services to terminate pregnancies and with health care afterwards. But in the sixteenth and seventeenth centuries, this was becoming more contentious. Some theologians and moralists labeled practitioners who participated in abortions sinners and murderers. Theologically minded medical authors increasingly pronounced on the sinfulness of procured abortion, depicted it as contrary to medical ethics, and urged healers to abstain from its practice for both their own souls and the spiritual and physical well-being of their patients. While health boards did not unequivocally prohibit the medical practice of abortion, they increasingly tried to regulate it by means of legislation. Only physicians were officially permitted to induce abortions and only for reasons of medical necessity. All other healers who participated in abortions by selling drugs or letting blood from pregnant women without a physician's prescription were threatened with fines and corporal or capital punishment should a woman die as a result of their interventions.

Moral invocations and official restrictions did not, however, reduce demand. Healers knew how to work around the medical restrictions on abortion and when and how to resist or ignore them. Women and men in need learned to navigate this terrain: they knew how to find healers who would be sympathetic and helpful and those who would sell products without asking too many questions. They also knew how to present their bodies to make such transactions easier and less risky for the healer. Women and men, like Marsilia and Lauro, could procure abortions by crafting illness narratives concealing their true intentions; medical practitioners, like the doctor Giuliano and the apothecary Teofilo, might unwittingly participate, though they, too, could fall back on these narratives if they needed to exculpate themselves from participating in a prohibited practice. The ambiguities of the female body, uncertainties surrounding pregnancy, and the availability of purgative medicines complicated attempts to regulate abortion.

This chapter investigates three sets of interlocking questions. First, what did medical authorities and practitioners think about abortion, and where was it situated in medical theory and practices? Second, how was abortion induced, and how widely known and available were products and techniques? Third, how did women perceive and communicate experiences of their bodies, pregnancy, and abortion? These questions will be addressed by exploring the connections and tensions between medical ideas and practices—as related in male-authored medical works, medical legislation, and the work of midwives, apothecaries, surgeons, physicians, and other healers—and women's narratives of their bodies, pregnancy, and abortion, as accessed through personal letters and verbatim testimonies in trial records.

"Hippocrates Is Not an Angel or an Evangelist"

Did doctor Giuliano and apothecary Teofilo feel any trepidation in giving don Lauro Sarrio drugs to purge the womb of a pregnant woman? Did they really believe the story of a priest's sister in childbirth danger? They told the judge they did, and this scenario would not have been uncommon—many women faced dangerous pregnancy and childbirth complications and these often proved fatal—but of course, neither the judge nor we could know for sure what the healers thought the medicine was really for. However, they likely knew they were on shaky ground. According to the medical establishment, the healers—especially the physician—should have been more careful. In theory, the physician was to see and evaluate the pregnant woman himself before writing a prescription for medicines that could cause abortion. In practice, and especially in rural settings, this was often impractical or impossible—doctor Giuliano could not do that on account of his debilitating gout. Men like don Lauro Sarrio could often acquire purgative drugs with little scrutiny.

Medical practitioners, from university-educated physicians at the top of the hierarchy to lower-status and informal healers at the bottom, knew participating in an abortion for a woman who simply did not want to be pregnant was prohibited. Theologians thought healers assisting in abortions were as guilty of sin as the women and men who procured them. In works on the moral, ethical, and spiritual aspects of healing, medical authors also spoke out against procured abortion and the medical establishment's complicity.[2] In his Latin work *On Christian and Prudent Means of Healing* (1591), the Bologna-trained physician and author Giovan Battista Codronchi emphatically condemned procured abortion and castigated healers who administered it or aided in its practice:

> A physician who prescribes abortive remedies for a pregnant woman, who has her bled [i.e., phlebotomy], or who helps or counsels her so that she has an abortion, for whatever reason, however much he might justify it, [even if he acts so] she does not come to infamy or scandal, or to avoid her murder, which might arise if the birth comes to light or the pregnancy discovered, or even to free her from infirmity or death, he commits homicide and a capital crime,... because he has caused a bodily and spiritual death.... At no time or occasion ever, whether the fetus is animated or not animated, is [a healer] to attempt abortion.[3]

About a decade later, the physician and Dominican friar Scipione Mercurio issued a similar condemnation, but with more powerful imagery, in his best-selling vernacular treatise *On the Popular Errors of Italy* (1603). In a chapter titled "On that Popular Error, Ungodly and Cruel, by which Some Persuade a Physician to Abort Fetuses," Mercurio depicted the physician, "the evil doctor," as "the principal agent" of abortion. "What is the state of the soul of those physicians who counsel and help [women and men commit abortions?]" he rhetorically asked. "It is blessed God's great mercy, . . . that prevents the heavens from striking [physicians] with lightning, or that does not allow the earth to open and swallow them, those horrendous monsters and enemies of the human race."[4]

Literate medical practitioners also knew that Hippocrates, whom early modern physicians considered "the founder of our profession," prohibited abortion in his *Oath* outlining the ideals and ethics of healing, which, in most early modern versions, was unequivocal: "I will never give a woman a pessary to have an abortion, I shall keep my life and art pure."[5] Physicians would find a version of this statement in every edition of Hippocrates's collected works. Italian readers could find the *Oath*, in a slightly different formulation, in Lucillo Filalteo's 1554 Italian translation and paraphrased in numerous other works.[6] By the seventeenth century, surgeons, trying to elevate the status of their art, would also look to the *Oath* as setting the ethical ideals of their profession. The surgeon Tarduccio Salvi paraphrased it in his influential *The Surgeon, a Brief Treatise* (1613): the good and Christian surgeon will "neither give a pregnant woman a tampon or a beverage to kill the fetus."[7] While the translations of the *Oath* from Greek to Latin and Italian differed, the essence of the prohibition was clear.[8]

Hippocrates, however, was apparently conflicted on the subject of abortion. Codronchi and Mercurio were troubled that the same Hippocrates who prohibited abortion in his *Oath* also admitted (in the treatise *On the Nature of the Child*) to instructing an enslaved woman singer (considered a prostitute by some early modern commentators) to jump up and down and make her heels touch her buttocks, so she could abort what was believed to be a seven-day-developed embryo.[9] The famous physician, humanist, antiquarian, and Hippocrates apologist, Girolamo Mercuriale, acknowledged that "sterilizing or preventing the development of the *conceptus,* or killing it" was morally problematic for a Christian physician. But he did not outrightly prohibit the practice or condemn the physician when it was done for health-related reasons. Mercuriale saw Hippocrates's seemingly contradictory words and actions as consistent with Christian understandings of embryology and medical ethics, specifically delayed animation. Mercuriale held that in the *Oath*, Hippocrates was discussing the animate fetus, but in *On the Nature of the Child,* "the fetus which is not yet living and which is not animate." Abortion of the former was prohibited; the latter, less so, Mercuriale argued, especially when healing a pregnant woman who might be fatally ill.[10] Mercurio was less committed than Mercuriale to saving Hippocrates's moral reputation. "Don't tell me that Hippocrates teaches this doctrine because I will respond that Hippocrates was neither an angel nor an evangelist, and not everything he says is true, but, like other men, he can err, and even when he does not err, he was not a Christian."[11] In the mid-seventeenth century, the Roman forensics expert Paolo Zacchia stated with seeming certainty that "there is no one who does not know how grave a sin that doctor [who prescribes drugs to cause abortion] is committing."[12]

Medical practitioners, like doctor Giuliano and apothecary Teofilo, therefore received mixed messages. On one hand, they had two important ideological frameworks bidding them to steer clear of abortion.

Both God and the "father of medicine" allegedly condemned the practice. But not always. Male-dominated religious, legal, and medical institutions officially prohibited abortion through moral and professional discourse and through legislation—in theory. In practice, things were less clear. Like their ecclesiastical counterparts who moralized on abortion, medical authors like Mercuriale, Codronchi, and Mercurio simplified a complicated issue for rhetorical effect. In practice, abortion had multiple medical meanings. It could be the result of an accident or the unintended consequence of therapeutic intervention. Pregnancy could be misdiagnosed, genuinely, incidentally, or intentionally, as illness. Medicines, prescribed and consumed in order to cure, could induce abortion. While some might forbid a healer from inducing abortion in order to heal a pregnant woman who was ill, at risk, or in the process of miscarrying or who was carrying a dead fetus and at risk of dying, others (and perhaps most) would have thought such interventions imperative, justifiable, and moral. Moreover, medical practitioners—from midwives and barbers to apothecaries and physicians—might empathize with individuals desiring abortions. Some were even in their shoes, seeking to terminate pregnancies for their familiars or women they had impregnated. While abortion could have several discrete medical meanings, in practice, the neat divisions between licit and prohibited, accidental and intentional, rarely matched the messiness of its lived bodily and medical experience.

Reading Women's Bodies

In autumn 1569, shock and terror gripped the thirteen-year-old noblewoman Costanza Colonna as she delivered a dead male fetus in the Convent of San Paolo Converso, near Milan. Costanza had gone there to wait out the final stages of her marital separation from her husband, Francesco Sforza, on the grounds of his sexual incapacity. Until the moment she expelled the six- or seven-months-developed fetus, Costanza, the convent nuns, her physicians, and her husband had all insisted she was a virgin because Francesco was impotent. Costanza and her attendants had noticed her growing belly, but this was diagnosed by her physician as a symptom of dropsy of the womb, a blockage of fluids stemming from menstrual retention. When investigated by the archbishop of Milan's vicar general for possibly concealing pregnancy and procuring abortion, Costanza and her maids shifted responsibility to the physician, Francesco Ra, who misdiagnosed the pregnancy and prescribed therapy that likely caused the abortion. In his defense, Ra maintained he was deceived, not explicitly by Costanza or her familiars but by her body. He admitted that when he first began to treat Costanza, he suspected a pregnancy "since she did not have her proper courses," but having been assured by everyone of her virginity, he followed standard medical practice in diagnosing her with dropsy of the womb and prescribing medicines and therapies designed to purge obstructed matter and encourage menstruation. Costanza, her maids, the nuns of San Paolo Converso, and the physician all claimed to have been misled by her body. They drew on convenient yet real discourses of ignorance and ambiguity to defend themselves against charges of concealing and intentionally terminating her pregnancy.[13]

Ecclesiastical and legal authorities appealed to and expected medical institutions and individual practitioners, like Francesco Ra, to try to regulate the practice of abortion. In the sixteenth and seventeenth centuries, civic health boards increasingly issued legislation and threatened disciplinary measures against practitioners who participated in it. However, these authorities conceded that strictly regulating abortion was beyond the medical establishment's capacities for multiple reasons. At a basic level, individuals often intensely desired to terminate unwanted and threatening pregnancies, and this was often done secretly, with or without the participation of a healer. Abortive methods and products were widely known and easily accessible, so much so that policing was impossible. And Costanza's example reveals another key difficulty: the ambiguities of women's bodies and the uncertainties surrounding generation, pregnancy, and childbirth. For medical practitioners, like Francesco Ra, women's bodies could be deceptive. Healers often found themselves in problematic positions when trying to heal women suffering from womb- or menses-related illnesses. Women, too, might perceive and experience their bodies as confusing and treacherous, as Costanza claimed to have. But this ambiguity was also a resource that could be manipulated to intentionally terminate an unwanted pregnancy, as it might have been for young Costanza, who was hoping for a marital dissolution.

Responding to social, political, and religious imperatives that held pregnancy and fertility to be of public and spiritual—and therefore male—concern, in the sixteenth and seventeenth centuries, European and especially Italian medical practitioners embarked on intense study of women's bodies, anatomy, illnesses, and therapy in order to better understand and intervene in women's health, to maximize fertility and minimize risks in pregnancy and childbirth.[14] With a new emphasis on hands-on experience, anatomists had increasing access to deceased women's bodies, and their dissections often focused on the reproductive organs, with the aim of discovering the "secrets" of generation.[15] Famous anatomists and professors at Italian universities, such as Andreas Vesalius, Realdo Colombo, Gabrielle Fallopia, Juan Valverde de Amusco, Giulio Cesare Aranzio, Girolamo Fabrici d'Acquapendente, Giulio Casseri, Adriaan van den Spiegel and Johann Vesling, devoted considerable attention to women's reproductive organs and the pregnant uterus. Discoveries were made—including Fallopia's discovery of the tubes linking the ovaries to the uterus, to which he gave his name—and knowledge was created and disseminated in text and increasingly sophisticated anatomical images. Anatomical interest in women's bodies coincided with and spurred investigation into female physiology, pathology, and therapeutics. Inspired by the early sixteenth-century rediscovery of Hippocratic texts on women's medicine, physician-professors, like Albertino Bottoni, Alessandro Massaria, and Girolamo Mercuriale, gave university lectures and produced books devoted to systematizing women's medicine, while others, such as Sylvio Lanceano and Girolamo Perlini, produced specialized treatises on illnesses related to and complications stemming from pregnancy and childbirth. An important innovation, with wide-ranging influence, was the production of vernacular works of women's medicine, including Giovanni Marinello's *On Medicines Pertaining to Women* (1563) and Scipione Mercurio's *The Midwife* (1595), the first Italian book intended for practicing midwives. General and specialized works on surgery and pharmacology also devoted attention to therapies specific to women's illnesses, as did popular works in the so-called medical secrets genre, which developed in parallel with professional literature on therapeutics. By the end of the seventeenth century, physicians could claim, at the theoretical if not necessarily the practical level, to be undisputed authorities in all matters pertaining to

women's medicine. The Roman forensics expert Paolo Zacchia devoted
many chapters of his groundbreaking *Medical Legal Questions* to women's
bodies, frequently berating midwives and other lower-order healers for
their ignorance, which he argued often had devastating physical and
legal consequences. The Franciscan friar and professor of medicine at
Padua Bernardino Cristini continued a similarly patronizing discourse
in his long and impressive treatise *Illnesses Particular to Women,* which
contained over four hundred case studies (*observationi*), many of which
contrasted the erroneous and dangerous practices of midwives with his
own expert knowledge.[16] By the eighteenth century, medical authorities
throughout the peninsula worked to circumscribe the practices of midwives and, in unison with their civic and ecclesiastical counterparts,
established systems of licensing and formal examinations.[17] Responding to society's deep-rooted anxieties surrounding fertility, generation,
pregnancy, childbirth, and maternal health, these projects reveal an unprecedented level of intellectual and institutional investment in researching and understanding women's bodies and establishing male
medical practitioners as its experts.

Yet, even under constant investigation, the female body often con-
founded. *Corporal ambiguity*—the understanding that bodily signs and
symptoms could have multiple and even contradictory meanings—was
a fact of early modern life. This was paradigmatically true for the female body, especially pertaining to generation and pregnancy. While
anatomists developed more sophisticated understandings of the womb,
that organ remained stubbornly opaque in living women. Children
were born every day, but generation remained hidden and mysterious.
Pregnancy could be both obvious and impossible to detect. One could
never know with certainty what was taking place inside a woman's belly,
and attempts to discover its contents often ended in frustration, disappointment, surprise, danger, and sometimes death. This considerably
affected healing practices and the regulation and experience of
abortion.

Scholars in various disciplines have argued that the availability of
accurate pregnancy testing and obstetric ultrasonography in the twentieth century changed the meanings and experiences of pregnancy in
profound ways. By making fertilization, implantation, and the development of an embryo and fetus observable (in the sense of detecting the

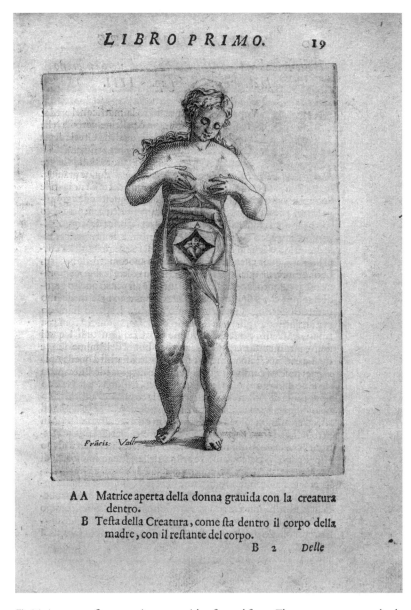

Fig 1.1 Anatomy of a woman's uterus with a formed fetus. The young woman modestly covers her breasts and looks down at her belly. Does she know that she is pregnant?

Girolamo (Scipione) Mercurio, *La commare o riccoglitrice* (Venice: G. B. Ciotti, 1601), p. 19. Courtesy of the Thomas Fisher Rare Books Library, University of Toronto.

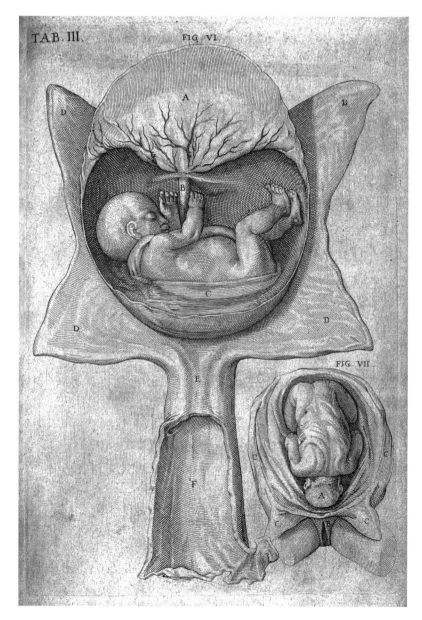

Fig 1.2 Disembodied gravid uterus with a formed fetus.

Girolamo Fabrici da d'Acquapendente, *De formato foetu* (Venice: Francesco Bolzetta, 1624), plate 3. Courtesy of Rare Books and Special Collections, University of British Columbia Library.

presence of the human chorionic gonadotropin hormone [hCG] in maternal blood or urine, suggesting implantation; and where sound waves are used to create visual images of a gestational and yolk sac, fetal pole cardiac activity, and an embryo or fetus in utero), these technologies have made pregnancy more easily knowable and, for those who use them and on whom they are imposed, a relatively unambiguous state of being. They have also made abortion politics fiercer.[18] Premodern individuals—and people today who lack access to these technologies or choose to forgo them—had no such certainties. Pregnancy, especially early in term, was not a fixed or objectively known state but depended on the way a woman perceived and interpreted her bodily experiences, influenced by age and education, fears and desires, and the evaluations and input of familiars, onlookers, and sometimes medical practitioners. The awareness of pregnancy developed in stages, growing in certainty over time and often influenced by more experienced women. A Roman woman Elena Cocchi expressed this gradual and collaborative awareness clearly: "When I began to know that I was pregnant, I had my midwife Dianora, who has [helped] deliver my other children, come and I told her I wondered whether I was pregnant and she looked at me and said I was and from that point I began to grow."[19] But pregnancy was only really confirmed with the delivery of a child, dead or alive. Prior to this, it was always uncertain—something people accepted. That uncertainty meant pregnancy was "to some degree negotiable."[20] While uncertainty was accepted, it was also cause for anxiety. It put women at risk of irrelevant, unnecessary, or dangerous medical interventions and exposed healers when they were called to diagnose and treat potentially worrisome symptoms. For individuals who wanted abortions and those who sought to provide them, uncertainty was a resource and a means to get around regulation.

Though it was accepted that the signs of pregnancy could be misleading, then as now, there was an intense desire to know as early as possible whether a woman had conceived. Male-authored medical treatises, letters women wrote to each other, and trial testimony from cases of abortion and miscarriage caused by assault allow some entry into perceptions and the phenomenology of women's bodies, pregnancy, and its termination. Learned and popular works of women's medicine and midwifery signaled the difficulty of identifying conception, as they

enumerated its "common" signs, including a "tightening and contrac-
tion" in the womb, fatigue, headaches, vertigo, decreased libido, loss of
appetite, unusual cravings, nausea, changes in the color and odor of
urine, increased urination, constipation, paleness, sunken eyes, weight
around the pubic bone and nave, and pain in the kidneys and lower
back.[21] While women, their familiars, and healers looked for these signs
as potential indicators of pregnancy, it was accepted that these were
relative—more pronounced in some, absent in others, and certainly not
specific to pregnancy.

Surer indications that a woman was pregnant appeared over time.
Absence of menstruation was one of the first signs women looked for to
discover pregnancy. Women, especially newlyweds and elites, often
monitored their menstrual cycles closely, as did their family members.[22]
The Grand Duchess of Tuscany, Christine de Lorraine, stated in a 1617
letter to her daughter the Duchess of Mantua, Caterina de' Medici
Gonzaga, that she thought Caterina was pregnant because she had not
menstruated in a while; as Christine regarded her daughter's menstrual
cycle as regular, she read its absence as potentially signaling pregnancy.[23] According to medical theory of the time, pregnant women did
not menstruate because the nutritive elements of menstrual blood were
needed to nourish a growing fetus; later, blood was transformed into
milk to feed the newborn. This transformation yielded another sign: a
pregnant woman's breasts swelled as they filled with milk that, further
along, might come out when breasts were squeezed. If nursing a child, a
woman was expected to stop lactating if she became pregnant. In 1634,
in her lawsuit against her abusive husband for causing her to miscarry a
three-months-developed fetus, Elena Cocchi explained that she knew
she was pregnant at the time of the assault because "I did not have my
times as I am used to having them and because the milk that was nursing my son dried up." Coupled with nausea and a loss of appetite, these
were "all similar signs that pregnant women have and that I had all the
other times I was pregnant."[24]

If retained menstruation suggested pregnancy, a growing belly
could make it public fact and a social experience. Early modern Italians
scrutinized women's bodies, and changes in shape and girth were topics
of conversation and gossip. For newlywed women hoping to be pregnant, a growing belly might be displayed with pride and different

clothing to alert observers to her soon-to-be status of matron. For single women lacking the prospect of marriage, a growing belly could be interpreted as the manifestation of sin and a wayward life; it could also alert onlookers to an episode of sexual violence. As such, it was threatening, something to be concealed, bound, and perhaps reversed by means of abortion. In 1586, "everyone" in the small town of Campugnano (near Bologna) knew Aorelia di Battista was pregnant—they saw she had a big belly—though Aorelia denied it. A widow with five children, Aorelia was described as poor, with a reputation of sleeping with migrant and temporary agricultural laborers for money. Townspeople stared at, scrutinized, and gossiped about her belly, because it might confirm her sins and desperation and justify her marginalized position in their community, but also perhaps, because it might lead to social disorder, as indeed it did when authorities from Bologna came to investigate the causes of her dead fetus.[25]

In other circumstances, a big belly on a single woman could be a shield and resource. In 1603, a seven-months-pregnant woman named Angela da Filletino, who self-identified as a courtesan, confronted her enemy Venere da Bologna, also a self-identified courtesan, on a busy street in Rome, in front of an audience of neighbors. Assuming Venere would not assault a woman with a big belly, Angela antagonized her and hurled shaming insults. When Venere could take no more, she started toward Angela ready to fight and may have struck her: an onlooker yelled out, "Stop, don't do it! You want to turn your back to Rome [i.e., be whipped by the authorities]? Don't you see she's pregnant?"[26] Bystanders intervened to break up the fight, but Venere was denounced to the criminal tribunal. Angela would later miscarry and successfully sue Venere for causing the miscarriage.[27] Knowing this episode ended in a dangerous miscarriage, it is indeed grim to think that Angela perceived her belly to be a protective barrier, behind which she could antagonize and shame her adversary without consequence. But her actions suggest this was how she saw it. Married women were also able to denounce their violent husbands to criminal tribunals and possibly sue for separation because their abuse caused miscarriages. This bleak reality underscores the social and micropolitical meanings of a growing belly beyond the indication of fetal life, future personhood, and future motherhood. A distended belly suggested pregnancy and shaped the way individuals perceived and interacted (or were supposed to) with a woman who bore it. For a married woman who desired it, a growing belly was a sign of hope and may have led to special treatment. For a single woman, it could bring shame and vulnerability, but it was also supposed to confer social and judicial protection, at least until childbirth. A growing fetus caused a growing belly and caught the eyes of neighbors, prompting gossip that shaped or reinforced a woman's social identity.[28]

For most medical practitioners and ordinary people, the most persuasive sign of pregnancy was the sensation of motion in a growing belly. The essayist Sperone Speroni reflected this: "I say, if the fetus moves, she is certainly pregnant."[29] In September 1618, Caterina de' Medici Gonzaga again hoped she was pregnant, and there were many signs, but she remained skeptical because she had not felt the fetus move.[30] While delayed or absent periods and a growing belly were relatively easy to observe, perceiving fetal motion, especially first movements, was often difficult. It was a subjective experience, influenced by numerous internal and external factors. Theologians and canonists equated motion with animation and theorized its date at forty days for a male fetus and eighty for a female. Medical authorities, unable to confirm or dispel these numbers (and likely thinking it was wise to leave the matter of animation to the theologians), related the timing of fetal motion to the fetus's level of formation or development. Determining an exact time frame was admittedly impossible, so these authorities preferred to give a range. Girolamo Mercuriale thought a male fetus could be formed anywhere from thirty-five to fifty days after conception. Following a formula found in the works of Hippocrates, physicians thought the time required for the fetus to be strong enough to move was approximately double the time taken for its formation. Using Mercuriale's numbers, this meant that if a male fetus was formed in forty days, it would begin to move around the eightieth day; if it was formed in forty-five days, it would begin to move around the ninetieth day.[31] While suggesting precision, medical authors (Mercuriale included) conceded there was no certainty in any of these numbers.[32] The Modenese physician Giovanni Marinello taught readers of his vernacular work on women's medicine to expect motion sometime after the third month for male fetuses and in or after the fourth for female fetuses, an opinion echoed by Juan Valverde de Amusco, professor of anatomy at the University of Rome.[33]

Waiting for the fetus to announce itself by moving could be a frustrating and anxiety-ridden disruption to everyday life. It indicates a uniquely gendered experience of time, where a woman's days might be dominated by intense concentration on perceiving and evaluating physical sensations in the hope or fear that another being was growing in her body. The perception of motion depended on the size and vigor of the developing fetus but also on what the carrying woman paid attention to, what she felt, and how she interpreted it. Class, marital status, and circumstances influenced this. Newlywed women, especially elites hoping to be pregnant with a male heir, likely felt substantial pressure to identify fetal motion as early as possible; the earlier pregnancy was determined, the sooner a regime of care could be undertaken to maximize chances of a healthy pregnancy. Women not wanting to be pregnant but fearing they were likely also ruminated on every abdominal rumble: the sooner they suspected pregnancy, the sooner they might try to intervene to terminate it. Every bodily sensation would have been scrutinized. Yet even women whose bodies were closely monitored could miss or misinterpret signs. Young women generally learned about the signs and sensations of pregnancy from seasoned matrons. In the mid-seventeenth century, the young Roman noblewoman Eugenia Spada-Maidalchini reported to her mother, Maria Spada, that she only began looking for signs of pregnancy after her more experienced relatives instructed her to: "I think I felt the baby because of what *they* said," Eugenia reported, "but I am not sure because I do not know if I can recognize it."[34] Recognizing "it" was not easy, requiring constant attention, education, experience, and often the oversight of experienced women. Above all, it required time. The attempts of Bianca Cappello, second wife of Francesco I de' Medici, to ascertain whether she was pregnant are illustrative. In the winter of 1587, there was suspicion that she might be but no confirmation, even after "four or five of [Florence's] best physicians looked and touched my body up to the meat."[35] Time revealed she was not pregnant. According to Paolo Zacchia, attempting to detect pregnancy before the fourth month was often a fool's errand.[36]

While the cessation of menstruation, a growing belly, the sensation of motion, and eventual lactation were all regarded as the best indicators of pregnancy, they were far from determinative or universal, and this made abortion difficult to regulate. And all these signs invited several medical readings. The signs suggesting pregnancy were also symptoms of womb-related illnesses. Retained menstrual blood could be shaping and nourishing a growing fetus, but it could also be trapped. Menstrual retention (*amenorrhea*) was commonly seen to afflict women, especially virgins, nuns, and widows whose sexual inactivity, it was thought, made them more susceptible to womb-related illnesses. Menstrual retention also caused milk-like secretions from the breast (*lactational amenorrhea*).[37] In the humoral system of medicine, a healthy and well-functioning body was one where humors flowed naturally throughout and were evacuated in a regular and balanced way. If humors became trapped due to a blockage (*oppilatione*), the body was unable to purify itself. Trapped humors could decay, making the body ill.[38] Many illnesses afflicting women were understood to stem from a clogged womb unable to purify itself through menstruation, a natural and vital form of purgation by which the female body expelled abundant or corrupting humors on a regular basis.[39] The longer a blockage persisted, the more danger of a woman developing ulcers, cancers, tumors, and severe fevers, which could prove fatal. There was also the risk of becoming infertile, as regular purgation was necessary for conception.[40] For all these reasons, absent periods were never regarded as a certain sign of pregnancy—in fact, Zacchia thought the cessation of menstruation was "the most deceptive." In many cases, women, especially those hoping to not be pregnant, would have interpreted delayed or absent periods as illness requiring healing rather than as signs of conception. A "missed" period never confirmed pregnancy, and the onset of a period was not considered evidence that a woman was not with child. Some women menstruated throughout pregnancy, Zacchia reported, and others menstruate rarely or never at all and "yet they conceive."[41]

A growing belly with the sensation of movement within also invited diverse medical meanings. If menstrual retention persisted too long it could develop into dropsy (*hidropisia*), a common illness in premodern Europe, in which a blockage of fluids in a limb or part of the body resulted in swelling. The sight of swollen cheeks, throats, forearms, hands, calves, or feet was not unusual, and women often suffered dropsy of the womb (*hidropisia della matrice*).[42] A clogged womb retained

blood, water, other fluids, and wind that a well-functioning body released on a regular basis. The buildup of fluids or winds caused the
womb and belly to distend: "The belly enlarges, and it seems to the
woman as if she is pregnant," Giovanni Marinello explained.[43] Furthermore, the bubbling and sloshing of the trapped fluids could be mistaken for fetal motion.[44] As well as looking pregnant, women suffering
dropsy of the womb were weak and lethargic, had trouble breathing,
and experienced pains in the belly and kidneys, all symptoms mimick-
ing pregnancy.[45] A woman's belly might also swell and look pregnant if
she developed a tumor or other growth in her womb, like a *mola,* a particularly dangerous and confusing generation.[46] Malign "fleshy"
growths, molae were described as roundish and hard to the touch,
growing in size and weight and rolling around in the womb like a ball.
Most medical authorities believed molae were generated through sexual intercourse; the mixture of insufficient or infirm seeds and blood
creating a mola instead of a fetus.[47] Medical texts described the mola as
a "generation gone wrong," a "corrupt conception."[48] Dictionaries, like
the one issued by the Accademia della Crusca, defined the mola as a
"false pregnancy."[49] Molae were much discussed in early modern medical literature; however, only a handful of physicians claimed to have
had actual experience with them. In this respect, molae were like "monsters"—real and not uncommon but observed by few.[50] While physicians
speculated on ways they, midwives, and women themselves might distinguish a mola from a true pregnancy, most agreed that only time
would tell. According to the physicians Scipione Mercurio and Alessandro Massaria, if a woman who appears pregnant has not given birth by
the eleventh month, she is likely not carrying a fetus.[51]

In the early modern period, the normative signs of pregnancy were
anything but. Pregnancy's shared signs with womb-related illnesses
created conditions for shock, disappointment, and fear when women
who hoped to be pregnant found they were instead suffering from a
dangerous illness requiring therapy. Scipione Mercurio reported several
instances of such missed diagnoses in his influential vernacular midwifery treatise. In one case, a woman of Tivoli believed herself pregnant
as her belly grew, but after fifteen months of waiting, she passed a great
amount of wind from her womb and her belly deflated, as did her hopes
of birthing a child.[52] In 1664, the Roman doctor and one-time papal

physician Mattia Naldi described the case of thirty-four-year-old Maddalena Simonetti, a married woman who appeared in all respects to be pregnant but in "labor" delivered only "a little fluid." Her menses subsequently returned, though her abdomen remained massively swollen until she died some twenty years later. An autopsy revealed she had carried a mola-like growth for over two decades.[53] For all these reasons, Paolo Zacchia thought no faith could be put in a swollen belly, an aphorism the Roman midwife Dianora Prosperi also held: testifying in a 1634 case of miscarriage caused by assault, Dianora, with over twenty years' experience, said, "It's not enough for a woman to be big to be able to know if she is pregnant, because there are many that are big and that are not pregnant."[54]

Conversely, women who thought themselves suffering from womb-related illnesses could discover they were actually pregnant. For some, this was joyous news; for others, devastating, creating a crisis in their lives. Mercurio recounts the case of an unnamed Venetian noblewoman who, after consulting several physicians regarding a mysterious illness, was diagnosed as "very sick" and in need of therapy. She traveled to Padua to be cured by the celebrated physician Ercole Sassonia of the University of Padua, who pronounced her not sick but pregnant. She gave birth a few months later to a "beautiful boy."[55] For Mercurio, this story served in part as evidence of pregnancy's slipperiness but also as professional boasting—only the best physicians could "read" women's bodies accurately. But even the most learned and distinguished physicians made mistakes, and these could prove disastrous. In autumn 1663, the Roman noblewoman Diamante Vecchiarelli was diagnosed by her physicians as suffering from dropsy as her belly swelled and she experienced abdominal pains. Neither Diamante nor her physicians entertained the possibility of pregnancy for several reasons: her husband, Andrea Muti, had been dead for approximately eight months; Diamante was thought to be infertile as she had produced no children in fourteen years of marriage; and she was known to be chronically oppilated. To address her dropsy, her physicians administered strong medicines to purge her womb of its trapped fluids. Much to everyone's surprise, Diamante delivered a healthy baby boy and named him Andrea Giuseppe Muti, after his father, who apparently impregnated her shortly before he died. Shocked, and relieved that the prescribed medicines had not caused an abortion, one of her physicians, the celebrated Gabriele Fonseca, admitted that his and Diamante's other physicians' incompetence was inexcusable.[56] Despite diligent effort, medical practitioners (including elite doctors like the papal physician Fonseca) and women themselves could misdiagnose pregnancy as illness.

While these cases ended happily, other instances of missed or misdiagnosed pregnancy could be traumatic, with higher costs. In the late seventeenth century, Bernardino Cristini described a situation he encountered while serving as the town doctor in Campitello (approximately ninety kilometers northeast of Trento). Virginia Roi, a twenty-eight-year-old widow, came to Cristini with a swollen belly thinking she was about six months pregnant. She said she felt all the sensations she had experienced in her previous three pregnancies. This was traumatic for Virginia because her husband was long dead and the "women of the town" were spreading rumors she had taken a lover, which Virginia vehemently denied. She even went to see her confessor to "certify that she was pregnant without knowing a man." Eventually she consulted Cristini, who told her not to worry because her pregnancy was in fact dropsy, which could be healed. Eager to publicly prove her innocence and honesty, when Virginia began to feel the "pains of childbirth," she called several women to her bedside to witness her expel a great quantity of water and wind, after which her belly subsided and her moral status was restored.[57] Besides harming a woman's reputation, a false pregnancy could have financial consequences. Paolo Zacchia was asked to give his opinion in a civil case where a woman named Violante Albenti was accused of living dishonestly and becoming pregnant after her husband's death. This was significant because Violante's husband's will left her his entire estate on the condition she remain faithful to him for the rest of her life; if she remarried or lived dishonestly, the estate would go to a specific (unnamed) charitable institution. Two years after her husband's death, the charity sued Violante for the estate on grounds that she was pregnant. Violante swore she had had no lover and was not pregnant, even though her belly was "swollen in a remarkable fashion." After several months, Violante passed a large amount of water with a fleshy growth.[58]

Pregnancy was both a bodily and a social experience. The cases summarized above reveal that social identity, reputation, marital status, and specific life circumstances influenced the way women's bodies were encountered, evaluated, and engaged with. For married elite women like Bianca Cappello-de' Medici, Eugenia Spada-Maidalchini, Diamante Vecchiarelli, and Scipione Mercurio's unnamed Venetian noblewoman, ignorance of pregnancy could be believed because these women had no apparent reason to deny it. While thirteen-year-old Costanza Colonna did have reason—she was hoping for a marital annulment from her reportedly impotent husband—she could credibly claim ignorance of her body due to her youth. Single women and those with dubious sexual reputations were judged differently. For Virginia Roi, a swollen belly led to malicious gossip and accusations; for Violante Albenti, similar accusations came with the risk of substantial financial loss.

Discourses ascribing ambiguity and duplicity to the female body influenced the perceptions of onlookers and also shaped women's relationships with their own bodies.[59] In some circumstances, they experienced them as baffling and treacherous terrain, reflecting contemporary medical views and cultural expectations. Women learned to interpret their bodies through instruction and experience. When asked by the vicar general of Milan, who had come to investigate why she had not admitted pregnancy, Costanza Colonna replied, "I didn't know I was pregnant, and the doctors treated me for an oppilation and dropsy." When asked, "Didn't your ladyship ever feel the creatura in your body in all those months?" Costanza responded, crying, "I didn't think of it"; "I didn't believe it until I saw the creatura." Ignorance of pregnancy and unintentional abortion, even by means of medical intervention, could be sincere and was accepted: "And seeing her in many tears and great anguish, and once more consoling her, [Costanza's examiner] said that, given her young age, she might not have known."[60] This was as true for elite women like Costanza Colonna and Diamante Vecchiarelli as it was for a single servant woman like Maria da Brescia, who, in 1577 Bologna, used a similar defense to exonerate herself from the accusation of intentionally aborting or smothering a fully developed fetus by delivering it into a latrine: "I had never been pregnant and I did not know what I had in my body. I thought I had a bubble in my body; I had no knowledge of being pregnant." Maria admitted to feeling strange pains in her belly but interpreted these as indigestion caused by some bad onions.[61]

For some women, absent periods, stomach pains, and a growing belly suggested pregnancy; for others, these same signs could be genuinely or willfully interpreted as indigestion, menstrual retention, dropsy of the womb, and other illness. Past experiences, self-awareness, and desire, as well as marital, familial, and social relationships, all shaped a woman's interpretations of her body and factored into how observers chose to interpret and interact with it.

While ambiguity often put women in precarious situations, it was also a resource that could be manipulated to intervene in reproduction. Ecclesiastical, civic, and medical authorities worried that women might choose to perform their pregnant bodies as ill, crafting convincing narratives to trick healers into misdiagnosis in order to procure medicines to induce abortion. Girolamo Mercuriale warned that "dishonest women seek such remedies from physicians to satisfy their lust and avoid reproach: all of them must be refrained."[62] Similarly, Bernardino Cristini cautioned, "There are women who are pregnant, from concubinage [or] adultery and they do not confess this, but rather try to fool physicians with the appearance of [menstrual] suppression, hoping to receive medicines and bloodletting [to induce] abortion. In these matters, physicians must be very warned."[63] This warning was difficult to heed. Costanza Colonna and her familiars may have pulled such a deception on the physician Francesco Ra in 1569. Medical practitioners acknowledged these situations put them at professional, legal, and perhaps moral risk, for which they had no solutions. The ambiguities of women's bodies made healing them tricky business. These same ambiguities also provided healers with convenient defenses should a criminal investigation materialize: doctor Ra may very well have known his interventions were intended to induce abortion, and this may have been okay with him; but it was also convenient that he could claim to have been fooled by the illness narratives and the ambiguous signs of Costanza's body in order to exculpate himself from any wrongdoing.

Purging the Womb

In spring 1613, Superio de Magistris, a wealthy man from the small town of Sezze, was trying to procure an abortion for his niece Maria de Vecchis, with whom he had been having sex for some time. Superio bought the purgative herbs calamint and aristolochia from a local empiric Cola Cocchiarello and the apothecary Pasquale de Tantis, respectively; he tried to get the town surgeon Mario Todesco and the barber Marzio Bracci to bleed Maria, though Bracci allegedly refused because there was no physician's prescription. Superio also convinced fra Maccabeo, a roaming Dominican friar and noted exorcist, to procure an infusion of colocynth and fresh savin from an herb seller in the Piazza Navona market in Rome. It appears the combination of all these drugs worked, and Maria aborted—allegedly, for she and Superio denied everything.[64]

Early modern Italians, like Superio, shared a common knowledge of medicines that were understood to be able to terminate pregnancy and knew where to get them. They knew because they often needed to and because the same medicines were routinely used to heal women of womb-related illnesses, such as retained menstruation and dropsy. Citing misogynistic literature of the period, some historians have represented knowledge of products that could terminate pregnancy as "women's secrets"—knowledge women possessed and transmitted to each other but not to men. A sixteenth-century commentator in the often-published *Secrets of Women*, a medieval work translated into several European vernaculars and purporting to expose men to women's alleged secret knowledge regarding sex, generation, and pregnancy, reported that "evil women" teach young girls how to abort "by boiling down certain herbs which they know well."[65] While women, especially midwives, almost certainly knew how to address womb-related illnesses and how to terminate pregnancy, and this knowledge was transmitted through networks of family, friends, and acquaintances, such tropes give the impression that men, including medical practitioners, were somehow denied this information and uninterested in acquiring it.[66] This does not ring true for sixteenth- and seventeenth-century Italy. Male healers and healer-merchants identified drugs that could contract the womb and stimulate menstruation and could therefore be used to induce abortion. Men responsible for unwanted pregnancies, like Superio de Magistris and priest Lauro Sarrio, learned what herbs and compound drugs could terminate pregnancy when they needed to and had their own, largely male, networks to obtain them.[67] That purgative medicines could be used to terminate pregnancy was not specialized knowledge restricted to medical practitioners; nor was it a secret that women in need whispered to each other. It was general health knowledge that women and men possessed or could learn through experience or social osmosis.

Knowledge of a rich array of simple and specialized medicines and their effects circulated on various social levels. It was acquired and transmitted through textual learning, personal experience, and relationships with a range of healers. Much information regarding herbs, compound drugs, and surgeries that encourage menstruation, induce cramps and uterine contractions, and purge the womb could be gleaned from learned and popular medical works discussing women's illnesses and how to treat them. Authors did not explicitly teach "what to do to have an abortion," but this was implied in discussions of what to avoid while pregnant for fear of causing miscarriage. The same laborious or jarring activities, traumas, medicines, and surgeries a physician, midwife, or experienced matron might warn a pregnant woman against or the therapies prescribed for menstrual retention, dropsy of the womb, or malign growths could be used to expel the unwanted product of a sexual encounter. The warnings a husband was given when his wife was expecting could be manipulated by a man seeking to rid himself of the consequences of fornication, rape or adultery. The relationship between purgatives and abortion was clear. According to the physician Giovanni Marinello, everything good for pulling out an obstruction could cause an abortion.[68] This duality gave women and men the means to try and control reproduction and exacerbated efforts to regulate abortion.

Early modern Italians appear not to have practiced invasive surgical abortion—inserting instruments into the womb to induce abortion. It simply does not come up in the historical record. My assumption is that invasive surgical abortion seemed too dangerous. Cesarean section was practiced, but specifically to extract a developed fetus when the pregnant woman could not deliver and might die, in the hope the fetus might survive or at least be baptized.[69] The most common methods for inducing abortion were bloodletting, especially from the saphena vein in the foot, the consumption of purgative medicines, vigorous activities, and blunt trauma to a woman's abdomen.

Letting blood from the foot might strike a modern observer as a peculiar way to heal an obstructed womb or terminate pregnancy;

however, it made sense within the humoral system of medicine and was a regular therapeutic practice from the time of Hippocrates until the eighteenth century. In his *Discourse on the Bleeding of the Human Body* (1584), the surgeon Pietro Paolo Magni taught that the saphena vein in the inner side of the foot was important for women because it was connected to the uterus. Anatomists, including Vesalius, Realdo Colombo, and Juan Valverde de Amusco, apparently confirmed this. (In fact, the saphenous vein, via its tributaries, stretches almost to the pubic tubercle but does not connect to the uterus.) Letting blood from this vein was thought to stimulate the womb and encourage blood flow downward, resulting in a menstrual purge. The vein was therefore commonly referred to as the "vein of the mother," "menstrual vein," or "virgin's vein," (it was thought that virgins often suffered illnesses due to insufficient purgation).[70] Giovanni Marinello prescribed that up to six ounces of blood be let from the saphena vein of a woman suffering from menstrual retention and related illnesses.[71] Barber-surgeons practiced this procedure, as did midwives, who also prescribed it for their patients, though they were often officially prohibited from doing so.[72] A woman being bled from her foot appears to have been a common sight in early modern Italy.

Because it was believed to encourage menstruation and purge the womb, such bloodletting was also used to terminate pregnancy. In medical works, physicians warned barbers against bleeding pregnant women.[73] Paolo Zacchia was explicit: "Blood let from the feet can induce an abortion so directly and rapidly."[74] Civic health boards officially proscribed the practice. In Bologna, barbers were forbidden to let blood from a pregnant woman's foot without the "expressed permission, either from the mouth or in writing from an approved physician," under threat of a twenty-five-lire fine.[75] In the first few weeks or months of pregnancy, a menstrual flow was thought to suffocate the fetus and wash it away; in later pregnancy, the return of menstruation and loss of blood from the venesection deprived the fetus of its source of nourishment, which could lead to its death.[76] These effects were well known throughout early modern Europe.[77] This was Superio de Magistris's hope when he sought out the barber Marzio Bracci in Sezze to bleed Maria. The bloodletting doctor Francesco Ra conducted on Costanza Colonna to cure her dropsy was understood to have contributed to her

Fig 1.3 Under the supervision of a physician, a barber surgeon and his assistant let blood from the foot of a sickly young woman, held up by a familiar. The saphena vein was believed to be connected to the uterus. Letting blood from this vein encouraged contractions and menstruation. It was commonly used to treat menstrual retention and to induce abortion.

Pietro Paolo Magni, *Discorsi . . . intorno al sanguinare i corpi humani* (Rome, 1584), p. 61. Hathi Trust Digital Library.

Fig 1.4 In contrast to the image in Magni's book, here the scene is dominated by women: the barber surgeon appears to be in a convent and is assisted by a nun in the bloodletting of a young nun who is being comforted by her fellow sister.

Cintio d'Amato, *Prattica nuova et utilissima di tutto quello, ch'al diligente Barbiero s'appartiene* (Venice: Giovanni Battista Brigna, 1669), p. 24. Hathi Trust Digital Library.

abortion.[78] The practice was so ubiquitous that the priest Girolamo Sertorelli mentioned it in his work on sin and confession: confessors were to ask penitent barbers and surgeons, "Have you drawn blood from the veins of [a pregnant woman's] foot to make her abort?"[79]

Letting blood was often used in combination with purgative medicines, fixtures in all healers' practices. In the humoral system of medicine, most illnesses derived from fluids and matter being trapped in the body and were healed by evacuation. Purgatives were commonly consumed to encourage bowel movements, urination, vomiting, and sweating.[80] Women frequently consumed them in a variety of forms to cleanse an infirm or blocked womb or encourage menstruation and fertility—conception was thought to be facilitated by a purified womb purged of corruptions and more receptive to male seed. Purgatives were also consumed to help women through childbirth by inducing contractions and encouraging delivery, to expel stubborn afterbirth or deliver a dead fetus trapped in the womb.[81] This meant they could also terminate pregnancy. Physicians explicitly advised pregnant women to avoid purgative medicines. Girolamo Mercuriale warned his Latinate readers that purgative herbs such as savin (a species of juniper) should be kept away from pregnant women because they were "inimical to life" and would corrupt the fetus. When used intentionally to terminate pregnancies, purgative herbs and drugs were referred to by some medical authorities, such as Albertino Bottoni, professor at the University of Padua, as *maleficia medicamenta*, medicines used for evil purposes.[82] It was not the nature of the drug but the intention behind its use that turned a purgative into an "evil medicine."

Information regarding herbs and drugs to purge the womb and induce abortion was widely available in medical works produced for various audiences. Literate medical practitioners and apothecaries learned of medicinal herbs ("simples") in works of materia medica and pharmacy, genres of medical writing that proliferated in the sixteenth and seventeenth centuries. The newly available *On Medical Material* by the ancient Greek author Dioscorides (translated into Latin and Italian in 1544 by the naturalist Pietro Andrea Mattioli) provided a wealth of knowledge regarding Mediterranean plants and their medicinal uses, inspiring the composition of many practical and theoretical works of pharmacy.[83] These described numerous herbs that could stimulate menstruation, unclog a blockage, encourage childbirth, dislodge a trapped fetus, or terminate one in development. The following outlines the herbs most commonly used for these purposes.

Under *aristolochia* (birthwort), readers found that this plant is so called because of its ability to help women with childbirth and postpartum purgation (i.e., it brings on the *lochia*). Aristolochia stimulates menstruation, purges retained fluids, induces birth, and expels afterbirth; it could also drive the fetus from the womb before it is due, which "most of the time ends up killing it." *Artemisia* and its subspecies *matricaria* (both belonging to the asteraceae family of plants and related to chamomile and sunflower) had similar properties. Boiled and consumed or steeped in a bath, these herbs induce menstruation, help in childbirth and the expulsion of the afterbirth, and purge a clogged womb. Made into plasters and rubbed into the pubic bone, they induce menstruation; their juice combined with myrrh and inserted into the womb "pull every [obstruction] out." The herb *sabina* (savin) was also widely used as a menstrual stimulator and sometimes to "kill the fetus in the belly." Grinding the fronds of the plant *calamintha* (calamint, lamiaceae family) into a paste or making *scammonia* (scammony) into a juice and inserting either of these into the womb (as pessaries) could release retained menses and also kill a fetus. *Bryonia* (bryony), also known as *vete* (or *vite*) *bianca,* purges the womb, encourages menstruation, removes the afterbirth, and "kills the fetus in the body." *Pulegio* (pennyroyal), *ruta* (rue), *centaurea* (in the asteraceae family, like *artemisia*), *coloquintida* (colocynth), *elleboro* (hellebore, in either its white or black varieties), and *mandragora* (mandrake root) were also well known and commonly used for purging the womb and to "kill the unborn and drive it out."[84] This list represents a fraction of the herbs with these properties described in works of pharmacy. Variously prepared and administered, purgative herbs stimulated menstruation, induced childbirth, expelled afterbirth, and other tissues from the uterus, expelled dead fetuses, and terminated ones in development.

Apothecaries also made more specialized compound drugs—by combining several purgative herbs and other medicinal substances—regarded as stronger and more effective but also more dangerous. In the sixteenth and seventeenth centuries, health boards and colleges of physicians throughout Italy issued official pharmacopeias or "antidotaries," books or lists of approved and standardized medical recipes, to

quo quis coniiciat , ſi lubet , hanc illis indigenis , corrupta Italica uoce Metti in borſa , ideo Pettimborſa nomina-
ri,quòd tot uiribus commendetur , ut perinde ac gemma,crumenis aſſeruari mereatur: aut quòd tantùm uiribus excellat,
ut medici ea utentes ingentem argenti,& auri copiam crumenis ſint repoſituri , Teuriani planta ſic Græcis,Gentiana ſimili
ter Latinis uocatur : Mauritanis, Gentiana,Gentiana baſilica,ſeu Baſateca : Italis,Gentiana : Germanis,Entzian,uurtz, Nomina.
ſiue Creutz uurtz : Hiſpanis, Gentiana : Gallis,Gentianne : Boemis horce : Poloniis Gonyczka .

Ἀριστολοχία.　ARISTOLOCHIA.　　　CAP. IIII.

ARiſtolochia nomen ex eo ſibi adoptauit,quòd exiſtimetur optimè puerperis opitulari.Tria eius genera traduntur . Rotunda, quæ fœmina uocatur, folijs hederaceis,præſtanti odore cum acri-

ARISTOLOCHIA ROTVNDA.

Fig 1.5 Aristolochia (birthwort) was one of the best known and widely used herbs for women's purgation. As its name suggests, the plant was celebrated for its ability to help women with childbirth and postpartum purgation. The botanist Pietro Andrea Mattioli wrote that aristolochia stimulates menstruation, purges retained fluids, accelerates childbirth, and expels afterbirth; it could also drive the fetus from the womb before it was due, which often resulted in its death.

Pietro Andrea Mattioli, *Commentarii in sex libros Pedaci Dioscoridis Anazarbei de medica materia* (Venice: Ex officina Valgrisiana, 1565), bk. 3, ch. 4, p. 647. Courtesy of the Thomas Fisher Rare Book Library.

protect consumers from erroneously prepared or fraudulent drugs that could harm and possibly kill.[85] In these technical and specialized works, apothecaries found approved recipes for compound medicines, along with brief descriptions of their uses and effects. All licensed vendors of simples and compounds were required to have a copy of their city's official pharmacopeia and follow its instructions when making medicines. They were expected to know that purgative drugs could terminate pregnancies and that they were, therefore, to take great care when selling them.

A survey of official pharmacopeias from several Italian cities suggests many powerful compound drugs that could cause abortion circulated commonly throughout the peninsula. The index of Bologna's 1641 pharmacopeia listed more than fifty compounds for "healing the womb." Most contained several of the purgative herbs listed above. Composed of black hellebore, aristolochia longa, artemisia, centaurea, cassia fistula, myrrh, rue seed, pennyroyal, apio, and savin, the *antidotum haemagogum* was one very strong purgative. As its name implies, this electuary was used primarily for encouraging menstruation, but it was also used to expel uterine obstructions, a dead fetus, and afterbirth.[86] The *Roman Antidotary* explicitly warned apothecaries against giving this compound to pregnant women because it would "kill the fetus."[87] The electuary *triphera magna* had similar effects. When enriched with artemisia, it was regarded as very effective in stimulating menstruation and terminating pregnancy.[88] The *trochisci hysterici,* a lozenge or pill composed of powdered myrrh, castoreum, savin, aristolochia, matricaria, and rue juice, ingested orally or inserted into the vagina and cervix, cured its namesake, hysteria (suffocated and wandering uterus), by pulling the uterus downward to its natural place. It could also release retained menses and expel a fetus, as would *syrup of artemisia* (a combination of artemisia, matricaria, pennyroyal, calamint, savin, rue, and betony), *hiera archigenis* (a pill made with black hellebore, myrrh, colocynth, and aristolochia), *trochisci of myrrh,* and many other drugs composed of or derived from purgative simples.[89]

Pharmacies from Venice to Messina were to stock the simples from which these purgative drugs were made and know how to compose them when needed. However, health offices also tried to regulate their traffic. In some places, apothecaries were officially prohibited from selling purgatives and other powerful medicines that could be used for "nefarious" purposes without a physician's prescription. The hierarchies of medical practice and the economics of medicine are explicitly evident here. In 1595, the head of Rome's health office (*protomedicato*), Marsilio Cagnati, issued a bylaw prohibiting apothecaries from selling poisons, opiates, solutives (purgatives and laxatives), and "[substances] that could make a pregnant woman abort" without a written prescription from a physician, under threat of a twenty-five-ducat fine and possible corporal punishments, depending on the circumstances surrounding the sale of the medicine and its consequences.[90] Similar prohibitions were issued in Bologna from at least 1581 onward. The Bolognese authorities warned that if apothecaries distrusted the dosage on such a prescription or suspected "any error" (tampering by the customer?), they were to go in person to verify with the physician; otherwise, they were not to give the substance to the customer. Apothecaries could be fined twenty-five gold scudi if something went wrong with the patient.[91] A certain level of medical competence on the part of the apothecary was required to make these assessments and catch any errors, but to ensure no misunderstanding, in 1653, in his second term as protomedico of Rome, Paolo Zacchia amended his earlier ban by explicitly naming simples prohibited from sale without a prescription; among others, he listed hellebore, savin, scammony, and castor bean seeds (*semi di ricino*), all simples used to both heal women of womb-related illnesses and terminate pregnancy.[92] Similar prohibitions were issued in Palermo in 1657.[93]

Behind these restrictions lay concerns regarding patient safety and the circulation of dangerous substances that could be used for illicit purposes. Many of these simples could be highly toxic if consumed in high doses, and some were used as poisons. On one hand, prohibiting the sale of purgatives without a physician's prescription may have been the expression of concern that certain drugs could be very harmful to pregnant women and might even cause death. Unintentional abortion stemming from medical intervention was considered serious and could lead to criminal proceedings; should the woman die from complications the healer could be prosecuted for homicide. On the other hand, prohibitions on selling products that could terminate pregnancy were also attempts by municipal health offices to monitor and regulate the practice of procured abortion. Authorities warned that the properties of some purgative drugs were so well known that young women often tried to acquire them from apothecaries under false pretense in order "to cover up their mistakes."[94] Though such sources suggest women tried these tricks, at the moment we lack evidence of women as direct patrons of apothecary shops. In most cases, it appears to have been men who purchased medicines for the women in their lives.[95] Without a prescription from a physician, apothecaries were to assume individuals, men or women, seeking to purchase these purgative drugs could use them for abortion and were therefore not to sell them. By restricting the prescription of drugs to learned and licensed physicians, the reasoning was, there would be fewer unintended consequences for patients and fewer procured abortions. And by making an individual get a prescription, a physician would also get paid.

Requiring a physician's prescription of course indicates that physicians could prescribe medicine with the explicit intention of inducing abortion. Physicians were permitted, in certain situations, to intentionally terminate pregnancies for health reasons. It was university-educated and licensed physicians, and not lower-order healers, who were to make these decisions. The need to publish legislation year after year, however, suggests that apothecaries and other vendors continued to sell prohibited substances without authorization. In another 1595 Roman bylaw, protomedico Marsilio Cagnati expressed frustration that vendors of medicines (droghieri) were illicitly selling purgatives "every day." Cagnati ordered his proclamation to be hung prominently in every pharmacy, so anyone walking in would see it and know they could not purchase such products from this type of healer without a prescription.[96] Such legislation was meant to introduce new laws but also to restate ones that were being disregarded. In fact, it is clear that consumer demand drove this "illicit" purgative trade. As a number of historians have shown, the sick often preferred to have apothecaries, barbers, surgeons, and midwives heal them rather than physicians.[97] The Neapolitan apothecary fra Donato d'Eremita stated that "common people hold an apothecary in higher regard than a physician," likely due to their knowledge of drugs and because they were more affordable and practical healers. If an apothecary knew which drug healed a specific illness, why would a consumer go to a physician, only to be sent to the apothecary later? Succumbing to pressures of competitive medical marketplaces, apothecaries often disregarded prohibitions and sold certain purgatives to those who sought them.[98]

Prohibitions against selling purgatives without a physician's prescription were likely difficult to enforce and often conflicted with social values, including male prerogatives and obligations to look after women of the household. An amended Bolognese bylaw of 1600 appears to confirm this: apothecaries were told they could not sell "dangerous, poisonous, abortive or analgesic" substances without having seen a prescription, "*except* to the head of the family / household," and if they kept a record of the buyer, the quantity of the product, and the reasons given for its purchase.[99] This bylaw does not suggest a head of a household could walk into a pharmacy—a space of sociability and that has been described as a proto-public sphere where medicines were sold but also where news was discussed and gossip circulated—and unproblematically request a *medicamento abortivo,* a drug to terminate a pregnancy.[100] It likely meant a person of good reputation could buy a purgative drug that might be used as a diuretic, to encourage menstruation, or for other womb-related issues for a woman in his household. The buyer of a decoction of aristolochia or savin, or perhaps an antidotum haemagogum, a triphera magna, or a trochisci of myrrh, might purchase these for his virgin daughter suffering from retained menstruation; for his wife requiring a menstrual stimulator to purify her womb in order to get pregnant or because she was ready to give birth and wanted to accelerate the process or to encourage a postpartum purge; or for his mother, just entering menopause and suffering from hysteria.[101] The fact that a head of household could purchase these same products for his unmarried daughter who might be pregnant; for his pregnant wife in order to avoid another mouth to feed; or for another woman, a servant perhaps, whom he, his son, or another man had impregnated might have been problematic for medical, civic and ecclesiastical authorities, but in many cases unavoidable. Only the reputation of the customer, it seems, enabled an apothecary to evaluate the intended use of the purgative. The physician Giuliano Amato and the apothecary Teofilo Mari told the authorities that they trusted the priest don Lauro Sarrio, believed the story of a childbirth emergency, and did not hesitate to sell him a purgative decoction intended to expel the creatura, dead or alive—perhaps his priestly vestments banished thoughts that Lauro might use this medicine to induce abortion? Perhaps they did not care what he intended to do with the product?[102] Sometimes even a sullied reputation did not prevent someone from acquiring herbs that could cause abortion. Superio de Magistris, whom everyone in his town of Sezze suspected was having a sexual relationship with his niece Maria, had no reservation asking the apothecary Tomeo Ciolli for a remedy to make a "woman from a good family" abort in order to spare her from scandal; nor did various healers hesitate to give him materials to that effect.[103] Apothecaries and herbalists were likely not centrally concerned with such issues or may have sympathized, even empathized, with the women and men confronting unwanted pregnancy. Some knew of theologians who thought it licit to induce abortion—especially if the fetus was not yet animate—to prevent scandal or when they feared the woman was at risk of violence or even death. Moreover, some apothecaries were in these very situations themselves, as we will see.

Midwives, of course, also had considerable knowledge of herbs and drugs that were efficacious for women's health and for abortions. The assumption has long been that midwives were the main practitioners of abortion. However, primary source evidence has not yet confirmed this to be true for early modern Italy. In fact, we know relatively little about actual midwives and their healing and child birthing practices.[104] In his influential vernacular midwifery treatise, Scipione Mercurio represented midwives as competent in the art of uncomplicated childbirth but ignorant when it came to women's anatomy, illnesses, and their cure.[105] He thought it his responsibility to teach midwives about illnesses commonly afflicting women and how to heal them, and in discussions of womb-related illnesses, he included information regarding purgative medicines. While he stated that giving women purgative medicines was officially a physician's job and not a midwife's, Mercurio thought it prudent to describe what herbs should be given to women suffering from dropsy or difficult or delayed labors; who could not expel the afterbirth or deliver a dead fetus; or women who harbored malign growths in their wombs. Mercurio assured his readers he was not trying to "turn midwives into physicians" but rather seeking to equip them with necessary knowledge and skills to do their job properly and safely. "I have taught her to give medicines out of care," he felt the need to explain.[106]

Mercurio's representation of midwives' ignorance and his self-assigned responsibility to educate them was self-aggrandizing and likely did not reflect most midwives' knowledge and capabilities. Midwives were indeed the experts on childbirth and were also regarded as knowledgeable about women's bodies and illnesses, sexual lives, and reproduction. They regularly served tribunals as witnesses in cases hinging on the examination and interpretation of women's bodies, including those concerning procured abortion, miscarriage caused by assault, infanticide, rape, and defloration, as well as cases of marital dissolution on grounds of impotence and sexual incapacity.[107] Midwives also offered a range of healing services to women, children, and possibly men and were sources of therapeutic information in their communities. This troubled health boards, and legislation was increasingly issued prohibiting women from engaging in healing practices outside of standard midwifery. In 1620, the Roman protomedico decreed that women could only participate in the medical establishment as midwives and in childbirth; any attempt at healing was subject to a twenty-five-scudi fine. The need for such legislation, repeated throughout the seventeenth century across the peninsula, suggests midwives were doing just that.[108] In 1642, Angela Rhighetti, a midwife in Bologna, was sentenced to pay a twenty-five-lire fine and forfeit the drug she "made and sold for women's purgation."[109] Later in the century, Bernardino Cristini related a case where a twenty-one-year-old (unnamed) woman from San Vito (in Abruzzo), four months pregnant and suffering from fevers, consulted a midwife who gave her purgative medicines. The medicines caused the fetus's death, which was reportedly not desired or intended, and it remained trapped in the woman's womb until Cristini expelled it with even stronger purgative medicines. In relating this case, Cristini's intention was clearly to show his learning and the midwife's ignorance—he accused her of "wanting to play the physician." However, the story also suggests women turned to midwives when they were ill and that midwives provided purgative medicines. For many women, midwives like Angela Rhighetti and Cristini's unnamed midwife from San Vito may have been primary conduits for these products. Testifying before a governor's criminal tribunal in a case of miscarriage caused by assault, the Roman midwife Dianora Prosperi said, "To be a good midwife, [a woman] must have many qualifications": alongside the usual skills in healthy and safe delivery and determining whether a woman was pregnant, how far along she was, and when she would deliver, Dianora told the judge a good midwife "should know how to proceed and to give opportune remedies" to a pregnant woman feeling certain types of pains and "to give medicines and [treat a pregnant woman] with waxes" when she sees signs suggesting the risk of miscarriage.[110] Although confined (perhaps strategically) to pregnancy, Dianora's words indicate midwives possessed therapeutic knowledge and procured, fabricated, and administered medicines. They also transmitted elements of their therapeutic knowledge and experience to university-educated physicians. Unlike Mercurio and Cristini, Giovanni Marinello had no problem admitting he had learned from a midwife that a simple decoction of pennyroyal steeped in wine was successful in expelling stubborn afterbirth.[111] Women in need of a purgative to encourage menstruation or those trying to have an abortion might turn to a trusted midwife for information and products. While physicians and health boards increasingly tried to circumscribe and regulate these practices, in the early modern period, many still used midwives as their primary "agents of health."[112]

Women and men also learned about therapies that healed womb-related illnesses and that could induce abortion from popular works of so-called medical secrets. These inexpensive and popular self-help manuals, with eye-catching titles such as *Medicinal Secrets*; *Secrets of Medicine, Surgery and Alchemy*; *Universal Secrets . . . Containing Remedies for all the Infirmities of the Human body and also for Horses, Cows, and Canines* developed in parallel and in competition with professional literature on therapeutics and flourished in the early modern print market. These publications were important vectors, transmitting knowledge in multiple directions. Authorship ranged from university professors to charlatans. Authors communicated the central tenets of Hippocratic-Galenic physiology and pathology, but with a clear focus on therapy, to broad audiences in a simplified and practical way. They also disseminated empirical, artisanal, and "folk" remedies to university-educated physicians. Historians have suggested these works were used primarily by lower-order healers and ordinary people, who learned from them how to self-medicate in relatively straightforward and accessible ways. As most healing took place within the household, such books would have proven quite useful.[113]

In these texts, a reader found remedies for various illnesses of the womb—how to induce menstruation, increase fertility, ease difficult labor and the passing of the afterbirth, and expel a dead fetus. Information was similar to but less intricate than that found in treatises for medical professionals. Authors of books of secrets recommended letting blood from the "vein of the mother" and decoctions and electuaries containing calamint, myrrh, pennyroyal, aristolochia, savin, matricaria, and many other purgative herbs.[114] For stimulating menstruation, Pietro Bairo promised savin was "the strongest" of all purgative herbs.[115] Such recommendations were often accompanied by warnings that if consumed during pregnancy these might "corrupt the fetus" and cause abortion.[116] After recommending a concoction of matricaria, savin, and other simples for inducing menstruation, the compiler of a collection of remedies (apparently gleaned from the work of the famous anatomist and professor of simples at the University of Padua, Gabrielle Fallopia) urged his readers not to give this to a pregnant woman because it would cause her to abort. It would not only harm her body but would cause the death of a fetus without a soul, a "very horrendous sin." The author assured his readers his remedies were published for good, not evil. Used appropriately, this recipe would heal womb-related illnesses; used for evil, it could cause great scandal.[117] Thus, the relationship of purgative to abortifacient was explicitly stated. No matter how adamant the author was that he was not teaching how to terminate pregnancy, that was indeed what he was doing, and this may have added to his book's appeal.

Women and men used some of these recipes to terminate unwanted pregnancy. Neither a physician nor an apothecary was needed to procure some of these products. Purgative simples could be purchased from informal healers, such as charlatans and herbalists, or even from grocers in public squares, who sold many of the same herbs as apothecaries but were less systematically monitored by medical authorities.[118] One could pick some purgative herbs wild, for free; according to the *Roman Antidotary*, aristolochia grew in the countryside just beyond the Quirinal Hill.[119] There was no way to control the consumption of such herbs in rural areas. Gardeners (*ortolani*) knew how to grow plants like aristolochia and that their roots, steeped in wine and oil, could expel a dead fetus.[120] Those who bred and cared for horses and other livestock also knew which herbs would purge a mammal's womb, help with difficult labor, or induce abortion. According to Carlo Ruini, Bolognese senator and author of a work on equine anatomy and care, "occasionally one needs to abort pregnant horses for the utility and accommodation of men," especially if they are noble, expensive, destined for racing or other exercises, or simply because they have been "impregnated against the will of the owner."[121] According to Mattioli, farmers, peasants, and "herb-women" often knew the healing properties of plants because of their experience with nature, an association, especially for women, insinuating magic and witchcraft.[122]

It is important to understand that purgative herbs like aristolochia and savin, compound drugs like triphera magna, and bloodletting from the saphena vein were not *abortifacients* in the sense that this was their primary application. They were purgative herbs used for general healing and to alleviate various ailments and they also had emmenagogue and abortifacient properties. As historians have argued, it would be a mistake to assume every menstrual regulator was covertly used by women to avoid or terminate pregnancy or that the phrase "to bring on the menses" was code for "have an abortion."[123] Most women used purgative medicines to promote health by means of encouraging menstruation and releasing trapped and corrupting fluids. In a 1629 letter to her father, the famous scientist Galileo, Sister Maria Celeste Galilei advised she was feeling much better since Doctor Ronconi gave her a purgative "in order to try to remove an obstruction that has troubled me . . . for the past six months." She also wrote that Sister Violente, who apparently suffered from similar illnesses, "continues purging" herself.[124] To treat the noblewoman Violante Corsa who suffered from dropsy of the womb, the celebrated physician, protomedico of Rome, and Pope Sixtus V's personal physician, Giovanni Zecchi, prescribed phlebotomy and purgative drugs (including syrup of artemisia and decoctions of savin leaves, matricaria, and pennyroyal), along with exercise, baths, and fumigations, all to encourage menstruation and expel obstructed matter.[125] Perhaps ironically in relation to contemporary Western medical views, these purgatives were also consumed to encourage fertility. Zecchi prescribed many of them to an unnamed Roman noblewoman having difficulty conceiving and to another unnamed woman from Macerata who had just suffered a miscarriage—he recommended she be purged at least twice before attempting to conceive again.[126] Apothecaries and health boards in Venice, Bologna, Rome, and Naples marketed triphera magna as a fertility drug: according to the Venetian apothecary Girolamo Calestani, "it helps [women] conceive and get pregnant."[127] And this was exactly how some women used purgative therapies. In a 1617 letter to her mother, Caterina de' Medici Gonzaga indicated her desire to be purged in order to maximize her chances of conceiving.[128]

Nonetheless, individuals also believed bloodletting from the foot and purgative medicines could terminate pregnancy. In 1603, Mennoca Liberatori, from the small town of Filletino in Lazio (approximately seventy kilometers east of Rome), debated consuming colocynth (*melo stricto* in her vernacular) to terminate her unwanted pregnancy—she thought this herb might work because she "heard it said that it is used when women give birth and their afterbirth has not been expelled."[129] Determining whether these purgative drugs or bloodletting worked in terminating pregnancy is a contentious issue and beyond the scope of this book.[130] What matters here is that early modern Italians believed these therapies worked and used them accordingly, but they also knew they could be unreliable and dangerous. Authorities tried to regulate their consumption because they were known to work and could be dangerous. Women suffering from retained menstruation and dropsy of the womb consumed decoctions of savin and aristolochia or the compound triphera magna with the expectation of expelling trapped blood or other fluids, regulating menstruation, and alleviating their illness. Pregnant women who consumed such drugs may have expected or feared abortion.

Women and men knew what to say to healers to procure purgatives, and to judges to exonerate themselves from accusations of procuring abortion. Although buying potentially dangerous medicines was becoming more difficult in an increasingly regulated medical marketplace, in the sixteenth and seventeenth centuries, purgatives could be acquired through numerous sources with relative ease. In 1613, one of Superio de Magistris's agents reportedly bought savin from an herb seller in busy Piazza Navona, no questions asked; in 1624, the eighteen-year-old seminary student Antonio d'Avossa reportedly procured a purgative beverage from a vendor in Naples, hoping to terminate his lover's pregnancy. The sources currently available suggest that, generally, women did not purchase their own medicines from apothecaries but relied on male proxies.[131] But apothecaries were not the only conduits for these materials. Mennoca Liberatori acquired colocynth without male assistance in her small town of Filletino in order to terminate her pregnancy. The physician Bernardino Cristini reported that an unnamed nineteen-year-old unmarried woman in the small seaside town of Ortona al Mare (approximately thirty kilometers south of Pescara) "procured some herbs to abort," apparently "from some women." It is unclear where these herbs came from—perhaps they were picked wild or grown in personal gardens.[132]

In cities, health offices and civic authorities sought to regulate abortion by regulating the practices of healers and healer-merchants. Primarily, the onus to police abortion was put on apothecaries, barbers, midwives, and herb sellers. Given the high demand for bloodletting and purgative medicines and that the intention of the procurer could never be known with certainty, most vendors would not have hesitated long before selling products that could be used as abortifacients. Depriving a sick woman of a healing purge on the chance she was pregnant could worsen her condition.[133] Moreover, many vendors may not have cared to inquire into their customers' intentions. As we will see in subsequent chapters, moralists' conceptions of the gravity of abortion were not necessarily shared by all or even most individuals. Healers and purveyors of medicines may have empathized with some women who found themselves pregnant or the men who impregnated them and came seeking a purge to escape the hardship and punishment a pregnancy could bring. Indeed, some apothecaries found themselves in these situations. In 1610, the apothecary Flaminio Danzetti was denounced to the criminal tribunal of Rome for allegedly giving his pregnant lover, nineteen-year-old Artemisia d'Europia, a beverage that, according to her sister Lavinia, caused her to abort an eight-months-developed male fetus and ended up killing her.[134] Around the same time, Giovanni Antonio Calander, an herb dealer in Naples, was tried for raping, deflowering, and impregnating his servant, Superna de Cyno, and giving her or forcing upon her an "abortion-inducing potion, one so strong and poisonous that one take was enough to take the life of both the fetus and the pregnant woman." According to the jurist Camillo Borelli, who consulted on the case for the Great Court of the Vicaria of Naples, there was much evidence to suggest Giovanni's guilt: "He is an apothecary and dealer of medicines, and so he could have easily procured the venomous potion."[135] We know about these cases because women died, allegedly of complications from attempted abortions; their impregnators were the prime suspects because they had motive and could easily procure the materials. This was likely not an uncommon situation, although one hopes most women had better outcomes than Artemisia and Superna.

An individual in desperate need might also turn to more mechanical and violent methods, for which they needed no medical practitioner. In discussions of how to avoid miscarriage, medical authors warned women to avoid certain physical activities, like running, climbing stairs, dancing, and jumping. Riding in carriages was regarded as especially dangerous because the bumps and jerking battered the fetus, weakened the membranes binding it to the uterus, and could cause it to slide out. Scipione Mercurio moralized that riding in carriages was so ingrained among Italian elites that pregnant noblewomen could not break the habit despite the harm that could arise from this vain amusement.[136] Some noblewoman did, however, pay heed. In an April 1617 letter, Christine de Lorraine warned her daughter Caterina de' Medici Gonzaga, believed to be in the early months of pregnancy, not to ride in carriages for at least another month because any jolt could dislodge the tiny fetus from its mother.[137] Pregnant women were also to avoid strenuous labors and, above all, violent encounters. Anything that shook or damaged the body and made a woman tighten or contract her belly could cause miscarriage.

Women wanting to abort might reverse this advice. The *Secrets of Women* compendium stated, "Harlots, and women learned in the art of midwifery, engage in a good deal of activity when they are pregnant. . . . They dance and take part in many other evil deeds. . . . They have a great deal of sex, and they fight with men. They do all these things so that they might be freed from their pregnancy by the excessive motion." An unidentified sixteenth-century Italian commentator on this added that these methods were common knowledge among "evil women," who taught them to "young girls who have become pregnant and wish to hide their sin."[138] Learned physicians like Albertino Bottoni also thought these methods were regularly practiced by prostitutes.[139] Tommaso Garzoni, author of best-selling encyclopedia *Universal Piazza of all the World's Occupations* (1585), associated this knowledge not with young prostitutes but with their pimps, male and female, who were more experienced in sexual matters and for whom a pregnant prostitute was a liability.[140]

Medical practitioners struggled to isolate the causes of miscarriage. Authors of medical works enumerated countless factors, internal and external to the body, that could terminate pregnancy. Internal causes referred to a woman's particular humoral complexion and her anatomy, which might predispose her to conditions causing sterility or an inability to carry a fetus to term. Wombs that were tightly packed, loose, overly large or small, too fat or thin, phlegmatic, humid, slippery, too cold, hot, moist, or dry were inconducive to generation and detrimental to fetal development. Aside from these inherent shortcomings, acute or chronic illnesses a woman might suffer during pregnancy could severely damage the fetus and possibly cause the woman's own death. Emotional health (*passione delle anime*) also affected pregnancy and was to be regulated. Depression, grief, fear, and anger were especially dangerous for pregnant women.[141] This discourse had moral and legal currency. The theologian Marco Scarsella warned that frightening a pregnant woman could cause her to abort, and the individual responsible for the fright would be guilty of a mortal sin.[142] In a 1603 case of miscarriage caused by assault investigated in Rome, the judge looked into whether fear of being attacked or hit with a stone caused six-months-pregnant Angela da Filetino to turn ill and later abort.[143] Environmental factors, such as quality of air, climate, and temperature, also influenced what transpired within women's bodies. Stagnant or pestilential airs and temperatures that disagreed with a woman's natural constitution could cause or worsen illness, potentially causing miscarriage. A pregnant woman needed to watch her diet and, of course, not consume purgative herbs.[144] Girolamo Mercuriale considered all these factors as he tried to construct a regimen for the exasperated Duchess of Parma and Piacenza, Maria Aviz-Farnese, who had suffered six miscarriages in four years. Mercuriale could not isolate one specific

cause but preferred to list several medical issues needing to be addressed prior to Maria trying to conceive again.[145]

In early modern Europe, pregnancy was often regarded as pathological; the growth of a fetus in the womb weakened a woman's constitution, made her more prone to illnesses, and augmented their danger.[146] For women hoping to be with child, pregnancy could be a happy
time but also a time of uncertainty and anxiety—maternal mortality
appears to have been high, although we lack demographic studies to
confirm this. Many women made wills and were urged to confess before
going into labor. Miscarriage, stillbirth and potential death from childbirth complications, it was believed, could arise from any combination
of factors influencing a woman's physical and mental health. Pregnant
women were responsible for the health of their fetuses and had to com-
port themselves appropriately—what they consumed, their activities,
social relations, and emotions were now particularly important and
had to be regulated. However, even the strictest discipline could not
guarantee the safe birth of a living child. The causes of miscarriage
could be something as distant as a malign celestial constellation, as
dreadful and inevitable as an outbreak of plague, or as simple as a
cough, a bout of gas, or an uncomfortable bed, which was blamed for
Maria Virginia Borghese-Chigi's miscarriage in 1658.[147] "Any little disturbance can cause abortion," Scipione Mercurio warned.[148]

For all these reasons, medical practitioners were often unable to
distinguish between miscarriage and induced abortion. Testifying in a
1613 case of suspected abortion, the midwife Adlotia Pomponi from
Roccagorga (approximately eighty kilometers southeast of Rome) assessed the body of the suspect, Maria de Vecchis, and concluded Maria
had given birth naturally, miscarried spontaneously, or had an abortion: "I cannot know which," the midwife told the judge.[149] Even the
foremost forensics expert of the period, Paolo Zacchia, admitted he
could not differentiate between induced and spontaneous abortion
early in pregnancy: "Investigating the signs of an early abortion seems
to me to be a pointless endeavor," he wrote, "since sometimes [sponta-
neous] abortion occurs so readily in the first months that women themselves experience it as a rather difficult purgation of the menses." Spontaneous abortion was common, and the physical traces were often
identical to those of induced abortion, leaving Zacchia to state it was

often impossible to distinguish "whether a woman has given birth, had an abortion, or none of the above."[150]

Medical authorities had more to offer in cases of abortion caused by violence. Criminal courts often investigated cases of abortions allegedly caused by assault, calling on medical practitioners to examine abused women's bodies and aborted fetuses to determine causes. In medical texts, as in manuals of confession and works of jurisprudence, abortion caused by violence was commonly, though not exclusively, associated with men.[151] In most cases, abortion was not the direct aim of an assault, but sometimes it was. In 1606, Marsilia Tomasi told a judge her abortion was caused by a purgative beverage that the priest Lauro Sarrio gave her and by her cousin Isabetta jumping on her back and kicking her kidneys.[152] In another seventeenth-century case reported by Paolo Zacchia, an unnamed priest allegedly caused a thirty-three-year-old woman to miscarry by beating her, specifically directing blows to her kidneys with a stick. Though details are lacking, the cleric may have been responsible for the pregnancy, and the beating intended to terminate it. Violence was likely a desperate resort for women and men seeking to terminate unwanted pregnancies. Though probably effective, abortion by violence would have been very dangerous; the woman in Zacchia's case hemorrhaged to death following the abortion.[153]

Abortions to Heal

Early modern medical authors discussed another context for abortion, where causes were less ambiguous and intentionality clearer: abortion induced for or as a foreseeable consequence of healing. So-called therapeutic abortion appears to have been a common yet controversial practice that figured prominently in medical, religious, and legal discussions of abortion.

It was widely believed that pregnancy weakened a woman, made her more disposed to illnesses, and could turn even a minor illness serious and potentially fatal.[154] In his work *Death caused by Pregnancy, Abortion, and Childbirth* (1607), the Roman physician Girolamo Perlini discussed the myriad illnesses and diseases that could arise and be intensified during pregnancy. Many stemmed from anatomical and humoral issues. While menstrual blood goes to nourish the fetus in pregnancy, in some cases it can go unconsumed, accumulate, drown the fetus, and corrupt in the womb, causing such illnesses as dropsy and various potentially fatal fevers.[155] Women could also simultaneously generate and nourish a mola and a real fetus, posing a threat to both the woman and the fetus.[156] In the case of a woman carrying twins, if one fetus died, both the living fetus and the pregnant woman were at risk. Confronted with such situations, some healers and their patients thought it appropriate to medicate a pregnant woman who was in considerable peril, even though the intervention could terminate the pregnancy.

Believing in prevention, physicians urged women to put their bodies in their care versus that of midwives, in advance of pregnancy, and to consult regularly to maximize the chances of a healthy pregnancy without dangerous complications. Evidence suggests some, generally but not exclusively elite, women did seek physicians' advice on how to manage pregnancy.[157] The physician would customize a regimen for the woman's specific physiological needs and alter it as needed in order to safeguard her from illness. If a woman's specific complexion predisposed her to certain acute or chronic illnesses, the physician would try to offset this imbalance through diet, activities, light exercises, and medicines if needed.[158] Some women, however, might be deemed "unfit for conception" altogether. Someone who was perpetually sick or whose womb appeared unable to support a fetus should, according to Girolamo Mercuriale, "dedicate herself to virginity" and life in a cloister rather than the marriage bed.[159] Midwives might be asked to probe a woman's genitals and digitally examine her cervix and uterus to ascertain whether she was capable of coitus and her anatomy conducive to conception and pregnancy. Such examinations were also standard in cases of marital dissolution on the grounds of sexual and generative incapacity.[160] If the woman's genitals, cervix, and womb were deemed too tight for sexual intercourse and too narrow to support fetal growth and childbirth, healers might try through various means to loosen and stretch them. We do not know how common these practices were, although we do know they were carried out in high-profile marriages where the birth of an heir was politically significant, but even then, examinations and interventions were no guarantee.[161] Trial and error was the only sure way to know whether a woman could conceive, carry a fetus to term, and deliver it alive. Women were warned to take every precaution to maximize the chances of a healthy pregnancy and delivery, and medical practitioners had to be prepared to intervene to minimize the risk of miscarriage or the death of the pregnant woman.

Physicians thought it better to prevent conception altogether for women who were likely to suffer complications, had a history of miscarriage, or suffered from dangerous chronic illnesses during pregnancy. Some medical authors—especially those writing in Latin—taught methods of avoiding conception, such as using liniments to prevent the meeting of seeds or having the woman jump around and take baths immediately following coitus to expel male seeds. In his 1562 vernacular collection of materia medica, Francesco Sansovino felt no trepidation listing eighteen medicinal substances that prohibit conception.[162]

But what should be done for women who thought or knew they were pregnant and were deemed at risk of serious health dangers or death? Inducing abortion to heal a woman at risk forced healers, in theory and perhaps in practice, to assess the moral value of a fetus in relation to the dangers threatening the pregnant woman. Theologians had long wrestled with the ethics of therapeutic abortion, questioning whether it was permissible to commit a "wrong" (the termination of the fetus) to bring about a "good" (healing a pregnant woman). The so-called doctrine of double effect, conceived of by Thomas Aquinas and elaborated on over the centuries, factored into medical discussions and perhaps practices. In print, physicians were seemingly conflicted. In practice, it seems they prioritized a woman's health and well-being.

Theologically conservative physicians such as Codronchi and Mercurio unequivocally rejected the practice, arguing that pregnant women should endure their ills, minor or fatal, and that, instead of medical intervention, "hope [should] be placed in Omnipotent God, who formed the fetus, [and] is able without our help, or aside from our hope, to save it."[163] Instead of administering purgatives, which would likely kill the fetus, Mercurio thought it better to appeal to the majesty of God with orations and votives that might save both pregnant woman and fetus. He urged midwives to get between the physician and the sick pregnant woman and convince them not to intervene but to endure and pray. The midwife, according to Mercurio, should tell the woman that choosing therapy might cause abortion, a great sin, and that she would be severely judged by God if she made her fetus "taste death before life" by introducing herself to her issue "as a murderer rather than a nourisher."[164] Mercurio assumed the physician believed the practice to be licit and unproblematic. He aimed to change this by convincing the pregnant woman and the midwife that abortion is a sin, inspiring them to resist the physician and to change his mind on such therapeutic interventions.

Not all healers agreed with Codronchi and Mercurio's black-or-white attitude. Girolamo Mercuriale thought that if the life of the woman was in significant risk, the physician should try to heal her even if it could result in the death of the fetus. In these cases, he argued, the physician should not be thought to have committed a mortal sin or crime. Mercuriale drew on theological discussion of direct and indirect causation to justify his position: "I say that it is never permitted for a physician to make killing the fetus his end. It is permissible for him to treat the woman with necessary medicines which may harm the fetus, but it is never permitted to pursue a treatment with the intention of killing the fetus." As long as the physician has acted with the intention to heal, he has not acted contrary "to our inviolable faith," Mercuriale argued.[165] His learned colleague Albertino Bottoni agreed, stating almost as an axiom that "a physician should first tend to the mother and then try to conserve the fetus."[166] After instructing surgeons never to bleed a pregnant woman because it could cause abortion, Tarduccio Salvi added an important qualification: "When forced by some urgent cause, like a continuous fever, or other accident, physicians order phlebotomy, reasoning that they are not phlebotomizing a pregnant woman as a pregnant woman, but as a fevered woman." He continued by urging caution, recommending only a little bit of blood be drawn and from the vein in the arm versus the foot.[167] Zacchia also concluded that "because pregnancy in some women is so deadly that it is unavoidable for them to die along with their fetuses unless they abort . . . then it seems to be not only permitted but fair to procure an abortion for the purpose of saving at least the mother."[168]

In practice, the issue was not so simple. Medical authors thought that inducing abortion was dangerous, especially when a woman was further along in pregnancy and if she was ill and weak.[169] Indeed, before the advent of modern medical technologies and practices that have made abortion safe, the termination of pregnancy could be dangerous and potentially fatal, though not necessarily any more dangerous or fatal than pregnancy and childbirth itself. Early modern people, and those today who lack access to legal and safe abortion, knew that complications could arise and result in trauma and death.[170] Although they used different terminology, they identified and experienced incomplete abortions (where a dead fetus or tissue remained trapped in the uterus), severe hemorrhage, infection, sepsis, and poisoning and, as we have seen, developed, as best they could, therapeutics to address these complications.

Mercuriale, who accepted the practice in theory in certain circumstances, was skeptical of whether a healer could induce abortion in a dangerously ill woman without causing her death. He noted that Aetius and Avicenna, two pillars of the Western medical tradition, "agreed that it should be permitted to kill an animate fetus" in these circumstances, but he challenged them on the limits of medical certainty: "I would like them to tell me, whether any doctor can be so skilled to not kill the mother with substances that destroy the fetus. This is certainly not a promise any doctor can make, since the substances which destroy the fetus are poisons, they are toxic and hostile to the mother. Moreover, it is clear that during an abortion, the woman undergoes the perils of death, and so I cannot see how a doctor can avoid the risk of killing the woman along [with the fetus]." Like his later contemporaries Codronchi and Mercurio, Mercuriale concluded prayers might be the best medicine.[171] Several medical writers echoed this concern, but it was disputed. In certain circumstances, Bottoni thought it better for a physician to carefully induce and manage an abortion rather than let a woman suffer, because the illness itself could cause miscarriage, which he judged more dangerous as it was more unpredictable. Because letting nature take its course was too risky, Bottoni thought physicians were better off intervening: "We ought to carry out the work of nature by facilitating and accelerating the abortion," he argued.[172] Bottoni suggested bloodletting and purgative simples and compounds, referring his Latinate reader to the remedies he described in detail in his discussion of menstrual retention. Mercurio dismissed this as medical hubris and tried to convince his readers that inducing abortion in an already dangerously ill woman was a surefire way of killing both the fetus and the pregnant woman.[173] He also challenged the practice on moral grounds: "It is not true that everything that the ancients allowed should also be allowed to the Christian and God-fearing physician, to whom I speak. Avicenna was a Turk. Aetius was not Christian."[174] The practice was both morally and medically fraught.

Medical practitioners, of course, preferred to heal sick pregnant women without harming the fetus, but this was never easy and, according to some, not possible.[175] The Spanish physician and author of an influential work of women's medicine Juan Raphael Moxius thought it possible and licit to medicate pregnant women in two periods: either very early in pregnancy (aborting an inanimate fetus—regrettable but morally licit) or in late term. He argued that abortion induced for health reasons after the seventh month was licit because the fetus is able to survive or at least be delivered alive and baptized before its death. Zacchia however was skeptical of such results. He thought the post-seven-month fetus more likely to be destroyed in the womb because the abortifacient drugs required to expel it needed to be very strong: "The larger the fetus, the more violence is inflicted, and the more powerful are the drugs needed to cause an abortion." The drugs and process of delivering a dead fetus would also, he thought, greatly harm the pregnant woman: "This procedure can on neither side be so secure that, after the abortion is induced, the health of the mother is sure to follow. Whenever we induce an abortion, that mother is surely exposed to a mortal risk to her life, as experience often demonstrates that women also meet their end with drugs of this sort."[176]

The fear of losing an unborn child and possibly their own lives may have led some pregnant women to suffer through illness and eschew therapy, at least to a certain extent. Maria Spada, writing to her pregnant daughter, Eugenia, who was experiencing bouts of debilitating nausea, warned her not to tell her physician about the illness, perhaps fearing any medicine he might offer could terminate the pregnancy and damage Eugenia's fertility and health.[177] Nevertheless, if illness was judged significantly dangerous, some women, their families, and their physicians thought administering purgative medicines was a necessary course of action, even if it threatened the unborn child. This held true in the highest echelons of society, who were most concerned with lineage. In the spring of 1551, a pregnant Eleonora di

Toledo, wife of Cosimo I de' Medici, was diagnosed by her physicians as dangerously oppilated. She was given strong medicines that healed her but caused the abortion of a six-months-developed female fetus. At the time, Eleonora was around twenty-nine years old and had already birthed nine children. With an heir lined up, Eleonora's family, handlers, and physicians judged this medical intervention to be necessary. Unfortunately we do not know how this decision was made or carried out, what Eleonora thought about it, or how she experienced it.[178] Approximately one hundred years later, in autumn 1649, a pregnant Olimpia Aldobrandini Pamphili (wife of Camillo Pamphili) fell ill with a sickness her physicians judged grave enough to warrant bloodletting, which appears to have resulted in abortion.[179] In these situations, the pregnant woman's health was valued above that of a fetus and the potential loss of a future child. No doubt, the marital status and class of these women helped make them candidates for such medical care and shaped the way their abortions would have been understood. We do not know how common such interventions were and whether they were as available to unmarried and non-elite women as they were to noblewomen. In theory, if not necessarily in practice, these abortions were morally and medically justified because they involved women who had accepted the social norms that were to govern them: women who had desired children and wanted to be or were already mothers. They were not for women who simply did not want to be pregnant or for whom pregnancy did not bring immediate and severe health risks, even if it brought immediate and severe social risks. Nevertheless, that authors devoted considerable and careful attention to the subject of abortion induced for or as a consequence of healing suggests purging pregnant women was part of standard healing practices but also that it was controversial and required justification.

Inducing abortion in cases where a fetus was believed to be dead in the womb was less controversial but still contentious. A dead fetus had to be expelled quickly before it began decomposing within the woman's body, which could quickly turn fatal.[180] If it could not be expelled naturally, healers had to intervene. In print, physicians recommended medicines to soften the womb and make it slippery, followed by strong purgatives designed to encourage contractions.[181] In 1608, the Roman

physician Pietro Bresciani prescribed a trochisci of myrrh to help
Ginevra Rossi expel a fetus he estimated had been dead for about one
week.[182] If medicines failed, a midwife might try to pull the dead fetus
out manually. If this proved too difficult or dangerous, a surgeon might
be called to extract it with hooked instruments; rarely was cesarean section an option on a living woman. The longer the dead fetus remained
in the woman's body, the greater the risk and urgency to remove it.

The opacity of the female body, however, rendered even these procedures problematic, the difficulty being determining with certainty that
the fetus was dead. Again, motion was the primary sign indicating fetal
life. If neither the carrying woman nor a medical practitioner could detect motion, the fetus was presumed dead. But this was never sure. The
priest and theologian Bartolomeo Gittio recounted a 1619 case he pur-
portedly witnessed in Benevento, where an unnamed pregnant woman
was in considerable pain and believed her fetus was dead in her body,
but she could not expel it. Her midwife agreed the fetus was dead "for it
made no motion" for some time. They requested a physician come to
the house to administer medicines to induce labor. (Evidently the midwife did not have purgatives to offer.) While they waited for the physician, the woman surprisingly delivered a living boy, whom Gittio was
able to baptize just before it died. Potentially a bit of pious fiction, Gittio's message was that, in uncertain situations, healers should not intervene in haste: "Women are very often deceived" into thinking their
fetus is dead because they do not feel motion. "While lack of motion is
a sign of a dead fetus," he continued, "their great pain does not allow
them to perceive this motion." Gittio laid the blame on women, without
addressing why medical practitioners were also deceived. He cautioned
that, prior to administering medicine to expel a presumed dead fetus,
some time should pass in case it begins moving or is born alive and that
before decisions are made, "not one but two learned persons" should be
brought in to assess the situation.[183]

Even for physicians and in circumstances of medical need, it was
never an easy decision to induce abortion. While Gittio worried that
women and their healers might mistake an immobile fetus for a dead
one, others feared individuals might manipulate this situation by
feigning dangerous illness or a dead fetus to terminate unwanted pregnancy, which is exactly what the priest Lauro Sarrio was accused of

doing in 1605. While lack of motion was considered the most indicative sign of a dead fetus, healers still looked for maternal signs to make the diagnosis, including sharp abdominal pains; unfamiliar heaviness; depressed eyes or pallor; an inability to hold urine or stool; a soft, slack belly; a hard, dense lump in the belly; fevers or shivers; belly and genitals cold to the touch; a fetid odor emanating from the vagina and through the mouth; the umbilical cord hanging outside of the vagina and turning black; or the expulsion of a lot of blood or the afterbirth but not the fetus.[184]

Yet, even when they were sure a fetus was dead and a woman's life was in danger, some healers hesitated to intervene. The Roman physician Timoteo Camotio confronted such a terrible scene in 1603. He was sent by a judge to Angela da Filletino's house to examine her and to later testify in her trial against Venere da Bologna for trauma caused by assault. Timoteo determined that Angela had been harboring a dead fetus in her womb for about a week. He was sure of this because he saw the umbilical cord, cold and black, hanging outside Angela's vagina—"manifest signs of a dead fetus," he told the judge. While he stated that the rotting fetus was increasingly putting Angela's life in danger, Timoteo thought it best not to intervene but to wait and hope the fetus would be expelled naturally, which happened the next day. Perhaps he knew it would be expelled imminently or feared a purgative drug or other medical intervention would prove fatal for Angela.[185] Other physicians, in different circumstances, did not hesitate to intervene. Bernardino Cristini's reported case from the seaside town of Ortona al Mare where the unnamed and unmarried nineteen-year-old woman "procured some herbs to abort (from some women)" is an example. The herbs half worked, and the fetus died but remained trapped in the woman's womb. After six days of agony and fear, the woman's "friend" begged Cristini to secretly come and help. Cristini did not hesitate. He gave several powerful purgatives, including a steeped broth of powdered aristolochia root, savin leaves, and a trochisci of myrrh, and inserted a pessary containing ground black hellebore root, colocynth, and myrrh into her vagina. These strong purgatives worked quickly, apparently taking only a quarter of an hour to induce contractions and expel the trapped fetus and afterbirth. According to Cristini, the woman recovered well. Evidently, Cristini, a Franciscan friar as well as physician, had no qualms about helping this woman; nor did he use her case as an opportunity to moralize on this issue.[186] Nevertheless, the contextual details he provided (that she was nineteen and unmarried and had tried to procure an abortion from a lesser healer) suggest an underlying point: abortion was risky and dangerous.

It is unclear how often healers were faced with the decision to induce abortion for healing purposes, but the fact that physicians, jurists, and theologians frequently discussed the matter suggests it might have been common enough to be controversial and to require justification. Officially, university-trained physicians were the only medical practitioners authorized to make the decision, but in practice, a variety of healers probably provided purgative medicines or prescribed phlebotomy for pregnant women who were ill, at risk of miscarriage, or carrying a dead fetus. While they preferred physicians make these decisions, jurists agreed that, as long as a purgative was given and consumed with the intention of healing, neither the provider nor the consumer should be tried for a crime. Most jurists thought no punishment should be meted out in these situations because, according to Giacomo Menochio, jurist and senator in Milan, an abortion committed for the sake of healing was similar to committing "murder in self-defense."[187]

Conclusion

Early modern medical discourses regarding the female body, pregnancy and its termination underpinned ecclesiastical and secular attitudes and practices surrounding abortion. Medical thought on abortion was interwoven with theological commitments and legal frameworks. However, medical conceptions emerged as paramount factors shaping how onlookers interpreted the signs of women's bodies and how women related their experiences and interpretation of their own bodies. Ambiguities and uncertainties surrounding women's bodies shaped the stories individuals could tell others and themselves to explain the appearance of those bodies, dispel accusations of pregnancy, and counter charges of intentionally procuring or assisting in abortion. The meaning of abortion was always open to interpretation because pregnancy, the operations of the female body, and its healing were always complicated.

Even under constant scrutiny, the female body remained unpredictable and opaque. Signs of pregnancy could be symptoms of illness and vice versa. Medicines procured for healing and even to encourage fertility could cause abortion. Credible medical explanations explained such incidents and accidents. At the same time, discourses of uncertainty and ambiguity could be manipulated by women and men to pursue a course of action best benefiting them. Women who suspected they were pregnant and did not want to be could choose to present their bodies as ill and in need of a purge. Women and men knew or could learn through experience, observation, and social networks or from reading medical books that ingesting herbs like savin, artemisia, and aristolochia and letting blood from the foot encouraged menstruation, expelled trapped fluids and corrupt humors, contracted and purged obstructed wombs, accelerated childbirth and the expulsion of afterbirth, and could therefore be used to induce abortion. These products were widely available in cities and the countryside. They could be purchased, with or without a prescription, from a pharmacy or grocer or picked from the earth; they could be combined with other herbs and made into compound medicines or steeped into simple beverages in kitchens and consumed privately at home. What is more difficult to ascertain is how decisions to procure and consume products to purge the womb were made in real time. At what point did a woman suspect she might be unhappily pregnant and try to procure medicines to abort? At what point would a man responsible for an unwanted pregnancy purchase medicines or resort to violence to terminate it? At what point would a medical practitioner judge a woman at significant risk to warrant medical intervention that might terminate pregnancy and put her life in danger?

Evidence of experience is, of course, elusive and always difficult to interpret. We can assume that awareness of pregnancy and actions taken to terminate it were likely proportional to levels of threat. As we will see in greater detail in the next chapters, pregnancy could sometimes be disastrous for women, their families, and their impregnators. A woman, a family member, and the man responsible for the pregnancy might monitor her body closely and procure purgative medicines at the first suspicion of pregnancy in order to encourage menstruation and purge her womb. While dominant discourses primarily associated abortion with unwed women, women in less threatening situations—married women or those in stable non-marital relationships—also procured abortion, though perhaps with less urgency. The meanings ascribed to abortion were shaped not only by medical discourses but equally by the social and political contexts and the circumstances in which they occurred.

Rosana and Giovanni

ROSANA DA POLI AND GIUSEPPE ANSALONI were married on a January day in 1596, in the Borgo neighborhood of Rome just east of the Vatican.[1] They were surrounded by family: Rosana's mother, Fantilla da Poli, a laundress; her sister, Pelegrina, and her husband, Giovanni Manello, a Sicilian rosary maker; and the groom's brother, Giacomo Ansaloni, a local barber-surgeon and friend of Giovanni Manello. Rosana's father was absent and may have been dead.[2]

The joy of the occasion apparently did not outlast the wedding night. Giuseppe found that his bride was not a virgin. He kept asking her what happened, "why she is not a virgin." After repeated denials, Rosana allegedly told him about her sexual past. She confessed that her brother-in-law Giovanni had violently raped her. Giovanni and Pelegrina lived upstairs from Rosana and her mother. In the middle of one night some months earlier, Giovanni had gotten up from his marital bed and gone downstairs to Rosana's room, which she shared with her mother. After muzzling her with a cloth, so she could not cry out, Giovanni had sex with her "with force." Her mother, who was sleeping with her—possibly in the same bed—woke up and saw what was happening. Fantilla began to shout, but Giovanni placated her and returned to his wife's bed.[3]

Fantilla apparently acted the next day, when she threatened to bring a lawsuit against her son-in-law for deflowering Rosana, but Giovanni pacified her by promising a dowry for her now compromised daughter. This arrangement, it seems, was beneficial to all: the household's reputation would not be damaged by making a shameful sexual transgression public; in the eyes of neighbors, onlookers, and prospective husbands, Rosana would still be regarded a virgin; and she would have a dowry with which to attract a husband. Fantilla would have known a trial against her son-in-law for this transgression (which in fact constituted three crimes: defloration/rape, adultery, and incest) would have been a shaming and uphill battle. Had she pressed charges, Giovanni could have argued that Rosana was a willing participant or that Fantilla allowed her daughter to be deflowered or had even pimped her, in exchange for money, and that what transpired that night was consensual or brokered sex, not violent rape, although it would still have been adultery and incest. Perhaps lacking a better chance for her now-compromised second daughter to marry, and likely fearful of notoriety and losing the financial contributions Giovanni had been making to the household, Fantilla apparently agreed to his proposal—money for a dowry would likely have been the most she could have expected from a court case anyway.[4]

But Rosana's troubles did not end there. About three months after the rape, she discovered she was pregnant. Before her belly could alert onlookers to the fetus growing inside, Giovanni put a plan in place to procure an abortion. By her husband's later account, Rosana resisted this intervention, knowing it to be dangerous and a terrible sin, but Giovanni convinced her, saying it would be "her good fortune and she would not be put to shame."[5] Of course, the abortion was intended to be his salvation as well.

To cover up the pregnancy (and Giovanni's crimes), the family told their neighbors that Rosana had dropsy stemming from menstrual retention that distended her belly. Rosana's compliance with this deception was necessary in order to procure the abortion. With the pregnancy concealed and reimagined as illness, Giovanni set about procuring an abortion. He acquired medicines from an unnamed source and arranged for his good friend Giacomo Ansaloni, the barber-surgeon, to bleed Rosana.[6] By the barber's account, both Giovanni and Rosana said she was suffering from dropsy and assured him a physician had prescribed that she be bled. Apparently, Giacomo trusted his friend and did not ask to see the physician's prescription, which he was legally compelled to do. Giacomo bled Rosana, allegedly to help his friend's suffering sister-in-law purge her body of its obstruction. Following the phlebotomy, Giovanni gave her a purgative beverage to drink and hit her in the belly.[7]

The bleeding, the beverage, and the beating worked, and Rosana, held and supported by her sister, Giovanni's wife, expelled the fetus into a chamber pot. It was judged to have been around three months developed. Rosana, "almost dead," was bedridden for about two months. To cover up the physical evidence of the abortion, Giovanni threw the fetus down the well in the courtyard of the house.[8] Contrary to his expectation, the well did not wash the evidence into the sewers of Rome and the Tiber: the fetus resurfaced a few days later as Rosana, helped by a neighbor, drew water for a bath. Rosana brought it back to the house and showed it to Giovanni, Pelegrina, and Fantilla. To put this unpleasant affair behind them, Fantilla took the fetus and buried it in the courtyard.

Soon, Rosana was wed to Giuseppe Ansaloni. Giovanni brokered the marriage, potentially in collaboration with his friend Giacomo, the eligible Giuseppe's brother. But Giuseppe's apparent indignation at finding his bride was not the virgin he'd been promised eventually resulted in actions that brought the entire affair into the public realm and record. Giuseppe and Giacomo first confronted their kinsman Giovanni. According to Giuseppe, Giovanni first denied the allegations but eventually said, "What do you want from sinners! Penitence? Even Saint Peter sins. And for this [affair] you two want me to leave my children and my wife? But let's see if I can find a remedy."[9] Giovanni presumably offered Giuseppe some financial settlement—perhaps he had not been able to pay out the promised dowry?—but instead of compensating his brother-in-law, Giovanni allegedly spoke secretly with Rosana and Pelegrina, telling them to keep quiet about the whole affair and admit to nothing. He threatened to make this ugly situation go away by finding witnesses to testify that Giuseppe was insane and had made the story up and that he would arrange for Giuseppe to be sent to the galleys. Apparently, Giovanni assumed Rosana would be an ally and would want her husband banished. Rosana, however, allegedly told Giuseppe about the scheme. The brothers-in-law were clearly at odds, but Giuseppe appears to have waited over two years for Giovani's promised "remedy" before acting on his injured pride.

On June 27, 1598, Giuseppe denounced Giovanni to the Roman Court of the Borgo. He charged that Giovanni had violently raped, deflowered, and impregnated Rosana and then forced her to have an abortion to conceal the pregnancy and sexual transgression. Of these serious offenses, abortion was theoretically the heaviest and the one Giuseppe highlighted in his denunciation. Judge Bennino, who was assigned the case, heard a lurid and terrible story of abuse from Giuseppe and his brother Giacomo, who accompanied him to the court and made his own deposition. The barber Giacomo told the judge that, until his brother came to him with Rosana's confession, he was unaware his bleeding of Rosana was not to treat dropsy. He said he initially did not believe the abortion allegations and had confronted Rosana himself. According to him, she confessed the whole story about the rape and how she and Giovanni tricked him into performing the phlebotomy that may have terminated the pregnancy. Potentially facing charges of performing an abortion, Giacomo attempted to exonerate himself by falling back on discourses of ambiguity, claiming that he had been fooled by the illness narrative and the unclear signs of Rosana's body. The brothers asked Judge Bennino that Giovanni "be punished in conformity with justice," a standard conclusion of a legal complaint.[10]

Giuseppe testified to all the violence and trauma Rosana had experienced as well as Giovanni's crimes and deceits knowing that, after so much time had passed, there was no way of proving Rosana was not a virgin at the time of their marriage, that she had been deflowered against her will by Giovanni, or that there had been an abortion to terminate the unwanted pregnancy. Judge Bennino may have recognized this or may not have believed the accusations or been willing to devote institutional resources and his time to investigating a family quarrel. Though the charges were grave, the trial went no further than Giuseppe's and Giacomo's testimonies. Giacomo was not investigated for his actions, and Giovanni was never questioned about his alleged crimes. And Rosana, who did not accompany her husband to court, did not speak for herself. Perhaps she wanted nothing to do with this matter.   ❧

CHAPTER TWO

Abortion and the Church

IN SPRING 1590, a woman from the town of Lodi went to her confessor to cleanse her soul. All year her priest would have urged her and her fellow parishioners to confess their sins regularly. But, like most, confession was a sacrament she likely received once a year, usually during Lent in preparation for Easter. Among the sins weighing on her conscience this year was an abortion. Like every penitent, she probably told her confessor she felt remorse for the abortion, and she may have genuinely meant it. She asked and likely expected forgiveness, with manageable salutary penance. We know little about this woman, not her name, age, or anything of her life, only that she had an abortion and confessed it. However, we know of this unnamed woman's existence because her decision to confess her abortion had consequences she likely did not foresee. She was denied absolution, deemed excommunicate, and cut off from the Church and God's grace. Thus she entered the historical record.

Things would have been different two years earlier. Her unnamed confessor would likely have absolved her for the abortion—his approach dependent on the facts of the case, his level of education, experience and compassion, and his commitment to curing souls. Perhaps he was a seasoned confessor, a man who had heard a lot of sad and unfair stories and interacted with many penitents. He may have empathized with her and understood the abortion to be both a sinful and desperate solution to a complicated yet not uncommon situation that many women faced. He might have concluded she was not to blame for this sin, that someone else forced the abortion on her or gave her no other options. Perhaps he'd have accepted it was an accident or the result of medical intervention intended to heal. He might have explained the gravity of the practice, the spiritual value of the lost fetus, and imposed manageable penance in a way that cleared the woman's soul without making her secret public and compromising her reputation. But by 1590, the confessor no longer had the authority to absolve this sin. Abortion was now deemed so heinous and grave that only the pope himself could absolve it. In October 1588, Pope Sixtus V had issued a papal bull making abortion, for the first time in Church history, unequivocally homicide and its procurers and accomplices—including priests—excommunicate, with absolution reserved to the Holy See alone. Sixtus sought to eradicate what he described as a "detestable," "abhorrent," and "evil act" by giving abortion a new meaning and imposing severe punishments for the practice.[1]

And so the confessor told the unnamed woman from Lodi she had a choice: go to Rome and beg the pope's forgiveness or live excommunicate. The thought of traveling to Rome would have seemed absurd—the trip would be long, expensive, and dangerous, and how could she explain it to her family and community without exposing her sin and potentially causing a scandal? Her decision not to go to Rome may have been easy, but that does not mean it was not agonizing. We do not know if she struggled with her excommunication and how to explain to her fellow parishioners why she could not receive the sacraments.

We know about this woman because she and her confessor did not give up hope for her local absolution. The confessor reported the case to his bishop, Ludovico Taverna. He, too, was troubled by her excommunication and the new papal law. And she was not the only woman caught in this predicament: "a few women" from Lodi had confessed to abortions that spring, and they, too, were fighting for local absolution. As the cases piled up, Bishop Taverna wrote to Pope Sixtus V explaining the situation and asking for permission to offer absolution locally.[2] Perhaps surprisingly, Sixtus granted Taverna's request.[3] The unnamed

woman from Lodi received absolution from her confessor. The ecclesiastical politics of her salvation resolved, she disappears from the historical record.

This interaction exposes various tensions at the heart of Catholic
religious thinking on abortion at the end of the sixteenth century. On
one hand, procured abortion was considered a sin, with which the post-
Tridentine Church was increasingly concerned. On the other hand,
abortion was something that women did, that they felt compelled to
do, or that was forced upon them against their will, for complicated
reasons. These reasons belayed simple moral prescriptions and even
papal prohibitions threatening eternal damnation.

Religious discourse shaped how individuals perceived, contemplated, experienced, and responded to abortion. This chapter investigates the evolution of this discourse in the sixteenth and seventeenth
centuries: how the post-Tridentine ecclesiastical establishment thought
about abortion and responded to its practice, how religious discourses
were created and disseminated, and how these discourses may have
been received and processed by the laity. We cannot know what an individual like the woman from Lodi thought about the morality of abortion and its spiritual consequences—sources offering unmediated access to this kind of interiority do not exist. But we have many and varied
sources produced by ecclesiastical authorities and institutions that
communicated ideas about abortion to both clergy and laity. These include prescriptive sources, such as theological treatises, confessor's
manuals, decrees, and legislation, and descriptive sources, like ecclesiastical trial records that investigated priests who were accused of procuring abortions and supplications that reveal what people did and introduce us to individuals like the unnamed woman from Lodi. Taken
together, these sources expose a Catholic Church—comprised of popes,
cardinals, bishops, theologians, canonists, and confessors, and also
laywomen and men—wrestling with how to define and regulate a practice that was motivated by seemingly immutable social realities.

A Mortal Sin

> In truth, I have never been able to understand the nature of
> those cruel and ungodly Fathers or Mothers that leads

them, with a soul so barbarous, ruthless, and ferocious, to
think of bringing death to their own children, to abort
those whom they have brought together, composed and
nourished with their own blood, who are housed in the in-
nermost viscera of their body, and in the most intimate
depths of their heart. This error, more cruel than ferocious,
. . . is not committed by any other species of animal other
than man and woman, and only to cover a foul dishonesty
and for fear of some dishonor. An infamous act, [because]
to conceal carnal fragility, one commits four even worse [ac-
tions], which are the homicide of that innocent fetus; forever depriving that unfortunate soul from the sight of God;
the condemnation of one's own soul; and finally [the condemnation of the soul] of the physician or whoever helped
to accomplish this great wickedness. . . . You should know
that depriving life from fetuses in the bellies of mothers is
nothing other than depriving them forever from seeing
God. [For this] most cruel wickedness, on the day of Judgment, Divine Majesty will [inflict] the most strict and most
severe [punishment] on those Mothers and Fathers who
have aborted their children, [who have deprived] them so
wickedly of life, and of heaven, a sorrow so atrocious that all
the sacred theologians conclude that, if the pains of hell are
very grave, the greatest punishment is that of not seeing
God. And because it is mostly women who are wont to fall
into this error, I call them not "mother" but "Megara", fury
of hell in human form, that wicked woman who, to conceal
her unbridled lust . . . procures the death of the body and
death of the eternal soul of that unfortunate Innocent, who
would have been born her child, who tastes death (so to
speak) before life, who dies before being born, . . . who, before walking the earth, is buried in it, and even sometimes
in a latrine, and finally, who before meeting its mother as a
nourisher, experiences her as a murderer. . . . It is such an
enormous and ungodly [sin] to abort a fetus that every law,
every Doctor, all reason condemns it and punishes
severely.[4]

Was this how the unnamed woman from Lodi understood the sin she had confessed to? According to the author of these fiery words, the Dominican friar and physician Scipione Mercurio, most Italians did not, and that was why they procured, participated in, and tolerated abortions. So, in a lengthy chapter in his *Popular Errors of Italy* (1603), a work intended to expose the dangerous practices, false beliefs, and grave moral errors apparently prevalent among the "popular" classes, Mercurio undertook to teach them. But he was not simply transmitting doctrinal information; Mercurio used provocative rhetoric with vivid and disturbing imagery to elicit an emotional response from his reader. Individuals who procure abortions betray God and are enemies of humanity; they are monstrous and selfish; to conceal a sexual transgression, a carnal weakness, and protect reputation, they murder their flesh and blood and betray divine law and plan; this murder deprives a being of its imagined human life and, more importantly, from its future in the embrace of God. They are both women and men, but women more so. This combination of frames was meant to convince the reader to include the fetus in the moral and spiritual community, induce guilt and disgust for tolerating the practice of abortion, and, Mercurio hoped, lead to widespread change in mentality and behavior. His words and aims reflect what we might expect from a cleric writing at the turn of the seventeenth century and in the throes of the Italian Counter-Reformation. The sentiments he expressed had been developing in the minds and writings of Christian thinkers for centuries, but Mercurio's words were a product of his specific time and place. Over the course of the sixteenth century and especially in its second half, the Catholic Church increasingly regarded abortion to be a grave mortal sin that demanded correction and put programs in place to change how individuals, both lay and clerical, thought about it.

At a very basic level, all Christians likely knew the intentional termination of pregnancy was a "sin," something they were not supposed to do, which affected their relationship with God and compromised their chances of salvation—this much would have been inculcated into them through centuries of direct and indirect moral and religious education.[5] Nevertheless, religious authorities perceived abortion to be widely practiced and socially tolerated. Of primary concern among reformers was a perception that both laity and some clergy practiced

abortion because they did not understand or accept its spiritual meaning. Exacerbating the problem was the belief that confessors easily absolved procurers of abortion and those assisting them without impressing the gravity of the sin on the sinner, either because the confessors
themselves remained ignorant in these matters or because they simply
did not care to. A developing discourse, fueled by Protestant and Catholic reformers alike, blamed priests and especially confessors for the laity's sinful behavior and general ignorance of doctrine and teachings
on sin.[6] If Mercurio's lay women and men procured abortions because
they did not understand its gravity, if they were in "error" and committed such "enormous and ungodly" sins, it was the fault of their negligent priests and confessors for not teaching them.

By the Council of Trent (1545–1563), it was widely held within the
upper echelons of the Church that many priests were unfit to care for
souls, some being as immoral, if not more so, in their behaviors and as
unorthodox in their beliefs as many of the penitents whom they were to
shepherd.[7] The ardent reformer Carlo Borromeo, archbishop of Milan,
believed penitents confessed their sins out of habit rather than guilt,
with no intention of changing their ways, and that absolution was too
easily given by lax or ignorant confessors.[8] Clerical discipline and professionalization were among the most important tasks and greatest
challenges of the reforming Church. This was a long, slow, uneven process. As much as some reforming authorities tried, by the end of the
sixteenth century, the Church had not been able to implement a standard, efficient, and widespread system of clerical education and oversight. The diocesan seminary was mandated at Trent (1563) for the precise purpose of training priests for the care of souls, but it too fell short
of its aim, especially in its first four decades. Priests were ordained with
or without completing seminary education. While some clergy, especially those in orders such as the Jesuits, were undoubtedly better educated by the end of the century, they were a minority.[9] Lack of incentives
or penalties for not attending seminaries, coupled with the ineffective-
ness of disinterested, unpopular, or under-resourced bishops, meant
most priests were no better educated than their pre-Trent predecessors.
Historians have argued that discernible results would only become apparent in the seventeenth and eighteenth centuries, and mostly in richer
northern Italy.[10]

Post-Tridentine ecclesiastical authorities wanted the confessor to be a genuine and authoritative moral power and strove to make the confessional a key site from which to convey and establish moral standards, save souls, and cultivate obedience. By inquiring into all aspects of penitents' lives, the confessor could take his community's pulse and teach the tenets of the faith, especially what constituted sin and how to avoid it. He could explain the gravity of specific sins, make his penitent understand how they harmed the soul and, finally, assign fitting penance. Successful confession would result in a clean soul for the penitent and would also teach them to examine their own conscience and monitor the conduct of their neighbors. Reform was to start in the confessional and, through it, be inculcated upon an individual's conscience and world view. It was to be maintained through constant self-examination and social watchfulness.[11] The confessional was regarded as the best location from which to regulate sins like abortion, and the pedagogy provided by the confessor, the best means through which to change broader mentalities surrounding its practice. An abundance of educational materials appeared in the second half of the sixteenth century instructing clergy on how to tackle this lofty goal. Surveying a number of these treatises reveals what priests were supposed to be learning about abortion and telling the laity.

Ideally, all confessors would read the seminal works of moral theology and summae (compendia or summaries) of cases of conscience in order to exercise their office competently; however, this was unlikely to happen since many could not read Latin. The *Catechism of the Council of Trent for Parish Priests* (1566), commonly known as the *Roman Catechism,* was composed to remedy this. Published in Latin but quickly translated into Italian (1567), the *Roman Catechism* taught priests the basic and standardized doctrines of the faith, enabling them to teach their congregations. As it addressed the basics of the faith, the *Roman Catechism* did not give abortion the same analytical treatment as the moral theologians did in their compendia of cases of sin; however, it is significant that it mentioned it at all. Discussing the "Sacrament of Marriage," the *Roman Catechism* taught priests to "communicate to the faithful" that, aside from companionship and support, the reason for marital union was the generation of offspring and propagation of the faithful. As the Apostle Timothy taught, "Woman shall be saved by bearing children."[12] It was "a great wickedness that those joined in matrimony, [through the use of] medicines, impede the conception of children, or if they are conceived, kill the creatura in the belly." Abortion, the *Roman Catechism* chided, is a "conspiracy of two homicidal people."[13] Both husband and wife were portrayed as murderers, equally complicit. This was the standard, if rudimentary, teaching the *Roman Catechism* sought to impart on all clerics and, through them, to all Catholics. More refined understandings would come with higher education.

Following Carlo Borromeo's model, several bishops ordered their confessors to always have in their "hands a few good books and several approved authors of cases of conscience" to guide them through the difficult task of caring for souls.[14] Bishops compiled lists of approved authors and works for their confessors to master because, according to the bishop of Ferrara Giovanni Fontana, "ignorance is inexcusable in a parish priest."[15] At the top of most of these lists were the influential summae of cases of conscience: the *Angelic Summa* (1480s) of the canonist Angelo Carletti; the *Summa of Summas* (1516) of Sylvestro Mazzolini, chair of theology at the University of Rome and Master of the Sacred Palace; the *Little Summa of Sin* (1525) by the important reformer Cardinal Cajetan (Tomasso de Vio); and the *Golden Armband Summa* (1547) of the Dominican preacher and inquisitor of Piacenza Bartolomeo Fumi.[16] Authors provided authoritative and simplified teachings of cases of conscience, drawn from the works of Church fathers, medieval theologians, and canon law, for clerics who needed straightforward answers to questions of morality relevant to their congregations' daily lives. For quick and easy access to information on sin, summae were arranged alphabetically and thematically cross-referenced. They varied in length and sophistication yet were highly formulaic.[17] Published in Latin, they were translated into Italian for wider readership. Popular and authoritative, they were textbooks for many seminarians well into the seventeenth century.[18]

Looking up the term *abortion* in these publications, the confessor would learn it was a mortal sin, but with distinctions. Like their predecessors, summists framed the issue around the status of the fetus and the spiritual consequences of its termination and summarized the standard theological and canonical position: abortion was considered homicide if the fetus was animated with a rational soul—around forty days from conception for male fetuses and eighty days for females; it was a lesser but still grave sin to abort a preanimated fetus.[19] The confessor would learn that abortion generally stemmed from the sin of lust, that single women often sought physicians for abortions to cover up illicit sexual encounters, but also that men were instigators, and that married couples sometimes practiced abortion.[20] Confessors learned to ask medical practitioners whether they participated in abortions. The morality of abortions intentionally administered or resulting of interventions intended to heal pregnant women suffering from life-threatening illnesses featured prominently. A confessor would learn this practice was licit and sometimes even encouraged, but only if the fetus was preanimate, for in this case the physician "will not be the cause of death of a human being, but rather will be freeing [one] from death." The abortion of an animate fetus, even to save the mother, was regarded as mortal sin and homicide and was therefore prohibited.[21] In these summae of cases of conscience, a priest learned simplified, almost axiomatic teachings he would somehow have to apply to very complicated real-life cases.

Another important work featuring prominently on confessors' lists of readings was the *Manual for Confessors and Penitents* by the Spanish Augustinian Martin Azpilcueta. First published in Italian in 1569, Azpilcueta's *Manual* was the most influential work on confession and sin well into the seventeenth century.[22] While summae were generally conceived as handbooks for clergy, Azpilcueta intended his work for both confessors and penitents. The book sought to prepare the confessor for his sacramental role and the penitent for the act of confession by providing instruction on how to examine one's conscience and think about the intentions behind actions that might be sinful. Departing from the alphabetical structure characterizing most summae, Azpilcueta's manual was organized thematically, discussing sin within a broader exposition of the rules of Catholic life as found in the Decalogue, the seven cardinal sins, and the sacraments. He also included a section on interrogations proper to the penitent's economic, civil, and occupational grouping, alerting the confessor to different penitents' specific needs.

While much of the content of Azpilcueta's book was unoriginal, its compelling systematization and repackaging of the teachings contained in authoritative summae made it very successful. It also inspired a deluge of derivative works that adopted its structure and sought to make doctrine relevant to clerical and lay audiences.[23] In many of these texts, authors asked their readers: "Have you committed x sin or y action?" "Have you thought this bad thought?" "Did you want this sinful thing to happen?" The interrogative style not only taught the confessor what questions to ask but also showed the penitent what to ask her- or himself before confession and in everyday life. A guiding principle of these works was to communicate simple, accessible, and unambiguous prescriptions. In terms of abortion, authors such as the Barnabite friar Antonio Pagani, the Jesuit Paolo Morigia, and Franciscan Giovanni Molisso repeated (sometimes verbatim) and summarized their predecessors' teachings. Their texts communicate the straightforward precepts that reached ever increasing clerical and lay audiences. Readers learned, first and foremost, that procured abortion was mortal sin and those who had abortions or participated in them sinned against the commandment "Do not kill." Some authors explained that the gravity of abortion depended on the fetus's development and introduced the concept of animation; others ignored this in favor of simple, unconditional condemnation.

But these texts offer more than this simple teaching. Authors used explicitly gendered rhetoric when discussing methods employed to terminate pregnancy and the gravity of the sin. Women were depicted as "seeking" abortion—that is, desiring it and intentionally procuring it. Knowing what one was doing and freely doing it was key to defining the action as a mortal sin. The confessor was taught that women "seek" to abort through the acquisition and consumption of products, through activities chosen for this end, and "accidently" through their social habits and activities. Pagani stated unequivocally that a woman committed homicide when "she procure[ed] things in order not to conceive or to terminate her pregnancy." The confessor was told to ask his female penitent if she had ever attempted to terminate pregnancy either by "taking things by mouth" or by physical means such as dancing, jumping, wearing too-tight clothing, or carrying heavy weights. Even if she failed in aborting, she still sinned against the divine commandment against homicide if she had intended or desired to do it. Even if she was "not seeking to abort [but did] various things [that put her in] danger of aborting," such as lifting weights, doing tiresome things, dancing or jumping around, she still committed mortal sin. Pregnant women were to be mindful of their activities and careful with their bodies—abortion caused by accident or negligence was not completely excusable. These warnings were meant to encourage women to be conscious of the risks of physical activity during pregnancy, but they were also intended to teach the confessor that women may "blame" terminated pregnancies on mundane physical activities in the hope of evading punishment. And it was not only single women who were suspect. A "married woman and mother of the family" had to learn it was sin not to want to have children and that abortion was similar to suffocating a newborn—both were homicide. In these works, procured abortion was depicted as a woman's practice, and confessors were taught to be suspicious of female penitents.[24]

In contrast, men's involvement in procured abortion was not always explicitly mentioned. When it appeared, men were depicted not necessarily as seeking abortion but as "causing" it, by beating their pregnant wives, "treating [them] badly," or having sex when they were pregnant. Authors agreed that such behavior was mortal sin, though some specified only if the abortion was intentional. Men were also implicitly included in the catchalls "anyone" and "others" who force women to abort, who "have made a woman abort," who helped or "has given a woman medicines to abort"—they too sin against the fifth commandment.[25] It is unclear whether such statements specifically targeted men responsible for aborted pregnancies, or if they addressed other women who assisted in abortions. Most likely they were meant for everyone, intended to inspire watchfulness over pregnant women and scrutiny over one's actions and conscience. Pregnant women were to be monitored, and in no way was anyone to take part in abortion by providing materials or knowledge to that end.

While authors did not directly implicate husbands, seducers, and rapists in procured abortion, most represented male healers as perpetrators and facilitators, assuming and teaching that physicians were the experts when it came to abortion, the ones who often administered it. Perhaps surprisingly, these publications were silent on the participation of midwives. On this point, all authors of popular works on confession followed the opinions of the previous generations of summists and authors of similar works: it was a mortal sin for a physician to give a

pregnant woman medicine that would cause the abortion of an animated fetus, but it could be licit to abort an inanimate one to spare a
woman from illness or death. The physician was warned not to induce
abortion hastily. Acting without knowing the developmental stage of
the fetus was a mortal sin. Confessors were to ask physicians and surgeons: "Have you given anything or counseled her in ways to abort" or
given a woman things "that will harm her fetus"? Apothecaries were to
be asked if they had given or sold poisons or medicines with incorrect
doses that could harm or kill the patient or cause abortion, or if they
had given such things to those who may have used them toward "evil
ends." Confessors were to teach physicians never to counsel the sick to
heal the body at the expense of their soul. A physician would not be excused if he told his patient, "I do not counsel you to do this, but if you
do it, you will be healed."[26]

Though simple and highly formulaic, the teachings regarding
abortion in these works on sin and confession are revealing. Many references to abortion, directed at both clergy and laity, were made in the
last decades of the sixteenth century, and the unnamed woman from
Lodi likely received some of them, either from her confessor or perhaps
from a book. Authors portrayed abortion as a common practice and serious spiritual problem requiring monitoring and active prevention. It
was only one of myriad immoral practices linked to sexuality condemned in these works: adultery, rape, incest, sodomy, and prostitution
were also featured and often received more attention than abortion, but
none of these was considered homicide. It was believed confessional
education and discipline could change attitudes toward all these sinful
practices. Through his intimate relationship with the penitent—
woman, man, married, single, mother, healer—the confessor was best
placed to discover cases of abortion and best suited to teach its sinfulness. Within the secrecy of the confessional, the penitent would confess
their abortion or their participation in one, and the confessor would
explain its meaning, consequences, and why it was a grave mortal sin.
Understanding what they had done, the penitent was to be contrite and
deeply distressed by their own actions; they were to vow to abstain from
committing this sin again, but according to the fathers of the Council
of Trent, they were also to "hate" and "detest" the sin they committed
and their past life that brought them to it. Following confession, a new

life began, where penitents questioned their own actions and scrutinized their consciences.[27] They would also keep watchful eyes on their
neighbors' conduct. The confessor in his practice and the confessional
education propagated in works of devotion were expected to instill
such awareness in the laity, with the hope of reforming mentalities toward abortion and curbing its practice. Yet, despite their investments in
confession as a tool of moral and social change, the ecclesiastical establishment increasingly believed this was insufficient to change thinking
and practices surrounding abortion.

A Bishop's Case

As the Tridentine program of moral reform tightened through the late
1500s, the confessor was paradoxically both more important as an
agent of change and increasingly limited in his ability to absolve those
who confessed certain sins. "Atrocious and grave crimes," as the fathers
of the Council of Trent labeled them, sins causing public scandal and
notoriety and potentially influencing others to act similarly, were "reserved" for absolution to only "the highest priests."[28] Abortion was increasingly deemed such a sin, and more and more bishops attempted to
assert their control over it by doing so.

The episcopal reservation of abortion was intended to impress the
gravity of this sin upon the laity and was also meant to ensure abortion
would not be easily dismissed or leniently handled by the confessor
himself.[29] In Milan, Archbishop Carlo Borromeo forbade his confessors
from absolving procurers of abortion from the time of his first synod in
1565.[30] Paolo Burali d'Arezzo went further, reserving procured abortion as well as procured sterility (i.e., consuming products that inhibit
conception) while he was bishop of Piacenza (1568–1576) and again
when he was archbishop of Naples (1576–1578).[31] Throughout the
1580s, Burali's successor in Naples, Annibale da Capua, also reserved
abortion, but he specified only of an animate fetus.[32] In 1580, the archbishop of Ravenna, Christophoro Boncompagni, put the case of
"women, or others" who seek to abort their fetus on his list of cases reserved to his office, and published the list in Italian lest anyone misun-
derstand.[33] In 1584, the bishop of Viterbo, Carlo Montigli, also listed
abortion among cases reserved to his office, but like Annibale da Capua,

he only reserved the abortion of an animated fetus.[34] In 1587, the bishop of Camerino, Girolamo Bovio, reserved any type of abortion to his office alone.[35]

These bishops did not define what abortion was; its meaning was taken for granted, as were the meanings of other reserved sins, such as heresy, demonic magic, incest, and clandestine marriage, which could certainly evoke varying interpretations. Nevertheless, penitents in Milan, Piacenza, Naples, Ravenna, Viterbo, and Camerino who admitted within the secret confines of the confessional to procuring abortion could not officially receive absolution within that space. The confessor had to persuade or pressure his penitent to take themselves to the bishop and confess to him for absolution. Forcing the penitent to go to the bishop for reconciliation with the Church and God would increase the sinner's sense of personal shame and make them realize the magnitude of their sin. Reforming bishops saw the system of reservation as a tool for establishing moral order, effecting reform and asserting their authority over both laity and confessor within their diocese.[36]

The enforcement of this system, however, proved difficult and often impossible. By reserving a case to his office, the bishop could make a secret sin public, potentially causing scandal within the community. This fear was particularly acute for women, especially the young and unmarried, who, caught in reserved cases of carnal sin, could not go to a bishop without attracting the attention of kin and community. A woman could not go to the diocesan center where the bishop resided and expose her lover, seducer, rapist, deflowerer, adulterer, or incestor without jeopardizing her own or her family's reputation. This was especially true if the man responsible for her pregnancy was a priest or married man, a man of some importance or of high status, or someone else with whom marriage was an impossibility. Such a public denunciation could strain familial, financial or political relationships, and might incite a vendetta, violence toward the woman or her impregnator, or even death. Admitting to abortion before one's confessor in complete secrecy and suffering private penance was one thing; traveling to the diocesan center for an audience with the bishop and reporting the details of illicit sexuality was another.

Bishops, of course, realized the repercussions of reserving sensitive cases like abortion—indeed, the threat of exposure was meant to

influence conduct: do not commit the sin if you cannot face the consequences. Nevertheless, while several bishops obliged procurers of abortion to come before them, it was widely accepted that, for the common
good, such cases were better absolved locally, in secret, by a confessor.
Archbishop Paolo Burali d'Arezzo thought it wise to allow his confessors in Naples to absolve women locally "from all carnal sins," including those he himself reserved, in order to avoid potential scandal.[37]
This was also the preferred practice of the rigorist Archbishop Carlo
Borromeo in Milan.[38] Because abortion was so closely tied to honor and
shame—that of the woman, her impregnator, and their families—and
had the potential to cause scandal and social disorder, bishops allowed
those confessing to be absolved in secrecy by their confessors. The
danger of revelation was judged greater than the benefits of making the
penitent go before the bishop. While the reservation of cases was a
tactic intended to influence conduct, it was impractical and, in some
cases, appears to have been readily circumvented. Some bishops, such
as Antonio Altoviti of Florence, Filippo Sega of Ripatrasone, near
Macerata, and Fantino Petrignano of Cosenza, seem to have acknowledged this futility and did not reserve cases of abortion at their provincial and diocesan synods of 1574, 1576, and 1579, respectively.[39]

That abortion was neither unequivocally nor universally held to
be a reserved sin posed other spiritual and jurisdictional problems. If
a priest moved from a diocese where abortion was reserved to one
where it was not, he might refuse absolution in ignorance or, conversely, absolve someone when he should not. What would this mean
for the penitent's soul? Theologians thought a penitent who experienced faulty or incomplete absolution was not fully rehabilitated. The
confessor was obliged to make this right. Upon learning of his error,
he was to admit to the penitent that their absolution was invalid and
either send them to the bishop or request permission to properly absolve them himself. The specter of scandal loomed over these situations: the penitent had to undergo another confession, potentially
alerting the community to her or his secrets, especially if the individual generally confessed only once a year. Moreover, the confessor
would appear ignorant in front of his bishop and, should word get
out, might lose the respect of his parish. Tommaso Zerola, bishop of
Minori (near Salerno), thought that if there was danger of such

scandal, the absolution of a reserved case should be given in absentia without troubling the penitent.[40] But this meant the penitent might not grasp the gravity of their alleged sin. A thornier circumstance, and one for which theologians had no easy answer or practical solution, was the fate of a penitent who committed a sin in one diocese where it was reserved and then traveled to another where it was not. Could a man or woman who procured an abortion in Naples, where abortion was reserved, confess it in nearby Cosenza where it was not? Would the absolution stand? These questions and uncertainties regarding reserved cases were theoretical and often academic, but they do suggest that sensitive and controversial cases, like abortion, even if officially reserved by bishops were likely not generally handled by a Carlo Borromeo or Paolo Burali but secretly and expediently by their confessors so as to avoid scandal and social disruption.

Priests Behaving Badly

The reservation of cases was also an episcopal attempt to discipline the confessor himself, on the chance he might be too lenient and quick to absolve an individual who procured an abortion. More importantly, the oversight of a higher office could guard against priests procuring abortions for women they impregnated. It was common knowledge and the stuff of popular literature and Protestant critique that Catholic clergy regularly, openly, and often without remorse engaged in fornication, concubinage, rape, solicitation in the confessional, sex with nuns, and sometimes sodomy with other men and boys. Many priests were not celibate. Communities tolerated a certain level of clerical sexuality and sometimes even long-term concubinage, and the Church expected and accepted a great deal of it while officially prohibiting it. Situations that were kept secret, relationships that were peaceful and where the priest's behaviors did not disrupt communal life or interfere with his religious duties, rarely caught the attention of authorities and therefore never made it into the historical record. The cases that did, and were investigated, were those where priests' behaviors went beyond what individuals or communities were willing to tolerate. Authorities and tribunals intervened when priests' actions caused scandal, where someone felt wronged and demanded justice.

The archives of ecclesiastical tribunals throughout Italy abound with trials investigating a wide variety of clerical misdemeanors, many of them involving sexual transgressions.[41] Episcopal investigations in cases of defloration, violent rape, concubinage, and adultery reveal that priests commonly procured and administered abortions for the women they impregnated. Some cases were scandalous and infamous. The case of the priest Giovanni Pietro Lion certainly made an impression on the ecclesiastical establishment and Venetian society. Lion was publicly executed in Venice in 1561 for seducing, raping, and violently harming his charges while confessor at the Convertite convent for reformed prostitutes and for inducing abortions "through medicines and other arts"—likely violence—in the ones he had impregnated.[42] In a 1570 case from Correggio (just east of Parma), the priest Giorgio Righetti was accused of having a year-long affair with the married Violante Gatti. When it was discovered she was pregnant, he gave her a beverage to make her abort. Violante reportedly drank the abortifacient for two consecutive mornings but decided she could not commit this sin and threw the rest away. Righetti confessed to having sex with Violante twice but denied being responsible for her pregnancy—he claimed she was already pregnant by her husband when they had sex—and vehemently denied giving her a beverage to abort.[43]

In another infamous case, in 1587, the vicar general of Caiazzo denounced his neighbor, the Spanish Dominican bishop of Telese (northeast of Benevento), Giovanni Stefano de Urbieta, to superiors in Rome on behalf of the laity of Telese for numerous violations ranging from public gambling, blasphemy, and eating meat during Lent to raping a virgin, committing the "great sin of sodomy with a boy in church," and causing the death of a nun whom he had impregnated by forcing her to drink a dangerous abortifacient beverage. The vicar reported that the people of Telese accused their bishop of sin that was not only appalling for a bishop but even for a Turk.[44] Although we do not know how authorities in Rome handled this case, we do know Giovanni Stefano vacated his office that year and, according to a nineteenth-century historian of the Telese episcopate, returned to his native Spain.[45] Even clerics highly placed in the ecclesiastical hierarchy behaved in morally reprehensible ways and were often called to task when their flock demanded better.

Ecclesiastical tribunals investigated these types of cases in order to respond to the moral demands of the laity and preserve social order, discipline wayward clerics, and propagate the image of ecclesiastical justice and reform. Some priests may have been punished severely; mostly they were disciplined mildly, sometimes not at all. Common opinion was that ecclesiastical tribunals protected their own, and indeed they did, but only to a certain extent. Clerical privilege meant that, in most cases, priests could not be tried in criminal courts but only in ecclesiastical ones, where they might be treated more favorably. However, we should not assume that every time a priest was absolved or when punishment did not match the penalties prescribed by theologians and canonists that Church courts were necessarily excusing these bad behaviors, though they often did just that. Cases of sexual transgression, especially abortion, were always difficult for tribunals to investigate. Most hinged on hearsay, and it was often the word of the priest against that of his denouncers. In both ecclesiastical and secular tribunals, women were inherently disadvantaged, and it was an uphill battle to pin defloration (whether by means of violent rape or seduction with a promise of marriage), rape, or pregnancy on a man, whether lay or religious. It was often claimed that another man was responsible, a claim that tribunals had to investigate, especially if the woman had a dubious reputation. Uncertainty and distrust of women was ubiquitous in these cases, strategically deployed by accused priests and always taken into account by investigating judges, meaning many priests, like lay men, who committed wrongs were let off.

A source that provides insight into the thoughts, feelings, and legal reasoning of ecclesiastical judges investigating cases of clerical abortion is the collection of legal briefs or opinions (*consilia*) composed by Martin Azpilcueta while he was consulter and canonist for the Sacred Apostolic Penitentiary, one of the most important ecclesiastical tribunals in Rome. The penitentiary did not investigate or try public cases; that was the job of episcopal tribunals and the Inquisition. The Apostolic Penitentiary was principally a tribunal of the "internal forum," a tribunal of private conscience and grace, where penitents could seek absolution for certain sins and crimes and dispensations for issues their bishops or other authorities might not have jurisdiction over or refused to grant.[46] It was a central tribunal dealing with issues of "irregularity"—a state of being, determined by past actions (sins or crimes) or disability (physical or cognitive), prohibiting an individual from receiving orders. For an ordained cleric, incurring irregularity meant that he was prohibited from exercising his office, celebrating the sacraments, maintaining benefices, and could result in the loss of clerical status. As it was considered a form of homicide, the abortion of an animate fetus was officially held by canon law to be a sin for which an individual incurred irregularity. In theory, a man who procured an abortion could not become a priest; a priest who procured an abortion could no longer care for souls. In practice, there was room for maneuvering. Martin Azpilcueta heard and gave his opinion on at least four cases of clerical abortion while he served the penitentiary in the 1570s and 1580s, under the pontificates of Pius V, Gregory XIII, and Sixtus V.[47] In their published form, his consilia were intended to guide theologians, canonists, and consultants of the penitentiary through difficult or extraordinary cases of conscience.

Two cases heard before 1586 are exemplary. In the first, a priest admitted that, before he took his orders, he had impregnated a woman and encouraged her to have an abortion. Forty days after their union, the woman said "she thought she was made pregnant." "Forty days" meant the unborn might have been animate. The man immediately counseled her to abort by means of letting blood, but he never learned if this was successful. He went on to take orders. Was his ordination in vain? Had his actions rendered him irregular and therefore disqualified from the priesthood?[48] Azpilcueta thought not. He pointed out that the priest did not know whether the woman was truly pregnant but only "suspected it because she said she suspected it." Could her testimony be trusted? Azpilcueta appeared to give no authority to the woman's suspicion of her own pregnancy. Perhaps she was mistaken. Perhaps she said this strategically to coerce the would-be priest into marriage, to pay a dowry, or for some other advantage. The assumption of women's "reproductive blackmail" was pervasive and shaped the esteemed theologian's reasoning. And Azpilcueta found more cause for skepticism and doubt. While it was dangerous to bleed pregnant women, Azpilcueta stated it was never certain this intervention would actually cause an abortion. He argued that because news of an abortion had not reached the priest, he could believe nothing came of this, that either the bleeding was not carried out or the woman had not really been pregnant. Because bloodletting was not a "sure thing," because the woman's suspicion of pregnancy was neither sufficient nor trustworthy, and because the priest did not hear of the results, Azpilcueta concluded this priest "can set aside his scruples."[49] In this case, it did not matter that the would-be priest sought the abortion of a potentially animate unborn. Doubt apparently rendered the priest's fear of irregularity easy to assuage: dispensation, it seems, was not necessary.

Another case Azpilcueta analyzed concerned a priest who counseled a pregnant woman to abort, giving and teaching her the means to do so. She refused to have an abortion, but after she delivered, she killed the infant. The question at hand was regarding the priest's responsibility in the infanticide. Azpilcueta conceded that issuing a definitive decision in this case was impossible because of the lack of information. But he did speculate. He thought the priest was not to blame for the infanticide and not irregular, especially if he had not fathered the child. After all, she did not do what he counseled—that is, have an abortion. Infanticide was graver because it was the killing of an actual human being rather than one *in via*; it was committed by physical violence directly on a human being—perfectly willful murder, whereas abortion was less direct, more uncertain and more likely for the "concealment of an offence."[50] However, if the priest was responsible for the pregnancy, "it can be presumed that [the woman] was more moved to killing on [his] account."[51] While his counsel was not for the killing of the newborn but rather the abortion of a fetus, he was certainly guilty of sin in the forum of conscience and perhaps for affecting her decision to commit murder. Establishing irregularity from the evidence available was, however, not possible. Azpilcueta certainly suspected the priest of wrongdoing but found insufficient evidence to censure him for the infanticide.

The circumstances motivating priests to procure abortions were similar to those that motivated lay individuals. Priests had intimate, longer-term or fleeting, and sometimes violent sexual relationships with women, often resulting in pregnancy. The pregnant body of a lover or victim was the site of a priest's sin and of possible future scandal for his bishop and the whole Church. Abortion was sought to conceal wrongdoing and evade punishment. It was a sin and a crime that ecclesiastical courts took seriously, but there were many variables in these cases that made investigation and adjudication difficult. There were many reasons for priests to procure abortions and many reasons for their superiors to excuse them.

Papal Interventions

While some reforming bishops attempted to change the way their clergy and their flocks thought and behaved, in cases of abortion there were often reasons to ignore, excuse, forgive, and even tolerate what was officially deemed a mortal sin. Much of this leeway was justified by ambiguities and uncertainties surrounding abortion, by the sexual and gender politics underlying its practice, and the social consequences of exposure. Nonetheless, reform-minded ecclesiastical authorities continued to seek solutions to what was perceived to be a common practice that carried heavy spiritual consequences.

The most dramatic and controversial attempt to change thinking on abortion came in 1588 from Pope Sixtus V, in the form of an apostolic constitution, a particular type of papal bull that condemned errors of the faith, established doctrine, decreed penalties, and was intended for the whole Catholic world.[52] Titled *Against those who Procure, Counsel and Consent in any way to Abortion* (promulgated on October 29, 1588, and first published on November 16, 1588), the bull was and continues to be referred to by its incipit, "Effraenatam," meaning "without restraint," an evocative term that linked abortion with the dangers of lust.[53] Frustrated by what he perceived to be a common and tolerated practice, Sixtus sought to definitively set the spiritual meaning of abortion and "eradicate" its practice through new ecclesiastical and secular policies threatening severe penalties. As official papal legislation, the bull was unprecedented.[54]

Against those who Procure, Counsel and Consent in any way to Abortion was consciously novel and a deliberate act of meaning making. The bull is divided into two parts: a preamble explaining what abortion is and why the bull is needed, followed by specific decrees on how to punish offenders in order to "eradicate" the practice. The central claim of the bull is that procured abortion is truly and unequivocally homicide, and its procurers and accomplices are truly murderers. Sixtus linked this claim to social problems with grave spiritual consequences: individuals

S.^{MI} D. N. SIXTI

DIVINA PROVIDENTIA
PAPÆ · V·

Contra Procurantes, Confulentes, & Confentientes,
quocumque modo Abortum

CONSTITVTIO:

R O M AE
Apud Hæredes Antonÿ Bladÿ, Impreffores Camerales
M. D. LXXXVIII·

Fig 2.1 Frontispiece to Sixtus V, *Contra Procurantes, Consulentes, & Consentietes quocumque mod Abortum. Constitutio* (Rome: Antonio Bladi, 1588), the first papal bull on abortion in the history of the Catholic Church.

Courtesy of Rare Books and Special Collections, University of British Columbia Library.

procure abortions to terminate the unwanted conceptions of lust; they and anyone who assists them kill souls and deprives them of salvation; religious and secular authorities tolerate the practice; all of this is a direct affront to God and greatly harms the *corpus christianum*. According to Sixtus, the situation required papal intervention and justified new laws with unprecedented penalties and which extended papal jurisdiction into matters that traditionally fell to other authorities. The distinct elements Sixtus used to frame abortion and the specific "remedies" he offered to solve the problem require close examination, for they were unprecedented and controversial and shaped the Catholic Church's thinking on abortion for centuries to come.

The first sentence of the bull justified its necessity: as Christ's vicar on earth, Sixtus had to repress the "audacity and daring of most profligate individuals who know no restraint, of sinning with license against the commandment 'do not kill.'"[55] From the outset, abortion was equated with killing and a violation of God's law. Sixtus used arresting descriptors and evocative imagery to depict the practice, its procurers, and anyone assisting them as "monstrous," "atrocious," "brutal," "cruel," "ferocious," and "inhuman," words intended to characterize individuals as enemies and separate them from God-fearing Catholics. Sixtus continued this tactic of "othering" by asking the reader a series of rhetorical questions:

> Who will not detest such an abhorrent and evil act, by which are lost not only the bodies but much worse also the souls? Who will not condemn to a most grave punishment the impiety of a person who will exclude a soul created in the image of God and for which Our Lord Jesus Christ has shed His precious Blood, and which is capable of eternal happiness and is destined to be in the company of angels, from the blessed vision of God, and who has impeded as much as he could the filling up of heavenly mansions, and has taken away the service to God by His creature? who has deprived children of life before they could receive from nature their portion of light, or defend themselves from bestial cruelty through the protection of their mother's body? Who will not abhor the cruelty and unrestrained debauchery of

impious people who have arrived into such a state of mind
that they procure poisons in order to extinguish the conceived fetuses within the viscera, and pour them out, trying
to provoke by a nefarious crime a violent and untimely
death and killing of their progeny? Finally, who will not
condemn to a most grave punishment the crimes of those
people who with poisons, potions and evil deeds sterilize
women or impede that they conceive or give birth by evil
medicines?[56]

Who would answer these questions affirmatively? The interrogative
conveyed information about abortion in a way that forced the reader to
align themselves with Sixtus's views on the issue and accept his solutions to the perceived problem. Neither here nor elsewhere in the bull
did Sixtus engage with any of the complex reasons motivating individuals to procure or assist in abortions; nor did he moralize on the sexual
arrangements that produced the aborted fetus—that would have dis-
tracted from his aim of defining abortion as murder and of providing a
universal and normative foundation for how to evaluate and decide
cases of abortion. Rather, simple and pathos-laden verbal images (loss
of bodies and souls, killing one's children, Christ's sacrificial blood,
union with God, etc.) were to render the morality of abortion clear and
universal. This rhetoric was meant to erase any ambivalence a reader
might have and incline them to empathize with the fetus and not the
procurer of abortion.

Sixtus also provided "supporting evidence" to reinforce his claims
and make his decrees easier to accept. In an attempt to minimize the
novelty of the bull, Sixtus explained he was "in part renewing old laws
and in part extending them." The "old laws" were decrees issued by the
bishops at the Council in Trullo (691), part of the Synod of Constantinople (the Sixth Ecumenical Church Council, 680–681), and the 546
Council of Lleida (Lerida in Castilian Spanish). The Synod of Constantinople, he explained, decreed that individuals who give abortive medicines and those who receive and use them to "kill fetuses are subject to
punishment applied to murderers."[57] The bishops participating in the
Council of Lleida took a somewhat more merciful stance: "Those who
kill fetuses conceived from adultery or extinguish them in the wombs

of mothers with potions, if with repentance would recur to the good-ness and meekness of the Church, should humbly weep for their sins for the rest of their lives." This ruling highlighted adulterers but also speci-fied penalties for clerics who participated in abortion: "If they were Clerics, they should not be allowed to recuperate their ministry and they are subject to all Ecclesiastical law's and profane law's grave pun-ishments for those who nefariously plot to kill fetuses in the uterus of childbearing women or try to prevent women from conceiving or try to expel the conceived fetuses from the womb." Sixtus positioned his bull within a lineage of conciliar attempts to eradicate the practice of abor-tion by equating it with homicide and harshly punishing its procurers and practitioners, including clergy, a point we shall return to below.[58] Sixtus also appealed to the authority of Church fathers. He turned to St. Jerome to explain the mysteries of generation and God's role in it: "While nature receives seed, after having received it nurtures it, nur-tured body distinguishes in members, meanwhile in the narrowness of the belly the hand of God is always at work, who is Creator of both body and soul and who molded, made and wanted [this child], and, mean-while the goodness of the Potter, that is of God, is impiously and overly despised by these people." A woman's body, her womb, is literally a con-tainer for divine presence: God is at work in the maternal body creating new life. Citing St. Ambrose, Sixtus emphasized that "it is no small and trivial gift of God to give children in order to propagate mankind." The faithful should know well that "the fecundity of childbearing women is a divine gift." How barbarous then that "by this cruel and inhuman crime parents are deprived of their offspring that they have engendered; the engendered children of their life; mothers of the rewards of mar-riage." Coupled with injunctions against parricide and powerful dis-courses portraying women being "saved through childbearing" (1 Tim. 2:15), Sixtus introduced what can be thought of as a pronatalist dis-course: abortion deprives "earth of its cultivators; the world of those who would know it; the Church of those that would make it grow and prosper and be happy with an increased number of devoted faithful."[59]

In sum, the questions and statements in the bull's preamble con-veyed the meaning that abortion was homicide: abortion kills bodies and souls; it deprives a soul (that God created in the womb and for which Christ was sacrificed) from seeing the light of the world, from knowing its parents, and most importantly from God's embrace. Abortion violates God's commandments and his intentions for women; it deprives the earth, the state, and the Church of citizens; it is inhuman. The point of the preamble was to establish the spiritual value of the fetus and, as a consequence, the immoral character of those who procure and participate in its destruction. Bolstered by biblical invocation, decrees of councils, teachings of Church fathers, and (an assumed) natural desire for the propagation of the faithful, Sixtus's language was designed to instill in the reader a desire to eradicate abortion and approve of his measures to do so. These measures were decreed in the second part of the bull.

> All and whosoever, men and women, . . . who procure the abortion of an immature fetus, whether animated or not animated, formed or not formed, will incur the punishments established by divine and human laws and by Canonic Sanctions and Apostolic Constitutions and which the civil law inflicts upon true murderers who have actually and really committed homicide, by the act and deed itself, and by this our perpetually valid constitution we state and order that the same punishments and laws and constitutions are to be extended to the aforementioned case.[60]

Departing from centuries of theology and philosophy, canon and criminal law, and common understanding, Sixtus disregarded considerations of animation and formation in the spiritual and legal meanings of abortion. By decreeing that the longstanding ambiguities about the beginnings of human life were irrelevant to the spiritual meaning of abortion, Sixtus consciously sealed off the space that allowed for a tolerant and ambivalent attitude toward the practice. From the date of the bull's promulgation, all Catholics were to believe that all intentional abortion was homicide. For clarification, Sixtus included methods of pregnancy termination: abortion meant "to kill . . . immature fetuses in the maternal viscera" through substances and physical means—medicines, poisons, violence, burdens, and labor imposed on a pregnant woman. His ban also included all substances promoting sterility and impeding conception, along with "other unknown and carefully researched means, so that abortion really follows."[61]

The bull's force also lay in its incursion into the jurisdictions of both secular and ecclesiastical authorities. "We give order and command" to all judges, both ecclesiastical and civil, "to punish the guilty of these crimes in accordance with our decrees and sanctions." This infringed on the standard and accepted jurisprudence of the time, which gave judges authority to issue penalties at their discretion. (Judicial discretion will be discussed in Chapter 3.) Recognizing that prosecution was difficult because abortions are "usually committed secretly," Sixtus instructed judges to proceed not only by accusation and denunciation, as was standard, but also by means of inquisition. As with other grave offenses, tribunals were to actively investigate cases of abortion: they must keep a watchful eye over their subjects, endeavoring to uncover secret and hidden cases of abortion; soliciting the voluntary reporting of suspicious behaviors; following up on leads given in other cases being investigated and launching cases ex officio. Judges were to take abortion seriously and investigate and punish its procurers vigorously.

Sixtus went further still, supplementing earthly punishments with spiritual ones:

> We want that the monstrous gravity of these brutal, cruel, ferocious and inhuman crimes be punished not only by temporal sanctions but also by spiritual censures and for this reason We decree that all persons . . . who, as principal parties or accomplices . . . besides the aforementioned sanctions, are also *"ipso facto"*, *"latae sententiae"*, automatically excommunicated by Us.[62]

Immediately and automatically, at the moment of procuring, providing, or assisting in an abortion, an individual is cut off from the faith. To ensure this spiritual censure was taken seriously, Sixtus reserved absolution to the papacy alone. An individual who participated in an abortion could no longer receive forgiveness from their confessor except *in articulo mortis,* on the point of death.[63] Sixtus also revoked bishops' authority over abortion, a move he knew would be controversial as it contravened decrees issued at the Council of Trent, a point he explicitly acknowledged. Invoking his belief in (and aspiration for) papal "full power" (*plenitudo potestatis*) in both spiritual and secular affairs, Sixtus reminded his reader that he was "placed by the lord in the supreme throne of justice," and no one could therefore infringe on his constitution. If anyone (including judges, princes, or cardinals) tried to resolve cases of abortion in any way contravening the decrees of his bull, "he will incur the indignation of Almighty God and of Blessed Apostles Peter and Paul."[64]

To reiterate, the bull was unprecedented. Through evocative and forceful language, Sixtus redefined Catholic doctrine on abortion, infusing it with spiritual, moral, and social meanings intended to influence his readers and, through them, broader audiences. The gravity of the offense, he declared, justified severe measures and papal encroachment into the jurisdictions of ecclesiastical and secular authorities.

Generations of scholars have drawn on Sixtus's bull, summarizing parts of this complicated source in a few sentences or paragraphs, to demonstrate a long line of Catholic thinking and papal legislation on abortion. However, the motivations that shaped the document, the social and political contexts in which it was created, and its reception have not been adequately investigated. Why did Sixtus issue this bull at this time? Who were his targets? Some scholars have assumed that Sixtus issued the bull as part of a campaign to curb prostitution in Rome. While the general regulation of sexuality and of women's bodies was certainly part of the context that shaped the bull, the assumption rests on unchecked inference that abortion was, and was regarded as, a "problem" of women's sexual behaviors. However, there is no mention of prostitutes in the bull; nor is there direct moralizing on "dishonest" women's sexual and reproductive behaviors. Rather, the bull's explicit targets are "audacious," "daring," "profligate," and "unbridled" *hominum* who break the fifth commandment and get away with it, and "impious *hominum,* full of lust and cruelty," who seek the "violent and untimely death of their own offspring." The bull asks: "Who will not condemn . . . those [*illorum*] who with poisons, potions, and evil deeds sterilize women or prevent them from conceiving and giving birth with evil medicines?"[65] While *hominum* and *illorum* could mean "people," there is evidence suggesting the bull targeted men more than women. Throughout, Sixtus depicted women not as active malicious agents but as passive victims of abortion. Women were being sterilized, impeded from conceiving and giving birth, given poisons and medicine to abort. Abortions happened to women; violence, burdens, and medicines were "imposed on pregnant women."[66] Only a few statements in the bull were explicitly directed to women. "The same women" who were given medicines, who suffered violence and were forced to carry heavy loads, sometimes "knowingly do the aforementioned." "Women who knowingly take" abortifacients were mentioned alongside those who gave and prepared them.[67] The adverb "knowingly" (*scienter*) is important: it modifies the only two statements in the bull directly addressing women who seek abortion. Nowhere did Sixtus mention a penalty (or lack of one) to be imposed on a woman who was forced to consume or who unknowingly consumed an abortifacient. Knowingly—that is, intentionally—seeking, consuming, and giving such substances for the purpose of terminating pregnancy constituted murder. That he only explicitly addressed women as active agents twice in the bull suggests he had other principal targets in mind.

Although the bull does not explicitly mention medical practitioners, it is clear they were among Sixtus's targets. The word "medicaments" was referred to four times in the bull, and "potions" and "poisons" five times each. Medical practitioners, widely construed, were included in the capacious category of "interposed third persons" who provide knowledge, services, and products for abortion. Anyone who has "helped, counseled, shown favor or knowingly given potions and whatever kind of medicine, written private letters, or prescriptions"—and here he was speaking about male physicians, for only they wrote prescriptions—as well as those who give women sterilizing potions and poisons to impede conception, are automatically excommunicated and tried as murderers. Medical practitioners were to completely abstain from participating in abortions and by doing so would help regulate the practice.

There is still other internal evidence suggesting the bull targeted men. Three of the bulls' ten decrees are directed exclusively to clergy involved in abortions; the other seven decrees explicitly list clerics alongside other delinquents. Sixtus decreed that clerics involved in abortions (as procurers or accomplices) would be deprived of their clerical privileges, their office, and any benefice they might have and declared incapable of receiving them in the future, as was the case for clerics who commit voluntary homicide. In direct violation of decrees established at Trent, Sixtus stated this penalty would be meted out even if the crime was secret and did not cause public scandal, and even if it was not proven judicially—and a bishop could not offer absolution or dispensation. A priest would lose his clerical status and be handed over to secular authorities to be tried and punished in the same manner "as laymen who are truly and really murderers."[68]

This foundational bull in the history of Catholic thought on abortion was directed equally toward the eradication of the practice *in toto,* the reform of sexual morality (male and female) in general, and the disciplining of clergy in particular. It therefore must also be read in these blended contexts. The bull was one element of this aggressive pope's broader campaign against deviance, sexual sin, and reprobate clergy.[69] In 1586 and 1587, Sixtus issued similarly harsh and unprecedented bulls against adultery and incest.[70] Neither of these, however, were universal, but specific to the Ecclesiastical States and the city of Rome, where Sixtus was the prince. This meant they could be vigorously enforced. His policies on adultery made an especially strong impression on Romans and foreign observers. In that bull, Sixtus sought to punish all sexual behaviors that betrayed the sacrament of marriage. He targeted both women and men. Examples included individuals who separate from their spouses to be with other people; women who are granted a separation from their husbands and vow to live in a monastery but then leave their enclosure and live "dishonestly"; married men who solicit prostitution and married women who engage in it (married women who live a "mala vita" were ordered to, within twelve days of the bull's issuance, report to designated officials and promise to live honestly); individuals who engage in concubinage; men who commit adultery or seduce or rape virgins or married women; fathers or mothers who pimp their daughters or husbands their wives. All these were to be punished by death, and many were. Contemporary newsletters (*avvisi*), the frightening and imaginative gallows stories (*relatione de giustizie*), and diaries that circulated in manuscripts entertained and terrified readers with stories of adulterers condemned to death, often without judicial process.[71] Famous stories include the execution of the nobleman Roberto Altemps, the legitimated son of the Cardinal (Mark Sittich) Altemps, for adultery and defloration / rape. While stories of nobles being punished for their sexual transgressions might titillate, Romans disapproved when the pope's discipline did not match popular assessments of justice. According to a newsletter writer, the June 1586 execution of a Roman woman who had prostituted her daughter was deemed excessively severe and cruel, especially because the daughter was made to look at her mother's corpse hanging from the scaffold for an hour, wearing her client's gifts.[72]

Sixtus also took a harsh stand with clerics. In his short but energetic five-year papacy, he issued a number of bulls and edicts targeting clerical conduct. In 1587 he issued new and stricter decrees against the ordination and continued practice of the ordained who were deemed irregular, either because they were born illegitimate, had a physical disability, or because they committed certain sins and crimes that should have disqualified them from orders—the important and influential Cardinal Santori referred to this constitution as Sixtus's "bull against bastards and malfactors."[73] Sixtus took this issue seriously, renewing and intensifying the bull only days before he promulgated the bull on abortion in October 1588.[74] That same month, Sixtus also issued an edict prohibiting regulars from owning coaches or carriages and riding through the streets of Rome, an increasingly fashionable practice among elites but one the pope deemed scandalous for religious.[75] This was followed, in 1589, by a bull decreeing penalties for ordained clergy not wearing their habit or being tonsured, therefore not distinguishing themselves from the laity, in violation of Tridentine decrees.[76]

Sixtus occasionally issued dramatic punishments for priests who did not live up to his ideals. In June 1586 he ordered the burning of a priest and a boy for sodomy.[77] In the spring of 1590 he sentenced to death a priest and a nun caught in a sexual relationship.[78] He certainly knew about the infamous case of the Venetian confessor Giovanni Pietro Lion, discussed above: Sixtus was the inquisitor general of Venice until 1560, when the government requested his removal due to quarrels stemming from the severity with which he exercised his office.[79] Sixtus would have been away from Venice for about one year when Lion's story broke and likely had strong opinions on the matter. He would also have been aware of the supplications to and decisions of the Apostolic Penitentiary concerning cases of clerical abortion and may have heard about cases investigated in episcopal tribunals. He certainly knew about the scandal Bishop Giovanni Stefano de Urbieta of Telese caused with his various excesses, including rape, sodomy, and causing the death of a

nun whom he had impregnated by forcing her to have a dangerous
abortion. Giovanni Stefano was forced to resign or fled his office in
1587, and Sixtus himself appointed the next bishop, a man he deemed
capable of reforming the dioceses clergy and laity.[80] While it is, at present, unknown whether a specific incident inspired Sixtus to issue his
bull on abortion at this time, it is clear he had clerical discipline in
mind as he drafted it: Cardinal Giulio Santori reported in his diary
that Sixtus asked him to look over the minutes of the bull against religious who do not wear their habit or tonsure, "ordering me to increase
the penalties against the ordained for the serious disorders that are felt
by everyone, *and it is for this reason that he also made the bull on abortion,
where he had shown himself so severe so that many could feel it.*"[81]

How did people "feel it"? The bull's harsh penalties were meant to
deter people from participating in abortion and ensure ecclesiastical
authorities fell in line. In this and his many other bulls, Sixtus sought
to reform morality while exerting authority over the ecclesiastical establishment and expanding the papacy's secular power by dissolving
the boundary between sin and crime. *Against those who Procure, Counsel
and Consent in any way to Abortion* was the legislation of a territorial
prince and Christ's vicar on earth. By rendering individuals who had or
helped in abortions excommunicate, reserving absolution to his office,
and voiding the powers of judges and officials to resolve the matter as
they saw fit, Sixtus was impressing the gravity of the sin on both laity
and clergy and trying to amplify the power of the papacy.[82] As of October 29, 1588, all Catholics had to accept that abortion was homicide,
that its agents were murderers and excommunicate, and that the sin
could only be forgiven by the pope himself. Challenging Sixtus's interpretation of the meaning of abortion or rejecting his decrees could be
interpreted as heresy and a matter for the Roman Inquisition.

All clergy and (in theory) all Catholic secular authorities were
therefore to know about the bull, communicate it to the laity, and enforce it, so it had to be widely disseminated. Within days of its promulgation, news of the bull was spread by the avvisi writers in Rome. It
was printed on November 16 in Rome and distributed throughout
Italy, Catholic Europe, and possibly to Catholic dioceses overseas.
Within months, it was also printed for local distribution by publishers
in Bologna, Florence, Venice, and Naples.[83] The bull was quickly and

widely broadcast to effect change in the meaning of abortion and the Church's policies regarding it. Bishops had to inform all their confessors of the new decrees, who were in turn to inform the laity. This was of genuine and urgent importance due to the automatic excommunication imposed on those procuring, administering, or assisting in abortion. On November 6, the bishop of Nola Fabricio Gallo had celebrated a diocesan synod, and it seems that before he learned about Sixtus's bull, his list of reserved cases had already gone to the printer in Naples to be published as part of the synodal decretals. The decretals informed all Gallo's confessors that abortion was reserved to his office but could be absolved by those to whom he had given authority to handle reserved cases. Deleting this from the list of sins reserved to him or introducing a new section for cases reserved to the papacy were apparently not options—perhaps the type had already been set? The preferred solution was a marginal note next to the listing of abortion, alerting the reader to Sixtus's new bull and the change in policy.[84] Other bishops also modified their lists. Agostino Valier, bishop of Verona, amended his list of reserved cases, which had been consistent in Verona since the 1542 episcopate of Matteo Giberti, explaining that procuring, counselling, or aiding in abortion was, as of 1588, reserved to the pope.[85] In the 1589 synodal decretals of Piacenza, Filippo Sega (by then bishop of Piacenza) summarized Sixtus's bull in a paragraph in a section on cases reserved to the papacy—noteworthy because eleven years earlier, as bishop of Ripatransone, Sega had not included abortion on his list of reserved cases.[86] In 1590, the bishop of Ancona, Carlo Conti, went further still, issuing a four-paragraph *sommario* of the bull. Written in Italian, the broadsheet summarized the decrees, omitting Sixtus's intense preamble, for all his confessors and curates, warning them to accommodate their practices to the new rules "to avoid incurring any penalty."[87] These publications indicate some bishops took the bull's reservation of absolution seriously and immediately (within weeks and months) informed their confessors, who were to advise the laity.

While its dissemination might be easy to track, the impact of Sixtus' bull is more difficult to assess. How did bishops feel about the papal incursion into what had been their jurisdiction, as decreed at the Council of Trent? Did priests tell their parishioners the new rules on abortion? Did confessors refuse absolution to those who confessed to abortions? Perhaps most importantly, what did the laity think about all this? There is significant evidence that both the theological redefinition of abortion and the political implications of Sixtus's bull, as they pertained to both matters of ecclesiastical jurisdictions and social and reproductive life, were immediately controversial and that clerics and laity alike resisted them, even attempting to have the bull changed.

The Politics of Absolution

In the months following the promulgation of the bull, bishops and vicars throughout Italy sent petitions to the Congregation of Bishops requesting special permission to absolve penitents who confessed to involvement in abortions.[88] Unable to secure local absolution, these individuals were living excommunicate—their souls in jeopardy. Traveling to Rome to have the Pope hear and deliberate their matter was a trip hardly anyone would or could take. In theory, refusing the trip meant they would remain excommunicated from the faith. Bishops found this situation spiritually unacceptable.

On June 17, 1589, not six months after the bull was promulgated, an (unnamed) vicar of Larino (in Molisse) asked the Congregation of Bishops to clarify certain points surrounding the pope's new bull, apparently becoming the first to question it in writing. Did Sixtus's condemnations apply equally to those who gave and caused abortion and to those who sought and had it? What about those who aborted "unintentionally" and "without malice from carrying weights or [suffering] beatings"?[89] The vicar sought clarification on whether and how to apply the pope's new bull to these situations. It is unclear whether he was faced with specific cases and needed to know how to act or whether he was preemptively seeking elucidation.

The spring of 1590 saw more letters from bishops and vicars from northern and southern Italy. And this is when the unnamed woman from Lodi, with whom this chapter began, entered the conversation. The bishop of Lodi, Ludovico Taverna, wrote directly to Sixtus requesting permission to absolve "a few women" who were "deceived and seduced by the Demon" and had abortions to avoid "dishonor and infamy." These women confessed to drinking beverages to impede conception and to terminate pregnancy, and others had contravened the bull by giving them aid and counsel. Lodi's confessors informed all these individuals they could not be absolved locally and had to appeal directly to the pope. But, Taverna stressed, it was impossible to convince them to go to Rome. Fearing exposure, for reasons of honor and shame, they could not and would not, leaving them no way to regain grace and reenter the Church. The bishop of Lodi "most humbly plead[ed]" for Sixtus to issue some expedient remedy around this matter in order to free these people from their sin and remedy the dangers to the health of their souls without increasing the chance of scandal.[90]

The vicar of Aversa (just north of Naples) Stefano Campanari felt the same way. He informed the prefect of the Congregation of Bishops, Cardinal Nicholas de Pellevé, that his confessors and penitentiary had recently informed him of "many penitents that have committed abortions of both animate and inanimate fetuses" within his diocese. The vicar requested a "remedy" from the pope on behalf of those principally concerned—the women who aborted, those who made them abort, and those who helped them. In total, he sought permission to absolve twenty penitents.[91] The congregation received similar letters from the archbishop of Milan Gaspare Visconti, the archpriest of Siena (unidentified), the bishop of Potenza Sebastiano Barnaba, and the archbishop of Trani Scipione da Tolfa, all around the same time, all seeking special permission to absolve penitents for the sin of abortion locally because they would not go to Rome.[92]

The congregation's registry indicates each of these requests was answered in the same way. Sixtus allowed all these procurers of abortion, both women and men, and their accomplices, who could not, "for legitimate reasons," come to Rome to be absolved locally "for this time only," not, however, by their bishops but by their confessors. Along with reprimanding these sinners and assigning "salutatory penance" appropriate to the "quality of the case," priests were to be instructed by their bishops to preach about the gravity of this sin and alert the laity to the difficulty of securing absolution.[93] "Proceed with prudence" and "with appropriate confidentiality," the pope warned, in order to avoid any "inconveniences": take care that the confessor confides in you these cases without expressing the names of the penitents—that is, in a way that does not break the "secret and seal of confession."[94]

These petitions and responses bare several important points. First, on a basic level, they reveal that quite a few people had abortions and consumed products to impede conception and that they had help: "twenty penitents" from Aversa; "some women" from Lodi; "some people" from Siena; "a few poor" souls from Milan. While vague references to "some" do not reveal precisely how common the practice was, they are significant, especially in aggregate and alongside Aversa's "twenty," because criminal and ecclesiastical tribunals certainly did not prosecute anywhere close to this many people for abortion every year. These expressions of quantity suggest abortion was indeed a common enough practice that "a few people" confessed to it each year. If the letter writers were exaggerating, this still tells us they expected their reader to find the numbers plausible. Unfortunately, the authors of these petitions did not offer any information about the penitents seeking absolution. According to the bishop of Lodi, it was women who confessed to procuring and aiding in abortions; the other supplicants did not specify gender. Were they predominantly women or men? Single or married? Adulterers, prostitutes, priests, or medical practitioners? Why did they procure abortions, and why did others assist them? Only Lodi specified that individuals were motivated to procure abortions to avoid "dishonor and infamy." Such motivation was likely genuine, but it was also to be expected. Time and time again people sinned to avoid hardship, and prescriptions were expected to be flexed to avoid scandal. By highlighting the vulnerability of the "poor women" who were "seduced by the devil," the bishop of Lodi urged the pope to recognize the social consequences of exposure and be more inclined to grant the requests. And it worked. It is not surprising that the other supplicants concealed all identifying details, because offering too much information might betray the secrecy of confession. If the episcopal reservation of abortion threatened exposure and the rupturing of the confessional seal, what would forcing an individual to go to Rome for absolution do? In these cases, it is likely the petitioning bishops and vicars were themselves in the dark, that only the confessors knew the whos and the complex whys of these cases.

This brings us to the second point: clerical knowledge of these abortions came from confession, in springtime, when most individuals fulfilled the minimum requirement of one confession a year during

Lent, in preparation for Easter. Here we have evidence that laity confessed abortions and expected absolution. It also suggests they considered abortion a sin that needed confessing. However, we only know about these individuals because their confessors knew of Sixtus's bull and took it seriously enough not to issue absolution, and because they reported the cases to their superiors who started a paper trail. Third, these ecclesiastical authorities recognized that sending individuals who had or participated in abortions to Rome was not an option and so appealed to the pope on the penitents' behalf. Fourth, Sixtus accepted this and allowed for absolution, not by bishops and vicars—which would break the seal of confession—but by the sinners' own confessors, with the stipulation that sufficient penance be given and that the case be handled discreetly. Again, the fear of scandal was deployed in the supplications to justify resisting the decrees of the bull, and this was accepted by Rome as legitimate. Furthermore, nothing in the supplications or the papacy's replies suggests these sinners and their accomplices were to be delivered to secular tribunals to suffer capital punishment as "true murderers who have actually committed murder."[95] Rather, it was clear these cases would remain in the internal forum and be dealt with through the sacrament of penance.

Careful attention to what was communicated in these letters and what was omitted further reveals how tactical the crafting of a supplication could be.[96] What reached the Congregation of Bishops and Sixtus V and what is preserved in the historical record are the versions of events the supplicants wanted read. While these letters have much to offer, it is also clear they are distortions of complex situations and events that are unrecoverable. An individual confessed to having or assisting in an abortion, but what exactly did the penitent tell the confessor and what did they conceal? The confessor processed this testimony and had to make decisions about whether, what, and how to tell his superior. The final communication is the written version sent to Sixtus, which represents what the bishop or vicar wanted him to know. At every level, the story of a woman who had an abortion was modified in conscious and unconscious ways. We do not know what specific politics, personal convictions, agendas, and potential gains shaped each version that led to the final bare-bones—and somewhat formulaic—portrayal sent to the pope. What we can know, however, is that women in Larino,

Lodi, Milan, Siena, Potenza, and Trani had abortions, that confessions were made, and that absolution was locally denied. We cannot know how this weighed on their souls, but we do know these "sinners" were willing to live excommunicate rather than expose themselves by seeking pardon from the pope. We also learn that some ecclesiastical authorities abided by the pope's decrees on abortion—at least on paper—but also that they were willing to question them in the form of a supplication. We might speculate that these supplications were cautious attempts to test the bounds of the pope's bull, his encroachment into episcopal prerogatives, and his general program of centralizing spiritual authority. In this respect, they were effective.

These supplications had a direct effect on curial politics. They showed the Congregation of Bishops that Sixtus's bull created serious spiritual, social, and administrative problems. Even before the letters arrived, everyone likely knew that penitents from Milan in the north to Potenza in the south—not to mention those from France, Spain and New Spain, Lima, Congo, Goa, Nagasaki, Manila, everywhere Catholics lived—would not travel to Rome to plead their case. Several high-ranking cardinals discussed these problems and wondered whether the bull might be amended. Giulio Santori, Costanzo da Sarnano, and Giovanni Antonio Facchinetti (the future short-lived pope Innocent IX) tried to convince Sixtus to issue an amendment restricting the bull to the Ecclesiastical States—where the pope was the territorial prince—and to altogether remove the reservation for women who could not go to Rome without scandal and danger to their lives. Sixtus refused to lift the reservation, to diminish the bull's force by restricting it, and to relinquish papal authority over the matter.[97] At the end of his pontificate (Sixtus died in August 1590), the bull remained universal and (theoretically) in effect.

The curia of Gregory XIV, Sixtus's second successor, had to deal with similar challenges from bishops and vicars. On May 7, 1591, the congregation responded to another request from the archbishop of Trani and again granted his confessors authority to offer absolution with the same warnings communicated to the penitent.[98] On May 22, the congregation received a letter from the archpriest of Altamura, Giangiacomo de Mansi, requesting the same permission but to absolve a physician who had administered an abortion to a pregnant woman suffering from what was believed to be a fatal illness. Mansi reported that, a year earlier, (i.e., 1590), a physician, in order to save a pregnant woman from death, had "ordered [and administered] appropriate and ordinary remedies," so she might give birth even though she was not yet due. He had acted with the counsel of another physician who was "older and more expert in the art of medicine." The "creatura was born alive," Mansi maintained, "and was baptized by the midwife," which was common practice in emergency births. Because of Sixtus's bull, Altamura's confessors and penitentiary refused to absolve the physician during Holy Week. Mansi judged this unfair, especially because the aborted fetus' soul was saved through baptism. Mansi sought permission to absolve the physician himself because the "crime" was not done maliciously: "This poor physician and good Christian so longs for absolution."[99] He was silent on the fate of the woman.

Mansi's letter demonstrates that physicians administered therapeutic abortions and confessors faced these trying medical situations. That the religious of Altamura refused to absolve the physician suggests they were interpreting Sixtus's bull quite literally, as Sixtus made no explicit mention of abortion administered to heal or as a consequence of healing. This physician lived excommunicate for about a year before the archpriest took on his case. The Congregation of Bishops replied to Mansi on June 18, 1591, almost one month after he sent his supplication, informing him that the physician, as well as anyone else "who has fallen [to this sin]," could now be freely absolved but ordering that confessors "use every diligence and effort to extirpate this grave sin." This time, however, permission to absolve was not granted as a "one time only" act of mercy and expediency; rather, Gregory XIV had decided to modify Sixtus's bull.[100]

Mansi's letter appears to have been the last straw. It had become clear to the cardinals of the Congregation of Bishops and Gregory XIV that Sixtus's bull was ineffective in regulating the practice of abortion, that it was not implementable and was in fact too radical. Mansi's letter prompted Gregory to convene a meeting with the Congregation of Bishops in late May, where "with speedy deliberation . . . and according to their advice" he decided Sixtus's bull needed to be moderated.[101] On May 31, Gregory issued a constitution of his own, *A Moderation of the*

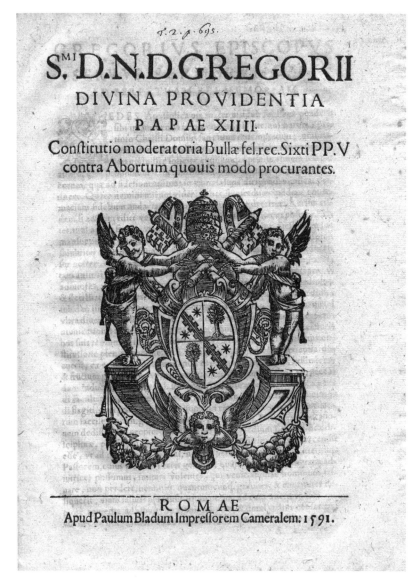

r.2.p.695.

S.ᴹᴵ D.N.D.GREGORII
DIVINA PROVIDENTIA
PAPAE XIIII·

Conſtitutio moderatoria Bullæ fel.rec. Sixti PP.V
contra Abortum quouis modo procurantes.

ROMAE
Apud Paulum Bladum Impreſſorem Cameralem: 1591.

Fig 2.2 Frontispiece to Gregory XIV's moderation of Sixtus V's papal bull, *Constitutio moderatoria Bullae Fel.rec Sixti PP. V. Contra Abortum quovis modo procurantes* (Rome: Paulo Bladi, 1591).

Courtesy of Rare Books and Special Collections, University of British Columbia Library.

Constitution set forth by Sixtus V, which marks another papal attempt to define abortion and intervene in its handling.

Referred to by its incipit, "Sedes apostolica" (the Apostolic See), Gregory's bull attempted two things: first, to justify Sixtus's motivations for issuing his novel and controversial bull, while at the same time acknowledging its inefficacy and the problems it created; and second, to solve those problems by "moderating" his predecessor's decrees. The *moderation* in the title of the bull and throughout the text is significant because Gregory was not officially revoking Sixtus's bull. Although papal infallibility did not become official doctrine until 1870, Gregory knew he could not openly criticize his predecessor and could certainly not say Sixtus was wrong in doctrinal and ecclesiastical matters without tarnishing the institution of the papacy and its claims on spiritual and secular authority. By "moderating" Gregory meant to lessen and restrict certain elements of the bull without rejecting it completely. He chose his language carefully. He wrote that the Apostolic See, always "feeling the gravity and the magnitude of the weight leaning on it in procuring the salvation of souls," sometimes seeks to discourage "the audacity of the obstinate faithful with severe punishments." However, the Church also "opens its maternal bosom to the same people if they should wish to return to her heart and humbly request pardon for their sin, and it lays out an easier road to penitence for them; it tempers hardness with suitable gentleness." Sixtus, "inflamed with the zeal of justice," apparently represented the strict disciplinary side of the Church; Gregory, the "maternal" and merciful side. In his preamble, Gregory made the case that both approaches were needed to save souls. Nevertheless, "experience showed [that] the utility and fruit that were hoped for [by Sixtus's bull] did not come into being." Not only had the bull not dissuaded people from abortion, but it had provided the opportunity "for very many sacrileges and for the most-grave sins and crimes." By this, Gregory meant that individuals continued to procure and assist in abortions, and because seeking absolution from Rome was not an option, they ignored or accepted their excommunication. Perhaps priests involved in abortions also concealed their irregularity and continued to participate in sacred rituals and the sacraments. Gregory was subtly admitting that Sixtus's bull was doing more harm than good. Judging that the sword of ecclesiastical discipline should be wielded so it "tends to the treatment and not the ruin of souls," Gregory found it necessary to moderate Sixtus's bull because it "block[ed] the way of salvation," something the Holy See could not allow, "no matter how gravely and enormously one sinned."[102] No doubt, he also recognized that a papal law that was ignored and unenforceable undermined the legitimacy and authority of the institution.

Gregory modified Sixtus's bull in three important ways. First, when abortion was neither "an issue of homicide or of an animate fetus," Gregory thought it "more useful" to return to the traditional and less harsh penalties of canon and secular law.[103] This reasserted the ambiguous distinction that Sixtus had removed between a preanimated and an animated fetus—once again, the abortion of the former was a mortal sin but not homicide, and its procurer would not become irregular; the abortion of the latter was to be treated as homicide, and the penalties Sixtus decreed in his bull would stand. Second, the penalties against clerics who participated in abortions were modified accordingly. Here, the bull is not explicit but refers the reader to the decrees of canon law and the Council of Trent on the reservation of cases and irregularity: bishops were again given authority to give dispensation in cases of irregularity and to absolve clerics from sins and crimes, especially if they were secret. The exceptions were cases of willful homicide and certain sins and crimes that were public, caused scandal, and found their way before a tribunal.[104] Third, Gregory reinstated the authority of confessors to "fully and freely" give absolution in cases of the abortion of a preanimated fetus and remove excommunication for "those who have sinned up to now and those who will sin in the same situations [in the future]." Prelates and officials who were confronted with these cases were to act "as if [Sixtus's] constitution had never been published."[105] By reinstating the distinction between preanimated and animated fetuses, reinvesting confessors with the power to absolve the abortion of the former, and giving bishops back their powers to dispense and absolve clergy, Gregory, in effect, rejected the central tenets of Sixtus's bull and its main solutions for deterring individuals from the practice of abortion. However, regarding the abortion of an animated fetus and the corresponding penalties for laity and clergy, Gregory left Sixtus's bull to "endure entirely in its own strength."[106] This is important, for while Gregory XIV significantly softened Sixtus's harsh stand, he was still committed to defining the abortion of an animated fetus as a form of homicide. Nevertheless, he thought a less harsh approach might be more effective in changing mentalities toward the practice.

Gregory's bull garnered immediate attention. The news writer in Urbino reported Gregory had "reformed" Sixtus's bull by "lifting" excommunication and the papal reservation of absolution and bringing the matter back to canon and secular law, *"ad viam iuris."*[107] Bishops informed their confessors of the new regulations in person, in synods, in their published decrees, and in printed Italian summaries for those who could not read Latin.[108]

"The Choice of a Lesser Evil . . . Is a Good Choice"

Sixtus's bull *Against those who Procure Abortion* was in force for two and a half years. As of June 1591, abortion was, once again, not unequivocally homicide, and canonical distinctions were reaffirmed. While the Church's position had more or less reverted to its centuries-old status quo, Sixtus V's and Gregory XIV's proclamations mark an important turning point in Catholic thought on abortion. Among all the issues preoccupying the papacy at this precise moment (e.g., food shortages and banditry in the papal states, the French "wars of religion," diplomatic difficulties with Spain, the perceived threat of the Ottoman Empire, ongoing struggles with heresy and the spread of Protestantism, supporting the expansion of Catholicism across the globe, etc.), it is significant that abortion became something so important and contentious that it took up the time of two popes and their curiae. Prohibiting abortion was part of Sixtus V's broader program of moral and clerical reform, but evidently it was an urgent and exceptional case, important enough to be singled out with a specific and unprecedented piece of legislation. But what were the immediate and longer-term sociocultural effects of the papal interventions on the spiritual meaning and ecclesiastical handling of abortion?

In the short term, the direct involvement of the pope in an issue that, until 1588, was handled locally by a confessor and (maybe) a bishop meant the lives of individuals who procured or participated in abortions could be profoundly changed beyond the physical, emotional, and local ways they might have anticipated. We cannot know how the unnamed woman from Lodi felt about having her life and eternal salvation hanging in the balance as the highest echelons of the Church and the pope himself discussed her case or how the unnamed physician from Altamura felt about his excommunication for trying to heal a woman at risk. Did the papal legislation and the politics of salvation influence their understanding of their "sin" and conscience, their sense of self, and their estimation of the institutional Church and its personnel? We cannot know precisely how individuals experienced their excommunication, what they thought about the interactions that brought them back into the fold, or how being caught up in ecclesiastical politics shaped their spiritual trajectories. What is clear however is that Gregory's moderation of Sixtus's bull did not mean anxieties surrounding the Church's thinking on abortion abated. The immediate and longer-term impact the bulls may have had on the laity resulted from the impact the decrees had on the ecclesiastical establishment. The remainder of this chapter therefore will explore how that establishment processed the messages of the two papal bulls on abortion, how they continued to debate meanings and negotiate best practices for regulating behaviors and disciplining individuals, including clerics, and how these ideas and practices were communicated to the laity in the first half of the seventeenth century.

While Sixtus's bull on abortion was, as of May 31, 1591, no longer official Church law, as a papal statement on the subject, it provided an important precedent and had to be reckoned with by all who thought and wrote about the spiritual and legal issues surrounding abortion. The bull did not raise new questions or offer new answers to old debates on the relationship between abortion and homicide or fetus and human being. It did, however, offer clarity: the unqualified statement that all abortion was homicide was to be taken as a universal moral principle. It also opened up the possibility that the pope was implicitly saying animation occurs at conception, an interpretation some commentators debated. Furthermore, the decree that all authorities were to pursue all cases of abortion as if they were cases of homicide and that only the pope could offer absolution removed the ambiguity and any flexibility regarding how individuals who procured and assisted in abortions ought to be punished. Conversely, Gregory's moderation was an explicit statement of support for the long-held traditional theory of delayed

animation and a return to juridical flexibility. While Gregory's bull officially stabilized the issue by returning it to the canonical formulation,
many theologians did not feel the matter was settled. The papal interventions inspired more questions and consequently more doubt: Who
had the authority to make doctrinal statements on this subject and on
what grounds? Who had jurisdiction over the handling of abortion?
What were correct and just punishments for those who had and participated in abortions, both lay individuals and clerics, and how were these
to be determined? These questions, of course, were not new, but the recent papal volte-face on abortion inspired theological discussion and
more nuanced analysis.

Inspired by new developments in casuistry (a method of decision
making emphasizing cases and their particulars over the application of
universal principles) and probabilism (a theological doctrine allowing
an agent to choose any probable opinion over other probable opinions
when certainty cannot be had), seventeenth-century theologians put
the morality of abortion through rigorous analysis. They raised new
doubts on accepted positions and devised new ways to deal with the
inherent uncertainties relating to the paradigm of animation, and, in
particular, the afterlives of aborted and miscarried fetuses. Catholic
theologians, philosophers, and medical theorists engaged vigorously
and provocatively in speculative or philosophical embryology. Novel
theses were proposed resulting in a growing sense of uncertainty. The
result was both more radical and more conservative interpretations.[109]

For instance, in a 1620 publication, Thomas Fyens, the celebrated
professor of philosophy and medicine at the University of Louvain, provocatively rejected the traditional opinion that set animation at forty
days for male and eighty days for female fetuses by arguing that human
fetuses are animated with a rational soul immediately or at latest by the
third day after conception. In 1635, Jan Marcus Marci, scientist, phi-
losopher, and professor of medicine at the University of Prague, challenged both Fyens's and the traditional hypotheses by arguing that the
fetus only receives the immortal soul after it is delivered fully formed
enough to survive on its own; before that time "the fetus in the uterus is
a part of the mother, like one of her fingers," he argued.[110] These interpretations of fetal development and animation had important consequences for the theology on abortion. In Fyens's view, all abortions were

the killing of human beings with souls; in Marci's, none were. Exasperated with the multiplicity of arguments, Paolo Zacchia lamented "that as time went by, uncertainty around these issues increased rather than decreased." Nevertheless, he too weighed in. Acknowledging that departing from the time-honored position (validated not only by ancient and modern theological, philosophical, and medical authorities but also by Pope Gregory XIV) for a "novel" opinion was perhaps risky, Zacchia nonetheless decided that Fyens's view that the "rational soul is created and infused by God immediately, at the exact moment of conception," was more convincing than the traditional position of delayed animation.[111] While Zacchia, a medical practitioner and personal physician to Popes Innocent X and Alexander VII, felt confident enough to make this statement in print and did so apparently without consequence, Italian theologians discussed the issue carefully and critically. By and large, most concluded the canonical assumption was the safest.

While many theologians and moralists focused their analysis of abortion on the spiritual value of the fetus, some, mostly casuist theologians, acknowledged that fetuses were not disembodied entities but were situated in the complicated social, political, and material lives of actual human beings and that their fates were often justifiably secondary and tied to those of the women carrying them. While certainly important, the spiritual value of the fetus was not the only factor that mattered in decision making and weighing the sinfulness of an abortion. The Sicilian Theatine Antonino Diana in particular took into account, in a profound way, the challenges, burdens, and traumas pregnancy could impose on women, men, and healers and the conflicting imperatives influencing decisions to have or to participate in abortions. He concluded that abortion always carried a heavy moral load but that in certain circumstances it was morally understandable, even licit.

Diana devoted twenty-four long pages of the seventh volume of his magisterial *Moral Explanations, in which Rather Specific Failures of Moral Sense are Explained, Briefly, Clearly, and as Humanely as Possible* (1628–1656), to discussing the sin of abortion, especially in light of the recent papal bulls of Sixtus V and Gregory XIV.[112] Diana analyzed thirty-four specific questions, arguing alongside or against a number of authoritative theologians. He began with definitions and with summaries of the two bulls, but the majority of his discussion pertained to "delicate difficulties" that arise in practice as individuals struggle with decision making. From the start, Diana thought it important to be as clear as possible regarding the meaning of the word "procuring," for almost everything pertaining to the morality of abortion rested on this word. Procuring abortion means "to plan diligently, either on one's own or through an intermediary, to prematurely remove a fetus from the womb of its mother." The procurer "is the one who intentionally acts such that the fetus is driven out of the womb."[113] Several of Diana's thirty-four subchapters on abortion wrestled with how to determine whether, how, by whom, and why abortion was procured. At stake were issues of intentionality, context, and circumstance, which together determined the meaning of abortion. Here I will focus on three complicated and rich discussions to illustrate aspects of Diana's thinking on the matter.

One of the most fascinating questions Diana wrestled with was "whether [individuals] are excused from judgement if they had an ignorance of the law or of the deed, even if this ignorance is negligent, self-inflicted and cultivated." These were very specific yet difficult-to-define terms: "negligent" seems to mean careless and without thought; "self-inflicted ignorance" could mean an individual knows there is information they do not possess but either cannot or will not acquire it before deciding on a course of action; whereas "cultivated ignorance" implies more actively avoiding the acquisition of knowledge. Diana argued that the answer to this question was yes: an individual who had an abortion in ignorance and one who did so intentionally but in ignorance of the law, whether that ignorance was genuine, negligent, self-inflicted, or cultivated, should not be punished according to the papal laws. Why would this be the case? Here Diana seems to be engaging with the inherent uncertainties and ambiguities surrounding the practice of abortion and women's bodies. Although he did not address the medical aspects at play, he knew abortions could happen unintentionally but as a consequence of intervention and that intentionality was therefore difficult to parse, both for the woman who had the abortion and for those judging her. When it was ambiguous, Diana thought punishment should not be inflicted. To justify this opinion, he argued that Sixtus himself specifically used the word "knowingly" before decreeing penalties for procurers. "Knowingly" was a heavy and all-important word,

meaning "when knowledge is [or has been] sought." "Knowingly" elimi-
nated any ambiguity and clearly indicated the agent knew what they
were doing and expected certain effects, knew what the law had to say
and what the consequences of their actions might be. When there was
doubt, when an individual was uncertain, when they did not know for
sure that they were pregnant, or when they did not know or fully understand the law, even if abortion resulted, the individual ought not to be
punished according to the papal bulls. This pertained both to the individual who had the abortion and anyone who helped, offered materials,
or participated in any way that contributed to an abortion: if this was
done in ignorance of the law or the deed, he or she should be exempt
from censure. Diana was not alone in this flexible opinion: he cited his
eminent contemporaries Martino Bonacina and Oliviero Mazzucchelli,
who agreed that "ignorance, even cultivated ignorance, excuses one
from incurring this judgement provided that extreme heedlessness is
not present." "Heedlessness" seems to mean that an individual pos-
sesses a strong suspicion they are committing a wrong and that it is
prohibited by specific laws but feigns ignorance: this is close to committing fraud. All three theologians agreed that as long as there was ignorance, the agent was not open to the harsh papal censors, "for the high
pontiff added this adverb, knowingly, which excludes ignorance of any
sort, unless it is conjoined to extreme heedlessness."[114] When abortion
was had in ignorance, it was not deemed procured.

Perhaps most importantly, Diana acknowledged the importance of
taking power and gender dynamics into account when trying to determine intentionality and responsibility, weaving this thread through
several questions. For instance, he asked "Whether a mother who procures an abortion incurs the excommunication ordered by Sixtus V."
He noted Sixtus only explicitly mentioned women as willing and intentional agents twice in his bull. Diana, citing several other authorities,
interpreted this as implying abortions were often forced on women or
that women were coerced into procuring abortions. Diana agreed that
women who desire abortions, who knowingly and intentionally procure
them of their own free will or as "partners"—that is, in collaboration
with their impregnators or another agent who wants them to abort—are
subject to all censures. But he also felt it important to note that "a
woman should be excused if she is forced to take a drug that causes

abortion as a result of fear caused by a man pressuring her. And the reason is that whenever a woman takes a potion that causes abortion because she is pressured, . . . she should not be said to have procured an abortion."[115] Diana continued this line of reasoning as he discussed "whether it is licit to suggest an abortion when a pregnant woman is prepared to kill herself to avoid infamy."[116] He cited theologians who argued it was immoral to counsel a lesser evil to avoid a greater one, but he rejected this. Here, too, Diana was in agreement with Mazzuchelli, whom he quoted: "Whenever a father has decided in his heart and is determined to kill his daughter, whom he had found pregnant due to illicit intercourse, or whenever the daughter herself is prepared to kill her own self to avoid infamy, and she is unable to be deterred from this intention by any means—in such a case, it would be permissible to offer counsel and serve as a guide towards procuring an abortion, because this would not be to serve as a guide towards an evil act, but towards the choice of a lesser evil, which is a good choice." Diana realized this was a controversial statement—he was essentially arguing that, in some circumstances, grave ones to be sure, an individual, perhaps a confessor, could advise and help a woman to have an abortion in order to prevent an even worse sin of suicide or murder. Diana thought this "the more reasonable thing to do," citing the influential Cardinal Juan de Lugo. De Lugo argued that such advice is never absolute but explicitly or implicitly conditional on the circumstances at hand. If one cannot deter an individual from a more serious sin or prevent a more serious sin from occurring, it is indeed "rational advice" to suggest they commit a lesser sin to prevent the greater one: "If you are going to do one of these things, do this lesser, and not that greater one."[117] What is especially interesting in this question is that Diana initially sets it up as a binary between abortion or suicide but also introduces, though without discussion, filicide—a dishonored father threatening to murder his pregnant daughter. Diana would likely have known this was a real threat. Women who found themselves pregnant outside of marriage feared their fathers, brothers, or other kin who claimed responsibility for them might feel dishonored enough to contemplate murder.[118] In this case, the pregnant woman and her adviser / confidant / facilitator were both procurers. It is interesting to note that Diana did not discuss what role or guilt, if any, belonged to the paternal figure influencing, perhaps unknowingly, the decision to procure an abortion. In both these questions, Diana acknowledged external pressures and dangers shaping a woman's decision to terminate pregnancy and motivating others to help her. In so doing he brought real power dynamics to bear on the question of intentionality and responsibility.

Diana advanced the debate over the morality of abortion by analyzing it both as an abstraction and as a situated and contextualized practice motivated by specific circumstances. Through this approach, he challenged the pretense of applying abstract and universal moral principles to complicated situations. For taking this approach and arriving at conclusions that sometimes justified and excused "sinful" actions, Diana was, in the second half of the seventeenth century, labeled morally "lax," and his theology dangerous, by rigorist theologians. Indeed, Diana was one of the main "malefactors" Blaise Pascal berated in his influential *Provincial Letters,* which satirized and ridiculed casuist and specifically Jesuit theologians. Echoing the concerns of mid-sixteenth-century reformers, more rigorist theologians, and especially the Jansenists of France, Pascal feared that case-based moral reasoning, like Diana's, could lead to moral skepticism or encourage laxity and an even greater tolerance of sin. Influenced by theologians like Diana, confessors might communicate their opinions to the laity, resulting in individuals reconciling themselves to practices rigorists deemed sinful as a matter of principle.[119]

Leaving the laxist-rigorist moral theological debates aside, what is of interest is the relationship between Diana's learned academic discussions and actual practices. Undoubtedly Diana's opinions were shaped by the realities of seventeenth-century life—he was, after all, a human being living and interacting with other human beings in the streets, ecclesiastical offices, and churches of Palermo and Rome. He was a high-ranking cleric, but he knew the pressures, vulnerabilities, traumas, and clashing imperatives that influenced individuals to procure abortions and moved others to help them. Consequently, it would be short-sighted to assume his discussion was purely academic. While most priests may not have read Diana's large Latin tomes, many did; some were persuaded by them, others may have rejected them. Diana was an influential and respected theologian with an important ecclesiastical career: he served on the pope's committee to examine bishops before their appointments and as a consultant for the Sicilian and Roman Inquisitions, two roles that brought him face-to-face with clerics who were directly responsible for the care, instruction, discipline, and rehabilitation of souls, both lay and clerical. While it is unclear how and to what extent his discussions of abortion influenced the thought and practices of bishops, confessors, and judges in ecclesiastical tribunals, my assumption is that they did. At the very least, what they demonstrate is that a high-ranking cleric and influential moral theologian took the context and circumstance within which individuals procured and participated in abortions into consideration as he tried to determine its spiritual consequences. In this respect, Diana's thoughts reflect and help us understand the tendencies and approaches of ecclesiastical authorities dealing with such cases.

The More Things Change

In the years following Sixtus's and Gregory's papal bulls on abortion, bishops, confessors, and ecclesiastical tribunals continued to wrestle with how to regulate the practice and make sense of those papal interventions. Bishops continued to view abortion as a threat to the spiritual life of their dioceses and continued to reserve it to their office to impress its gravity upon laity and clergy. In his 1591 synod, the bishop of Lodi, Ludovico Taverna, reserved abortion to his office.[120] Not two years earlier, Taverna had faced an awkward situation in seeking permission from Sixtus to absolve procurers of abortion locally. Taverna included abortion on his list of cases but also appended Gregory's entire bull moderating Sixtus's to his synodal decretals, so all the priests of Lodi would see that Church legislation on this matter had changed and Taverna now had the authority to reserve this sin to his office.[121] Similarly, the bishop of Nola Frabrizio Gallo removed the marginal note alerting confessors to Sixtus's bull from his published list of reserved cases.[122] Many bishops followed suit, including Gabriele Paleotti in Bologna, Giulio Cesare Riccardi in Bari, Giovanni Fontana in Ferrara, Napoleone Comitoli in Perugia, Claudio Rangoni in Piacenza, Pietro Aldobrandini in Ravenna, Domenico Bollani in Brescia, Erminio Valenti in Faenza, Lorenzo Castrucci in Spoleto, Marcantonio Corner in Padua, Marcantonio Bragadin in Vincenza, and likely many others. Some re-

served abortion unequivocally; others, only the abortion of animate fetuses.[123] While many bishops returned it to their reserved list, it is probable that confessors absolved those who admitted to procuring
abortion, perhaps with their superiors' permission, most likely during
Lent, and with secret penance to avoid scandal. Young and unmarried
women were likely given absolution with ease in order to avoid exposure. Even if bishops resisted such accommodations, by 1593 their
hands were once again officially tied. Pope Clement VIII issued a papal
bull stating superiors of religious orders could offer absolution from
certain sins, including abortion, that were episcopally reserved. He also
stated that, like bishops, superiors could allow their responsible confessors to hear and offer absolution from these cases in certain circumstances. This decree was reaffirmed in 1624 by Urban VIII, likely due
to ongoing jurisdictional tensions between bishops, superiors, and
regular confessors.[124] Bishops seeking to reform the sexual morality of
their dioceses by restricting absolution ran up against the ever-men-
acing specter of scandal and the long arm of Rome.

The confessor remained the most appropriate and best placed me-
diator, and the confessional the best forum from which to regulate sin
and change lay thinking on abortion. So vernacular works on sin and
confession rolled from the presses at even greater speed than they had
in the sixteenth century. Like their predecessors, most seventeenth-
century authors eschewed speculative discussions and analysis of contentious issues for simple, authoritative positions to convince their
reader to internalize the belief that abortion was mortal sin. As such,
authors like Luca Pinelli, Girolamo Sertorelli, Augostino Gotutio, and
Bartolomeo da Salutio ignored the recent papal legislations and presented their discussions of abortion in much the same ways as their
late-sixteenth-century predecessors.[125] Authors with a clerical as well
as lay audience in mind thought it prudent to mention the papal
interventions.[126]

In the seventeenth century, confessors may have asked their penitents more questions and moralized more about the sin of abortion,
explaining what it meant and why it was a grave sin. If the confessor
found the penitent unremorseful or beyond pity, if the context and circumstances prompting the sin were unconvincing, if the confessor was
a rigorist, absolution might be denied. However, depending on the

circumstances, many confessors would have offered absolution with the satisfaction of penance. This is what most penitents expected. In 1613 Sezze, Superio de Magistris tried to convince the apothecary Tomeo Ciolli to give him medicines to cause an abortion. Tomeo resisted, saying "that he could not because this was a sin," to which Superio responded "that [Tomeo could] confess it, because it was for a woman from a good family, and it would remedy the scandals that could come to light, [Tomeo could tell the confessor] that he did it out of mercy."[127] Superio's words were clearly self-serving—he sought an abortion to conceal his sin and crime of raping and impregnating his niece—but that does not mean he was not reflecting a pervasive belief that such a confession would result in absolution. What mattered here was the framing, context, and circumstance of the sin the apothecary was asked to commit. The expectation was that the confessor would understand the motivation and moral reasoning that guided such decisions.

Ecclesiastical tribunals also continued to be important sites for shaping and disseminating religious discourse on abortion, although perhaps not exactly in the ways the reforming Church intended. Recall that Sixtus wanted his bull to be greatly felt by misbehaving clerics. Priests continued to be investigated for a variety of excesses, including sexual practices and abortion. More local and comparative research on ecclesiastical tribunals is needed to know whether they pursued clerics for these offenses more vigorously after the papal bulls on abortion than before; however, the current research suggests similar levels of interest, engagement, and approaches to discipline. Cases continued to come to tribunals when individuals or communities denounced troublesome priests. Generally, this only happened when someone felt personally wronged by a cleric and demanded compensation or another form of justice or when a cleric greatly scandalized his community and they wanted him out. Cases investigated by different tribunals over a period of four decades after Sixtus V's bull suggest ecclesiastical authorities continued to wrestle with how to investigate cases of abortion and discipline troublesome clerics.

In 1590, the Sicilian Inquisition investigated Dario Ferraro, a thirty-four-year-old priest, for sexual activities with multiple unnamed women as he served the community of Petralia (approximately one hundred kilometers southeast of Palermo). When questioned, "these girls" admitted to a sexual relationship with the priest and "said that he would give them remedies in order not to get pregnant." The remedies consisted of soft snake skin and saffron leaves to be eaten in the mornings and having the women wash their bellies with vinegar. "One [of the women] heard [Dario] saying that if the unborn child was not animated, having an abortion was not considered sin and that it was not sin as she was his spiritual daughter." Dario's punishment for these heresies—it was heresy to claim that what the Catholic Church considered a sin was not a sin—was that he could no longer hold mass or administer sacraments for ten years; banishment from Petralia for ten years; and three years of penitential labor at a hospital or charitable institution.[128] Dario would certainly have felt these penalties to be significant—it was not easy to be exiled for a decade from one's home and lose one's livelihood—but they are remarkably lenient considering that, in 1590, Sixtus V's bull was still officially law and, according to that law, Dario should have been defrocked and handed over to secular authorities to be tried for homicide. Evidently, the Sicilian Inquisition—a Spanish institution but one that still fell within the Italian clerical universe—did not follow Sixtus's law.[129]

Many such examples reveal that ecclesiastical tribunals often protected priests, men who represented and were supposed to be embodiments of their institution, at the expense of those they harmed. Judges often trusted their own more than the women and their familiars who made accusations against them. It was a truism that women sought to entrap priests in sexual relationships or commit fraud by denouncing a fictional sexual relationship, usually rape, in order to profit from an innocent priest. It was also assumed and believed that parents colluded with or coerced their daughters to these ends. Even if the priest had a bad reputation and was not to be trusted, ecclesiastical tribunals sought to resolve cases against them as expediently as possible to minimize scandal. These cultural tropes were both self-interested and genuine. They are particularly evident in the attitudes and methods of two judges of the tribunal of the archbishop of Naples, who investigated two cases of clerical sexual transgression, ensuing pregnancy, and abortion tried in the 1620s.

The first case involved Antonio d'Avosso, an eighteen-year-old cleric who was investigated in 1625 for deflowering sixteen-year-old Portia de

Pastena, a relative who worked as a servant in his mother's house, one year earlier while he was a seminarian. According to Portia and her father, who made the denunciation, Antonio seduced her with the promise of marriage, which of course could never happen if he became a priest. When it was discovered Portia was pregnant, Antonio procured beverages to induce abortion, but Portia (reportedly) refused them. Her father brought the case to the archbishop's tribunal to redress the dishonor this would-be priest had brought on his daughter and his house. Along with honor, Portia's father wanted a dowry for her to wed. Antonio denied the charges and produced a letter from his seminary stating he was in residence at the time of the alleged affair. As part of their investigation, the court had Portia physically examined by two midwives, who confirmed she was pregnant. The judge then inquired into her sexual reputation, asking neighbors whether she worked in homes other than Antonio's mother. The aim, it seems, was to discredit Portia and discover another man who might be responsible for her defloration and pregnancy, but none was found. In the end, the court sided with eighteen-year-old Antonio, who had just embarked on an ecclesiastical career.[130] Evidently, his sins, if he did in fact commit them, did not impede him from the priesthood. Portia's body and that which grew inside it appear to have only mildly threatened this future priest and the ecclesiastical establishment.

In 1627, the Naples tribunal was again investigating a case of clerical sexual transgression and attempted abortion. This time, twenty-seven-year-old Mattia de Fusco, a priest at the Annunziata Basilica of Naples, was denounced by Giulio della Starita for violently deflowering and impregnating his thirty-year-old daughter, Martia, and trying to get her to have an abortion.[131] Martia testified that about one year earlier, Mattia, on a few occasions, ambushed her inside the main entrance of her apartment building, forced her to lie down on the stairs, and violently raped her. When it was discovered she was pregnant, Mattia gave her a "white powder," which she consumed, but it did not cause an abortion. Martia carried the child to term, apparently in secrecy, and gave birth to a boy, who was deposited by the midwife in the Annunziata orphanage attached to the basilica where the priest served. Mattia visited Martia after the delivery and apparently gave her money for her ordeal, explaining it was all he could do.[132] The judge questioned Martia's witnesses, who corroborated her pregnancy and delivery. Her close familiars said definitively that Mattia impregnated her; others said they only knew what she told them and could neither confirm nor deny the allegation.

Mattia was arrested and detained in the archbishop's palace jail. The priest denied all charges. He said he knew Martia because he saw her when he visited his brother, who lived in the same apartment building, but claimed he had never actually spoken with her and certainly had never touched her. Mattia gave the judge a list of individuals whom he hoped would provide exonerating testimony. All were men, including several clerics. His witnesses described Mattia as a good man from a good family, "an honest and modest man, a respected, God- and justice-fearing-man," who celebrated mass at the Annunziata with devotion and edification and to whom everyone listened. They reported Mattia visited other homes where young and beautiful women lived, and no one ever complained that he did or said anything untoward—one witness was emphatic that "he was always, always serious and presented himself with much honor, modesty and respect" when he was around young women. His witnesses said Martia della Starita was old and ugly. This "evidence" apparently mattered to the men testifying and to the judge, who later asked other witnesses to evaluate Martia's attractiveness—their evaluation of her looks apparently meant she was undesirable and therefore could not have been raped.[133] Mattia's witnesses also indicated the apartment building was busy, containing three units including an accountant's office, and it was highly unlikely the two could have an undetected sexual encounter in the narrow stairwell by the main door.

As was standard in cases of sexual assault, this became a "she-said-he-said" match. It is unclear what the judge thought or how he was going to resolve the suit because, in the end, he did not have to: Martia's father returned to the archbishop's court and withdrew the charges against Mattia. "I have come here to relieve my conscience [regarding] the complaint I made against don Mattia de Fusso under the pretense that he raped my daughter. I made this complaint on account of my daughter, who told me that said don Mattia raped her. [She confessed] that it was not [Mattia] but my son-in-law, Giovanni Bernardino Castellano, who at present is dead and was killed a year ago. For this reason, I have come to exculpate don Mattia."[134] Did the judge buy it? Should we? Had Martia really tried to pin her illegitimate pregnancy on an innocent priest to conceal an affair with or rape by her brother-in-law? Had someone, perhaps her own father, put this plan in place to extort Mattia? The (conveniently) dead son-in-law on whom the rape and pregnancy were now blamed could not remedy the situation, but priest Mattia might offer money to protect his honor and clerical position. The della Starita family clearly had something to gain by accusing the priest and, whether or not he was guilty, Mattia had much to lose. Perhaps here we see the sexual fraud trope deployed by a woman, with or without the collusion of her family, against an innocent priest in action. Had it not been for Giulio's last-minute rush to do the right thing and clean his conscience, Mattia de Fusso might have faced serious and shaming punishment for defloration, rape and attempted abortion. But this eleventh-hour confession feels too convenient. Perhaps Mattia was guilty of everything that was claimed and decided it was better to make extrajudicial arrangements with the "damaged" woman's father. Perhaps the judge himself brokered the deal to make the case go away. The judge asked Giulio whether he was paid or influenced by anyone to drop the suit, to which Giulio said no. The trial ended there. We cannot know what really happened to Martia, who her illegitimate child's father was, or what the priest Mattia did or did not do. What we do know, however, is that allegations of sexual assault made against priests were difficult to investigate, let alone prove.

We can assume most cases of clerics procuring or assisting in abortions to conceal their sins never made it to court, either because no one cared to report them or because extrajudicial solutions to problematic relationships were preferred. That does not necessarily imply that a priest did not worry about how his sins affected his soul and his clerical status. Priests feeling the weight of the sin of abortion or men who had participated in abortion in the past and now pursued the priesthood continued to supplicate the Sacred Apostolic Penitentiary in Rome for absolution and dispensation. Two mid-seventeenth-century works composed by consultants for the penitentiary suggest that its handling of cases of clerics or prospective clerics involved in abortions had not changed following Sixtus's and Gregory's bulls. The Jesuit Valentino Mangiono, who served the penitentiary as theologian and consultor from 1634 to 1660, discussed abortion in relation to irregularity and impediment in an unpublished formulary he composed for internal use, titled *Simple Method of Supplicating the Penitentiary.* Mangiono listed all the information the penitentiary needed to adjudicate a case and offer absolution or dispensation: The supplicant must specify whether he was responsible for the pregnancy and how he contributed to the abortion—that is, whether he offered or provided medicines or money to buy them or whether he assaulted the pregnant woman with punches and kicks to her womb. He had to specify whether the fetus was en-souled and if it was born alive or dead and, if alive, how it died and whether it was baptized beforehand.[135] The archive of the Apostolic Penitentiary abounds with tens of thousands of supplications, making it a Herculean task, one I was unable to accomplish, to sift through them all to find cases of priests petitioning for absolution and dispensation from the irregularity incurred by participating in an abortion. Nevertheless, it is safe to assume priests did submit such supplications and that they followed Mangiono's instructions. His colleague and fellow Jesuit Marco Paolo Leone offered for analysis a supplication he adjudicated in his published treatise, *Practice of the Major Penitentiary and the office of the Sacred Apostolic Penitentiary* (1644).[136]

Leone's unnamed supplicant was a priest who confessed to a sexual relationship with a woman for whom he arranged or perhaps forced an abortion upon after it was discovered she was pregnant. No information regarding the nature of the sexual relationship was provided. The priest specified the fetus was animated, although he did not say how he knew that or whether he saw the aborted fetus. After the abortion, he continued with his duties and pastoral care. The priest knew that for the sins of procuring the abortion of an animate fetus and not respecting the irregularity he incurred ipso facto, he should receive ecclesiastical censure and penalties. However, the supplicant explained that he "greatly grieves for the above acts, which were carried out in secret." He was compelled to continue his ecclesiastical duties and administer sacraments to avoid the scandal that would have arisen had he conspicuously stopped. He implored the Apostolic See via the penitentiary for absolution from his sins "for the sake of his peace of mind." He was also asking for something tangible: a letter of dispensation to present to his superior, or anyone else needing to see it, stating he had been cleared of any wrongdoing and could continue his ecclesiastical work and keep his benefice.[137]

After summarizing the supplication, Leone offered his opinion to the head of the Apostolic Penitentiary, Cardinal Antonio Barberini. Once again, the central and determinative issues were the developmental stage of the fetus and the circumstances and nature of the scandal that motivated the priest's actions and kept him celebrating mass and administering the sacraments. On a broader level, however, Leone wrestled with how universal principles might come to bear on a specific situation. Leone summarized Sixtus V's bull and explained Gregory XIV's modification, stating that only the abortion of an animate fetus rendered a priest irregular. Ignoring the embryological controversies being debated by philosophers and theologians, Leone held the traditional canonical position of forty and eighty days for the animation of male and female fetuses respectively to be the common opinion, but he acknowledged the fundamental uncertainty of it all. Leone stated that in cases where it was unknown whether the fetus was male or female, animate or not, it was necessary—this being a spiritual matter—to choose the safest and more conservative solution and consider the fetus animate. However, he specified this ought to be understood as applying in the forum of the conscience, that is, in the confessional and for the purposes of assigning penance. In cases tried in court, "the opposite principle should hold sway. . . . When there is a disagreement concerning the penalty that has to be applied in an ambiguous situation, the gentler option should be chosen."[138] Regarding scandal, Leone stated the level of threat had to be high and genuine for it to justify the priest's actions but conceded that this could not be assessed "through mathematical reasoning but rather through plausible conjectures." He thought that, in all likelihood, the priest could not refrain from carrying out his duties for a long time without scandal arising—"a serious loss of honor and reputation"—thus revealing his crime. So Leone concluded that because the case remained secret and was not being investigated by a court, the priest should keep his benefice and required only "rehabilitation." Following a full confession, the priest should be absolved from his sins and penalties and must undergo grave and perpetual penance, both personal (fasting, praying, charitable labors) and financial (almsgiving and donations) depending on his wealth. Leone advised that the head of the Apostolic Penitentiary should "deal mercifully with him" and issue the letter of absolution and dispensation.[139] The fear of scandal, dishonor, and social disorder that exposure would bring such a priest, the woman he convinced or forced to have an abortion, their families, their community, and, no doubt, the Church he represented meant that priests would not be punished for procuring or forcing abortions, even of animate fetuses, on the women they impregnated.

One wonders how the woman who had (or was forced to have) the abortion felt about Leone's decision to absolve this priest and offer him dispensation. She, the unnamed women from Petralia, Portia and Martia from Naples, and no doubt many others may have wanted to punish the priests who (reportedly) coerced them into sexual relationships, raped them, impregnated them, and gave them products or forced them to have abortions. How did these women, their familiars, and the broader communities interpret the decisions of these ecclesiastical tribunals? What implications did this have for understandings of abortion?

The lenience priests who procured abortions received might lead twenty-first-century observers to assume that early modern individuals understood the courts to be biased, unfair, and hypocritical: "the Church says one thing and does another"; "priests chastise the laity for their sins but then they do the same and even worse"; "priests protect other priests." Such reactions are, naturally, influenced by recent events and public discourse surrounding clerical sexual abuse, especially pertaining to children and adolescents. And how could it be otherwise? While such comparisons run the risk of anachronism and universalizing an ever-changing Catholic Church and its diverse personnel, it is nonetheless likely that early modern observers harbored feelings of resentment when authorities forgave and protected priests at the expense of individuals they wronged. Despite efforts to quash it, anticlericalism and negative attitudes toward the institutional Church remained a significant phenomenon in seventeenth-century Italy, much of it rooted in resentment over clerical abuses, privilege, and immunity.[140] Catholic reformers feared the failure of priests to live up to the Church's standards compromised its moral authority, undermined its legitimacy, and reduced the laity's faith and trust in the institution. Clerical transgression and its toleration by ecclesiastical tribunals might lead laywomen and men to be skeptical of doctrine and Church discourse on sin and salvation: it set "bad examples" that might encourage the laity and give them license to sin and even reject doctrine that defined certain practices as sinful. In fact, laywomen and men often used the language and concept of clerical exemplarity when they denounced troublesome priests to their superiors. Did the examples of priests procuring and forcing abortions on women and the lenience with which ecclesiastical tribunals dealt with them foster a belief among the laity that abortion was not as grave a sin as Sixtus V, Scipione Mercurio and other clerics depicted in their scathing condemnations?

Perhaps, but we should not go too far with this line of speculation, not only because more research is needed on early modern Italian anticlericalism and the sources and nature of popular morality but also because we might be anachronistically applying twenty-first-century Western notions of corruption, hypocrisy, moral authority, and justice onto sixteenth- and seventeenth-century actors. In the case of abortion, I suspect many early modern Italians expected ecclesiastical tribunals to be lenient, just as they expected and accepted that priests would behave in morally questionable ways. The laity understood that prescriptions could and often would be flexed, and penalties mitigated when scandal loomed and complicated social and political circumstances were at play. This was especially true for clerics, who were a privileged class, but it was also true for the laity. As we will see in the next chapter, secular criminal tribunals that tried laywomen and men for abortions rarely meted out the penalties prescribed in codes of law. There was an accepted difference between doctrine on sinful practices and the meaning of acts committed in the tangle of clashing imperatives and desperate circumstances. Similarly, there was an accepted difference between prescribed penalties and expedient distributive justice that focused on outcomes and was usually described as "merciful." Confessors, moral theologians, and ecclesiastical and secular judges knew this, as did regular people. At the same time, clerical self-interest, which was part of a much broader and entrenched system of patriarchy, was real and had the effect of condoning sexual transgressions and tolerating (if not explicitly permitting) abortions to conceal them. Consequently, the practices of ecclesiastical tribunals also had the effect of silencing victims of sexual assault and, no doubt, in many instances completely erasing them from the historical record.

Conclusion

Throughout the second half of the sixteenth and into the seventeenth century, the Catholic Church came to identify the practice of abortion as a particularly grave sin, one perceived to be common and tolerated. Moralists depicted abortion as "ungodly," a violation of the divine plan and law, an affront to its creator, "inhuman," and going against an assumed universal human nature by depriving an imagined future human being of earthly life and heavenly salvation. Reformers proposed direct and sustained education alongside the threat of increasingly harsh punishment to get laity and clergy to internalize the spiritual meaning of abortion and eradicate its practice. However, beneath doctrinal formulations lay debate and ambiguity; beneath decrees and legislation, complex human dramas and institutional politics.

While most ecclesiastical authorities and theologians may have agreed that the intentional termination of pregnancy was a sin, the nature of the sin, its gravity, and how it ought to be handled were matters of contention. For most, the spiritual value of the fetus determined the gravity of the sin and was the primary reason for its regulation. Throughout the early modern period, the official Church position was the centuries-old theological-canonical consensus that procured abortion was a mortal sin but that only the abortion of an animated fetus was a form of homicide. Delayed animation allowed for flexibility: the earlier in pregnancy the abortion occurred, the less sinful; the later, the more sinful. In the second half of the sixteenth century, this flexibility was, for some, increasingly seen as a morally problematic loophole allowing individuals to procure abortions and authorities to tolerate them. Confessors were urged to teach their penitents about the spiritual consequences of abortion and were supplied with new educational materials to that end. Bishops seeking to reform the sexual morality of their dioceses attempted to impress the gravity of abortion on laity and clergy by reserving absolution to their office. However, Sixtus V officially and dramatically changed Catholic doctrine and policy on abortion with the controversial 1588 papal bull *Against those who Procure,*

Counsel and Consent in any way to Abortion. Though it was overturned two and a half years after its issuance, Sixtus's decree that all abortion was homicide, that anyone who procured or participated in abortion was a murderer and were to be tried as such, that they were automatically ex-communicate, and that absolution was exclusively reserved to the pope was unprecedented and marks a critical moment in Catholic thinking on abortion. As doctrine and law, the bull was short-lived, but as a papal statement it had deep and far-reaching impact. Its central tenets were discussed throughout the early modern period and shape religious dis-course on abortion to the present day.[141] Sixtus's bull and its reception also illuminate the political and jurisdictional issues at stake in chang-ing Catholic doctrine and policy on abortion. The bull was challenged and moderated due to its doctrinal innovations and disciplinary sever-ity, which most clerics were not ready to accept, but also, and perhaps mostly, for its jurisdictional incursions into matters and privileges tra-ditionally belonging to bishops. While Gregory XIV's bull was closer to what most ecclesiastical authorities thought and deemed acceptable, it is clear that the matter was far from settled, at least in the theological arena. The "paradigm of animation" was increasingly challenged and it would finally give way, in the nineteenth century, to the opinion that the fetus is infused with a soul at the moment of conception. Conse-quently, the Catholic Church would decree that all abortions are un-equivocally homicide. The roots of current Catholic thinking on abor-tion therefore can be directly traced to late sixteenth-century debates. However, these debates must be understood in their own contexts.

While early modern ecclesiastical authorities genuinely perceived abortion to be a wrong requiring regulation, it is also clear they saw it as a complicated matter, tied to broader social issues precluding simple solutions. Theologians, bishops, and popes knew women chose or were forced to have abortions to terminate pregnancies that were socially and physically threatening. They also knew that increasingly severe penalties exacerbated risks to personal and familial reputation, social order, and even individuals' lives. Harsh penalties bred resentment. Catholic religious discourse on abortion was shaped and contextually bound by the realities of early modern life; the struggles, injustices, and clashing imperatives that shaped decision making; and, ultimately, moral experience. As such, while officially moving in a more rigid direction, ecclesiastical authorities generally took into account the circumstances and moral weighing that persuaded an individual to have or participate in an abortion. Even Scipione Mercurio would have been hard pressed to defend his statement that women selfishly have abortions "to conceal . . . unbridled lust." Rather, clerics knew the stresses motivating individuals to terminate pregnancies in specific circumstances. In confession and ecclesiastical courts, they heard about pregnancies generated through violent rape, concubinage, seduction, adultery, and incest. Crucially, they knew men often forced abortions on women they impregnated and that clerics were often the malefactors. Reforming bishops, even the hard-liner Sixtus V, agreed that in practice such cases were better handled secretly and expediently in the confessional rather than in a tribunal. The instinct to suppress scandal lay deep in the consciousness and was part of the connective tissue of the Church and Italian society in general. Clearly, clerical and male self-interest was at play, but an awareness of the devastating consequences that non-marital sex, pregnancy, and abortion could have for some women and their families also factored in. Curiously, clerics were mostly silent on, and apparently disinterested in, the practice of abortion in the context of marriage. Perhaps this was something only broached in the privacy of the confessional.

All these debates and practices also reveal that Catholic discourse on abortion was dynamically shaped by both clergy and laity. Neither was willing to accept that abortion was unequivocally a mortal sin that damned their souls. Rather, most likely understood its morality to be contextual. "Sinners," like the unnamed woman from Lodi, negotiated with their confessors, resisted the involvement of their bishops, and challenged or ignored the decrees of their pope. Many were accommodated. The harsh penalties that, in theory, were to be imposed on those who procured abortion were meant to deter women, men, and clerics from its practice by emphasizing the gravity of the sin. For many, however, the Church's official teaching on abortion might have been irrelevant compared to the urgent situations they faced. At the same time, it was likely clear to all that these penalties were difficult to enforce, and it is questionable whether they were intended to be.[142] The Counter-Reformation Church, as historians have increasingly argued, put more effort into meaning making and discipline by threat and indoctrination than into implementing harsh punishment, although sometimes it did that too.[143] This appears to have been the case with abortion. Official Catholic ideology on abortion was moving in a more conservative direction and was increasingly and relentlessly being inculcated into Italians' world views, so much so that we might, with caution, say it would eventually become hegemonic. But this was not a given in the sixteenth and seventeenth centuries. Early modern Italian conceptions of abortion were under constant negotiation, both from above and below.

Femia and Antino

IN 1590, Femia de Andreozza of Trevignano became a widow, though it took some time to learn the news. Her husband had been laboring at a farm near Rome, a ten-hour journey from Trevignano on foot, when he was murdered at a tavern under unknown circumstances. Femia was young, just eighteen, and it does not appear that before her husband's death they had spent much time together. Nonetheless, she had been dependent on him and on his earnings. So was Femia's mother, Andreozza, who had been widowed herself years before. Femia's sister would herself be widowed two years hence. Marrying was a survival strategy for Trevignano women, but it was also often a losing strategy.

Trevignano was a small town on the banks of Lake Bracciano about forty-five kilometers north of Rome, in the Diocese of Sutri and Nepi. In a town like this everyone knew each other, but the Battaglioni women not only lacked husbands; they also lacked kin and were left to fend for themselves. "I cannot find anyone to marry my daughters because I am a poor woman," Andreozza lamented.[1] These were not easy times for anyone. A decade-long famine was devastating most of southern Europe, and the people of Trevignano all felt the pinch.[2] To survive, the Battaglioni women cobbled together a living from agricultural work.

Soon, though, another man came into their lives. Antino de Benedictis was the sacristan of the parish church, the Cathedral of Santa Maria di Trevignano, and the beneficiary of three income-earning benefices. He hired the Battaglioni to keep house for him. This was a common arrangement priests and other single men made with women, often older widows or female relatives. But there was a catch: many townspeople had reason to hate Antino, who had a reputation as a nasty, thieving, and scandalous cleric. The urgency of the moment, however, outweighed the risks of becoming his intimates. The Battaglioni women were desperate.

We know far more about Antino than we do about Femia and her mother and sister. Antino had been born in Vicarello, just outside of Trevignano. His parents likely died or abandoned him when he was quite young, and he was raised by a priest who set him on course for an ecclesiastical career.[3] There is no record of Antino's clerical trajectory except that he was installed as the sacristan of Santa Maria di Trevignano around 1584 and had obtained three benefices. Antino was a priest with minor orders: he had received the first tonsure and thus had clerical privileges, but he was not charged with the care of souls, and he could not administer sacraments, although sacristan was often a first step toward higher office. He lived in an apartment attached to the cathedral and was responsible for the sacristy, its sacred objects, and the church more generally. Antino was to ensure that the church was dignified, that its services ran properly, and that the priest and parishioners had everything they needed to perform and engage in the sacred rituals. This made him a key figure in the religious life of the town. "It is manifest that this is an office of great dignity," the fathers of the Congregation of Christian Doctrine in Rome proclaimed, and "therefore, [one] must elect to this office a very circumspect, devout and exemplary person."[4]

But Antino was anything but an exemplary cleric. Townspeople reported that he stole from them and that he even physically fought with them. To most he was "the sacristan" or "*prete* Antino," but they also had other words for Antino. Court witnesses later testified that he was an "evil person," "committing many wickedness," "always turning Trevignano upside down," "barking at and insulting everyone without showing anyone respect."[5] "It does not appear to me that he ever held a priest's life," said one man.[6] The archpriest of Santa Maria di Trevignano, Giacomo Filici, who worked with Antino and was his superior, explained that the three churches from which Antino drew beneficiary income were once venerated and well attended but that Antino had run them into the ground; congregants had abandoned them.[7] He allegedly sold a consecrated bell from one of the churches, the Madonna dell'Immagine, and pocketed the proceeds.[8] He was said to have stolen between ten and twenty-five bottles of oil from the Confraternity of Discipline, pouring the oil into his own barrel and filling the emptied bottles with water, which he then returned to the confraternity's cellar.[9] He appropriated a whole basket of candles from the Confraternity of the Corpus Christi, perhaps to avoid buying candles for the churches he was responsible for equipping.[10] Antino was also accused of stealing a gold ring that had been given to the Madonna del Rosario by a townswoman as a votive offering in return for a healing miracle; Antino allegedly took the ring off the Madonna's finger and pawned it for a small loan.[11] In retaliation against a perceived insult by Archpriest Filici, Antino twice smeared excrement on the door of Filici's brother. "It couldn't have been anyone else but him," said the brother.[12] "Everyone in this *castello* speaks with one tongue," a congregant said. The sacristan was "a bad example to the whole community."[13] But Antino was never sanctioned or disciplined because he could count on his good friend, the bishop of Sutri's vicar, to protect him. The townspeople objected to the friendship and resented the abuse of ecclesiastical power.

Antino's most-talked-about wrongs were sexual. Beginning around 1588, he was having an affair with Bernardina Paris, a recent widow known by her nickname, Gnogna. She had three children, and Antino was godfather to the youngest. Through the sacrament of baptism, Gnogna and Antino were relatives, so not only was Antino violating his vows of celibacy; he was committing the sin of incest; the sacrament of baptism had made him and Gnogna family. The relationship greatly shamed Gnogna's sons, and her eldest, Agostino, tried to kill Antino after he once caught the two having sex.[14] The people of Trevignano objected to the affair but the relationship ended only when Gnogna died, coincidentally around the same time as Femia de Andreozza's husband.

The deaths of Gnogna and Casciolo intersected and conspired to push Antino and Femia together. Femia knew Antino's reputation and that she was taking a risk in bringing him into her life. She may have felt like she had little choice. Femia and her mother provided domestic services to Antino, who spent more and more time in their little rented house because, according to Femia, "he did not have anyone else."[15]

Within months Femia and Antino's relationship developed into something more complicated when it became sexual.[16] Femia described their first sexual encounters as rape, nonconsensual and violent: "He forced me and I would not have agreed otherwise." But over time the violence subsided. "At first he had me always against my will," Femia said, but eventually "prete Antino enjoyed me peacefully [*pacifica-mente*]." Femia, it seems, surrendered to Antino's sexual demands. She sometimes referred to their relationship as a "friendship [*amicitia*]."[17] Townspeople went further and characterized their relationships as "marriage-like." Christiana Zizzi, a neighbor with a watchful eye, reported that Antino "held her as if she were his wife, governing Femia and her mother, bringing them and sending them wine, bread, meat, fish and staying to eat [with them]; . . . in short, Antino, day and night, came and went to [Femia's] house, as he wanted, and he slept there." Similarly, Catterina Venanti reported that Antino and Femia "ate and stayed happily together, and all the land always said and [continues] to say that prete Antino and Femia enjoyed each other." According to Vittorio Guidi, they "have been enjoying each other for four years now [carrying on] as husband and wife."[18]

In the estimation of many townspeople, Femia and Antino had formed, for a few years, a stable concubinal relationship.[19] They knew that, from the perspective of the post-Tridentine Church, this was a terrible sin. In theory, it was better to tolerate and forgive a cleric visiting prostitutes than one who kept a concubine; the former could be a discreet and occasional way of satisfying urges with "appropriate" women and could be dispensed with in the confessional as a sin of human weakness. Longer-term and public clerical concubinage could be perceived as a tacit and sometimes explicit criticism of the Church's demand of clerical celibacy—in fact, long-term and unrepentant concubinage could have been interpreted as having Protestant sympathies and, therefore, as heresy. In practice, ecclesiastical authorities only intervened when local communities considered relationships problematic enough to denounce them. The people of Trevignano expressed simmering disapproval, labeling Antino sacrilegious and a scoundrel, and Femia a whore, especially after she started spending nights with Antino in his apartment in the clerical residence attached to the cathedral and when she flaunted the several pairs of expensive shoes Antino had made for her, no doubt paid for with church money.[20] But for several years, they did not appeal to their bishop for intervention. They were not too concerned with Antino and Femia's relationship.

Based on the judgments of observers, Femia's term "friendship" seems to have meant something more than just sex and domestic services in exchange for goods. Their relationship started with and was periodically punctuated by violence. It was sustained by economic dependence and mutual assistance, but it may also have been, at times, satisfying for both Antino and Femia. Femia was pragmatic and sought to preserve herself and maneuver as best she could. She likely had to find peace in a situation in which she may have felt she had few choices and feared violence, but one in which she also had opportunities for material gain, security, and perhaps intimacy.

Pregnancy changed things. The townspeople gossiped that Femia had been pregnant on two occasions and Antino had arranged for and forced her to have abortions. Some said he threw the first aborted fetus in Lake Bracciano and buried the second in a neighbor's stable, where wild dogs dug it up and ate it. These abortions were considered the gravest of Antino's sins and crimes and greatly disturbed the community.[21] They also put Femia in considerable danger and made her rethink her relationship with the sacristan. However, their relationship only came to an end after Antino ruined Femia's opportunity to marry.

At some point in early 1594, Femia met a man named Francesco da Urbino, a foreigner in Trevignano doing seasonal labor. A few months later, they were planning to wed. Francesco knew about Femia's relationship with Antino, but it did not deter him because, according to one observer, he loved her.[22] When Femia told Antino about her engagement, he became very angry and caused a scene, mocking and threatening: "Wear the nuptial belt . . . but not even three days will pass that you will not wear it [anymore]." He then went to his friend the vicar of Sutri, Francesco Mezzaroma, and told him Femia's husband, Casciolo, was still alive, and therefore she would be committing bigamy should she marry Francesco. Two or three days later, an edict was posted on the Church of Santa Maria di Trevignano decreeing that one could not marry without proof that they were not already married or that their spouse was dead. It was only through word of mouth that Femia had learned of her husband's death, and everyone knew this was Antino's way of impeding her plans. Neighbor Marina heard Femia yell at Antino: "You are the one who [posted] this edict and is preventing me from taking Francesco [as a husband]. . . . Ah! I wanted to get myself out of sin . . . and you prevented me!" To which Antino replied: "Be quiet, be quiet, be quiet!"[23] Francesco and Femia went to speak with the bishop of Sutri, Orazio Morone, directly, but the bishop said he would not grant a marriage license unless it was proven that Casciolo was dead. In Trevignano, Antino threatened to have anyone who said Casciolo was dead tortured.[24] As time passed and all efforts to procure a marriage license failed, Francesco finally gave up. "Francesco wept a few times with me," Femia said, "complaining that this priest Antino prevented [the marriage] . . . and, in the end, grieving and weeping, he departed from me . . . saying that he was leaving in despair." Femia was unequivocal: "I say that it is clear that prete Antino is the one who has prevented this marriage . . . for no other reason than that he can continue to frequent me as he did before."[25]

But things did not go back to what they were before. The alleged abortions and fallout from the stymied engagement caused further scandal and gave the people of Trevignano the opportunity they may have been waiting for to denounce Antino and demand he be disciplined. Perhaps Femia would now be on their side and testify to all the hardship Antino had put her through. By the end of August 1594, a request was made of the vicar of Sutri, Francesco Mezzaroma, to send a notary and conduct an investigation into "the good and bad reputation and life" of Antino de Benedictis.[26] The vicar eventually obliged, and he and his notary conducted a two-day investigation that was immediately judged a sham. The vicar asked no questions about the alleged abortions and refused to listen to or transcribe what witnesses said about them. Christiana Zizze told the vicar and the notary everything she knew about Antino and Femia's relationship, about the abortions and the sabotaging of the marital plans, "but [the notary] wrote down little of what I said and did not want to write any more, saying that he did not believe me."[27] Vittorio Guidi said the vicar's notary "only recorded and examined what interested him. . . . I believe that he did not record anything of these things [that I said] because he said to me 'I am not researching these matters.'" The town was deeply disturbed by this abuse of power and the legal process. Several men went to Sutri to request a copy of the investigation documents for the community of Trevingano, but the vicar refused them.[28]

The people of Trevignano had had enough, and in October 1594, they bypassed their bishop and appealed to the pope. A formal denunciation was made by several town notables representing the whole community to the papal Tribunal of the Auditor of the Camera. The people of Trevignano charged that the sacristan held "a bad and scandalous life" and that the townspeople "suffer very much and receive most pernicious examples for their souls." They explained that Antino had never been disciplined because his ordinary favored him. They requested that a judge be sent from Rome to investigate "the crimes and sacrileges of this evil man," to uncover the truth, and to remedy the great damages Antino's deeds had caused to the health of their community and to their very souls.[29] The case was transferred to the Congregation of Bishops and Regulars, where Cardinal Alessandro Ottaviano de' Medici (the future pope Leo XI) received the letter. The ire of the community, the gravity of Antino's sins and crimes, the corruption of Vicar Mezzaroma and possibly Bishop Morone, and the disgrace they posed for the reforming Church as a whole compelled Cardinal de' Medici to act. He dispatched the experienced judge Giovanni Battista Pelingotti as an apostolic commissary and sent appropriate documentation stating his mission and his judicial powers to conduct a thorough investigation, arrest and detain anyone he deemed necessary, and, in the end, to suggest a verdict. However, in March 1595, just before Pelingotti arrived in Trevignano, Antino de Benedictis was whisked away to Sutri, allegedly under arrest by his friend Vicar Mezzaroma. Commissary Pelingotti would not question him. With the involvement of the Congregation of Bishops and Regulars, Femia and Antino's relationship had become a political battle between Rome and the bishop of Sutri. The bishop and his vicar based their claim regarding jurisdiction over the sacristan and the spiritual lives of the people of Trevignano on the decrees of the Council of Trent, while the townspeople turned to Rome for reform and justice.

Judge Pelingotti had Femia imprisoned in a back room of a tavern in the main square, where she would remain for a month while he questioned her and over forty other individuals. Almost everyone was forthcoming with details about the priest's *mala vita*. The abortions were particularly important as they were the gravest crimes Antino was accused of. If Pelingotti found concrete evidence that the sacristan had procured abortions, Antino could lose his clerical status, be exiled from Trevignano, and even handed over to secular authorities for corporal or capital punishment. Evidence of the abortions was, however, elusive and equivocal. That the abortions took place a year or two earlier (witnesses were imprecise about their dating) made physical evidence impossible. The only evidence available was testimony. Townspeople repeated the gruesome stories, but, problematically, no one could (or would) admit to having any direct evidence. Most simply told the judge that they had heard about the abortions from another person, that "it is said publicly." Perhaps fearing the consequences of testifying against the connected priest, witnesses preferred to attribute knowledge and thus transfer legal responsibility away from themselves and onto the community as a whole.

Femia, however, set the record straight. In two rounds of questioning from her makeshift jail cell, she testified to having been pregnant and described in agonizing detail how Antino had forced her to have a dangerous abortion. Contrary to what the town was saying, Femia told the judge she had been pregnant only once, about two years earlier (i.e., spring 1593). When she had felt sure she was pregnant, she told Antino. At first, he refused to acknowledge the possibility, and when she insisted, he became angry and saw to it that she had an abortion. While Femia was unequivocal that Antino forced her to abort, she gave two versions of how it happened.

First, she told the judge that two or three days after she told Antino she was pregnant, he came to her house and wanted sex, but she refused. Because "prete Antino is a man quick to rage," he began to beat her and threw her on the ground two or three times, leaving her badly bruised and in pain. As he was leaving the house, he warned her not to say anything about the pregnancy or the beating to anyone, even her mother. Femia took to bed, became ill, and aborted a few days later. "I believe that I aborted because of the blows that said prete Antino gave me," she told the judge.[30] In this version of events, it was the refusal of sex that drove Antino to violence that caused the abortion.

In her second examination, one day later, Judge Pelingotti asked follow-up questions to get Femia to be more explicit about Antino's knowledge of her pregnancy and the nature of the violence that caused the abortion. He wanted to know whether Antino knew what he was doing, whether the violence was intended to terminate the pregnancy. Femia now changed her story and confessed there was an abortifacient drink involved, that Antino had come to her house while her mother was at church and forced her to drink a yellow beverage. Not knowing what it was, Femia refused to drink it. She asked Antino what it was, but he would not tell her and pushed the glass to her face, saying, "Drink this, drink this, it is a good thing for you." Eventually he forced her into submission, and she drank a bit. She described it as very bitter. "As soon as I drank it, my whole stomach became disturbed and then started to turn . . . with great affliction and pain." Perhaps sensing her mother was on her way home, Antino left, taking the rest of the beverage with him and leaving Femia in writhing pain. The next day, Antino returned to the house, again when the mother was at church, and forced the drink upon Femia. She again resisted, explaining that it made her sick and demanding to know what it was. Eventually Antino made his intentions clear, allegedly saying, "Take it, take it because if you are pregnant, as you told me, [it] will make you abort." Knowing what the beverage was for, Femia now absolutely refused it, but Antino became violent and forced her to consume the rest of the drink. Shortly, Femia became very ill, began to expel a great quantity of blood, and aborted. She now told the judge, "My abortion could not [have come] from anything other than the [beverage] that Antino gave me to drink, which he told me was good for this, and from the blows that Antino gave me."[31]

Femia's testimony was damning, but Commissary Pelingotti questioned her credibility. Why had she withheld the information about the abortifacient beverage in her first examination? Femia told the judge that she had lied "out of fear that you would castigate and do some harm to me because I drank the thing." The act of consuming the beverage that caused the abortion, she feared, might render her culpable, an active agent, even though she claimed it was entirely against her will.[32] The judge likely wondered whether Femia was claiming force and violence to minimize her own participation—perhaps she willingly drank the beverage or even asked Antino to procure it.[33] Another thing that counted against Femia was that she had told no one about the pregnancy or the abortion, even her mother. Femia told the judge she had concealed the pregnancy from her mother because Andreozza strongly disapproved of and yelled at her over her relationship with Antino, and she also feared Antino would hurt her.[34]

Femia's description of the aborted fetus raised more questions. Because the legal and moral gravity of procured abortion depended on the gestational age of the fetus, Pelingotti needed information regarding its appearance. Specifically, he needed to discern whether it was animated. Femia told him she had not seen the expulsion. She said that, along with a great quantity of blood, she had expelled "a thing like a piece of flesh that I did not see." She explained that her mother had discovered it as she washed the bloody sheets and then told her what she'd seen.[35] How could she have failed to notice it? Femia explained that she was in such pain following the consumption of the beverage and the beating that "I did not notice anything other than the great quantity of blood that I made."[36]

When questioned, Andreozza confirmed the story but was adamant that she knew nothing of Femia's pregnancy until after it had been terminated. Andreozza said she believed her daughter had been sick with the flux, which manifested itself in a heavy expulsion of blood, and only discovered the truth when she went to clean Femia's blood-soaked sheets in the lake and "found in said cloths a small fleshy figure." She described it as long and wide as a folded piece of paper that was on Pelingotti's table. "According to me this flesh was a fetus that Femia my daughter aborted and I threw said flesh and abortion along with the other filthy things in the sheets in the lake." The judge asked for more information about the piece of flesh: Had it been animated, and was she sure it was a fetus? Andreozza replied that she had not felt it move and that she had not looked at it closely enough but was sure "this flesh was a fetus that [Femia] aborted." When she returned to the house, she told Femia what she had found in the sheets, but Femia denied the possibility and scolded her mother for bothering her with "such fantasies." When the judge asked about the causes of the abortion, Andreozza said she did not know for sure but suspected Antino must have given Femia something to cause it "because he is unscrupulous."[37]

With Femia's confession and all the testimonies he had collected describing Antino's other wrongdoings, Commissary Pelingotti had enough evidence to move the investigation onto the next phase, which likely meant Antino would be charged, probably taken to Rome, and would have to prepare a formal defense. Pelingotti took Femia to Rome, where it seems she was to be questioned again by other officials of the congregation, perhaps Cardinal de' Medici himself. Problematically, however, the trial dossier appears to be missing pages at this crucial moment in the case's development—there is a gap and no mention of what transpired in April 1595. We pick up the story again in May, and with a surprising development. Acting on the authority of Bishop Morone, Vicar Mezzaroma requested Femia be transferred to Sutri along with a copy of the trial documents Pelingotti had assembled during his investigation. Although the remaining documents are not explicit, it seems Vicar Mezzaroma and Bishop Morone refused to allow the trial against Antino to be handled by the congregation in Rome. For reasons not mentioned in the trial documents, Cardinal de' Medici obliged, and Femia was taken to Sutri and detained in the episcopal jail. She was now a prisoner of Antino's good friend Vicar Mezzaroma.

Shortly after her arrival, Vicar Mezzaroma cut to the chase, asking whether she had told the truth in her testimonies to Commissary Pelingotti. In this setting and in this new context, Femia said almost everything she had told Pelingotti about Antino was a lie. She now claimed she had been coerced into saying they had a sexual relationship and he impregnated her and forced her to have an abortion. She named several individuals who forced her to lie, including the townspeople Antonio di Cola, Mercurio Fasarolo, Giovanni Bastianello, and Bastiano Carpino, several of whom wrote the letter of denunciation to Rome and requested the investigation in the first place. Surprisingly, Femia also named Commissary Pelingotti, along with his notary. Femia told the vicar that the first time Pelingotti had questioned her, she had told him it was not true that she'd had a sexual relationship with the priest, that he had impregnated her and forced her to abort, or that he was responsible for her failed attempt to marry Francesco. However, swayed by Antonio di Cola and other townsmen, Pelingotti was set on punishing the sacristan. She said Antonio di Cola had gone to convince her mother that it was in Femia's best interests to lie, that he and several others promised to help her marry Francesco and even to give her a dowry if she said Antino had forced her to have an abortion. Andreozza was reportedly swayed and went to her daughter's cell in the tavern and urged her to lie:

"My daughter, it is best if you say that Antino impregnated you and made you abort." In his next examination, Pelingotti asked Femia if she wanted to add anything to her testimony: "What have you thought about? Is it true that Antino impregnated you and made you abort?" Femia told him what he and the other men allegedly wanted to hear: "I did not say the truth in my examination [before Commissary Pelingotti], that which I said, they forced me to say. [They said] they would marry me and give me a dowry, and I believed them."[38] Andreozza was also questioned again, in Trevignano as she was too old and sick to travel to Sutri, and she too changed her story, now testifying that she had been coerced into lying by Antonio di Cola and had persuaded her daughter to do the same: "Everything that I said in my examination against the Sacristan and my daughter, and that I told my daughter to say, I did not say this because it was true but because of what Antonio and [Commissary Pelingotti's] notary said. I wanted my daughter to get married."[39]

Vicar Mezzaroma sent transcripts of Femia's new testimonies admitting to false confessions on her part and asserting fraud and corruption on the part of Commissary Pelingotti to Bishop Morone. The bishop studied the about-face and concluded it was necessary to have Femia tortured to ensure she was now telling the truth.[40] She was questioned one last time on October 21, 1595, and she maintained that she had been forced to lie by the townsmen who wanted Antino punished. She was submitted to the *corda* torture for three-quarters of an hour. Femia's hands were tied behind her back; another rope was tied around her wrists and thrown over a beam in the ceiling from which she was hoisted up above the ground. She was repeatedly hoisted up and dropped from various heights. Her body's weight bore down on her inverted shoulders. Between anguished screams and begging for release, she maintained that she was now telling the truth: "If I have said otherwise, I said it because they forced me to say it."[41] Having seemingly gotten what he wanted, Vicar Mezzaroma released Femia, and she returned to Trevignano "absolved" of any wrongdoing. Antino was kept in Sutri for a few more months. He was not found guilty of abortion, but Bishop Morone knew he had to discipline the sacristan whom all Trevignano loathed and who had caused scandal and brought the Congregation of Bishops and Regulars and the long arm of Rome into their lives. Bishop

Morone sentenced Antino to two years of spiritual punishment tending to the sick and needy at either the hospital of San Giovanni Laterano or of the Consolazione in Rome. It would appear Bishop Morone hoped the two-year banishment from Trevignano might appease the townspeople and allow their tempers to cool, and for Antino, it provided an opportunity to atone for his misdeeds by helping the needy. He would hopefully return to Trevignano a better man and cleric.

But Antino never went to serve his term of penance in Rome. He returned to Trevignano and his old ways. In 1598, the community again appealed to Rome. Antino was accused of new and varied wrongdoings. He had continued to harass Femia. On Holy Thursday, when Femia went to the Church of Santa Maria di Trevignano to receive communion, Antino was tending to the sacramental wine. As Femia approached to take the sacrament, he said, loudly enough for everyone to hear, "Cow, scoundrel, you should be ashamed to come drink from me."[42] Such words uttered by a cleric as a worshipper was trying to receive the sacrament on this holy day were blasphemy. Antino's control of the sacred and his use of it to abuse Femia troubled everyone who witnessed it enough to incite the new appeal for Rome's intervention. But this second investigation does not contain a verdict. Would Antino finally be disciplined? Would Femia ever be free of him? We do not know.

CHAPTER THREE

Abortion and the Law

OLOGNA, January 2, 1578

The following has come to the ears and notice of the illustrious and excellent Lord Auditor Tursoni and his court: within the house of [Enea], an eminent nobleman of the Desideri family of Bologna, a certain serving-woman, attached to and dwelling within that same house, gave birth, and she disposed of the child in a certain drain or latrine, utterly without of any fear of the divine.

Responding to this matter, [the lord auditor] ordered me, the Minor Notary, to go in person with court bailiffs to the house of [Enea Desideri], the aforementioned nobleman, for the intent and purpose of understanding all the charges necessary for the matters outlined above. And he also ordered me to send her to the Torrone prison, once she had been found at the house or otherwise by the bailiffs, along with the body of the boy.

And so, in execution of the commission laid upon me, I went personally to the house of the aforementioned [Enea],

eminent Lord of the Desideri, located in Capella San Tomaso. Then, together with the said Lord [Enea], the bailiffs,
and Lana, one of the pages, I entered into the lower rooms of
the house, the so-called *stanza delle boccate* [laundry room
with pipes where waste was collected]. In that place, in my
presence and with the others around, [we located] the boy,
or rather his body, and, once he was found, of identifying
him and doing everything else that had to be done. Then,
once the body, covered in mud and excrement, was recovered
. . . I had it washed. And so, after the body was washed, I sent
the dead body to the Torrone prison with the woman Maria,
the serving-woman, found in a certain bedchamber.[1]

The notary, whose name was not recorded on the trial transcripts,
described a gruesome and tragic scene. His dry, matter-of-fact Latin description of what he and the other Criminal Tribunal of Bologna personnel saw and did appears to omit any sign of emotion or evaluation.
Were these men of the court accustomed to this sort of situation? An
indication that this notary did however feel and evaluate was that he
described the being found and pulled out of mud and excrement as a
"boy" but immediately edited himself by calling it a "body." This was
not a fetus in formation but a fully developed and possibly newborn
baby. The notary also decided the woman who had given birth and tried
to conceal the body did not fear God. He did not however record how
this case came "to the ears and notice" of the court. Perhaps the nobleman Enea Desideri himself brought the happenings of his household to
their attention in an attempt to control the narrative. What is clear is
that from their arrival at the Desideri palazzo, the tribunal's men knew
who was responsible for the dead body stuck in the drain: Maria da
Brescia, a young woman of unspecified age who was chambermaid to
Desideri's wife, Isabella. While the men of the Torrone retrieved the
body and washed it, Maria waited in her room. She then walked with
them to the Torrone prison, approximately fifteen minutes through the
heart of the city. What was Maria thinking? Was she rehearsing her defense? Did she stare at the wrapped infant cadaver paraded through
town? Was she wondering what neighbors were making of this scene?
Was she reconciling herself to the punishment she might receive? Would

she confess and plead for mercy? Or was she regretting not running away before the dead child came to the attention of the state?

In the menacing prison, Maria admitted to Judge Tursoni that she was responsible for the body in the pipes, which she called a creatura rather than a boy. However, she was adamant she had not committed a crime, explaining she had not known she was pregnant until the creatura slipped out of her body onto the floor of her room. It was dead. Shocked, panicked, and wanting to conceal it from the household, she picked it up and placed it in the latrine in the small room attached to her own. She stated repeatedly that she had no idea she was pregnant—she said she wasn't showing. She did admit to a sexual relationship with a man who was by then missing. Apparently, the noble household had also failed to notice Maria's pregnancy, or perhaps they jointly refused to admit knowing. No one knew anything about the missing impregnator.

The judge almost certainly thought Maria's claims of ignorance and a surprise delivery of a fully formed creatura / boy highly suspect. These were well-worn defenses criminal tribunals across Italy and Europe heard from single women and servants, like Maria, accused of procuring abortion or committing neonaticide. The laws of Bologna regarded the abortion of an animated and viable fetus to be similar, although not identical, to infanticide. The penalty was execution. However, there were important mitigating factors: to issue the maximum penalty, the court required either a full confession or certain proof that the woman knowingly and intentionally terminated her pregnancy or killed the newborn. In Maria's case, the court had neither. A forensic examination of the cadaver by experienced midwives was inconclusive, although they thought it had probably died in Maria's womb. This may have exculpated her from neonaticide charges, but not from intentionally procuring the abortion of a potentially viable fetus that could have lived outside her womb and been baptized. According to the laws of Bologna, Maria could face capital punishment.

As the primary phase of the investigation came to an end, the governor of Bologna, Giovanni Francesco di San Giorgio, received a rushed letter from Rome. Cardinal Filippo Boncompagni, cardinal nephew of Pope Gregory XIII and superintendent general of the Papal States, had directions on how this case of a lowly servant charged with such a crime ought to be handled. He wrote: "Although that Maria, servant of sir Enea Desideri, who is in prison and deserves capital punishment (for the matter that Your Lordship will hear about from the judge of the Torrone), nevertheless, considering the fragility of her sex, [it is advised] to change her penalty [into something else], so that it would not bring shame to her kin [*parenti*]. But it is for your lordship to establish what punishment will have to be given."[2] Boncompagni was a native of Bologna and had deep familial ties to the Desideri. He was almost certainly compelled to write on account of Enea. Although no one expressed it or recorded it in the case files, it was certainly possible—even probable—that it was a Desideri, perhaps Enea himself, who had impregnated Maria and helped or forced her to abort or commit neonaticide. While acknowledging that Maria might deserve capital punishment, the cardinal urged the governor to handle the case with care, "considering the fragility of her sex." This legal concept of *fragilitas sexus,* fragility or weakness on account of sex, was a legal concept of ancient Roman origin that held that women's responsibility in crime to be less than that of men because of women's inherent physical, cognitive, and emotional "weakness" and vulnerability. The cardinal suggested that Maria ought not be condemned to death but rather to a lesser penalty. Cardinal Boncompagni may have pitied the young servant woman, but sparing her from the scaffold would also prevent a scandal for the noble Desideri; he suggested a penalty that would not bring infamy upon her "parenti," a term that implied both her kin and the household she served. Cardinal Boncompagni's intercession appears to have worked. The investigation into the circumstances that resulted in a dead creatura discarded in the pipes of the Desideri palazzo ends with his creased letter. While the trial documents do not reveal what happened to Maria, the fact that the cardinal's letter was included and preserved in the dossier indicates it was a key element in the resolution of the case. Governor Francesco di San Giorgio likely took the cardinal's advice.

Maria's case illuminates important and tragic realities that underpinned and shaped legal conceptualizations of abortion and neonaticide, and their handling by civic authorities. Like theology and the Church, the law and its institutions considered abortion a moral wrong that disturbed society and required regulation and discipline. It was a crime, to be punished by the state. The theologically rooted belief that abortion was a form of homicide, combined with pervasive anxieties linking undisciplined sexuality and pregnancy outside of marriage with disorder, motivated civic authorities to attempt to regulate it through legislation and prosecution. When procurers of abortion were denounced or the cadavers of fetuses and infants found, criminal tribunals investigated and threatened punishment, including execution. However, like their ecclesiastical counterparts, civic authorities were sensitive to context and circumstances, and judges chose not to actively pursue procurers of abortion or to impose prescribed penalties. As Maria's case reveals, abortion could be a socially and politically sensitive crime. It was also legally contentious, resisting easy categorization. Civic authorities, state legislators, and legal scholars debated what abortion meant and how and why it should be considered a crime; they deliberated over the legal status of the fetus and what penalties were appropriate for procurers of abortion and those causing miscarriage by assault. The most influential jurists of the period agreed that the criminal nature of abortion was contentious. They were also skeptical that judges could discover—with the certainty needed for conviction—the causes of terminated pregnancies and fetal death or distinguish between natural or accidental miscarriage and abortion procured intentionally, as the result of violent assault or the consequence of medical intervention. Most agreed these issues were too uncertain to be decided in a courtroom, especially when the life of the suspect hung in the balance. Judges were acutely aware that behind many cases of abortion lay abuse and injustice that men perpetrated on women, as was perhaps the case with Maria da Brescia. The law, in theory and in practice, took all these factors into account.

In this chapter I explore legal conceptualizations of abortion. Like theology and medicine, the law was a major discourse through which individuals understood and communicated about abortion. However, trying to determine what the law on abortion was in early modern Italy is complicated. Before unification, the Grand Duchy of Tuscany, the Republic of Venice, the Papal States, the Kingdom of Naples, and all other discrete political entities governing the people of the peninsula and nearby islands had their own articulations of law and systems of enforcement. Even within a single state, however, there was often not a single source of criminal law. Legislation was important, but not

all-encompassing. In the sixteenth and seventeenth centuries, a handful of states criminalized abortion in legislation through codified statutes and civic ordinances and edicts. Most states had no specific legislation, yet abortion was considered a crime. Alongside legislation,
criminal law was developed in technical works of jurisprudence and
penology. Jurists operating in the continental common law tradition
(*ius commune*), a blend of ancient Roman civil law and Church canon
law, discussed the criminal nature of abortion, analyzed various factors
influencing its legal meanings, debated how it should be punished, and
instructed readers—other jurists and judges—on issues of trial procedure, investigation, and evaluation of evidence.

While codes and books shaped legal understanding, law was given
concrete meaning through its application and enforcement in courts.
Legal discourse on abortion was therefore also produced "on the
ground" in tribunals where judges encountered it, its procurers, agents,
and victims in specific contexts. In trial records, we see how judges and
generally non-elite individuals produced meanings at the situational
level and how doctrinal and prescriptive categories and understandings
of abortion fit or clashed with the messy and often tragic experiences of
real life.

Not surprisingly, these three main sources of law—legislation, jurisprudence, and trials—address abortion in different ways, often pro-
ducing inconsistent pictures of what abortion might have meant to the
state agents responsible for its regulation and to society at large. For
instance, some legislators and jurists categorized abortion as a form of
homicide, deserving rigorous investigation and capital punishment.
However, criminal tribunals rarely prosecuted cases of abortion. The
vast archives for the years 1575–1650 of the criminal tribunals of the
governor of Rome and of the city of Bologna, two of the busiest courts
of early modern Italy, yield only a handful of trials for abortion. There
are several reasons. Procured abortion was considered a "hidden" and
"concealed crime" (*crimen occultum, delitto nascosto*), generally kept secret,
and therefore rarely coming to the attention of the courts. While courts
could investigate cases ex officio, by means of inquisition, most cases
came to the court's attention because of individual denunciations of
women and men for troublesome or scandalous behaviors. When no
one cared, courts did not investigate.

We know prescription almost never determines practice. However, instead of accepting inconsistency and assuming a simple gap between law as a body of theoretical discourse preoccupying the minds of elite men, on one hand, and the ad hoc meting out of local justice in court, on the other, it is more productive to consider legal thinking and practice on abortion as formed in a dialectical relationship. Doctrinal commitments, civic preoccupations with notions of stability and order, and jurisprudential standards of investigation all interacted with the local moral economies of assorted social actors and varied notions of justice (both abstract and concrete) in an inherently unequal and unjust world.[3] Theoretical considerations and normative law both spoke to and ignored the untidy realities of social life. While the relationship between legislation, jurisprudence, and criminal investigation is indeed tangled, it is clear that the polished thought and detailed analysis found in print guided, as best it could, the messy business of questioning frightened, traumatized, and self-interested individuals and the evaluation of complicated forms of evidence in the context of lurid, scandalous, and socially disruptive cases. Jurists often said in print what judges investigating cases may have been thinking. At the same time, what judges encountered in dramatic and often disturbing cases often influenced the development of jurisprudential thought.

Criminalizing Abortion

"Aborting fetuses is such an enormous and impious act that every law, every doctor, and all reason condemns it and punishes it severely," wrote Scipione Mercurio.[4] This was not exactly true. While all states likely held procured abortion and miscarriage caused by assault to be crimes deserving punishment, they did not agree on what exactly abortion meant, whether and how they would issue abortion legislation, or what penalties offenders merited. In the sixteenth and seventeenth century, the criminalization of abortion was a matter of contention.

State legislation offers a starting point for examining the framing of criminal abortion. Statutes were a standard and somewhat uniform type of state legislation issued regularly by cities, towns, communes, republics, and kingdoms from the Middle Ages onward.[5] As a strategy for state building, the reiteration and elaboration of criminal statutes during the sixteenth and seventeenth centuries gave civic authorities the opportunity to amend, cancel, and add to their existing laws. In some states, statutes published in the sixteenth and early seventeenth centuries remained official codes of law for over a century.[6] Homicide, different types of violence, carrying arms, poisoning, theft, kidnapping, slander, defloration and rape, adultery, and sodomy, to name the most common, were criminal offenses punishable by the state. Abortion, however, appears in only a handful of early modern Italian criminal statutes. Of these, some made abortion a homicide, while others treated it sui generis, as a crime of its own.[7] Within these two classifications, important distinctions pertained notably to penalties, which ranged from fines—that fed state coffers or charitable institutions—to exile and corporal or capital punishment.

In keeping with canon law, most secular statutes that criminalized abortion calibrated penalties according to the fetus's level of development. The sixteenth- and early seventeenth-century statutes of Milan, Genoa, and Benevento followed the canonical formulations framing the abortion of an animated fetus as graver than that of a preanimate one.[8] In these states, the abortion of an animate fetus was a capital crime, and the procurer was to be executed. For example, the statute of Benevento, part of the Papal States, specified that the abortion of an animate fetus was equivalent to infanticide, and the "mother," along with any accomplice, was to receive capital punishment. Alternatively, the statutes of Perugia, Senigallia, Macerata, and Monterubbiano did not use the terms "animate" and "preanimate" but rather wrote visual cues into their abortion laws. In Perugia, a person causing the death of an "obviously pregnant woman" was to be twice punished, once for the death of the woman and once for the unborn.[9] The statutes of Senigallia and Monterubbiano stated that the abortion of a fetus when the woman was at least "three months pregnant" was a crime.[10] The visual markers "obviously pregnant" and "three months pregnant" likely meant the woman had to be showing, which also meant the fetus was advanced in its development and, therefore, animate. That these qualifiers were written into laws suggests legislators recognized that pregnancy was difficult to detect in the first few months and that this was legally relevant in the criminalization of abortion. Animation, in and of itself, was too imprecise to set judicial culpability.

Penalties—sometimes fines, sometimes corporal—also varied according to the gender and class of the perpetrator. The criminal statutes of Sezze framed abortion as a woman's crime and decreed that a woman who knowingly terminated her pregnancy would be put to death by burning.[11] In Senigalia and Macerata, if the person who provided the abortion was a man, he would lose his head; if a woman, she would burn unless she was able to pay five hundred lire within fifteen days.[12] In Benevento, social status mattered: for the abortion of a pre-animate fetus, an individual of modest class could be beaten or sentenced to pay a fine of two uncia; if of better condition, they could expect a fine of five uncia or a term of penance in a monastery or nunnery, at the discretion of the judge.[13] In Genoa, the offender, here assumed to be a non-elite male, could expect a sentence in the galleys, a common form of disciplinary labor.[14] Some statutes explicitly stated the penalty would be left to the judge's discretion (*in arbitrio*)—more on this concept below.

Because the laws criminalizing abortion are not easily contextualized, their force is difficult to assess. We do not know precisely when, by whom, or why these statutes were framed. Was Genoa's 1580 abortion law motivated by specific circumstances or pressing social issues, and how might they differ from those preoccupying the authorities and legislators in Milan, Macerata, and Benevento? It is likely that some statutes were vestiges and local permutations of ancient Roman and medieval customary law, reproduced and tweaked throughout the centuries, rather than responses to specific social concerns or intended for regular enforcement. Fuller answers depend on further research.

For scholars, the abortion laws described here are suggestive, but they are not representative. An examination of sixteenth- and early seventeenth-century statutes issued by many Italian states has turned up only this handful with specific laws against abortion. Florence issued no statute on abortion; nor did Modena, Parma, Cremona, Bologna, Treviso, Ferrara, or Venice. Strikingly, the renewed statutes of the city of Rome—issued under the pontificates of Gregory XIII in 1580, Sixtus V in 1590, Paul V in 1611, and Urban VIII in 1636—made no mention of abortion either in their laws on homicide, poisoning, parricide, and violence or in sections on sexual offences, such as rape and defloration, incest, and adultery.[15] This statutory silence on abortion is all the more surprising given the direct papal interventions on the matter by Sixtus V in 1588 and Gregory XIV in 1591.

What could this pattern of omissions mean? Might they suggest that most states did not consider abortion a punishable offense or that the criminality of abortion was so obvious that it needed no statute? More likely, the absence reflects the relative simplicity of this genre of legal literature. Criminal statutes were often framed only in general terms.[16] Homicide laws, for example, usually distinguished neither different types of killing nor the circumstances and motivations behind actions that resulted in death. Typically, they imposed a blanket penalty: he who kills will be killed.[17] The important question was whether abortion fell by implication under homicide statutes. In his annotations to the statutes of Bologna (1582) the jurist Annibale Monterenzi stated that it was a widely held assumption that abortion was a form of homicide but noted that Bolognese laws for homicide, in their current articulations, made no mention of it. Monterenzi clarified that only if the fetus was animated might an abortion be considered homicide. He did not explain how a judge should apply this distinction in the courtroom nor whether the abortion of an inanimate fetus was a crime at all.[18] In contrast to Monterenzi, the papal secretary Leandro Galganetti and the senator Giovanni Battista Fenzonio said nothing about abortion as they annotated Rome's early seventeenth-century homicide statutes.[19]

Local ordinances (*bandi* or *editti*), issued by civic authorities, tell more about the criminalization of abortion. These one-page proclamations or short pamphlets, written in Italian, appeared with greater frequency and were widely distributed. They were often posted around town and read out loud by a crier in order to alert inhabitants to new rules and to remind them of existing ones. Ordinances highlighted the most troublesome infractions and the most ignored prohibitions. Common criminal themes included violence, banditry, theft, and carrying weapons. In the late sixteenth and seventeenth centuries, civic authorities in both Bologna and Rome increasingly included specific prohibitions on abortion.[20]

While the abortion laws found in this type of legislation reached a broader audience, they were no more standardized or unambiguous than those in criminal statutes.[21] For instance, in his *General Ordinances* of 1588, the vice-legate of Bologna, Anselmo Dandino, included abortion under the law on poisoning and regarded it as a capital offense: anyone who sold poisons that caused a woman to abort an animate fetus, even if meant for other purposes, was to face capital punishment. Strictly speaking, this was not directed at or intended for the individual who sought abortion but for its provider. Furthermore, the clause "even if it was meant for another purpose" suggests the law, like the bandi of the protomedicato examined in Chapter 1, might have as much to do with fears of poisoning and medical malpractice as with policing procured abortion per se.[22] New prohibitions on abortion were issued in Bologna in 1608 and 1610 by Cardinal Legate Benedetto Giustiniano, this time in sections on homicide and parricide. In 1608, Giustiniano declared that "mothers" who willfully killed their animate fetuses by abortion were as guilty of homicide as "mothers who suffocate their babies."[23] In 1610, he refined this by adding important distinctions: if abortion was committed without intent or if the fetus was inanimate, punishment was at the discretion of the judge.[24] Giustiniano also addressed medical practitioners in a section on crimes committed by healers, declaring no one was to give a woman products to cause abortion. If a healer did so and the woman aborted or died, the healer would be tried for a capital offense.[25] Forbidding healers to participate in the termination of pregnancy was also a warning against medical negligence, although the law made no explicit provision for abortions induced as therapy, which, as we saw in Chapter 1, contrasts with the decree issued by the protomedicato of Bologna around the same time.

Ordinances concerning abortion from the governors of Rome were fewer and less precise than those in Bologna. Abortion first appeared in a Roman regulation in November 1591, just five months after Gregory XIV's moderation of Sixtus V's bull. The governor of Rome at that time, Gugliemo Bastoni, listed abortion among a slew of offenses ranging from poisoning, blasphemy, and violence toward women to prostitutes dressing as men, singing bawdy songs, and other activities and behaviors deemed immoral or subversive. Including abortion in this range of behaviors suggests that it was viewed as a morally problematic but not a particularly pressing issue. No details explained what abortion was, why it was a crime, or even what penalty it earned.[26] A 1595 ordinance from the governor, Cardinal Domenico Toschi, a celebrated jurist, offered slightly more: anyone who gave poison and caused a woman to abort an animated fetus "without the counsel of a physician" would incur the death penalty.[27] Toschi's prohibition aimed primarily at healers and providers of drugs, but it was not a wholesale prohibition. It stated that, where an abortion needed to be induced, it had to be done by a physician, a position also maintained by the Roman protomedicato. The important caveat "without the counsel of a physician" contrasted with the Bolognese laws of Cardinal Giustiniano issued a decade later.

While civic legislation in both Bologna and Rome prohibited abortion, authorities did not define it in the same way nor prescribe like penalties for procurers or administrators. Seeking to centralize authority and establish some consistency over criminal matters, in 1599 Pope Clement VIII published an authoritative set of *General Ordinances* for the entire Papal States.[28] Regarding abortion, he declared that causing a woman to abort an animated fetus, even if unintended, merited death and the confiscation of property; if the fetus was preanimate, the procurer should be sent to the galleys and suffer the loss of goods.[29] As women were not punished with terms on galleys, this declaration was directed, it seems, at men, perhaps those responsible for aborted pregnancies, including forcing them upon the women, as well as healers who participated in abortions. Clement's formulation was repeated in Roman ordinances until at least 1632. However, as evidenced by Cardinal Legate Giustiniano's 1608 and 1610 ordinances for Bologna, the declaration was not necessarily followed throughout the Papal States as Clement had intended.

There was no single explicit and consistent abortion law in early modern Italy. As late as 1673, the cardinal and jurist Giovanni Battista De Luca wrote, regarding abortion, that "one cannot give a definite and general rule applicable to all [states], the main reason being the great diversity of styles of Principalities."[30] While the legal systems and the criminal doctrines taught in universities and practiced in cities across the Italian peninsula were similar,[31] local social and political contexts probably gave different meanings to crimes and accounted for some of the variety we see in legislation on abortion. De Luca cited the papal bulls of Sixtus V and Gregory XIV as examples of difference. And a pope's goals were not necessarily those of the grand duke of Tuscany.

This sample of state and municipal legislation indicates that in some places abortion was explicitly criminalized. Nevertheless, the penalties to be meted out to offenders both differed across the peninsula, and even within some areas, and changed over time and from authority to authority. The relative scarcity of legislation on abortion—compared, for example, to rape, adultery, sodomy, prostitution, poisoning, or bearing arms—likely suggests that most authorities did not address abortion as a pressing issue that required direct legislative intervention. However, it also reveals much about the nebulous nature of abortion in the minds of early modern Italian lawmakers.

Although some civic authorities deemed abortion a crime, they had difficulty defining it and assigning clear or consistent penalties. For instance, the seventeenth-century jurist and judge of the Criminal Rota of Florence Marc'Antonio Savelli discussed abortion at some length in his influential work of criminal jurisprudence and penology. Yet he could not cite a single disciplinary regulation on the matter either included in republican Florentine statutes or promulgated by the Medici grand dukes. In contrast, he readily referenced numerous statutes and edicts addressing disruptive sexual behaviors such as adultery, incest, sodomy, and premarital defloration.[32] Legislation was not understood as an end but rather one layer of legal discourse among many. Thus, jurisprudential commentary on abortion, to which we will now turn, reveals it to be a complex and controversial subject for which simple laws, tidy categories, and blanket penalties did not reflect—as they seldom did—the messiness of real experiences and the difficulties of investigating cases and making judgments in actual situations.

In works of criminal jurisprudence and penology, a genre of legal writing that flourished in the early modern period, Italian jurists devoted substantial attention to abortion. After long and celebrated careers hearing cases in court and teaching legal doctrine and procedure, some jurists composed, for a professional audience, treatises on the practice of criminal law (*practica criminalis*) and collections of exemplary cases and sentences (*decisiones*) issued by royal and senatorial tribunals. Works like Prospero Farinacci's *Practice and Theory of Criminal Law* were massive and multivolume works containing analysis and citations on many subjects from legal doctrine to points of procedure.[33] In this genre, authors offered insight into how a jurist might categorize a type of crime or investigate cases, what problems or controversies might arise, and what penalties were appropriate for the offense committed. Most of the time, authors preferred to cite as many authoritative opinions as possible on a given subject rather than directly state what they themselves thought and did in practice—this was partly because every case of crime came with a unique set of circumstances, and therefore a judge was supposed to render a decision based on his judgment of these circumstances in relation to the wisdom provided by eminent jurists and the legal tradition. However, within a maze of citations, the jurists sometimes stated their own views or appeared to side with one authority, interpretation of doctrine, or moral and social imperative over another; these personal opinions will be privileged here. In the decisions genre, jurists curated collections of decisions made and sentences given by important appellate courts, such as the Sacred Royal Council of Naples and the Senate of Turin. Though legal historians continue to debate whether the concept of precedent had weight in early modern Italy, the rationale for publishing these decisions was clearly to present historical examples of how judges might engage with specific criminal offenses.[34]

These works reveal that abortion often preoccupied the minds and writings of the most influential jurists of the sixteenth and seventeenth centuries and occasionally took up the time and resources of important courts. While most jurists agreed that abortion was a crime that generally fell under the category of homicide, they also acknowledged that there were too many uncertainties, at both the doctrinal and practical level, to really treat it as such in court.

To be sure, there was a long legal tradition of debating doctrinal issues relevant to the criminality of abortion. When working to sort out abortion as a crime, sixteenth- and seventeenth-century jurists relied heavily on ancient Roman law and its medieval commentators. The Roman legal tradition was the main source of the continental common law (ius commune) that jurists learned in university and later used, in relation to local political and social contexts, to make and judge cases. Concerning abortion, ancient Roman law, particularly three precepts found in the *Digest of Justinian,* deemed neither procured abortion nor miscarriage caused by assault a homicide, because the unborn fetus was not legally a human being. In this Roman tradition, abortion was a crime but not a capital one; exile, fines, and the confiscation of property were appropriate penalties.[35] Medieval Christian commentators were uneasy with these laws because they overlooked the soul and were, therefore, at odds with theology and canon law and their paradigm of animation. A rich medieval legal discussion developed.[36] Some jurists drew a clear distinction between abortion pre- and postanimation; others wondered whether and how to apply this principle to actual criminal cases. Later, in a post-Tridentine context, and especially after the two papal bulls on abortion, early modern jurists again confronted the risks of challenging theological orthodoxy. Most commentators balanced moral and theological commitments with legal reasoning, the practicalities of investigating cases, and the social consequences of prosecution and meting out penalties. Where statutes and municipal ordinances represent a diversity of concerns in their abortion laws, jurisprudential writings, even though they might differ on points of interpretation, reflect a movement toward consensus. Like their predecessors, early modern jurists contemplated several themes: the circumstances under which abortion could be homicide, whether a fetus could and ought to be regarded as a human being, and whether a procurer or administrator of abortion or someone who caused a miscarriage by assault should be tried as a murderer.

Most jurists began their discussion of abortion with the legal status of the fetus. On this point, civil law aligned with theology and canon law. Civil jurists accepted the distinction between the abortion of a pre- and postanimate fetus, and that the latter was considered homicide and the procurer open to due punishment. However, animation was always regarded to be a problematic form of evidence; it was clear to all that gestational age and development dates for animation were contentious. Farinacci cited theological, scientific, and medical authorities variously claiming that male fetuses could be animated in thirty, forty, sixty, and even eighty days and females at forty, sixty, eighty, and ninety days.[37] Commentary by the forensics expert Paolo Zacchia was influential. Although he found Thomas Fyens's new theory of immediate animation more convincing than the traditional view of delayed animation, Zacchia concluded that a precise moment of animation could not be determined with certainty.[38] Most jurists, however, clung to the canonical opinion that was reaffirmed by Pope Gregory XIV in 1591.

While jurists acknowledged the importance of the soul and baptism to eternal life, most thought animation too ambiguous a basis for defining a homicide that could result in capital punishment. Giacomo Menochio explained that, even though the statutes of his own city of Milan (where he was a judge, professor, senator, and consultant to Philip II of Spain) distinguished between the abortion of animate and inanimate fetuses, most states did not because the matter was too ambiguous.[39] Nevertheless, at the end of the seventeenth century, the standard legal doctrine (*communis opinio*) on abortion went unchanged. In 1673, Cardinal De Luca repeated the distinction between animate and inanimate fetuses and the corresponding penalties for abortion but noted in a deprecatory way that these distinctions mattered more to jurists "who speak in generalities and in abstractions."[40]

Some jurists thought that physical fetal formation was a better measure than animation for determining the gravity of abortion and its punishment. They spoke of "perfect formation" (*formatus perfectus*), which meant a fetus completely developed and able live outside the womb, at least for a time. While animation gave the fetus a soul, in the transition from fetus to human being, viability and live birth was what legally mattered. Yet jurists discussed the haziness of this boundary, too. Asking whether one should speak of a "child" (*infans*) and "person" (*homo*) from conception, animation, or only from birth, Giacomo Menochio concluded that before it is born, a fetus is not a person or a child.[41] Antonino Tesauro, senator and judge at the Royal Court of Turin, was especially firm in his assertion that a fetus in utero does not have the same legal status as a born child. "It is one thing to *be* a thing," he argued, "and another to be *held* as a thing." A human being is never called "a true human [being] except after [she or he] has been born"; "a fetus that has not yet come out is not rightly said to be a person [homo]." Tesauro was unequivocal: "There is a difference between killing [a child] already born, and [killing] an immature [fetus] still in the womb."[42] The latter was not homicide or a capital offense, the former was.

These considerations were also important in the civil law arena. Because a fetus was not considered a human being, it could not affect the course of inheritance until after its emergence, alive and viable, from its mother's womb.[43] Fathers or other heirs sometimes resorted to delivery by caesarean section after the death of the mother, even if the child was certain to die during the process or shortly after drawing a few breaths, in order to direct the flow of inheritance.[44] In general, then, although timing was always debatable, jurists, often citing Hippocrates and, in the seventeenth century, Paolo Zacchia, regarded a fetus to be fully formed and viable around eight months from conception.

Although jurisprudence tended to require a fully formed and viable fetus born alive for abortion to qualify as a homicide, the legal commentators remained ambivalent and even anxious. All jurists who wrote on the subject felt the need to discuss the nature of fetal personhood and the criminal categorization of abortion (whether or not it might be homicide) and, ultimately, to defend the common opinion. Discussions generally started from the premise that abortion was widely assumed to be a form of homicide because it meant the loss of a soul and a potential and imagined future human life. This was partially due to the fact that theological thinking on the nature of the fetus and the subject of abortion permeated all forms of discourse. Nevertheless, even with the papal incursions at the end of the sixteenth century, the legal consensus until the end of the seventeenth century continued to be that the criminal severity of abortion increased with the gestational age of the fetus, only becoming unambiguously homicide with the intentional killing of a perfectly formed and viable infant—De Luca specified that this crime should be called infanticide and not abortion.[45] But the moments of transition remained hazy and subject to varying views. It was generally agreed that determining a penalty, and therefore what type of crime had been committed, based on fetal animation or level of formation was, according to the Florentine jurist and judge Antonio Maria Cospi, "[a] matter of great controversy" and "beyond the legal profession."[46] Civil law, like canon law, struggled with the resulting conflict: the crime of abortion had to be discouraged, but the earlier in the pregnancy, the less severe the crime. In the case of the Desideri maidservant Maria da Brescia, capital punishment was an option because her creatura was considered fully developed and viable, and she was suspected of neonaticide.

While often focused on points of doctrine, jurists could not separate abortion's abstract meanings from the lived experiences of gender and social status. Sometimes social norms and practices coincided and collaborated with legal doctrines; other times custom challenged and resisted the application of precept. In the following two sections, I explore some of the ways in which legal doctrine on abortion both ran up against and incorporated social facts; how it struggled with evidentiary standards; and how, in turn, individuals on trial made creative use of gender and body assumptions to exculpate themselves from wrongdoing. In doing so, ordinary people contributed, albeit unwittingly, to the formation of legal discourse on abortion.

Mitigating Circumstances

Amid academic discussions of animation and formation and whether to punish abortion as homicide, jurists often addressed the question of who procured abortion and why. Their answers identified women as the primary agents of the crime and acknowledged the gender, age, and social pressures that often motivated the practice. Unsurprisingly, almost all legal explanations linked the words "women," "honor," "shame," and "scandal." For example, in his published collection of decisions drawn from the Royal Court of Naples, the protonotary Vincenzo de Franchis titled his discussion of abortion "Whether a woman who procures abortion ought to be punished with the death penalty."[47] Similarly, the Florentine Cospi discussed the question "Which women are suspected of abortion?"[48] Answers spoke of status and life stage. Abortion was, according to De Luca, a practice of young, unmarried women (*zitelle* or *donniciole*), but widows and married women pregnant from adultery were also among the usual suspects. All these women had motives in common. According to Farinacci, abortion was a means of "concealing disgrace" and preserving honor and reputation.[49] Cospi echoed that women procured abortions to "escape the disgrace of their shamelessness."[50] For De Luca, abortion was committed by "those women who are dishonest to hide their dishonesty, and to continue to remain in the opinions of others as honest, because they are afraid of their family, or for their own reputation."[51] In printed works of jurisprudence, the gendering of abortion and its motivations often were clear and uncontroversial.

Unlike the moralists and religious writers examined in the previous chapter, who wrote to mold popular conscience and behavior, jurists addressed a professional audience, usually in Latin, and generally avoided inflammatory language. Rather than scolding hypothetical unmarried, adulterous, or widowed women for their debauchery, jurists often displayed a marked paternalism. The law and its officers accepted gender, age, and the need to preserve honor and avoid disgrace as legitimate factors that ought to diminish penalties for this crime. First, because of their inherent weakness, the law regarded women to have diminished responsibility in many legal and criminal matters.[52] Cardinal Boncompagni invoked this concept of fragilitas sexus in his letter where he sought to persuade the governor of Bologna to soften the penalties against Maria da Brescia. Second, jurists recognized youth and social vulnerability as mitigating factors. For example, they agreed that a "young girl" who had an abortion to conceal sexual relations and to avoid infamy and the wrath of her family merited rather milder penalties (*poena extraordinaria*) and left these to the judges' discretion. In most jurisdictions, the legal category of "minor" included women under the age of twenty-five.

Legal commentators were well aware that in the matter of seeking an abortion, young women might be subject to others in positions of power and authority. In print, rather than signaling the man responsible for the pregnancy, jurists usually blamed a young woman's mother, who likely convinced her daughter that abortion was the only way to avoid disgrace and hardship. According to Tesauro, the "impious mother" should be held responsible "if she allowed her daughter to be so unchaste that she could so easily be committed to the embrace of a man." Tesauro counseled, however, that the hypothetical mother or other matron responsible for a young woman should try to conceal the pregnancy and after delivery abandon the illegitimate child at an foundling hospital.[53] Recommending a similar solution, De Luca reported that in big cities women could easily bring their newborns to an orphanage. Yet he worried that in smaller places without these institutions, women might abandon their newborns in the streets or squares, where, he lamented, if no one took them in, the infants could die from exposure.[54]

Jurists were, on the other hand, glaringly silent regarding men's roles in procuring abortions. This omission did not imply that writers assumed men's innocence; rather it reflects broad misogyny and patriarchal privilege enacted in legal institutions and in print. In actual criminal investigations, however, the law did confront varying degrees of men's participation in and responsibility for abortions. Judges heard that it was often men who desired, arranged for, or administered abortions. But they also knew that men were responsible for abortions in less direct, more insidious ways. Men also caused abortions by putting women into situations where they had to decide between trying to terminate an unwanted pregnancy and carrying and giving birth to a child in the face of social, economic, and even mortal dangers. Unsurprisingly, women investigated for procuring abortion or committing neonaticide made these arguments. In doing so, they drew on and adapted discourses of fragilitas sexus, of female weakness, vulnerability, and victimhood, to shift blame to their impregnators. A common narrative was to explain non-marital pregnancy as the product of violent rape or of a sexual relationship where the man reneged on a promise of financial support or marriage. In these framings, pregnancy and its termination came not from reckless abandon or misjudgment on the part of women but rather the abuse and duplicity of men. Three cases investigated by the criminal tribunals of Rome and Bologna reveal this defense in action and illuminate the social realities that underpinned its legitimacy.

In 1602, Mennoca Liberatori, from the small town of Filettino (about seventy kilometers east of Rome), tried to abort the product of a violent, adulterous rape.[55] Mennoca was married, but her husband, Antonio, had been away for six years fighting in the company of the nobleman Orazio Caetani. At the time of the trial, no one knew whether Antonio was alive or dead. Mennoca lived with her young son and a kinswoman named Lucretia and her daughter. According to Mennoca, one night in January when her companion was away, Don Cinthio d'Andrea Palocho forced open her tightly locked door and entered her bedroom. Startled awake by his cold hand over her mouth, she cried, "Help me, Our Lady." To quiet her, Cinthio allegedly said, "Have no fear, it is me." Cinthio was related to Mennoca through marriage, but perhaps his statement "it is me" also implied a closer intimacy. He got into her bed, kissed, touched, and disrobed her, and said he wanted to do with her what husbands do with their wives. "I said that I did not want to, and resisted him, but, in the end, I being naked and him having more strength than me, he jumped on top of me and knew me carnally."[56]

Mennoca's description of their sexual encounter fit the legal requirements of rape of a married woman. In cases of defloration, women and their families seeking redress from the deflowerer had to prove nonconsent and resistance, which was evidenced by screams, torn clothing, bruises, wounds on the body, and bleeding. This was also required in cases of adulterous rape—minus the bleeding—where the woman had to clear herself of any willingness or acquiescence. Mennoca may have described what transpired, but she also knew what she had to tell the court. She said this was the only time she had had sex with Cinthio, explicitly stating that she was not engaging in a sexual relationship with her rapist, and insisted that she had not had sex with anyone else, a statement that was necessary to establish her sexual reputation. Her testimony reflects the formal and professional culture of the law and codes of sexual morality as much as it might reflect what she actually suffered that night with Cinthio.[57]

While Mennoca described the sex as forced and nonconsensual, some elements of her language were ambivalent. Several times in her testimony she described the sex as a sin and a misdeed that *she* committed: "this sin, by which I mean that I find myself pregnant since January"; "I have committed a misdeed with a man other than my husband"; "I have committed this misdeed only one time with don Cinthio"; "I find myself pregnant from this sin which I committed with don Cinthio"; "my husband Antonio was not in these lands at the time that I committed this sin with don Cinthio."[58] Mennoca's penitential and active rather than passive language gives the impression she also thought herself an agent in this wrongdoing. She articulated a conception of sex where nonconsent and force did not necessarily exculpate a woman from responsibility—the sin lay as much in the act as in its intention. However, remorse could also be strategic and may have been intended to move the judge to sympathy. Both sincerely and tactically, Mennoca described herself as a victim but also as a penitent sinner.

Mennoca's shame turned to fear as she discovered she was pregnant. Fear turned to action as she tried to have an abortion. She knew what to do and may have even been preparing for such an eventuality. Mennoca acquired the herb colocynth and a purgative beverage (of undisclosed ingredients), though she did not say from whom. The reason for the attempted abortion was obvious: it would conceal the sinful sex, and she and her family would avoid shame and stigmatization. Mennoca, however, also feared violence: she told the judge she feared her brothers might beat or kill her in vengeance for the disgrace her adulterous pregnancy would bring to their family. While it was sinful, criminal, and potentially dangerous, Mennoca decided abortion was a necessary course of action. She allegedly told her sister-in-law, "Oh for the love of God, I want to recover as best as I can, I want to eat a *melo scricto* [local idiom for colocynth] in the hope that it will make my belly go away."[59] But this did not happen. She consumed the purgative for a few days but then decided to stop. She did not explain why she abandoned the plan, and the judge did not ask. As her belly grew, her neighbors began to talk, and her pregnancy became public. Mennoca took refuge with a sympathetic kinsman for fear her brothers would kill her in her own home.[60] The commotion caught the attention of the vicar, who imprisoned her and began the investigation. At the beginning of the trial, Mennoca's father, Christophoro, came to court to officially state Mennoca's rape and pregnancy was an affront to his and his family's honor, for which he demanded justice in the form of the rapist's punishment. He also disavowed his daughter: "My Lord, I come [to court] because I understand that Your Lordship has imprisoned my daughter . . ., who, I understand, is pregnant, and because this pertains to my reputation and to the honor of my house, I have come to launch a lawsuit against my daughter and against the person who has done this wrong and dishonor to me, as well as against anyone who aided or showed favor. . . . I demand that [the court] proceed with the full rigor of justice."[61] Christophoro's public condemnation of both his daughter and her rapist / impregnator, and anyone else who aided and abetted them, was an attempt to recoup his and his family's damaged honor. It seems he either assumed Mennoca was somehow complicit in the illicit sexuality, or he did not care either way and was willing to sacrifice her to protect his own and his family's honor.

Had Mennoca gone through with the abortion, the events of that fateful night may never have come to light. However, something prompted her to stop taking the colocynth. Perhaps she was afraid of the physical dangers of abortion. Or perhaps, reflecting on the advice of familiars or even a confessor, she decided that terminating the creatura in her womb was a sin she could not live with. Or maybe she tried more times than she admitted, it simply did not work, and, in her retelling, she transformed inefficacy or fear into a moral decision to stop.[62] Mennoca did not say, the judge did not ask, and we cannot know.

The court tried to find her impregnator, but Cinthio had escaped in the night to the Kingdom of Naples, an act implying guilt. He clearly thought he would be punished for his behavior. Cinthio's misconduct may have provided him with short-term satisfaction, but it turned the lives of two families upside down. The consequences were grave for him as well—he was officially banished from Filettino and would have to piece together a life away from family and friends, unless of course he and his family found a way to compensate Mennoca's father and brothers and restore their honor. While the court tried to locate him, Mennoca, seven months pregnant, faced the wrath of her dishonored family, communal stigmatization, and potentially punitive action by the court, although there is no indication in the trial records that that was how the judge was leaning. Unfortunately, we do not know how this case ended. In her testimonies, Mennoca presented herself as vulnerable and susceptible to multiple forms of violence: physical, emotional, and now, facing pregnancy alone and the birth of an illegitimate child, social and economic. What would happen to her should her husband return from war? Would she keep the illegitimate child or abandon it at an orphanage? Would her disgraced family support her? Her attempted abortion, she told the judge, was sinful and wrong, and she had therefore abandoned that plan. But it was also completely understandable given the stakes. The real malefactor, she made clear, was don Cinthio.

A 1586 case investigated by the Criminal Tribunal of Bologna reveals another example of highly gendered vulnerability, this time economic in nature, used to explain a non-marital pregnancy that ended in a late miscarriage or stillbirth. The accused was Aorelia di Battista, a widow from the Apennine town of Camugnano (about fifty-four kilometers southwest of Bologna). Aorelia was suspected of neonaticide or abortion—the charges were not specific as it could not be determined whether the creatura died inside or outside her womb. Aorelia denied any foul play and vehemently argued that she had delivered a dead creatura, which she buried under a chestnut tree.[63] Forensic examination of the exhumed creatura revealed it to be fully formed and "perfect" in all its parts, but witnesses could neither confirm nor deny whether it was born dead.[64] With the cause of death unclear, Aorelia's reputation was the best evidence available. The context surrounding her pregnancy might make the claim of an abortion procured later in pregnancy or of neonaticide more or less plausible.

Aorelia was forthcoming. The dead creatura was the product of her sexual relationship with Pietro di Lazzaro, an unmarried agricultural laborer from Cavaliera (about fifteen kilometers south of Bologna). In Aorelia's version, Pietro had propositioned her many times, but she only yielded to his advances after he began helping her support her five children from her deceased husband. According to Aorelia, Pietro promised to help her raise the children; he gave her money and food and, according to one witness, may have proposed marriage. Their public relationship lasted over two years. Pietro ate and drank at her house, slept over, and acted "as if he was my husband." Aorelia emphasized the public nature of their relationship to imply she had nothing to hide and that the community did not object. While the evolution of their relationship cannot be known in greater detail, in her retelling, Aorelia portrayed it as both affective and self-interested. She told the judge several times she surrendered to Pietro's advances because she was poor: "Seeing as I am poor and that I cannot sustain my aforesaid family . . . he helped me and did what he could to help raise my children."[65] Trading sex for help raising her children was, in Aorelia's calculus, moral and responsible behavior. At the same time, she knew it was also a gamble. About one year earlier, she had been pregnant with Pietro's child; when she gave birth, Pietro demanded the child be given to the Ospedale degli Innocenti.[66] The couple continued their relationship, but when she became pregnant again, Pietro abandoned her. Aorelia then found herself more vulnerable than before.

When he was questioned, Pietro unsurprisingly gave a radically different account of their relationship. He told the judge that Aorelia was a prostitute whom he paid for sex: "I came and went, both day and night, from the said Aorelia's house, as I wanted and as it pleased me, and I slept there, and I screwed her at my convenience, and I gave her money, when I had it, and I screwed her like the whore that she is, as did other [men]. I cannot say who else screwed her, but I heard it said publicly that this woman is screwed by diverse people."[67] To exculpate himself from responsibility, Pietro labeled Aorelia a whore, exploiting typical stigmatizing assumptions about sexual commerce with unmarried women. Furthermore, saying that Aorelia had sex with many men meant that her impregnator could be any one of them. Pietro's language discounted a more intimate relationship akin to stable concubinage. He also denied getting her pregnant or sending a baby to the orphanage. Aorelia's pregnancy was her problem. Although no other witnesses called Aorelia a prostitute, neither did they intimate that Pietro owed her anything.

Aorelia's case offers an example of how non-marital sex might have been negotiated between desire, promise, and economic need but also clearly shows this was a dangerous gamble for women. Pregnant by a man who may have reneged on a promise to support her and her children, this widow and mother of five faced the prospect of another shaming, energy- and resource-draining pregnancy, and another mouth to feed, or perhaps another trip to the orphanage in Florence. Rather than shying away from it, Aorelia linked her pregnancy to her poverty. A hungry brood of children justified sinful sex; temporary economic security and potentially affective attachment resulted in non-marital pregnancy, which ultimately brought the relationship to an end. When Aorelia delivered a dead creatura, onlookers assumed foul play; to the judge who investigated her case, the alleged miscarriage or stillbirth appeared to have been a convenient end to a stressful relationship. The court had Aorelia tortured to see if her story would change, but she steadfastly maintained her innocence.[68]

Pregnancy was also not an uncommon result of sex with a false promise of marriage, as Lucia Pivinelli, a woman in her early twenties from the small commune of Montagu just outside Bologna, learned in 1610. Like Aorelia, she was impregnated and abandoned by a man who made promises. Knowing that she was pregnant, she concealed it from her neighbors and planned to give birth in Bologna and to pass the child to the Ospedale dei Bastardini. Unexpectedly, at about seven months she delivered a stillborn fetus. Like Aorelia's, Lucia's stillbirth was investigated by the criminal tribunal.

Lucia explained she was deflowered and impregnated by Sabatino Masotti, who, like Pietro di Lazzaro, was a roaming laborer. A few months earlier, Sabatino spied Lucia, identified her as vulnerable, and took advantage of her. Lucia lived with her sister and did not have male protectors or providers. Sabatino pestered her for sex and promised money and even marriage: "You are poor, I will take care of you or take you as my wife," he allegedly said. He would come to her house and molest her every other night. She resisted until she surrendered: "Being poor and hoping he would give me something, I consented," she explained to the judge. Lucia described the sexual intercourse that followed as fitting the requirements of defloration: it was painful and she bled. More frequent sex followed the first time; afterward, Sabatino sometimes gave her a gift or money.[69] A few months later, she thought she might be pregnant and told Sabatino. As their relationship cooled, she accused him of reneging on his promise to take care of her. Later, he broke off communication entirely, leaving her to deal with the pregnancy alone.

Sabatino turned up one and a half months after the stillbirth and was arrested and brought to the Torrone prison in Bologna, where Lucia was also being held. When asked about his relationship with Lucia, Sabatino claimed to have talked with her only once in church. The officials then read him portions of Lucia's testimony about having sex and getting pregnant, but Sabatino denied it all and accused Lucia of framing him for her own misdeeds. In a face-to-face confrontation before the judge, Sabatino called Lucia a liar. She agreed to confirm under torture her testimony about his mistreatment of her and did so steadfastly.

Mennoca, Aorelia, and Lucia blamed men for the criminal and potentially life-threatening situations they faced. All three women tried to shift responsibility away from their alleged wrongdoings and toward the injustices committed against them that led to the pregnancies and dead fetuses the criminal tribunals were investigating. Although absent from jurisprudential analysis, it was men like Cinthio, Pietro, Sabatino, and many others who lay behind abortions, stillbirths, and neonaticides. With her husband away at war, Mennoca was prey to the desire and overwhelmed by the physical force of Cinthio. Pregnant against her will, she contemplated and attempted but ultimately abandoned abortion as the solution to her woes. A poor widow struggling to raise five children, Aorelia was tempted by a promise of economic security for herself and her children into a non-marital relationship that resulted in pregnancy and ended with a dead fetus. Lucia was younger than Mennoca and Aorelia and more inexperienced when it came to men. A poor woman without protectors and providers, she was coerced into a sexual relationship with a man promising security and marriage. Like the judge, we cannot know whether Aorelia and Lucia suffered late miscarriages as they claimed or whether they procured abortions or committed neonaticide as some suspected. It is possible that they did not know how to interpret their terminated pregnancies themselves. Like Mennoca, they too would face social stigma and potential punishment.

Trial records such as these bring into sharp relief facets of gender injustices that are completely effaced in jurisprudential literature. Mennoca, Aorelia, and Lucia did not fit the stereotypical image of sexually wanton and dishonest young women and widows who procured abortion to maintain honor. Rather, these women portrayed themselves as prudent and deliberate; their respective judges encountered them as vulnerable, targeted, and self-described victims of men's abuse of power. These representations may have accurately reflected the way these women perceived themselves and felt about their situations, but they were also fashioned with hopes of eliciting sympathy from their judges. For Mennoca, admitting to procuring abortion was partly utilitarian, as it shifted culpability onto the man responsible for the pregnancy— "Look what he drove me to." This strategy could only work for her because she did not actually terminate her pregnancy and because her brothers threatened her with violence for the dishonor she brought them. While Aorelia and Lucia did not admit to procuring abortion or committing neonaticide, they did link their dead fetuses to Pietro's and Sabatino's immorality and exploitation—these men caused their pregnancies and hardships and therefore were also, in an essential way, responsible for the stillbirths. Although they did not articulate it explicitly, it is hard not to interpret their testimonies as implying that the root cause of the contemplated abortion and the miscarriages suffered, as well as the troubles they now faced, was the malice of men and the cruel circumstances they took advantage of and exacerbated.

The law recognized women as the weaker sex, and expected women on trial to present themselves accordingly. Women knew they had to be victims to elicit mercy and protection from paternalistic authorities: to be absolved or forgiven, these women could not be agents. While

Mennoca, Aorelia, and Lucia likely never read the works of jurists, they knew to play up the fragilitas sexus assigned them by the law. In doing so, they reproduced and made creative use of misogynistic gender assumptions to mollify an intimidating and asymmetrically powered institution.[70] Judges used this principle to mitigate their criminal responsibility. Regardless of what jurists failed to say in print, judges knew that men were responsible for unwanted pregnancies and often for abortions. Judges sometimes sympathized with women in these situations, but dispensing discretionary mercy, a quintessential feature of early modern justice, also reinforced their own power and fortified gender and social norms.

Bodies of Crime

For a mix of reasons, abortion was difficult to prosecute. Besides the potential social costs of scandal and even violence, from a purely legal perspective, the acquisition and interpretation of evidence about such an intimate crime posed major obstacles. The courts recognized and sought several kinds of evidence. Reports of local knowledge about both specific events and personal reputations were, although circumstantial, central to trials. Judges listened carefully to accounts of gossip and rumors regarding an illicit sexual relationship, pregnancy and its termination. *Fama,* a person's publicly acknowledged reputation for bad behavior, spurred courts to investigate, might justify the use of torture, and contributed to conviction. Nevertheless, for cases of alleged abortion and neonaticide, where a death sentence might follow, the court needed less fickle forms of evidence.[71] In such prosecutions, for a capital sentence, the law required clear demonstration that the fetus was fully formed and viable and that the abortion was committed knowingly and intentionally (*scienter, scientemente, studiosamente*) and with, as we might say, "malice aforethought" (*con sceleratezza, con dolo*).[72] This level of certainty best rested on a confession. Since even with torture these were rare, judges depended on evidence drawn from the body.

Judges primarily relied on the two main "bodies of crime": that of the accused woman and the product of her womb. These were both the material substances of the alleged crime and its primary witnesses. A body, when studied by experts, could have objective, evidentiary value.

The mouth might lie, but the corpus delicti, laid bare, could betray its possessor and confess its past. While all bodies challenged interpretation, the female body and its products, as we saw in Chapter 1, were deemed notoriously enigmatic. Engrained in law, the intrinsic ambiguities of women's bodies shaped judicial practice. Jurists assumed that both women and men exploited these ambiguities to fabricate illness narratives and procure abortions, and if caught, to exculpate themselves in court from intentional wrongdoing. Similar narratives of ambiguity were used in cases of miscarriage caused by assault. Although jurists lacked good answers for how to bypass these difficulties and to test intentionality, they did try. Works of criminal jurisprudence and trial records document the standards of bodily evidence for procured abortion and miscarriage caused by assault, and show how judges used them.

Legal discussions on abortion and its investigation in tribunals reflect the increasing importance placed on forensic medicine (medical knowledge and practitioners at the service of justice) and contributed substantially to its development. Judges relied on medical practitioners as expert witnesses in cases ranging widely from physical and sexual violence (including homicide, poisoning, and sodomy), to mental illness and spiritual offenses (such as witchcraft and demonic possession), to establishing sainthood.[73] In a context of necessary skepticism, expert testimony was regarded as a particularly high form of truth telling. It was their duty to put unpartisan words and objective narrative to the evidence of the body.

Although most forensic medical experts were men, in abortion cases, midwives with years of specialized experience were the preferred authorities. Despite women's losses to professionalization, Italian midwives remained instrumental agents in the legal system well into the modern period. For reasons of propriety and perhaps for consequent lack of experience, male physicians and surgeons were infrequently called on to testify in cases involving the physical examination of women's genitals and reproductive organs. As well for a fetus or a stillborn infant, judges first turned to midwives. The Roman midwife Angela Ferranta testified that she often delivered women of dead fetuses in various stages of development; furthermore, clients paid her—generally five giulii—to come to their houses to determine whether a uterine expulsion was a miscarried fetus, if it was male or female and how many months developed, or whether it was actually some other object of the womb.[74] This expertise made midwives indispensable to the criminal justice system and crucial to the development of forensic medicine.

While midwives and male medical practitioners were the experts, many judges were trained to evaluate their forensic testimonies. Early modern jurists increasingly possessed a sophisticated knowledge of medicine, and some authors incorporated a thorough discussion of the slippery signs of pregnancy and the ambiguities of the female body in their published work. These discussions aimed to equip judges with relevant medical information and to instruct them on the pitfalls of hasty assumptions and unwarranted evidentiary interpretations. Commentaries cited both ancient and modern medical authorities, but by the late seventeenth century, jurists relied mostly on Paolo Zacchia's influential compendium *Medico-Legal Questions*. This text included authoritative discussion on the signs of pregnancy, fetal development, and the bodily signs of abortion, childbirth, and neonaticide. Still, jurists knew and accepted that the mysteries of the female body would often prevent the certain discovery of whether a knowing and intentional abortion had occurred. This uncertainty allowed judges further lenience to issue discretionary clemency to women and men on trial.

In abortion trials, according to jurists, the body of the aborted fetus or dead infant provided primary evidence of whether a crime had been committed and how grave it was. The status of perfectly formed and viable could only be determined when the fetal body was available for examination. Yet an aborted fetus was often easy to hide, especially in the countryside.[75] Younger fetuses were quickly disposed of. Testifying in Rome in 1634, midwife Angela Ferranta reported that "we throw aborted fetuses that do not have a soul in the latrine, and I do not baptize them because they are not alive."[76] If a miscarried fetus was further along, a woman or her familiars might call a gravedigger to collect and bury the body, though not in consecrated ground.[77]

Lacking a fetal body, judges relied on witnesses for firsthand observation of pregnancy and delivery. Family and neighbors routinely monitored women's bodies. In court, witnesses often linked a woman's swelling and diminishing belly to a non-marital sexual relationship and to abortion or a secret delivery and neonaticide. In 1574, several

women from the commune of Capugnano, southwest of Bologna, told
the court that Pellegrina d'Angelo had been pregnant from adultery
and must have either aborted a creatura or killed it after birth. They
had watched Pellegrina's belly grow over several months, but then one
day it suddenly subsided. One neighbor, Sandra de Lancialini, told the
judge: "I said to [Pellegrina], grabbing her belly: 'what did you do to
your belly which was so big and now is gone?'"[78] Sandra's tone was
mocking and her touch threatening. Pellegrina was married, but her
husband had been away working for some time. Neighbors described
her as a dishonorable woman, but they refused to speculate on who impregnated her or what she had done with the creatura. In her defense,
Pellegrina denied adultery and pregnancy, explaining that her swollen
belly was a symptom of a womb-related illness that she regularly suffered in the late summer and early fall.[79] Without compelling evidence,
the judge dropped Pellegrina's case.

Jurists were preoccupied with the ambiguity of the signs of sexual
intercourse, pregnancy, and delivery, which had as much bearing in
cases of abortion, miscarriage caused by assault, and neonaticide as
they did in cases of rape and defloration, impotence, and civil cases
where the flow of inheritance depended on the generation and delivery
of living offspring. The ambiguities of the female body as they pertained to medicine were discussed in Chapter 1. Here we shall revisit
them in the discussions of jurists and examine how they were encountered by judges in actual cases and how they shaped criminal
investigations.

Following medical authorities, jurists expounded on the signs of
pregnancy and childbirth only to cast doubt on their accuracy as indicators. With the Roman Zacchia and their own cumulative courtroom
experience as their guides, the Florentine jurists Antonio Maria Cospi
and Marc'Antonio Savelli taught that a growing belly could be as much
a symptom of womb-related illness as a sign of pregnancy. They warned
that pathological retention of menstruation, forms of dropsy, and the
generation of molae and other "pieces of flesh" mimicked the signs of
pregnancy but were actually dangerous illnesses that required therapy.[80] The traces that recent delivery or abortion left on a woman's body
might be more pronounced. A woman who had been pregnant and
aborted or gave birth to a later-term fetus would have a saggy and

wrinkled belly. Lactation, one of the most potent signs of pregnancy, could start before delivery but was especially noticeable afterward. Finally, the conditions of a woman's reproductive organs—swollen, stretched, and loose labia; a wide vagina, cervix, and uterus; and the disappearance or division of the *myrtoides caruncula,* "little pieces of flesh" inside the vagina and the walls of the uterus—were signs of recent delivery. When all these signs are combined and sufficiently pronounced, Zacchia wrote, "it is permissible to suspect that, although she bore it in her womb, such a woman has gotten rid of her fetus through abortion."[81]

Since Zacchia and his readers knew that alternative medical explanations might account for all these signs, what was the legal force of the words "permissible to suspect"? An important case from early seventeenth-century Rome, analyzed by Zacchia and cited by jurists well into the eighteenth century, demonstrated the need for caution and skepticism. Mattia de Bello, whose husband had been exiled from Rome for a crime, earned the distrust, even the "intense hatred," of her neighbors, who denounced her to the authorities for adulterous pregnancy, attempting abortion, delivering in secret, and throwing the child in a latrine. According to Zacchia, Mattia's neighbors suspected first pregnancy, because her belly had swollen, and then childbirth, because it suddenly subsided. Some witnesses allegedly heard a baby's cries coming from Mattia's home. When the notary searched the house and the latrine carefully, he found no infant cadaver. What he did see was a blood-stained floor and some rags with pieces of coagulated blood. Denying the charges, Mattia explained that her swollen belly had been a symptom of severely retained menstruation; it deflated following a strong purge that expelled copious amounts of obstructed blood. Three midwives and a surgeon were brought in by the court to examine Mattia's body and its expulsions. They confirmed that Mattia's belly had recently and rapidly deflated, that her genitals were swollen, and that she was still emitting blood. Two midwives concluded that these signs indicated recent delivery, and therefore Mattia stood guilty of at least some charges—of adulterous pregnancy and childbirth, if not of abortion or neonaticide. The third midwife and the surgeon, however, read these signs as more consistent with a lengthy and stubborn bout of menstrual retention and its recent release.

Zacchia was asked to review the evidence and resolve the deadlock between the medical witnesses. He did not examine Mattia himself but rather formed his opinion from the witnesses' reports. He concluded that the available evidence did not indicate that Mattia had been pregnant or had an abortion but rather was consistent with her own diagnosis of a severe and pathological menstrual retention. In making his judgment, Zacchia relied on the more detailed reports given by the midwife and surgeon who judged Mattia innocent. He identified and expounded on several important points that led him to concur. First, Mattia's swollen labia was only slightly swollen; had she given birth, her entire pudenda would have been greatly swollen. Related to this, the midwife and surgeon who judged her innocent said that they detected myrtoides caruncula, small fleshy protuberances, inside her vagina and womb, which, had she given birth, would have been imperceptible because the whole area would have been swollen. Second, the blood that stained rags and the floor of her home and that Mattia was still emitting was not the mixture of blood, urine, and milk that postparturient women normally expel but rather was menstrual blood, "pure blood," containing blood clots. The former blood mixture usually flows abundantly, "like that of a sacrificial animal," he wrote; the latter flows heavily, moderately or thinly, depending on the woman's health. Third, Mattia's belly had deflated quickly, which was an effect of a strong and violent menstrual purge; the belly of a postparturient woman subsides slowly and regularly as the uterus contracts back to its prepregnant size. Fourth, Mattia was energetic and healthy, not weak and bedridden as women naturally are following childbirth. Fifth, no one mentioned whether she was lactating—an ambiguous sign but still a crucial one that could have been easily observed. Lastly, Zacchia interpreted Mattia's behavior as a sign of her character: had she been pregnant and either aborted or delivered and killed her newborn, she would surely have cleaned up the blood on the floor of her home and washed the stained rags. The fact that she left them there, Zacchia thought, indicated that "she was not afraid for herself, knowing that her conscience was clear, and she certainly knew there was no foundation for any suspicion of her."[82]

In his analysis of the evidence, Zacchia transformed Mattia into an object of medico-legal knowledge and emphasized a hierarchical regime of truth that privileged elite medical practitioners like himself over lower-order practitioners, like midwives. In its published form, Zacchia's consilium was intended to impress upon his readers the danger of putting faith in the testimonies of lower-status medical practitioners who focus on "trivial and equivocal signs and conclusions."[83] Their opinions could lead a judge astray. Zacchia's learning allowed him to understand the precise meaning of specific phenomena and identify other things that had been missed but were crucial to understanding what Mattia's body had experienced. To the untrained eye and the ignorant mind, Mattia's body might suggest pregnancy and crime, but what it really indicated was illness and cure.

Jurists and judges who read Mattia's case would have recognized Zacchia's aim to diminish lower-status healers' authority in legal matters and to increase that of university-educated physicians. However, they primarily cited Zacchia's discussion of Mattia's ordeal as an example of the difficulties they might face when investigating similar cases that rested on the ambiguities of women's bodies. Cospi and Savelli treated these evidentiary problems at length. They warned judges that, for example, not all women who had been pregnant and given birth had a drooping and wrinkled belly. Zacchia had taught that "there are some women, particularly among the nobility, who avoid this kind of unpleasantness or deformity by artifice and medicines," using straps and waistbands to hold up the belly during pregnancy and apparently preventing it from stretching too much. Cosmetics could also conceal what a woman's body had gone through. Women applied creams, ointments, and plasters after delivery to reduce stretch marks and tighten the belly. Because cosmetics could conceal the body's experiences, it was "not safe to declare that these women have not given birth from the smoothness of their bellies, since they could have given birth despite that." The opposite was also true: the wrinkles commonly associated with a postpartum belly also occurred in virgins and even in men who had suffered from dropsy and at one time had a large and distended belly and then had it subside. Judges were "to inquire beforehand as to whether the woman has experienced one of these illnesses in the past so that we are not misled by this sign," warned Zacchia.[84] The appearance of a woman's reproductive organs could also deceive because there was no "normal." Some women had stretched, flaccid, and loose genitals and a wide and loose womb by nature. Women could also have an unusually narrow and tight womb and retain their "vaginal integrity" even during labor. Women also used cosmetic products to tighten their genitals after sexual intercourse and childbirth. Some women would be judged "incorrupt [i.e., virgins] because of the narrowness and tight form of their uteruses . . ., although they have been corrupted and have given birth"; "other women will be judged corrupted and accused of abortion or secret delivery, even though they are virgins and innocent of these charges."[85] Even lactation was ambiguous, because, as Cospi explained, "when menstrual blood is not expelled from the uterus, the superfluity is transmitted to the breasts, just as we see in pregnant women."[86] A virgin or a chaste nun could have milk come out of her breasts due to irregular purgation, and even men were prone to lactate from time to time.[87] Zacchia warned that the ambiguities of the female body made it so that "even being virgins [women may] appear corrupted."[88] Judges were to accept that there was little certainty.

The fact that both Mattia and Pellegrina d'Angelo were suspected of having extramarital affairs as married women living apart from their husbands shaped their neighbors' and the court's perceptions of their bodies and the expectations of what had taken place within them. And yet these perceptions remained suspicions, powerful to be sure, but not certain or unimpeachable fact. In terms of the prevailing standards of evidence, the physical signs of pregnancy and delivery were considered "fallacy," "conjecture," and "presumption" (*fallacio, coniectura,* and *presumptio*).[89] The degree of uncertainty and doubt encountered in cases of alleged abortion was often great, and judges struggled to find secure and unambiguous physical evidence (*indicia indubitata*) on the body of crime. The quantity and combination of observable signs in relation to the confidence interpreters had in their meanings might incline a judge to presume a woman had been pregnant and had an abortion, but jurists urged skepticism and caution. Cospi insisted judges learn about the ambiguities of women's bodies because "their passions might be moved to believe that a woman might [have been] pregnant," and they might torture her and pass a harsh sentence, only to later discover that she had been sick rather than pregnant and was actually innocent.[90] Zacchia's analysis of Mattia's case and Cospi's and Savelli's commentary on it make clear that even in cases involving women with dubious sexual reputations, accusations of hiding pregnancy, having abortions, or committing neonaticide could be unfounded. These authorities urged caution and moderation.

Of course, if a fetus or the cadaver of a newborn was found, the accused woman had a harder time in court. But, here too, ambiguity loomed. Women could employ legitimate and well-used defenses to try to exonerate themselves. They could claim they had not known they were pregnant until they miscarried or delivered a stillborn child. The "ignorance defense" was common throughout early modern Europe.[91] Prospero Farinacci warned judges to expect a woman to claim she did not know she was pregnant until she felt "pain in the belly" and delivered a fetus into a latrine while performing "natural functions." Though jurists viewed the defense with suspicion, especially when coming from an unmarried woman, they had to contend with it because it was plausible, perhaps somewhat common, and difficult to disprove.[92]

Maria da Brescia, the young chambermaid with whom this chapter began, used this defense on the judge of the Criminal Tribunal of Bologna in 1578 to exculpate herself from charges of committing abortion or neonaticide. Maria admitted delivery—which she described as a stillbirth—but claimed she did not know she was pregnant until she saw the fetus slip out of her body. She told the judge that the night before the delivery she felt pain in her stomach but attributed it to digestive disturbance—some bad onions she had eaten earlier that caused what she interpreted to be painful gas. She went to bed hoping it would dissipate, but the next morning the pain was more intense. She felt the need to use the latrine, and as soon as she got out of bed, "I expelled that creatura on the floor, dead, it did not cry." Panicked, she picked it up and threw it in the latrine because she feared her brother would beat or kill her for the disgrace she brought to her family; no doubt, she also feared dismissal from the Desideri house. When pressed, Maria named her impregnator, a certain Pierino with whom she had had a sexual relationship before getting the job serving the noble family, but the court did not seem interested in this man. Perhaps the judge suspected or even knew a Desideri was responsible for the pregnancy. Nevertheless, Maria never swayed from her story that she delivered a dead creatura onto the floor of her bedroom and that it was a complete surprise. Her defense rested on the claim of bodily ignorance and inexperience of pregnancy: "I didn't know I was pregnant—I had never been pregnant and I did not know what I had in my body."[93] Apparently Maria had not been noticeably ill or unable to do her household chores, and the rest of the household staff who testified had also failed to notice her pregnancy or, perhaps fearing a charge of complicity, refused to acknowledge it to the judge.

Another important and difficult element for a judge to investigate was the claim that the fetus was born dead. Jurists, of course, knew and took into account the frequency with which women miscarried, especially in the first months of pregnancy. According to the jurist and judge from Bari Francesco Vivio, the fetus "hangs like a fruit on a tree" and any jostle or rumbling, as a cough, a bout of gas, or even a sneeze, could shake it loose.[94] Paolo Zacchia conceded that "investigating the signs of an early [term] abortion seems to me to be a pointless endeavor since sometimes a miscarriage occurs so readily in the first months that women themselves experience it as a rather difficult purgation of the menses."[95] Later in pregnancy, strenuous labor, fatigue, stress, and violence were often identified as causes of terminated pregnancies. Aorelia di Battista claimed her 1586 stillbirth was caused by stretching to reach and straining to pull a heavy load of grain toward her the day before. A single mother of five, Aorelia could not take time off work just because she was pregnant. That night, after she pushed her house door closed and locked it, she felt her belly turn, and the creatura fell out of her body without any effort.[96] In a 1593 case of alleged father-daughter incest in the Venetian countryside, Mattia Stanghelin purported to miscarry from labor in the fields: bending and lifting reportedly caused the fetus to slip out "like a slice of ham."[97]

Judges were suspicious of such claims of ignorance of pregnancy, strain, accelerated delivery, miscarriage, and stillborn fetuses, yet even with the help of the most experienced midwives and physicians, they often could not distinguish between causes that brought pregnancy to an end and that resulted in a dead creatura. When available, the examination of fetuses and infant cadavers for signs of foul play was crucial. Judges and notaries often inspected cadavers themselves first before turning to midwives and sometimes physicians and surgeons for professional examination and interpretation.[98] Medical witnesses carefully examined the body and gave detailed and somewhat standardized reports regarding its physical state and level of development. They recorded its sex and size, the articulation of limbs, whether it had hair and nails, and other essential features. They also described any marks or bruises on the body and assessed its level of decomposition. The aim was to establish the developmental stage of the creatura, for the gravity of the crime could be measured only by reference to the body's maturity. Finally, these experts were asked to pronounce on the causes that led to its death and expulsion from a woman's womb.[99] While the general level of development could be somewhat easily determined, especially the closer the fetus was to what might have been considered full term, medical experts often struggled to determine the cause of death.

In Maria da Brescia's case, the court had two experienced midwives examine the fetus found in the latrine. Both agreed it was a fully developed male *putto*; however, the cause of death was uncertain. The midwife Lucrezia said: "Having to give my judgment on whether it was born dead or alive, I will say that this is dubious, but that I lean more on the side that it was born dead than otherwise." Her reason was simple: if this woman really wanted to kill a live newborn, she likely would have suffocated it immediately, so its crying would not alert the rest of the household. Suffocating it would have left marks on the body, which this fetus did not have.[100] The midwife Veronica agreed with her colleague's assessment and added the curious statement that, in her experience, women "even with help [i.e., with a midwife], make dead babies all the time, which we midwives, with our learning, give them breath, by various means, so that within an hour they return to life."[101] This last statement is intriguing and difficult to interpret but seems to suggest midwives tried to intervene on stillborn, or seemingly stillborn, babies in hopes of getting them to draw breath or appear to draw a breath (perhaps a premodern form of CPR?), so they might live long enough for emergency baptism. It seems Veronica's statement was meant to impress on the judge that midwives regularly confronted situations where it was unclear whether the putto had died in the womb or after its delivery. Like cause, the time and place of death could be ambiguous.

In Lucia Pivinelli's case, the court had two Bolognese midwives examine her body and assess the reports of witnesses in Montagu who saw and described the fetus. Virginia Vigorosi and Elisabetta Jacobi

both examined Lucia in a cell in the Torrone prison. They digitally examined her genitals and womb and determined she had recently delivered. They also reported Lucia told them during the exam that she had
not yet expelled the afterbirth—this would have been nine or ten days
postpartum—and could feel it throbbing in her uterus. The midwives
told the judge she ought to be given medicine to expel it immediately,
as it was decaying and would cause fevers and might lead to her
death.[102] Regarding the fetus, the midwives based their interpretation
on the reports given in Montagu. The fetus was described as female,
three-quarters of an arm long, with proportioned limbs, reasonably
long hair, nails, and toenails. Those who saw it noted it was wrapped
in Lucia's shirt and was warm, suggesting it had recently come out of
her body. They noted there were no marks or signs of violence or suffocation. The report also mentioned the umbilical cord had been sev-
ered but not tied or clamped. Based on these descriptions, the midwives thought the fetus was about seven or eight months developed, no
more because Lucia was not lactating.[103] Regarding causes of death,
the midwives stated newborns could die without violence or force by
simply having their umbilical cords left untied, which allowed their
breath to escape their bodies little by little, so they died within a few
hours. The midwives also added that when a fetus was born dead, it
came out of the mother's body cold and did not seem to have blemishes
or rashes but was white, like washed cloth. They also explained it was
more difficult and painful for a woman to deliver a dead fetus than a
live one, because it did not collaborate in the process and the woman
had to do it entirely by force. Although they did not explicitly say so,
the assumption was that, had Lucia delivered a dead fetus as she
claimed, it would have been very difficult, and she would likely have
needed help, which would probably have caught the attention of neighbors. Moreover, the fetus would have been described as cold rather
than warm. Lastly, that the umbilical cord was not tied raised suspicion Lucia had left it open to allow the newborn's "breath" to escape,
leading to its death.[104]

The judge arranged for Lucia to go to the Ospedale della Morte and
receive medical attention, and when she was out of harm's way and
deemed strong enough, he questioned her again about how her putto
came into the world, when, and why it had died. Lucia confirmed its

level of development and said that, by her count, she was in the seventh
month of pregnancy, so the fetus would have been more than six but
less than eight months developed, but she could not be more precise.
The judge read the midwives' testimonies to Lucia and insinuated she
had intentionally left the umbilical cord untied to kill the living newborn. Lucia's response was blunt and logical: Why would she have tied
its umbilical cord if it had been born dead?[105] Evidently, the judge
thought this a reasonable response and did not mention it again. Regarding its temperature, Lucia maintained it was cold to the touch,
"not ice-cold, but cold." The judge pressed her repeatedly to admit the
child was born alive and she had killed it, but Lucia was steadfast: "It
was not alive, my lord, and I will never be able to say why it was not, and
I cannot do anything about this, I cannot supersede the one who is the
master of the whole world: it pleased God that it was born dead, and I
don't know what to make of it."[106] She ended her testimony by restating
she had not hurt the creatura, that it had been dead when she delivered
it, and therefore "I do not think I deserve any punishment." "May God
pardon me all my sins, but may he never pardon me this one [because I
didn't do it]."[107]

    In the sixteenth and seventeenth centuries, forensic examination
was often unable to confirm whether a creatura died inside or outside a
woman's body and whether a woman had an abortion, miscarriage,
stillbirth, or committed neonaticide. Early modern jurists, medical
practitioners, and laypeople alike looked for observable traces of violence on the body, but the absence of these signs did not confirm innocence—as the midwives Virginia and Elisabetta said, the newborn's
"breath" could leak out of its untied umbilical cord. The contentious
"lung flotation test" (which assumed the lung of an infant born alive
and having drawn breath before dying would float due to its expansion,
whereas one from a fetus that had died in the womb would sink because it was compact and dense) does not appear to have been practiced
in Italy before the eighteenth century.[108] Without visible marks of violence, no certainty could be had. Women's claims of miscarriage and
stillbirth, therefore, had to be taken seriously. Even though judges assumed women like Maria and Lucia could take advantage of the quo-
tidian nature of miscarriage and stillbirth to obfuscate intentionally
procured abortion or neonaticide, there was no way of knowing with

certainty. Because it was often impossible to distinguish between miscarriage and intentionally procured abortion, stillbirth, and neonaticide, jurists agreed that a woman who claimed innocence, especially
under torture, as a general rule, should not be given the ordinary capital punishment; if there was substantial plausibility, judges could issue
a milder penalty according to the specifics of the case.[109]

The ambiguities surrounding maternal and fetal bodies of crime
also characterized criminal investigations into miscarriage caused by
assault. While criminal tribunals took all forms of *aborto* seriously, they
encountered cases of miscarriage by assault more frequently than cases
of procured abortion and neonaticide. Some women suffered terrible
violence and traumas during pregnancy, a time during which, contemporaries agreed, they were at their most vulnerable and ought to be
treated with care and sensitivity. While early modern Italians were accustomed to seeing varying degrees of gender-based violence in their
daily lives, everyone knew assaulting a pregnant woman was anathema,
and courts actively prosecuted violators of these norms, sometimes including abusive husbands.[110] Women, their husbands, and kin brought
lawsuits against individuals they deemed responsible for a miscarriage
and the ensuing health traumas women faced. Jurists categorized miscarriage caused by assault as a form of potentially fatal violence. The
termination of pregnancy and the death of the fetus were treated as a
grave loss, but generally not as a form of homicide unless the pregnant
woman died from the assault or complications of the miscarriage.[111]
The standard penalty for causing a pregnant woman to miscarry was
monetary compensation to the aggrieved and potential corporal punishment; should the woman die, her assailant could be exiled or potentially executed. Women turned to family, friends, and neighbors for
help and support, and to courts as a resource against their assailants,
whether they were strangers, enemies, family members, or husbands.

Cases of miscarriage caused by assault came with evidentiary ambiguities similar to cases of procured abortion and were as difficult to
investigate. Establishing whether a woman's body and the objects it expelled constituted evidence of crime was contentious. Defendants accused their accusers of fraud: they claimed that women tried to pass off
natural or spontaneous miscarriages as caused by assault and even alleged women faked miscarriage altogether. Judges also struggled to

determine intentionality. Those accused of causing a woman to miscarry might admit to violence but could claim they did not know the
woman they assaulted was pregnant because she was not showing; they
also argued that the violence they enacted was mild and could not have
caused miscarriage. Defendants, both women and men, mobilized discourses of ignorance and uncertainty against pregnant women: assailants claimed that women used the ambiguities of the female body to
frame them, in the same way women might exculpate themselves from
procured abortion.

In cases of miscarriage caused by assault early in pregnancy, defendants often pled ignorance. In 1608, Ginevra Rossi, a candy maker's
wife who helped run the family shop in Rome, suffered a miscarriage
allegedly caused by being forced by inspectors, who threatened her and
her husband, Guglielmo, with criminal charges for allegedly selling
fraudulent candy, to climb up and down stairs and move heavy boxes
under duress. Ginevra died of complications resulting from the miscarriage. To justify their rough treatment of Ginevra, the inspectors
claimed they did not know she was pregnant—the implication being
that had her pregnancy been obvious, they would not have treated her
so roughly.[112]

As in cases of procured abortion, jurists held the "ignorance defense" to be convenient and expected but also valid, and conceded that
determining culpability was very difficult. Farinacci and Savelli favored
lenience, especially if the assailant "unknowingly or inadvertently per-
secuted a pregnant woman," if the woman did not yet have a noticeable
belly, or if it was not public knowledge that she was pregnant. The burden of proof fell to accusers: women and their witnesses had to make
the case that she was visibly pregnant and her assailant should have
known not to assault or treat her improperly. The earlier she was in
pregnancy, however, the less the law required others to treat her with
care; her assailant could be charged for violence and injury, but not necessarily for terminating the life of an unborn.[113]

Defendants also claimed their accuser had not been pregnant or
had not suffered a miscarriage but was trying to pass off menstrual or
other blood and objects as a miscarriage.[114] In 1632 in Rome, the abusive Domenico Cocchi accused his wife Elena and her aunt Polisana of
faking miscarriage to get him in trouble. Although he admitted to

assaulting his wife, he claimed she could not have been pregnant because she was still nursing their young son, had recently had her period, and did not have a distended belly. He told the judge that her aunt Polisana had a reputation for helping women fake miscarriages to get their husbands to treat them better: she had recently given her friend "some mass of blood" to present to her husband to make him "think that his wife had aborted on account of some sort of harm [he had] done her . . . so that from then on [he] would not harass her, and [instead] treat her with affection." "All these suppositions are great lies that come from deceitful women," Domenico argued.[115] Such misogynistic tropes about women's bodies and women's dishonesty were culturally pervasive, and Domenico used them to good effect. Men on trial could use this discourse of deception to exculpate themselves because it was plausible. And indeed, the judge took Domenico's claims seriously, but could not send medical witnesses to inspect the miscarriage, which Elena, her familiars, and her midwife friend all claimed was an approximately three-months-developed male fetus, because it had been disposed of. While there is no way of knowing whether Elena suffered a miscarriage or feigned it, what is clear is that she was seeking justice against and protection from her very abusive husband. As bleak as it might sound, miscarriage could be a resource against domestic violence and grounds for a marital separation.[116]

Cases of miscarriage by assault later in a pregnancy were also contentious. Aside from determining whether the accused actually assaulted the pregnant woman, in these cases, the difficulty lay in making a causal connection between violence and terminated pregnancy, and jurists summarized medical opinions on how to assess this. A blow to the viscera, especially near the kidneys, was thought likely to cause a miscarriage; a blow to the head or upper body less so. If the pregnancy was further along, more than four or five months, it would take greater violence to cause the miscarriage because the unborn would be more robust and tightly fixed to its mother. Facilitating investigation, such a beating, it was thought, would leave marks on the woman's and the fetus's body, and likely cause a scene drawing witnesses. Closer to delivery, even a mild beating was thought sufficient to cause miscarriage because the fetus was more exposed to the impact of a blow. The time between an assault and miscarriage also needed close inquiry.

According to Copsi, if a miscarriage occurred two or three days after a beating, the assault was likely causal and the assailant responsible; beyond three days, causal likelihood diminished and the judge was to consider other explanations, such as illness or even intentionally procured abortion.[117]

Of course, things were less clear in practice. In 1603 Rome, Angela da Filettino denounced Venere da Bologna for assault and causing her to miscarry a six-months-developed fetus. Both women were self-described courtesans. Venere confessed to an altercation with Angela but vehemently denied hitting her obviously pregnant rival, to which witnesses gave mixed and conflicting testimony. Venere also rejected the possibility that the argument had somehow caused Angela's miscarriage, which occurred almost three weeks later. Venere argued that the miscarriage must have had another more proximate cause: Angela continued to have sex with "rough men" and this likely injured her growing fetus. Venere alleged she was being framed.[118] The court sent the midwife Chiara Tibaldi and physician Timoteo Camotio to tend to Angela, examine the miscarried fetus, determine when it had died in Angela's womb, and whether violence could have been the cause. The medical practitioners concluded that the fetus had been dead for about six to ten days before Angela expelled it. They felt it was conceivable that the assault Angela said she had suffered led to the death of her fetus approximately seven to ten days later. However, both practitioners were cautious when it came to stating that assault was *the* cause of its death. "I cannot judge whether Angela's fetus died because of the blows that she said she was given," midwife Chiara testified, "because [the miscarriage] could have been caused by her sexual encounters or from illnesses she might have. . . . For this reason, I cannot judge whether the fetus died because of the alleged beating, but perhaps the physician might tell you."[119] But Doctor Timoteo was also cautious and disinclined to speculate, giving a similarly elusive response. The experts recognized multiplicity of meaning and may have thought that certainty about the specific cause of Angela's miscarriage could not be had.

Evidence based on women's bodies and fetal cadavers was as contentious in cases of miscarriage caused by assault as it was in cases of procured abortion and neonaticide. As in the latter, judges's perceptions were influenced not only by the nature of the available evidence

but also by the reputation of the accuser and the accused and the circumstances that brought cases to court. Suspicion ran deep that
women used the ambiguities of their bodies to their advantage, and to
commit fraud. But judges also knew that their assailants, both men
and women, mobilized these same discourses to exculpate themselves
from charges of assault and causing miscarriage. The claims and coun-
terclaims of all the litigants, as well as the attempts of medical practitioners to discover whether bodies were truly bodies of crime, all contributed to the shaping of general and legal perceptions and conceptions
of women's bodies and abortion. In these cases, the same judges who
investigated cases of procured abortion and neonaticide confronted
brutal violence inflicted on women, including their experience of
trauma and death. These experiences no doubt shaped how judges
thought about and would investigate cases of procured abortion.

Punishment to Fit the Crime

How did criminal tribunals punish individuals who they decided were
guilty of procured abortion or of neonaticide, or who were responsible
for miscarriages caused by assault? Let's consider these types of *aborto*
separately, for the law conceptualized them differently.

As we have seen, the developmental stage of the fetus was supposed
to determine the penalty for its termination: the rule was that if the
fetus was considered animated, fully formed, and viable, the ordinary
penalty (*poena ordinaria*) was execution, as it was for homicide. However,
jurists also agreed that in practice there were too many evidentiary uncertainties and social imperatives making the ordinary penalty legally
unsound, morally severe, and socially unproductive. The registers of
the Bolognese Compagnia di Santa Maria della Morte, a lay confraternity whose brothers tended to individuals on the eve of their executions, indicate that between 1570 and 1700, no one was sentenced to
capital punishment for committing abortion or causing miscarriage by
assault; in comparison, at least ten individuals were executed for infanticide.[120] Luckily, Maria, Aorelia, Pellegrina, and Lucia's names do not
appear on the registry of individuals comforted before their execution.
It seems capital punishment would only be meted out should a case be
cut and dried and an individual confess to neonaticide. In most cases,

jurists thought extraordinary or lesser penalties (*poena extraordinaria*) issued at the judge's discretion (*ad arbitrium iudicis*) were more suitable for individuals they believed guilty of wrongdoing. The judge was to assign a sentence he thought appropriate to the "quality of the case," the evidence available, his opinions regarding the culpability and character of the suspects. He had the discretion to determine what justice meant in a particular situation.[121] This was even the case in trials for unambiguous infanticide. Cardinal De Luca wrote that, while infanticide is truly voluntary homicide and therefore capital punishment was justified, generally this crime was "committed by young women not because they have soul so perverse as to murder a creatura, but only to protect their honesty." When committed for this reason, "it can be said that it is a crime committed for the defense of one's own life . . . and the individual is excused from the ordinary penalty of life [i.e., capital punishment]."[122] De Luca was silent on men's participation in infanticide.

What then were the extraordinary and actual penalties individuals on trial might expect? Trials investigated by criminal tribunals can be problematic sources for discovering sentences. For the governor of Rome's criminal tribunal, sentences are generally not included in the trial dossier but in a separate series of documents, and unfortunately many, if not most, are lost, damaged, or in an unreadable condition. Aside from archival loss, difficulties also lie in the fact that official decisions were often not rendered. Judges dropped cases for myriad reasons at various stages of investigation. For instance, the Criminal Tribunal of Bologna, which sewed its sentences into investigation packages that are well preserved, appears not to have issued official decisions in the cases against Maria da Brescia in 1578 or Aorelia di Battista in 1583, suggesting they were likely absolved. On the front page of Pellegrina d'Angelo's trial dossier, next to her name, there is a marginal note simply stating "absolved."[123]

We do, however, have some sentences related in printed works that are suggestive and might allow for extrapolation. Antonino Tesauro reported in his *Decisions of the Sacred Senate of Piedmont* on a case he heard in December 1554, where an unnamed woman delivered a dead fetus into a latrine. Like Maria da Brescia, she maintained she did not know she was pregnant until the moment the fetus came out of her body. Tesauro reported his colleagues in the Senate thought she was lying and had intentionally committed a later-term abortion or neonaticide. She was tortured twice, but her story did not change. Tesauro and his colleagues debated how to punish her. Four senators allegedly thought she should be put to death; Tesauro however argued that murder with malintent was not proven, and therefore a milder penalty was more appropriate. He was able to sway the other senators, and in the end, she was sentenced to a lashing and banishment from her town. Tesauro did not discuss why he thought she deserved a punishment at all. Rather he congratulated himself as this woman's "savior."[124] He also reported a similar 1563 case from the town of Vercelli (approximately seventy kilometers northeast of Turin), where a woman claimed she had delivered a stillborn child but was suspected of abortion or neonaticide. The town magistrate sentenced her to death, but the senate convinced the Duke of Savoy, Emmanuele Filiberto, to pardon her and lessen the penalty to a lashing and five years' exile.[125] Vincenzo de Franchis reported that in 1597 in Naples, the Grand Court of the Vicar, the main criminal tribunal of the city, sentenced a woman to death for procuring the abortion of an animated and well-developed fetus; however, the case was appealed to the Sacred Royal Council (the primary court of appeal), where the sentence was overturned: by a vote of six to two, the court sentenced the woman to a lashing and exile.[126] The Sicilian jurist Girolamo Basilico reported that in the summer of 1636, a man named Francesco Basili was investigated by the Royal Court of the Kingdom of Sicily for providing "drugs and a medicated potion to induce abortion." We do not know whether Francesco had impregnated the unnamed woman for whom he procured the abortion, but this seems likely. Although he was subjected to torture, he did not confess. The judge evidently thought Francesco guilty but lacked enough evidence to have him sentenced to death—according to Basilico, because Francesco's defense was strong and he had refused to confess under torture, the court could only sentence him to five years of exile "due to the seriousness of the crime." Unlike the women Tesauro and de Franchis wrote about, Basili was not whipped. Basilico was silent on the fate of the woman who consumed the abortifacient medicines.[127] Later in the seventeenth century, Marc'Antonio Savelli reported having seen two women convicted by Florence's criminal tribunal, the Eight on Public Safety, for procured abortions and sentenced to permanent incarceration in the Stinche prison.[128] Unfortunately, these jurists gave few details regarding these cases and we are left to wonder what evidence and circumstances led courts to these sentences.

If these examples are anything to go by, corporal punishment in the form of lashings, banishment, and sometimes incarceration were expected sentences for procured abortion and neonaticide—execution was not. In their books, jurists recommended moderation, and judges investigating complicated and sensitive cases operated with this maxim in mind, although particularly scandalous cases that troubled communities may have been punished more severely. Criminal tribunals, like ecclesiastical ones, sought to punish deviance and transgression in ways that disrupted social order as little as possible.

The concluding pages of Lucia Pivinelli's case seem to reflect this: "It seemed conclusive to the lords" of the Criminal Tribunal of Bologna that Lucia "had killed the aforementioned little girl . . . and therefore that she is not able to evade the penalties imposed against those who commit crimes of this sort." However, several Bolognese notables, including a senator and the prior of the Archconfraternity of Santa Maria di Vita, presented an apostolic brief of indemnity given by Clement X "for the purpose of freeing one person condemned to death, whomsoever the aforementioned lord officials desired." The archconfraternity had the privilege of "interrupting justice" and pardoning an individual they deemed worthy of mercy, which usually meant women who were deemed vulnerable.[129] Unfortunately, the trial records do not indicate what it was about Lucia or her case that moved these men to come to her defense and demand she "not be condemned." The governor accepted the intervention, and Lucia was pardoned, handed over to the archconfraternity, and likely entered an asylum for women at risk.[130]

Individuals found guilty of miscarriage caused by assault appear to have been sentenced to pay fines and sometimes to exile. For causing Angela da Filettino to miscarry, Venere da Bologna was fined thirty scudi—fifteen scudi to be paid to Angela and fifteen to the court. This was a substantial sum, and it is unknown whether Venere, a self-declared courtesan, could or did pay the fine.[131] In contrast, the candy maker Guglielmo Rossi asked the judge of the Criminal Tribunal of Rome to sentence the inspectors whom he blamed for his wife Ginevra's miscarriage and her death to a much higher fine: he demanded one thousand scudi for the loss of a miscarried child and four thousand for the death of his wife. It is unclear what the judge thought of this claim for damages or whether these amounts were representative or extraordinary. Nevertheless, Guglielmo's demand for one thousand scudi for the loss of his sixth-months-developed fetus renders the fifteen scudi Angela was to receive for her loss and life-threatening injuries rather minor. Cases of miscarriage caused by domestic assault were investigated less frequently and came with their own set of complications. Like ecclesiastical court judges who tried cases of marital separation, criminal judges likely preferred to rehabilitate marriages rather than break them up. However, they did punish husbands who severely abused their pregnant wives. Tesauro wrote that, in 1591, the Senate of Piedmont sentenced a man named Bota de Eugenia to several years' exile for causing his wife to miscarry by severely beating her—although Tesauro did not mention marital separation, it seems unlikely the couple would be expected to reunite after his five-year banishment.[132] Unfortunately we do not how Elena Cocchi's case against her abusive husband ended.

Conclusion

Civic authorities joined their ecclesiastical counterparts in identifying abortion as a crime requiring regulation and discipline and tried to change thinking toward its practice by issuing laws threatening severe penalties. Legislation and civic ordinances reflected agreed-upon norms and values meant to govern behavior; however, they were imprecise and varied from place to place. In works of criminal jurisprudence, jurists analyzed the intricacies of abortion and fetal personhood and discussed the acquisition and interpretation of evidence and the ambiguities of intentionality. Criminal investigations situate these discussions in specific settings and particular contexts, illuminating personal dramas and their social and physical consequences. Judges, representing the state, sought to balance the moral requirements and prescriptions of Romano-canonical law with the particularities of individual cases. What emerges from these different sources of law is tension and ambivalence.

In technical treatises, jurists discussed and debated what criminal abortion meant, how it was to be categorized, investigated, and punished, and the numerous factors judges should consider before making decisions and issuing sentences. While they were professionally obliged to treat abortion as a grave crime, sixteenth- and seventeenth-century jurists were reluctant to grant the fetus in utero legal personhood, even if it was animated and formed: live birth and viability was needed to influence the flow of inheritance and to make the death of a creatura homicide. Aside from doctrinal issues concerning the nature of the fetus and of the crime, cases of abortion were difficult to investigate from an evidentiary perspective. Jurists were increasingly medically literate and regularly consulted and learned from experienced midwives and physicians, but still, the uncertainties of women's bodies and of pregnancy and its termination made conviction difficult. Without a confession, determining intentionality was often impossible, and, therefore, the ordinary penalty of capital punishment was inapplicable. Sometimes abortion was procured intentionally; sometimes it was an accident; often it was hard to distinguish between the two. When judges felt there was enough evidence of wrongdoing, they sentenced procurers of abortion and individuals who may have caused miscarriage by assault to fines, corporal punishment in the form of lashings, disciplinary labor, or banishment. More often than not, they issued no punishment at all. The ambiguities surrounding women's bodies and the termination of pregnancy gave women and men exculpatory narratives to use in court, but they also gave judges pretense to absolve them when they thought it was in the best interests of justice and social order.

Alongside evidentiary uncertainties, judges weighed the social factors motivating women and men to procure abortions. Civic authorities did not try to regulate abortion by means of widespread surveillance, prosecution, and harsh punishment. Authorities appear to have been responsive to the social pressures that might lead women to have abortions and prioritized honor and the suppression of scandal and its effects over the rigorous enforcement of laws. The toleration of the practice also clearly served male prerogatives; men of all classes procured abortion to regulate reproduction stemming from their own illicit, transgressive, and violent sexual behaviors. On one hand, authorities demonstrated paternalism when they showed mercy and absolved women who had abortions; on the other, they had to because it was often their impregnators who caused, demanded, and orchestrated the ordeal or put women into situations where they may have felt they had little choice. Procured abortion was tolerated, to a certain extent, because it was inevitable and needed. When it worked, it allowed women to escape the social and economic perils of threatening pregnancy and single motherhood, and men to evade punishment for their sexual behaviors. The toleration of abortion simultaneously served overlapping moral and social imperatives.

Tensions and ambiguities in these sociolegal frameworks created spaces where women and men who found themselves in court for abortions could maneuver. Individuals on trial, both defendants and plaintiffs and their witnesses, made creative use of gender and body assumptions to cast doubt on their accusers or elicit their sympathy, exculpate themselves from wrongdoing, and evade harsh punishment. Some women shifted blame and guilt onto the men who impregnated them; others deployed discourses of corporal ambiguity to buttress their defense of unintentional abortion, late miscarriage, or the surprise delivery of a dead creatura. In doing so, they contributed to the formation of legal discourses and practices by astutely manipulating and simultaneously fortifying assumptions regarding female vulnerability and the ambiguities of the female body. Legal thinkers, judges, and civic authorities anticipated and often accepted these defenses—they may have even encouraged them. While they might regard abortion to be the destruction of a potential, if not actual, human life, they also understood it to be a comprehensible and not unexpected response to untimely reproduction, gender-based violence and various forms of injustice. The ambiguities surrounding women's bodies gave women, men, and healers exculpatory narratives to use in court, but they also gave judges pretense to absolve them or grant discretionary mercy when they thought it was the just thing to do. In sixteenth- and seventeenth-century Italy, social realities and practical considerations shaped legal thinking and judicial practices in general and on abortion in particular. Most of the time, these realities trumped doctrinal and moral commitments.

Maria and Superio

MARIA DE VECCHIS, from the small town of Sezze (eighty kilometers southeast of Rome), spent a lot of time in front of medical practitioners in 1613. A young, unmarried woman of undisclosed age, Maria was physically impaired and sickly, often suffering from various illnesses, fevers, general weakness, swelling, and bodily emissions caused, it was believed, by menstrual irregularities. She received regular therapy from the physician, surgeon, and apothecaries of Sezze. That year, Maria was also forced, on more than one occasion, to remove her clothes and present her body to court-appointed medical practitioners for forensic examination. The townspeople of Sezze believed she had been having sexual relations with her uncle, Superio de Magistris, a local man of wealth. They believed that she had been pregnant and that she had had an abortion. They asked the criminal court of Rome to investigate.[1]

Maria lived with her mother, Cornelia, and older brother, Mutio. Maria's father is absent from this story and was likely dead. Another older brother, Tolomeo, died a few years earlier. By all accounts, the de Vecchis family was respectable, but Maria was allegedly unmarriageable due to her health and appearance: Maria described herself as visibly impaired and chronically suffering from a cough or lung illness, an illness of the ear, and "every [other] illness."[2] Her bodily and health issues apparently framed her position in Sezze society. Records reveal less about Superio de Magistris. A member of a noble family with branches in Sezze, Terracina, Priverno, and Rome, Superio was wealthy and locally powerful—the current-day town hall of Sezze is located in Piazza de Magistris, a testament to Superio's familial prominence.[3] Superio had at least four acknowledged sons. The de Vecchis and de Magistris families were related; Superio was Maria's kinsman—she used the word "uncle"—by virtue of him being a first cousin to her mother, Cornelia. The two families also collaborated in a legume business: crops were stored in a supply room attached to the de Vecchis house, and Superio would visit to take count of the stock, which he would later sell in Rome. The de Vecchis family, it seems, depended on this business and their relationship with Superio for their livelihood.

Townspeople believed that Superio had been taking advantage of his power over the de Vecchis family and that he and possibly his son Simone had been having regular sexual relations with Maria for at least two years.[4] It was assumed that the de Vecchis family knew and either turned a blind eye or even allowed this. Maria's neighbors claimed Superio kept a mattress in the legume storage room at the de Vecchis house and that they had seen him and Maria spend time there together. The transgressions were held to be public knowledge. The people of Sezze admittedly disapproved of this sexual relationship, but their clamor seems to have intensified after Maria allegedly became pregnant in early 1613 and had an abortion in May. Everyone in town "knew" she had been pregnant, but only a few witnesses testified to seeing Maria with a distended belly. Maria was apparently shut up at home and did not leave her house for a few months.[5] During this time, Superio allegedly went to great lengths to procure an abortion, reportedly soliciting the services of various local and foreign healers. Maria's mother was said to be fully aware of these efforts. In May, when Maria was five or six months pregnant, they were apparently able to make "the creatura go away."[6] Everyone believed Superio or his son had impregnated Maria and that she had had an abortion: "Even the chickens know," one witness ardently reported, "so much is this fact known."[7]

The criminal statutes of Sezze stated that a woman who procured an abortion was to be executed by burning, but the townspeople were more interested in punishing Superio than Maria.[8] The magistrates of Sezze had apparently begun to inquire into the incestuous relationship and abortion a few months earlier, but Superio allegedly "corrupted the authorities" with a bribe of five hundred scudi. Others kept quiet because they feared Superio or one his henchmen might shoot them. Angelo Cima, a local prosecutor linked to the papal government, apparently refused Superio's bribe and was not afraid to proceed. He wrote to the Governor of Rome, detailing Superio's crimes and corruptions and requesting a judge be sent to investigate and bring justice to Sezze.[9] Although Superio claimed Cima was fabricating accusations to further a personal feud against him and perhaps to advance his own career, the governor agreed that a full inquiry was needed.[10] The apostolic commissary Ottavio Giandi was sent to investigate. Over several weeks in August, he questioned many townspeople. Having amassed enough evidence, he transported the accused and key witnesses to Rome, where they were detained in the Savelli and Tor di Nona prisons, for further questioning by Judge Girolamo Felicio Lunte.[11] While the charges against Superio included defloration, incest, and abortion, it was this last offense that most preoccupied the court, both because of its gravity and for reasons of evidence. Much of the trial focused on interpreting the signs of Maria's body for pregnancy and delivery and on investigating the healers who may have contributed to the abortion.

Superio and Maria were questioned three times in Sezze and once in Rome. Each time, the judges urged the defendants to freely confess their crimes, but they maintained their innocence. Maria expressed disgust at the accusations of incest with her uncle and his son: "They are my relatives," she said. "I have done no such thing." "I have never been known carnally by anyone and I have never been pregnant, nor have I aborted, or sought out to commit an abortion or to make myself abort with any kind of remedy."[12] Superio, too, angrily denied any sexual relationship with Maria and soliciting healers for an abortion. He admitted to visiting Maria often and to bringing healers to see her but said this was on account of her chronic bouts of illness. He explained that he engaged healers as a favor to Maria's mother, who may not have been able to afford the treatment on her own.[13] In her only testimony during the trial, Maria's mother confirmed Superio's story and cataloged her daughter's illnesses and the appropriate medical therapies she received.[14] The family's story was consistent: Superio was a caring and honorable relative, and Maria was a sickly girl in need of regular medical intervention, which the town physician also confirmed.[15] Confronting their accusers, Superio and Maria called them "mad liars and infamous," accusing them of telling "a thousand lies" and saying terrible things because they wished Superio ill.[16]

With witness testimonies called into question, the court turned to what it perceived to be more objective evidence: Maria's body. At the very beginning of the trial in Sezze, Maria was examined by three midwives: Giulia, Adlotia, and Beatissima who were brought in from Roccagorga and Ceccano, towns just outside Sezze. All three women were experienced, having helped many women through pregnancy, childbirth, and related issues but had likely not examined a body in a forensic capacity. Nevertheless, the court considered them expert witnesses. They were asked to carefully examine Maria's body and identify any signs of sexual experience, pregnancy, and childbirth.

In a room in the town hall, Maria was forced to expose her body to these three strangers who were specifically tasked with finding evidence of mortal sin and crime. Examining Maria's genitals, the midwives found her vagina to be larger and more stretched than it ought to be, not only for a virgin but for a woman who claimed never to have given birth. After prodding and manipulating Maria's belly, the midwives also explained that an unmarried woman who had never been pregnant was supposed to have a tight abdomen, but Maria's looked like a "flabby" and "wrinkly" sac. In addition, when the midwives squeezed her breasts, milk came out, the most certain sign of pregnancy and recent delivery, they said.[17] Maria's body had betrayed her. But the midwives could not determine how her pregnancy had ended: Maria had "either given birth or had aborted," midwife Adlotia said. "I cannot know which."

When it was her turn to account for her body, Maria ascribed different meanings to its shape and emissions. She admitted she was not a virgin but still insisted she had never had sexual intercourse with a man. She told the judge "how this disgrace has happened to me." About one year earlier she had been staying in the countryside outside Sezze with her since deceased brother, Tolomeo. Staying with them was a woman named Silvia and her little boy. One day, Maria and the boy had gone off to play, and as they were running around, they came across a ditch. Maria tried to jump over it, but, "being small, I ruptured myself." "I began to feel a great heat down below, that is in my vagina, and then I began to leak out a great quantity of blood." Silvia later examined her and determined that Maria was now deflowered. She told the judge that Tolomeo was furious when he found out what had happened—that is, "that I had been deflowered by jumping." He began yelling, calling Maria a disgrace. He said that "I have ruined myself for nothing." Had

Maria been marriageable, Tolomeo told her, they would have to report her accident to the court, so a prospective husband might not assume she had been deflowered by a man, "but because I am crippled I did not have to." Tolomeo could not confirm this tale for the court because he had died the same year the event occurred.[18]

Continuing to address the midwives' findings, Maria could not deny emitting liquid from her breasts but insisted her menstrual issues, not pregnancy, were the cause. "When my purge comes, I usually get milk in my breasts." Her flabby stomach, she explained, also came from her illnesses. A bout of dropsy might have stretched her stomach to make it appear as though she had been pregnant, while menstrual retention transformed blood into milk and escaped through her breasts. "My illnesses made me like this," she explained.[19]

Commissary Giandi had the midwives confront Maria with their testimonies to see if she would change her story, but she did not. The midwives specifically pressed her on her lactation. Midwife Giulia said, "My girl, a young woman who has not been pregnant and who has not given birth cannot have milk the way that you do."[20] Midwife Adlotia mocked Maria and asked whether the milk she expressed "came from the heavens," and Giulia impatiently said, "Show your breasts because I want the lord judge here present to see the milk!" Maria angrily replied, "Is it not enough for you to see it once? I have already confirmed to him that milk comes out of my breasts, the lord Commissary does not need to see it."[21] Referring to Beatissima's description of her body, Maria told the judge, "Everything that she says is true. I only assert that it is not true that I was pregnant, because I have never known a man."[22] In their testimonies, Superio and Cornelia also drew attention to Maria's frequent bouts of illness to dispel the accusations of incest, pregnancy, and abortion.

Once Maria's body had said what it could, both Commissary Giandi and, later, Judge Lunte in Rome concentrated their efforts on discovering the individual or individuals who might have participated in the alleged abortion. According to witnesses, Superio solicited several local and foreign healers—all men with whom he had varying relations—to terminate Maria's pregnancy. He allegedly approached Cola Cocchiarello, a young man who was a healer to whom locals turned when they had minor ailments. Superio asked Cola for herbs to purge

Maria, and Cola agreed to provide them, although it is unclear whether he understood they were intended to cause an abortion. The apothecary Pasquale de Tantis testified that, around the time everyone gossiped about Maria being pregnant, Cola came to his shop to grind aristolochia, which he had picked wild. Pasquale permitted Cola to use his grinder, knowing he was a healer, but on this occasion he warned him: "Cola, be careful of what you do because it is not your job to give things by mouth, and you can make some mistake."[23] But Cola would not be questioned by the judge; his mother, Tarquinia, said that, around ten days earlier, her son left home, saying he was going to his brother's vineyard in the countryside, but she was skeptical about his actual whereabouts. Searching Cola's things in her house, the authorities found a handwritten book containing various remedies, as well as several herbs and roots. These were shown to the apothecary Pasquale, who identified a good quantity of aristolochia, rue, centaurea, roots of valeriana, and powdered colocynth, all purgatives.[24]

Superio allegedly also asked the town physician, Ortensio Simeoni, who had a history of treating Maria, for a prescription to have her bled, but the doctor would not comply without examining her first.[25] According to the tailor Emilio de Bonis, the apothecary Tomeo Ciolli told him that Superio had explicitly asked him for a purgative remedy to make a woman abort—apparently he did not say Maria's name. Tomeo said he refused because "this was a sin and he cannot do it." But Superio tried to convince him, saying "that he can confess it, because it was for a woman from a good family and it would remedy possible scandals that might occur, that [Tomeo] would be doing it out of mercy." Tomeo said he was not persuaded.[26] Superio was allegedly also direct with the barber Marzio Bracci, who witnesses said was offered the very high sum of fifty scudi to bleed Maria without a prescription.[27]

When questioned by the judges, all these healers accused their denouncers of fabrication or misinterpreting what they had told them. The barber Marzio vehemently denied the claim that Superio offered him fifty scudi to bleed Maria. The physician Ortensio wanted to be clear about his interactions with Superio: he said that on several occasions Superio had indeed approached him, saying Maria was not feeling well and suggesting she be bled. Ortensio was adamant that he refused to give Superio a prescription without first examining Maria and maintained that Superio never brought her or divulged the reasons he wanted her bled.[28]

The apothecary Tomeo Ciolli received more judicial scrutiny than the other healers. Tomeo was a foreigner in Sezze. Originally from Bassiano, he had practiced as an apothecary in Priverno and in Rome before coming to Sezze in 1610. He had been jailed several times in his life but stipulated only for minor offences. He had also amassed quite a large debt: approximately 260 scudi to various creditors. In Sezze, he worked at the Pillorci shop for three years but had recently been fired.[29] Superio may have thought that, being out of work and in considerable debt, Tomeo would have little trepidation in providing him with purgative drugs. Tomeo, however, denied Superio had ever solicited him for this purpose. In Rome, Judge Lunte had the apothecary tortured on the corda to see if he would change his story. As Tomeo hung in agony, the judge urged him to confess that Superio had tried to buy remedies from him to make a woman abort. He endured this torture for a quarter of an hour without a confession. The judge evidently did not buy it; the notary wrote that Tomeo "persisted in his lies."[30]

After two months of investigation, the case rested on gossip and an ambiguous body—all suggestive, to be sure, but not conclusive. But a break in the investigation came when the court in Rome was able to locate another individual who witnesses said had helped Superio with the abortion. This was the roaming Franciscan friar Giovanni Giuseppe da Siccolo, better known as fra Maccabeo. After some effort, the court found Maccabeo in Terracina (approximately eighty kilometers to the southeast) and transported him to Rome's Savelli prison for questioning.

Fra Maccabeo was a Franciscan friar, originally from Sicily, but primarily living at a convent in Terracina. He went to Sezze and Rome somewhat regularly, stopping at small towns along the way. He testified with almost no interruption from the judge. He said that he was in Sezze in January of that year (1613), and one day, Superio approached him in the town's piazza, whispering that he needed "a great service." Without mincing words, he told Maccabeo he had deflowered and impregnated a young woman—Maccabeo said he never learned her name— that she was two or three months pregnant, and he wanted to procure an abortion. Superio told him he had tried a few remedies, including

savin, and had had her bled from the foot, but these had failed to terminate the pregnancy.[31] He "wanted me to teach him remedies to make
her abort." The friar replied that he had no remedies available, but Superio begged him to acquire some, and finally, Maccabeo obliged, saying he was returning to Terracina the next day but would be back in
Sezze in three or four days and would bring remedies "to make this
abortion happen." Superio promised that if they worked, he would buy
Maccabeo a new habit to replace his shabby-looking Franciscan robe,
but the friar said he did not need one, that he lacked nothing. The next
morning, Maccabeo found Superio waiting for him outside the convent
to beg him not to let him down.

Maccabeo soon returned to Sezze and gave Superio a flask containing an infusion of colocynth, saying, "If the woman drinks the infusion
that is in the flask in the morning, without anything else, she will
abort." However, one or two days later, an angry and nervous Superio
told him that all the potion did was make the unnamed woman empty
her bowels and throw up. Maccabeo was preparing to leave Sezze for
Rome, and Superio asked him to find a better remedy in the big city.
Superio specifically requested fresh savin, which Maccabeo told the
judge was very efficient at causing abortion. Superio told Maccabeo he
had already used savin, but it had not caused the abortion because it
was dried—evidently the fresh herb was stronger. Although the head of
Rome's health office prohibited its sale without a written prescription
from a physician, under penalty of twenty-five ducats, possible corporal
punishment, or even execution, fra Maccabeo had no difficulty acquiring savin from an herb seller in bustling Piazza Navona.[32] After giving
the savin to Superio, Maccabeo returned to Terracina, but a few weeks
later, Maccabeo learned from his friend and fellow friar Pietro that the
fresh savin had not worked either. Superio allegedly told Pietro to tell
Maccabeo this and to let him know he had found something else that
would get the job done. That was the last thing Maccabeo heard about
the affair.[33]

Even though, of all the witnesses questioned, Maccabeo was the
only one who admitted to being explicitly solicited by Superio and to
helping him procure an abortion, Judge Lunte had few follow-up questions for the forthcoming Franciscan. He did however ask why, with all
the medical practitioners available to him, Superio had asked a

Franciscan friar, and specifically fra Maccabeo, for this service. The friar told the judge he was a healer and well known for treating women for bewitchment. Maccabeo may have been an exorcist (licensed by his order or not).[34] Officially, exorcists were supposed to combat supernatural illness with spiritual cures. In practice, they often blended prayer and sacramentalia with drug therapy to literally purge visible "evils" from suffering bodies.[35] In varying degrees, exorcists knew a great deal about pathology and pharmacy. Maccabeo demonstrated a sophisticated knowledge of purgatives when he explained to the judge that his first remedy, the infusion of colocynth, had not caused the woman to abort because she was further along in her pregnancy than Superio had said, colocynth being a milder purgative best used in the first two months of pregnancy or in a higher dose.[36] Maccabeo did not however disclose why he agreed to help Superio. He did say that it was not for compensation—he made a point of telling the judge that he had refused Superio's offer of a new habit. Although Maccabeo claimed not to know the abortion was for Superio's niece Maria, he did know it was for a young woman from a good family who was supposed to be a virgin and for whom pregnancy could cause social trouble and even physical harm or death. Did the Franciscan friar agree to procuring an abortion because he sympathized with her hardship? Did he see it as the lesser of two evils? Judge Lunte did not ask.

When presented with Maccabeo's confession, Superio denied it, and Judge Lunte had them confront each other in the investigation room. When Maccabeo confirmed his testimony, Superio called him a liar, "pathetic," a "defrocked scoundrel sorcerer!" And he accused the friar of making up the story to get him in trouble, likely at the behest of Superio's enemies.[37] Maccabeo told the judge that, in the end, the remedies he provided had not resulted in abortion, but Judge Lunte must have felt Maccabeo's confession was suspicious, because he ordered the friar be tortured "to remove any doubt that could arise concerning [Maccabeo's] character or statements . . . due to the fact that he made himself a partner to the crime, and in order to remove any stain . . . and to aid and fortify his deposition." But before specifying the torture, Lunte asked Maccabeo how old he was and was told, "This September I finish my eighty-ninth year, and you can see that I have only four teeth left in my mouth, the rest have fallen out [during my many] years." The notary checked Maccabeo's mouth and confirmed he indeed had only four teeth.[38] Maccabeo's age meant he could not be strung up and tortured with the corda. Judge Lunte did, however, threaten him with the *stanghetta* torture: his right ankle would be placed in a metal vice that would be tightened, causing crushing pain and stopping blood flow. He urged Maccabeo to tell the truth and warned him that if he had given false testimony against Superio, "he would be called to render an account not only in this world but also in the other [world], especially because [Maccabeo] was a priest and a religious of the order of Saint Francis, therefore he should take good care to speak the true truth, which is all that was required of him."[39] To this Maccabeo replied: "My lord, what I have said in my examination is the truth, and if it weren't true, how could you ever think, for I am a priest and a member of a religious order, that I came here to bear witness in such a fashion as to put my soul at risk."[40] In the end, the stanghetta was a scare tactic and Maccabeo was not tortured. Judge Lunte released him, and with this last testimony, Maccabeo disappears from the historical record.

But—unlike the apothecary Tomeo, the barber Marzio, and the physician Ortensio—Maccabeo had confessed to having been solicited by Superio and to providing him with substances to terminate a young, albeit unnamed, woman's pregnancy. Likely hoping to extract more definitive evidence from Maria's body, Judge Lunte had her examined again by Roman midwives and this time by a surgeon. In a room in the Tor di Nona prison, Maria was again forced to bare her body to the menacing sight and touch of strangers. Again, her genitals, abdomen, and breasts were offered to three women the judge had brought in to "see and discover whether she had had children." All three midwives agreed with the previous assessments: "Having carefully seen and touched [her] where it was necessary, I say that this woman has certainly given birth and had children." The midwife Ginevra did not need her thirty-plus years of experience to know Maria had been lying: "The signs are so obvious that a blind person would know" that Maria had been pregnant and had recently delivered.[41] When the midwives left Maria's cell, the surgeon Vincenzo Pastore entered. He, however, examined only her feet, finding a scar on the right one, which he deemed caused by a lancet used to draw blood from what is "popularly called the vein of the mother."[42] The surgeon did not speculate as to why this vein might have been cut or even when the phlebotomy occurred, and Judge Lunte would have known there was no way of proving blood was let from Maria's foot to induce abortion. On Maria, however, the scar, in tandem with the bodily evidence the six midwives found and fra Maccabeo's confession, must have confirmed what the whole town was alleging: "Even the chickens know so much is this fact known."[43]

The investigation into Superio and Maria's alleged sexual relationship, her pregnancy, and the abortion concluded on October 8, 1613. Judge Lunte did not issue a sentence. Rather than punishing anyone for wrongdoing, he exercised judicial discretion and decided the best way to bring this affair to an end was to force Superio to make peace with Angelo Cima, the prosecutor from Sezze who had denounced him to the Roman court in the first place. The court made them pledge "that they would neither offend nor cause [each other] to be offended," on pain of a three-thousand scudi payment to the offended.[44] About the incest and Maria's alleged abortion, the judge said nothing. Presumably, the enigmatic fra Maccabeo resumed his business. The other witnesses returned to their lives in Sezze, including Maria and her corpus delicti.

Conclusion

$\mathcal{I}$n 1582, several elite Japanese converts to Catholicism boarded a Portuguese ship in Nagasaki and sailed for the lands of their converters. The head of the Jesuit missions in the East Indies, Alessandro Valignano, had organized this delegation of the sons of Christian feudal lords (*Kirishitan daimyo*) with two objectives in mind: to show his brothers and superiors in Portugal, Spain, and Rome the headway the Jesuits were making in Japan by displaying these noble, refined, and pious converted young men, thus encouraging further investment in the mission, and to impress upon the young Japanese men the glory of Catholic Europe, which they would report back to their people upon their return, inspiring more to join the faith. With stops along the way, the Tenshō embassy reached Lisbon in 1584. They spent time in Portugal and Spain and had an extended sojourn in Italy, visiting Pisa, Florence, Siena, Bologna, Venice, Milan, and Naples, before reaching Rome, their primary destination, where the men had audiences with Gregory XIII and the newly elected Sixtus V. By all accounts, the delegation was well received and, after two years in Europe, the young men returned to Nagasaki in the summer of 1590.

Valignano set to work on a book based on the young Japanese men's travels and, in Macao in 1590, published *A Dialogue Concerning the Mission of the Japanese Ambassadors to the Roman Curia*. The book describes two of the young travelers talking about their trip (what they saw, who they met, what they learned) with their kin back in Japan. Alongside conversations about sea travel, the ecclesiastical hierarchy, the kingdoms of Europe and their political affairs, the men tell of the riches of European cities, urban institutions, churches, and religious and charitable houses. One, Michael (or Miguel Chijiwa Seizaemon, nephew of the early convert daimyo Bartolomeu Ōmura Sumitada), tells his cousin Leo, who had never left Japan, about the many charitable institutions proliferating in Europe:

> There are other [charitable institutions] called *brephotro-phia*, in which babies abandoned by their mothers whether because of poverty or for some other reason, are taken in and cared for, and handed over for feeding to various wet-nurses; and this kind of work of mercy is of special importance, since babes of that tender age are so vulnerable to danger. There are, finally, others which, not deserving the title of nunnery, can be referred to generally as houses of women. Many women ask permission to resort to these, after years spent living less modestly; they commit themselves to a better way of life, and pass their lives imitating holy virgins in praising God and in other works.

Leo is impressed and concludes that these charitable institutions prevent "so many evils":

> It seems to me that all those places are extremely valuable, since they mean that so many evils which are common here in Japan can be avoided; such as the ravishing of virgins, bawdy houses of lewd women, wretched abortions procured with herbs or other pestiferous medicaments, the atrocious killing of tender babes by their own mothers by suffocation or some other form of cruelty. . . . In comparison with these evils the good things of Europe point to the truth of the Christian religion.

> *Michael:* You do well indeed to compare the two cases, and
> you seem to be gathering not a little fruit from our col-
> loquia, and to be weighing matters European in an ac-
> curate balance.[1]

Valignano claimed the work was based on the impressions the men had recorded in their diaries during the trip; it is beyond doubt, how-ever, that the author took liberties. Much of the dialogue reads as un-abashed Catholic-European propaganda. The book was written in Latin and intended to be used in teaching the language to students at the Jesuit colleges in Japan, but it also taught them the version of Cath-olic-European society and culture that Valignano wanted to project, from the very mouths of the Japanese elite converts who had allegedly witnessed them in action. The students at the Jesuit college, it was hoped, would disseminate this image to their compatriots, inspiring more to the faith and helping to inculcate its ethical and social codes.

The message of the cousins' exchange is clear: life is more valued in Catholic Europe than in Japan; the lives of human beings (here includ-ing fetuses and neonates) are better in Europe because they are cared for; and this is because of Catholic Christianity. The Christian impulse to charity inspires Europeans to create enclosures for vulnerable women, preventing men from "ravishing virgins" and "lewd women" from creating opportunities for sexual sin and social disorder, as hap-pened in Japan. This impulse to charity inspires Europeans to create orphanages so that "wretched abortions" are not procured and mothers do not kill their "tender babes," as happened in Japan. Comparing the two cultures through his cousin's observations, Leo concludes that the "truth of the Christian religion" allows Europeans to avoid the "many evils" that the non-Christian Japanese commit. Michael confirms that Leo is learning.

But, of course, the characterization of Catholic Europe that Leo was learning (and spreading) was propaganda and wishful thinking. Like Valignano, many Catholic missionaries throughout the early mod-ern world sought to propagate similar images of false realities to im-press and convert their targets and continuously thereafter to indoctri-nate neophytes in prescribed ways of thinking and behaving. From Nagasaki in the east to Lima in the west, converts were told that God prohibits abortion and neonaticide, and therefore those who commit these acts betray God and humanity; they are sinners and monsters. However, if missionaries truly thought the eradication of these practices was a godly ideal that demonstrated moral, social, and cultural superiority, the early modern Italian Church, states, and people were wanting. Had Michael Chijiwa Seizaemon been permitted to walk freely around the cities of Italy and speak candidly with a variety of inhabitants, he would have learned that Italians were quite ambivalent about abortion.

Though controversial and subject to increasingly heated debate, abortion was commonly practiced and generally tolerated in early modern Italy. It had multiple meanings and factored into women's and men's lives in different ways. It was a contested physical event and a practice that elicited varied, inconsistent, and contradictory responses. *Aborto* was a word used to describe a terminated pregnancy, but the significances ascribed to it changed in relation to context and circumstance. In some situations, abortion was interpreted as mortal sin and crime, a practice that many believed violated religious precepts and had to be punished and eradicated. In other situations, abortion was deemed forgivable, acceptable, necessary, moral, and unproblematic. Attitudes, experiences, and responses were shaped by gender, social status, family structure, age, and, of course, the motivations behind decisions to terminate pregnancy. They were also shaped by the uncertainties surrounding generation and pregnancy and by the physical ambiguities of the female body. Abortion was open to interpretation and negotiation at the institutional and communal levels, in regular interactions with neighbors and familiars, in the dynamics of a romantic or abusive sexual relationship, and at the level of a woman's personal and embodied experience. For all these reasons, an exploration of abortion reveals important insights into some of the broader issues confronting Italian society and culture in the sixteenth and seventeenth centuries.

Against the backdrop of the dramatic religious and social transformations that characterized the early modern period, this study has found both changes and continuities in attitudes toward abortion. Shifts can be detected at the institutional level in particular, as seen in official ecclesiastical, civic, and medical rhetoric. Authorities expressed a growing discomfort with the practice, which they believed was widespread and tolerated at all levels of society. They aspired to change attitudes and behaviors through education, legislation, and the threat of discipline. As part of broader campaigns of moral and religious reform and state building, the Catholic Church and secular governments in Italy increasingly condemned abortion as a form of homicide and linked it with sexual immorality. Abortion was often framed as a crime against a potential life, a sin against God's plan, and viewed as especially grave if the fetus was animated, as an unbaptized soul would linger in limbo, deprived of the vision of God—a concern that carried an increasingly heavy moral load. Non-marital sex was often assumed to be the root cause of the practice: If women and men did not engage in non-marital sex, the rhetoric went, they would not find themselves in situations where they had to terminate a potential human being to escape dishonor, public censure, or the burden of children.

Changes in institutional attitudes were especially pronounced at the legislative level. Harsh laws and the threat of severe punishment for those who procured, caused, or assisted in abortions, it was thought, would move individuals to accept the gravity of the practice and encourage women and men to abstain from non-marital sex. Authorities told their subjects that procuring abortion put one's own soul in jeopardy and deprived an unborn soul of salvation, therefore inviting harsh retribution. Ecclesiastical and civic authorities sought to regulate the practice with the threat of increasingly severe penalties, including spiritual sanctions, fines, banishment, and, in some places, corporal and even capital punishment. Had Michael Chijiwa Seizaemon remained in Italy a few more years, he would have seen that the practice of abortion was considered to have been prevalent and, for some, so problematic that it required the concerted efforts of Church and states to change attitudes by means of education, moralizing, legislation, and the threat of retribution.

However, Michael would also have learned that these efforts were more aspirational than implementable. Moral indignation and criminalization do not appear to have led to diminished practice or increased prosecution. Sharp discipline was not possible, nor does it appear to have been genuinely desired—even Sixtus V was unwilling to mete out the harsh penalties prescribed in his own bull, which resolved to eradicate the practice of abortion. Statements that clearly demarcated licit from illicit sexual relationships and licit from illicit abortions and that imposed harsh penalties for crossing the line reflected ideals and threats that could not materialize in the messiness of daily life. Prescriptions certainly shaped consciences and may have influenced behavior, but they did not determine an individual's decisions or how communities, institutions, and authorities might respond to them. In early modern Italy, abortion was practiced because it was needed.

Despite being a sin, abortion was tolerated for epistemological, moral, and pragmatic reasons. The termination of pregnancy was ambiguous. In the sixteenth and seventeenth centuries, neither Church nor states had consistently defined the meaning of procured abortion or agreed on how to regulate its practice. In fact, they couldn't. Procured abortion was often hidden and, without a confession, one could never know with certainty whether a woman had had an abortion or what caused it. Women's bodies were difficult to read and the evidence of alleged abortion was always contestable. Medical practitioners scrutinized female bodies and sought to discover and establish standards of proof with which to determine whether a woman was or had been pregnant and whether she had had a miscarriage or induced abortion or had delivered a stillborn or live, viable child. While there were important signs suggesting what a woman's body might have experienced, what it might be harboring, what it may have expelled, and what caused the death of a fetus or neonate, it was universally accepted that, without a confession, the intentional termination of pregnancy could not be proved beyond doubt.

The uncertainties and ambiguities of the female body were often as real for women themselves as they were for onlookers, including medical practitioners. For some women, the signs and sensations of pregnancy could be genuinely experienced as illness and vice versa. For a woman who was not trying or who did not expect or desire to be pregnant, the lack of a menstrual period, a growing belly, and lactation were causes for concern, as they signaled illness. Addressing these apparently common health issues was routine: women acquired and consumed purgative herbs and had blood drawn from the saphena vein in the foot to encourage menstruation, expel obstructions, and restore well-being. In many situations, women and onlookers interpreted the expulsion of blood and fleshy matter as a sign of healing, not abortion, although this may very well have been what these expulsions were. Treating women for womb-related illness was risky business, as the goal was often to evacuate the womb's contents. Both learned and lay individuals knew that the same drugs and surgeries women used to promote health and enhance fertility, and that pregnant women used to accelerate childbirth or expel afterbirth or a dead fetus from their bodies, could also bring pregnancy to an end. This knowledge circulated on various levels, and related products and services were widely sought and available. Physicians claimed to be better equipped to distinguish between womb-related illnesses and pregnancy than lower-status healers, including midwives, surgeons, and apothecaries, and tried to carve out a monopoly over these aspects of therapy. But restricting the traffic of purgative medicines and the practice of bloodletting was never a real possibility because these treatments were ubiquitous and used to heal many and unrelated illnesses. For all these reasons, in early modern Italy, the concept of a "back alley abortionist" selling secret products did not exist. Of course, women and men could and did procure abortions by deception. For individuals seeking abortions, and those selling materials and services to that end, ambiguity was a resource and a means to circumvent regulation and evade punishment. Claims of ignorance and ambiguity, miscarriage and stillbirth were standard narratives in the street and defenses in court because they were plausible and could not be easily discredited. Had Michael Chijiwa Seizaemon spoken to Italian medical practitioners, jurists, women, and men about abortion, he would have learned that ambiguities surrounding women's bodies, pregnancy, and its termination created gray zones that enabled the practice and its toleration.

Abortion was also tolerated for social-moral reasons, even though these were sometimes at odds with strict religious precepts. There were often wide gaps between official prescriptions on abortion and the beliefs and moral experiences of women and men, including ecclesiastical, medical, and civic authorities. The contexts in which abortions were sought and procured mattered. Gender, social status, reputation, circumstance, and the potential for scandal and social disruption influenced responses.

Abortion was perceived as addressing the consequences of early modern Italy's gender and sexual politics. Like prostitution, it was justified as an "evil" that was permissible because it prevented worse evils, primarily infanticide; the termination of fetal life, especially early in gestation, was deemed significantly less grave than the killing of a born child. But there were other evils perceived as worse than the intentional termination of pregnancy, chief among them, social disorder and scandal. Everyone knew and appreciated that pregnancy could be disastrous for some women. Women attempted to induce abortion as early as possible to terminate pregnancies resulting from sexual violence, intercourse with a promise of marriage or material support that was not fulfilled, sexual relationships with priests or relatives, or other problematic or illicit sexual relationships. Individuals, communities, and authorities often thought abortion was justified in circumstances where pregnancy and childbirth exacerbated already vulnerable women's hardships. Single working women might lose their wages and be thrown deeper into poverty. Unwed and poor mothers were often marginalized and stigmatized in their communities. Women feared violence and even death should their fathers and brothers discover they were pregnant without the prospect of marriage or compensation, or if their husbands discovered they were pregnant from an adulterous relationship. Some women contemplated suicide to evade the consequences of pregnancy. For some, pregnancy was medically perilous and abortion was sought and prescribed to alleviate potentially fatal illnesses and threats to future fertility. In all these situations, a woman's social and physical well-being often justified interventions that could result in the potential loss of a fetus. Had Michael Chijiwa Seizaemon paid attention, he would have learned that pregnancy often brought Italian women many and diverse dangers, and abortion offered a means of self-preservation.

Of course, abortion was not only a woman's practice. Men were intricately involved as procurers, facilitators, and administrators. Laymen and clerics, elite and non-elite, sought abortions and forced them on women they impregnated. Priests, while preaching against the practice, procured abortions to conceal their own transgressions and to avoid punishment. Members of the class and families of the authorities prohibiting the practice also procured abortions to conceal their own or a kin's transgressions. Men knew who to turn to for assistance and what to ask for. Male healers sold products and services to this end and often gave and forced them on women they impregnated. Men beat women to terminate pregnancies, sometimes killing them. Had Michael Chijiwa Seizaemon been clear-eyed, his diary entries might have indicated that it was often men, like the rosary maker Giovanni Manello, the sacristan Antino de Benedictis, and the nobleman Superio de Magistris, and many others, who were the active agents behind abortions because they desired and benefitted from the practice. He also would have learned that they rarely got in trouble for it.

Communities and authorities accepted that for both women and men caught in trying circumstances, the need to terminate a pregnancy could be pressing, making prescribed responses to the practice of abortion seem irrelevant. This was likely also true of abortions procured in the context of marriage for the purposes of reducing economic strain on a household and community and for maternal health, practices that are, however, almost completely invisible in the historical record. At all levels of society, prescribed responses were often flexed to avoid the difficulties that could ensue from allowing pregnancies in some contexts and circumstances to continue or from exposing one that had been terminated.

Tolerance, however, had limits. Individuals and communities objected and denounced procurers of abortion to the authorities when their behavior and personalities disrupted social peace and violated moral norms. Abortion was denounced as a symptom of a broader problem that could not be mediated privately or locally. Targets were usually men and often priests who were disliked, whose sexual relationships scandalized, and whose behaviors bred resentment and caused turmoil. Women were treated as evidence of men's misdeeds and often represented themselves as victims. Cases that came to court, therefore, must be examined through a lens considering social relations between plaintiffs, the accused and their accusers, witnesses, broader communities, and institutional authorities, and not primarily as examples of the top-down disciplining of sexuality and women's bodies. Yet, even in these exceptional cases, ecclesiastical and secular tribunals preferred moderation to harsh discipline. In practice, judges did not treat abortion as homicide nor sentence its procurers to capital punishment: depending on the particulars of the case, fines, disciplinary labor, corporal punishment, or exile were deemed more appropriate. More often than not, the accused received no punishment at all.

Even as ecclesiastical and civic authorities sought to impose stricter discipline through legislative sternness, institutional reach, and moral-theological education, they were well aware and accepted that abortion fulfilled a need and provided benefit, both for individuals caught in trying and desperate circumstances and for broader society. When it required justification, it was framed as a "necessary evil" that benevolent authorities tolerated to redress systemic gender-based injustices and maintain social order. More often than not, abortion did not require explicit justification.

Nevertheless, the early modern Catholic Church and Italian states were moving in a more rigid direction on the issue. Widespread moral and religious education, broadcast by institutions and through various media, sought to inculcate the belief that the intentional termination of pregnancy was the killing of a human being and a mortal sin. In 1679, Pope Innocent XI reopened the issue by officially condemning the proposition that it was licit to procure an abortion before animation for any reason, including sparing a woman's honor and even her life. In 1869, Pope Pius IX returned to Sixtus V's 1588 position and declared all abortions were homicides and would incur excommunication.[2] Catholics were to internalize the message and shun the practice or feel guilt when they terminated their own or other people's pregnancies and seek forgiveness to reenter God's grace. Doctrine crystallized and positions hardened.

The intervening years have seen violent struggles over who has authority over women's bodies and women's access to healthcare throughout the modern world. Post-Unification Italian governments promoted Catholic prohibitions against abortion and birth control to further pronatalist and colonial ambitions.[3] Today's Code of Canon Law and the Catechism of the Catholic Church hold life to begin at conception, prohibit induced abortion, and declare that procurers and administrators are automatically excommunicated. In Italy today, abortion is legal and has been since 1978, but in many parts of the country it is almost completely inaccessible, even in cases of medical emergency—a situation the United Nations Human Rights Committee, the Committee on the Elimination of Discrimination Against Women, and the European Committee of Social Rights have declared a violation of women's rights to health.[4]

This study of abortion in the early modern period reveals that these later and current developments were not necessarily inevitable. Institutions that are often portrayed as absolutely antiabortion have a less clear-cut history. In the sixteenth and seventeenth centuries, the Catholic Church held procured abortion to be a sin but was not unequivocally antiabortion. Italian states held abortion to be a crime but rarely prosecuted its procurers. The medical establishment sought to regulate the practice, but physicians, apothecaries, surgeons, and midwives often provided abortions to those who sought and needed them. Prescriptions and proscriptions were of course important and powerful, but they did not determine, nor have they ever determined, understandings, behaviors, experiences, and responses to abortion. We must resist representations that distort history to further self-interest, legitimize authority, and create a desired present. Historical study examining the issues from different angles and discovering what various people said and did reveals an obvious truth: Abortion was not a simple matter, not for authorities, not for communities, and certainly not for women.

NOTES

INTRODUCTION

1. *Catechism of the Catholic Church*, part 3, section 2, "The Ten Commandments," article 5, "The Fifth Commandment," "I. Respect for Human Life—Abortion, 2271," accessed May 27, 2020, http://www.vatican.va/archive/ccc_css/archive/catechism/p3s2c2a5.htm.

2. Sixtus V, *Contra Procurantes, Consulentes, & Consentientes quocumque modo Abortum. Constitutio* (Rome: Antonio Blado, 1588), f. 2r.

3. The following exemplary studies have influenced my approach to recovering and examining varied voices on this subject: Leslie J. Reagan, *When Abortion Was a Crime: Women, Medicine and Law in the United States, 1867–1973* (Berkeley: University of California Press, 1997); Cornelie Usborne, *Cultures of Abortion in Weimar Germany* (New York: Berghann Books, 2007); Susanne M. Klausen, *Abortion under Apartheid: Nationalism, Sexuality, and Women's Reproductive Rights in South Africa* (Oxford: Oxford University Press, 2015); Nora E. Jaffary, *Reproduction and Its Discontents in Mexico: Childbirth and Contraception from 1750 to 1905* (Chapel Hill: University of North Carolina Press, 2016); Cassia Roth, *A Miscarriage of Justice: Women's Reproductive Lives and the Law in Early Twentieth-Century Brazil* (Stanford: Stanford University Press, 2020); Natalie L. Kimball, *An Open Secret: The History of Unwanted Pregnancy and Abortion in Modern Bolivia* (New Brunswick, NJ: Rutgers University Press, 2020).

4. For recent surveys of sixteenth and seventeenth century Italy, see Gregory Hanlon, *Early Modern Italy, 1550–1800: Three Seasons in European History* (New York: St. Martin's, 2000); Christopher Black, *Early Modern Italy: A Social History* (London: Routledge, 2001); John Marino, ed., *Early Modern Italy, 1550–1796* (New York: Oxford University Press, 2002); Elizabeth S. Cohen and Thomas V. Cohen, *Daily Life in Renaissance Italy* (Westport, CT: Greenwood, 2008); Domenico Sella, *Italy in the Seventeenth Century* (London: Routledge, 2014). For the global perspective, Geoffrey Parker, *Global Crisis: War, Climate Change and Catastrophe in the Seventeenth Century* (New Haven, CT: Yale University Press, 2013).

5. For reviews of recent work on religious reform in Italy, see Ottavia Niccoli, *La vita religiosa nell'Italia moderna: Secoli XV–XVIII* (Rome: Carocci,

1998); Simon Ditchfield, "In Search of Local Knowledge: Rewriting Early Modern Italian History," *Christianesimo nella storia* 19 (1998): pp. 255–296; John J. Martin, "Religion, Renewal, and Reform in the Sixteenth Century," in *Early Modern Italy*, ed. John A. Marino (New York: Oxford University Press, 2002), pp. 30–47; Ann Jacobson Schutte, "Religion, Spirituality, and the Post-Tridentine Church," in *Early Modern Italy*, ed. John A. Marino (New York: Oxford University Press, 2002), pp. 125–142; Wietse De Boer, "Social Discipline in Italy: Peregrinations of a Historical Paradigm,' *Archiv für Reformationsgeschicte / Archive for Reformation History* 94 (2003): pp. 294–307; Christopher Black, *Church, Religion and Society in Early Modern Italy* (New York: Palgrave, 2004); Nicholas Terpstra, "Italy," in *Reformation and Early Modern Europe: A Guide to Research*, ed. David M. Whitford (Kirksville: Truman State University Press, 2007), pp. 228–249. For recent assessments and reassessments of the Counter-Reformation, see Alexandra Bamji, Geert H. Janssen, and Mary Laven, *The Ashgate Research Companion to the Counter-Reformation* (Farnham, UK: Ashgate, 2013); Elena Bonora, "Il ritorno della Controriforma (e la Vergine del Rosario di Guápulo)," *Studi Storici* 2 (2016): pp. 267–296; and Massimo Firpo, "Rethinking 'Catholic Reform' and 'Counter-Reformation': What Happened in Early Modern Catholicism—a View from Italy," *Journal of Early Modern History* 20 (2016): pp. 293–312.

6. Merry Wiesner-Hanks, *Christianity and Sexuality in the Early Modern World: Regulating Desire, Reforming Practice* (New York: Routledge, 2010). On marriage reform, see Daniela Lombardi, *Storia del matrimonio: Dal Medioevo a oggi* (Bologna: Il Mulino, 2008), and Silvana Seidel Menchi, *Marriage in Europe, 1400–1800* (Toronto: University of Toronto Press, 2016).

7. Along with other studies on attitudes and responses to sexual deviance cited below, see Guido Ruggiero, *The Boundaries of Eros: Sex Crime and Sexuality in Renaissance Venice* (New York: Oxford University Press, 1985); Guido Ruggiero, *Binding Passions: Tales of Magic, Marriage, and Power at the End of the Renaissance* (New York: Oxford University Press, 1993); Nicholas Davidson, "Theology, Nature and the Law: Sexual Sin and Sexual Crime in Italy from the Fourteenth to the Seventeenth Century," in *Crime, Society and the Law in Renaissance Italy*, ed. Trevor Dean and Kate Lowe (Cambridge: Cambridge University Press, 1993), pp. 74–98; Thomas Cohen, *Love and Death in Renaissance Italy* (Chicago: University of Chicago Press, 2004); Silvana Seidel Menchi and Diego Quaglioni, eds., *Trasgressioni: seduzione, concubinato, adulterio, bigamia (XIV–XVIII secolo)* (Bologna: Il Mulino, 2004); Cesarina Casanova, *Crimini Nascosti: La sanzione penale dei reati "senza vittima" e nelle relazioni private (Bologna, XVII secolo)* (Bologna, CLUEB, 2007); Joanne Ferraro, *Nefarious Crimes, Contested Justice: Illicit Sex and Infanticide in the Republic of Venice, 1557–1789* (Baltimore: Johns Hopkins University Press, 2008).

8. On the development of Catholic theology surrounding abortion, see the foundational work of John Noonan, *Contraception: A History of Its Treatment by the Catholic Theologians and Canonists* (New York: New American Library, 1965); John Noonan, "An Almost Absolute Value in History," in *The Morality of Abortion: Legal and Historical Perspectives*, ed. John Noonan (Cambridge, MA: Harvard University Press, 1970), pp. 1–59. See also Paolo Sardi, *Aborto ieri e oggi* (Brescia: Paideia, 1975); John Connery, S. J., *Abortion: The Development of the Roman Catholic Perspective* (Chicago: Loyola University Press, 1977).

9. Scipione Mercurio, *De gli errori popolari d'Italia* (Venice: Gio. Battista Ciotti, 1603), bk. 2, ch. 26, f. 108r–v.

10. In addition to works cited in note 8, see Adriano Prosperi's rich discussion of this history, *Infanticide, Secular Justice, and Religious Debate in Early Modern Europe* (Turnhout: Brepols, 2016), pp. 187–230 (the English translation of *Dare l'anima: storia di un infanticidio* (Turin: Einaudi, 2005).

11. On the criminalization of abortion in the medieval west, see Zubin Mistry, *Abortion in the Early Middle Ages, c. 500–900* (Woodbridge, UK: York Medieval Press, 2015), ch. 6; and Wolfgang Müller, *The Criminalization of Abortion in the West: Its Origins in Medieval Law* (Ithaca, NY: Cornell University Press, 2012). For early modern England, see Carla Spivack, "To 'Bring Down the Flowers': The Cultural Context of Abortion Law in Early Modern England," *William and Mary Quarterly* 107 (2007): pp. 107–151. For early modern Germany, see Ulinka Rublack, "The Public Body: Policing Abortion in Early Modern Germany," in *Gender Relations in German History: Power, Agency and Experience from the Sixteenth to the Twentieth Century*, ed. Lynn Abrams and Elizabeth Harvey (Durham, NC: Duke University Press, 2006); and Margaret Brannan Lewis, *Infanticide and Abortion in Early Modern Germany* (New York: Routledge, 2016).

12. John Riddle's work on the history of pharmacology has shown that ancient Mediterranean societies identified certain herbs as potentially capable of terminating pregnancy, and passed this information down through the centuries through a rich textual pharmacological tradition. John Riddle, *Contraception and Abortion from the Ancient World to the Renaissance* (Cambridge, MA: Harvard University Press, 1992); John Riddle, *Eve's Herbs: A History of Contraception and Abortion in the West* (Cambridge, MA: Harvard University Press, 1997).

13. The words of Giulio Folco, one of Santa Caterina's financiers, *Effetti mirabili de la limosina* (Venice, 1608), f. 4v, quoted in Vittorio Frajese, *Il popolo fanciullo: Silvio Antoniano e il sistema disciplinare della controriforma* (Milan: Franco Angeli, 1987), pp. 90–96.

14. The historiography on women's custodial institutions is vast. Here I cite some of the most recent and influential studies. Sherill Cohen, *The Evolution of Women's Asylum's since 1500: From Refuges for Ex-prostitutes to Shelters for*

Battered Women (New York: Oxford University Press, 1992); Angela Groppi, *I conservatori della virtu. Donne recluse nella Roma dei Papi* (Rome: Laterza, 1994); Nicholas Terpstra, *Lost Girls: Sex and Death in Renaissance Florence* (Baltimore: The Johns Hopkins University Press, 2010); Nicholas Terpstra, *Cultures of Charity: Women, Politics, and the Reform of Poor Relief in Renaissance Italy* (Cambridge, MA: Harvard University Press, 2013); Brian Pullan, *Tolerance, Regulation and Rescue: Dishonoured Women and Abandoned Children in Italy, 1300–1800* (Manchester: Manchester University Press, 2016), pp. 106-124.

15. According to Robert Davis, most women would have felt threatened walking the streets of early modern Italian cities, "The Geography of Gender in the Renaissance," in *Gender and Society in Renaissance Italy*, ed. Judith C. Brown and Robert C. Davis (London: Longman, 1998), pp. 19-38. For a less threatening picture, see Monica Chojnacka, *Working Women in Early Modern Venice* (Baltimore: Johns Hopkins University Press, 2001); and Elizabeth Cohen, "To Pray, to Work, to Hear, to Speak: Women in Roman Streets, c. 1600," *Journal of Early Modern History* 12 (2008): pp. 289-311.

16. For similar reassessments of the history of the sexual double standard in Spain and France, see Edward Behrend-Martinez, "'Taming Don Juan': Limiting Masculine Sexuality in Counter-Reformation Spain," *Gender and History* 24 (2012): pp. 333-352; Julie Hardwick, "Policing Paternity: Historicising Masculinity and Sexuality in Early-Modern France," *European Review of History* 22 (2015): pp. 643-657; and Julie Hardwick, *Sex in an Old Regime City: Young Workers and Intimacy in France, 1660–1789* (New York: Oxford University Press, 2020).

17. Domenico Ottonelli, *Alcuni buoni avvisi, e casi di coscienza intorno alla pericolosa Conversatione, Da proporsi a chi conversa poco medestamente* (Florence, 1646), pp. 372-373.

18. Giovanni Battista De Luca, *Il dottor volgare, overo il compendio di tutta la legge, civile, canonica, feudale, e municipale, nelle cose piu ricevute in pratica* (Rome: Giuseppe Corvo, 1673), bk. 15, ch. 5, p. 129.

19. Elizabeth Cohen, "Seen and Known: Prostitutes in the Cityscape of Late-Sixteenth-Century Rome," *Renaissance Studies* 12 (1998): pp. 392-409; Tessa Storey, *Carnal Commerce in Counter-Reformation Rome* (Cambridge: Cambridge University Press, 2008); Vanessa McCarthy, "Prostitution, Community, and Civic Regulation in Early Modern Bologna," Ph.D. diss., University of Toronto, 2015; Joanne Ferraro, "Making a Living: The Sex Trade in Early Modern Venice," *American Historical Review* 123 (2018): pp. 30-59.

20. Ferraro, *Nefarious Crimes.*

21. Garthine Walker, "Everyman or a Monster? The Rapist in Early Modern England, c. 1600-1750," *History Workshop Journal* 76 (2013): pp. 5-31.

22. We should follow Nicole von Germeten's injunction to "at least entertain the idea that women made choices when it came to their sexuality and

that they actually experienced sexual desires, even if they were heavily influenced by economic necessity and social and gender hierarchies." *Violent Delights, Violent Ends: Sex, Race, and Honor in Colonial Cartagena de Indias* (Albuquerque: University of New Mexico Press, 2013), p. 233. See also Elizabeth Cohen, "Straying and Led Astray: Roman Maids Become Young Women circa 1600," in *The Youth of Early Modern Women*, ed. Elizabeth Cohen and Margaret Reeves (Amsterdam: Amsterdam University Press, 2018): pp. 297–296; Hardwick, *Sex in an Old Regime City.*

23. Pregnant domestic servants might be thrown out of the household they served, but sometimes they received dowries from their masters if they or someone close to them were responsible for the pregnancy; see Dennis Romano, "The Regulation of Domestic Service in Renaissance Venice," *Sixteenth Century Journal* 22 (1991): pp. 666–667; Thomas Kuehn, *Law, Family, and Women: Toward a Legal Anthropology of Renaissance Italy* (Chicago: University of Chicago Press, 1991), pp. 83–88; Ferraro, *Nefarious Crimes.*

24. Thomas Cohen, "A Daughter Killing Digested, and Accepted, in a Village of Rome, 1563–66," in *Murder in Renaissance Italy*, ed. Trevor Dean and Kate J. P. Lowe (Cambridge: Cambridge University Press, 2017), pp. 62–82.

25. Sandra Cavallo and Simona Cerutti, "Female Honor and the Social Control of Reproduction in Piedmont between 1600 and 1800," in *Sex and Gender in Historical Perspective*, ed. Edward Muir and Guido Ruggiero (Baltimore: Johns Hopkins University Press, 1990), pp. 73–109. For similar legal approaches in Spain and France, see Abigail Dyer, "Seduction by Promise of Marriage: Law, Sex and Culture in Seventeenth-Century Spain," *Sixteenth Century Journal* 34 (2003): pp. 439–455; Hardwick, *Sex in an Old Regime City*, pp. 91–109.

26. Lucia Ferrante, "La sessualità come risorsa: Donne avanti al foro arcivescovile di Bologna (secolo XVII)," *Mélanges de l'École française de Rome* 99, Part II (1988): pp. 989–1016; Elizabeth Cohen, "No Longer Virgins: Self-Presentation by Young Women of Late Renaissance Rome," in *Refiguring Woman: Perspectives on Gender and the Italian Renaissance*, ed by Marilyn Migiel and Juliana Schiesari (Ithaca: Cornell University Press, 1991): pp. 169–191.

27. Philip Gavitt, *Charity and Children in Renaissance Florence: The Ospedale degli Innocenti, 1410–1536* (Ann Arbor: University of Michigan Press, 1990); Philip Gavitt, *Gender, Honor, and Charity in Late Renaissance Florence* (Cambridge: Cambridge University Press, 2011); Nicholas Terpstra, *Abandoned Children of the Italian Renaissance: Orphan Care in Florence and Bologna* (Baltimore: Johns Hopkins University Press, 2005); Pullan, *Tolerance, Regulation and Rescue*, pp. 125–176.

28. According to Joanne Ferraro, pregnant women set on abandoning future children could tap into networks and informal industries in order to receive services that would help them give birth abroad in secrecy and for the newborn to be taken care of afterward. Ferraro, *Nefarious Crimes.*

29. Neonaticide is commonly defined as the killing of an infant within twenty-four hours of its birth; infanticide is the killing of an infant after twenty-four hours and before its first year. Early modern Europeans did not always articulate this distinction.

30. Richard Trexler, "Infanticide in Florence: New Sources and First Results," *History of Chidhood Quarterly* 1 (1973): pp. 98–116; Claudio Povolo, "Note per uno studio dell'infanticidio nella republica di Venezia nei secoli XV–XVIII," *Atti dell'Istituto Veneto di Scienze, Lettere, ed Arti* 137 (1979): pp. 115–131; Claudio Povolo, "Aspetti sociali e penali del reato d'infanticidio: Il caso di una Contadina padovana del '700," *Atti dell'Istituto Veneto di Scienze, Lettere, ed Arti* 138 (1979–1980): pp. 415–432; Claudio Povolo, "L'imputata accusa: un processo per infanticidio alla fine del Settecento," in *Veneto e Lombardia tra rivoluzione giacobina ed eta napoleonica. Economia, territorio, istituzioni,* ed. G. L. Fonata and A. Lazzarini (Bari: Laterza, 1992), pp. 563–575; Gregory Hanlon, "Infanticidio dei coppie sposate nella Toscana moderna, secoli XVI–XVIII," *Quaderni Storici* 38 (2003): pp. 453–498; Gregory Hanlon, "Routine Infanticide in the West, 1500–1800," *History Compass* 14 (2016): pp. 535–548; Casanova, *Crimini nacosti,* pp. 184–193; Ferraro, *Nefarious Crimes,* ch. 4; Laura Hynes, "Routine Infanticide by Married Couples? An Assessment of Baptismal Records from Seventeenth Century Parma," *Journal of Early Modern History* 15 (2011): pp. 507–530; Prosperi, *Infanticide, Secular Justice and Religious Debate*; Colin Rose, *A Renaissance of Violence: Homicide in Early Modern Italy* (Cambridge: Cambridge University Press, 2019), pp. 151–154. For scholarship on infanticide in other early modern European contexts, see, for England, Mark Jackson, *New-Born Child Murder: Women, Illegitimacy and the Courts in Eighteenth-Century England* (Manchester: Manchester University Press, 1996); Laura Gowing, "Secret Births and Infanticide in Seventeenth-Century England," *Past and Present* 156 (1997): pp. 87–11; Garthine Walker, "Child-Killing and Emotion in Early Modern England and Wales," in *Death, Emotion and Childhood in Premodern Europe,* ed. Katie Barclay, Kimberley Reynolds, and Ciara Rawnsley (London: Palgrave Macmillan, 2016) pp. 151–172; Josephine Billingham, *Infanticide in Tudor and Stuart England* (Amsterdam: Amsterdam University Press, 2019); for Germany, Ulinka Rublack, *The Crimes of Women in Early Modern Germany* (New York: Oxford University Press, 2001), 163–196; David Myers, *Death and a Maiden: Infanticide and the Tragical History of Grethe Schmidt* (Dekalb: Northern Illinois University Press, 2011); Lewis, *Abortion and Infanticide*;

for France, Alfred Soman, "Anatomy of an Infanticide Trial: The Case of Marie-Jeanne Bartonnet (1742)," in *Changing Identities in Early Modern France*, ed. Michael Wolfe (Durham, NC: Duke University Press, 1997), pp. 248–272; Alfred Soman and Robert Muchembled, "Fils de Caïn, enfants de Médée. Homicide et infanticide devant le parlement de Paris (1575–1604)," *Annales. Histoire, Sciences Sociales* 62 (2007): pp. 1063–1094; Hardwick, *Sex in an Old Regime City*, pp. 183–200.

31. Martin of Azpilcueta, *Consiliorum sive responsorum* (Rome: Aloysii Zannetti, 1595), consilium, 59, p. 457.

32. For the treatment of abortion by assault in the Middle Ages, see Sara M. Butler, "Abortion by Assault: Violence against Pregnant Women in Thirteenth- and Fourteenth-Century England," *Journal of Women's History* 17 (2004): pp. 9–31; Müller, *The Criminalization of Abortion in the West*.

33. For thoughtful reflections on the medieval and early modern Church's fear of and practices surrounding clerical sexual scandal, and comparisons with the contemporary situation, see Dyan Elliott, "Sexual Scandal and the Clergy: A Medieval Blueprint," in *Why the Middle Ages Matter*, ed. Celia Chazelle et al. (London: Routledge, 2012), pp. 90–105; Wietse de Boer, "The Catholic Church and Sexual Abuse, Then and Now," *Origins: Current Events in Historical Perspective* 12.6 (March 2019), accessed May 27 2020, http://origins.osu.edu/historytalk/secrecy-and-celibacy-catholic-church-and-sexual-abuse.

34. I take this wording from Katie Watson, who distinguishes "ordinary abortion"—procured to terminate unintended or untimely pregnancy—from "extraordinary abortion"—procured in fewer and more extreme cases such as rape, incest, fetal anomaly, and health issues that put women's lives in danger. Commenting on the contemporary abortion wars in the United States, Watson notes, "The absence of the ordinary means that the cases we discuss most are the ones that occur least." *Scarlet A: The Ethics, Law and Politics of Ordinary Abortion* (New York: Oxford University Press, 2018), p. 7.

35. See the important methodological and ethical challenges raised by Saidiya Hartman, "Venus in Two Acts," *Small Axe* 12 (2008): pp. 1–14; Marisa J. Fuentes, *Dispossessed Lives: Enslaved Women, Violence, and the Archive* (Philadelphia: University of Pennsylvania Press, 2016).

36. George Lakoff and Mark Johnson, *Metaphors We Live By* (Chicago: University of Chicago Press, 2003).

37. John Florio, *A Worlde of Wordes: A Critical Edition*, ed. Hermann W. Haller (Toronto: University of Toronto Press, 2013), p. 457; Tommaso Porcacchi, *Vocabolario nuovo di M. Tomaso Porcacchi*, published alongside Francesco Alunno, *De la fabrica del mondo* (Venice: Gio. Battista Uscio, 1588), p. 1.

38. *Vocabolario degli accademici della crusca . . . seconda impressione* (Venice: Iacopo Sarzina, 1623), p. 16.

39. Girolamo Ruscelli, *Vocabolario delle voci latine dichiarate con l'Italiane* (Venice: Valerio Bonello, 1588), f. 1v.

40. See entries for *sconciamente, sconciare, sconciatura,* and *sconcio* in Antonio Bevilacqua, *Vocabulario volgare, et latino* (Venice: Aldo Manuzio, 1573), f. 60v; Filippo Venuti da Cortona, *Dittionario volgare et latino* (Turin: Gio. Dominico Tarino, 1590), p. 990; *Vocabolario degli Accademici della Crusca,* pp. 760-761; Florio, *Worlde of Wordes,* p. 617.

41. See *guastare* and *guasto* in Venuti da Cortona, *Dittionario volgare et latino,* p. 488; Bevilacqua, *Vocabulario volgare, et latino,* f. 28r; Florio, *Worlde of Wordes,* p. 288; *Vocabolario degli Accademici della Crusca,* pp. 396-397.

42. See entries for the verb and nouns *disperdere, disperdo, dispersi, disperso,* and *disperdimento* in Venuti da Cortona, *Dittionario volgare et latino,* p. 331; Bevilacqua, *Vocabulario volgare, et latino,* f. 19r; Florio, *World of Words,* p. 203; *Vocabolario degli Accademici della Crusca,* p. 284.

43. *Disertare* also meant "to make desert." See entries for *disertare* and *dolere, dolersi* in Florio, *Worlde of Wordes,* pp. 200, 209; *Vocabolario degli Accademici della Crusca,* pp. 278, 296.

44. Giovanni Boccaccio, *Il Decamerone di Messer Giovanni Boccaccio . . . Di nuovo riformato da Luigi Groto Cieco d'Adria . . . Et con le Dichiarationi Avertimenti, & un vocabolario fatto da Girolamo Ruscelli* (Venice: Fabio & Agostin Zoppini, 1590), p. 451.

45. Compare the 1569 and 1584 editions of Martin de Azpilcueta, *Manuale de confessori et penitenti . . . tradotto di Spagnuolo in Italiano dal R. P. Fra Cola di Guglinisi* (Venice: Gabriel Giolito di Ferrara), p. 166 and f. 179v-180r, respectively.

46. Compare the wording in the *Manuale de confessori et penitenti . . . tradotto dalla linguia Latina nella nostra Italiana da Camillo Camilli,* (Venice: Giorgio Angelieri, 1584), f. 180r, with that in the *Manuale del Navarro, ridotto in compendio da Pietro Giuvara theologo e tradotto dal Latino nella lingua Toscana da Camillo Camilli* (Turin: Gio. Dominico Tarino, 1591), f. 44v.

47. Sperone Speroni, *Orazione contra le cortigiane* in *Orationi del sig. Speron Speroni dottor et cavalier Padovano* (Venice: Ruberto Meietti, 1596), p. 194.

48. Daniello Bartoli, *Dell'Istoria della Compagnia di Giesu. L'Asia. . . . Parte Prima* (Rome: Stamperia del Varese, 1667), p. 134.

49. Bartolomeo Fumi, *Somma armilla del rev. padre Bartolomeo Fumo, . . . Gia tradotta in lingua volgare dal Rever. P. Maestro Remigio dell'istesso Ordine, & dal R. M. Gio. Maria Tarsia, Fiorentini* (Venice: Domenico Nicolini, 1588), f. 2v.

50. ASR, TcG, Processi, 1595, b. 269, f. 635v.

51. ASR, TcG, Processi, 1613, b. 116, f. 160v.

52. *Vocabolario degli Accademici della Crusca,* p. 7.

53. Pietro Aretino, *Sei giornate,* ed. Giovanni Aquilecchia (Bari: Laterza, 1980) p. 112. See Rosenthal's English translation, but note that he translates *sconcia* not as "miscarriage" or "abortion" but as "badly hurt." Pietro Aretino, *Dialogues,* trans. Raymond Rosenthal (Toronto: University of Toronto Press, 2005), pp. 118–119.

54. Pasquale Stoppelli, *La* Mandragola: *storia e filologia. Con l'edizione critica del testo secondo il Laurenziano Redi 129* (Rome: Bulzoni editore, 2005), act 3, scene 4, p. 211. For the English translation, see *Five Comedies of the Italian Renaissance,* ed. and trans. Laura Giannetti and Guido Ruggiero (Baltimore: Johns Hopkins University Press, 2003), pp. 91–93.

55. Giovan Battista Marino, "Nella sconciatura della Signora Veronica Spinola," in *La lira,* ed. Maurice Slawinski (Turin: Res, 2007), p. 274.

56. Florio, *Worlde of Wordes,* p. 156; *Vocabolario degli accademici della crusca,* p. 202.

57. Bartolomeo Dotti, *Per un aborto conservato in un'ampolla d'acque artificiali dal signor Giacopo Grandis fisico anatomico eccellentissimo,* in Bartolomeo Dotti, *Delle rime di Bartolomeo Dotti. I sonetti* (Venice, 1689), p. 167. For a brief discussion of the sonnet in the context of poems on the body and on monstrosity, See Marino Niola, *Il Corpo mirabile: miracolo, sangue, estasi nella Napoli barocca* (Rome: Meltemi editore, 1997), p. 102.

58. For *conceputto / concetto,* see *Vocabolario degli Accademici della Crusca,* p. 202; for *embrione, Vocabolario degli Accademici della Crusca,* p. 308; for *feto, Vocabolario degli Accademici della Crusca,* pp. 308, 336; Florio was less precise: *Worlde of Wordes,* pp. 217, 240.

59. The Latin word *vitalis* and the Italian words *vitale* and *vivace* were defined "as having life, that is able to sustain life." Venuti da Cortona, *Dittionario volgare et latino,* p. 1199. Florio translated *vitale* as "vitall, lively, that may live or hope for life. Also that whereby we live, and doth either bring or preserve life, any thing pertaining to the maintenance of life," and *vivace* as "lively, breathing, quicke, nimble, active, full of life, of long life, strong of nature, valiant, lustie greene, that liveth and continueth long." Florio, *Worlde of Wordes,* pp. 780–781. While *vital* can mean "maintaining, supporting, or sustaining life" in contemporary English, the medical-legal term *viable*—the ability of the fetus to live independently of the maternal environment—seems a more appropriate choice in the context of abortion. See entries for "vital" and "viable" in the *Oxford English Dictionary Online* (Oxford: Oxford University Press, 2020).

60. Paolo Zacchia, *Quaestionum medico-legalium* (Rome: 1621; the Lyon: Joannis-Antonii Huguetan and Marci-Antonii Ravaud, 1661 edition is cited here), bk. 1, tit. 2, quest. 7, pp. 43–45 and quest. 10, pp. 48–49.

61. Zacchia, *Quaestionum medico-legalium,* bk. 1, tit. 2, quest. 10, n. 17, p. 49.

62. For instance, Zacchia was called on to give advice on an inheritance case that hinged on the gestational age of fetus and therefore whether it had been legally "born" or "aborted." Zacchia, *Quaestionum medico-legalium*, bk. 10, cons. 37, pp. 209–212.

CHAPTER ONE ∾ ABORTION AND WOMEN'S BODIES

1. Giuliano Amato: "Et io gli feci una ricetta piccola che era suficiente a fare che detta donna havesse partorito o viva o morta che fosse stata la creatura dicendogli che se la creatura era viva questa ricetta mia haverebbe aggiutato la detta donna a partoritla et se la creatura fosse stata morta l'haverebbe aggiutato ad uscire." ASR, TcG, Piocessi, 1606, b. 53, f. 387v–388r.

2. See Winifred Schleiner, *Medical Ethics in the Renaissance* (Washington, DC: Georgetown University Press, 1997), for discussion of this genre of writing.

3. Giovan Battista Codronchi, *De christiana ac tuta medendi ratione* (Ferrara, 1591), bk. 1, ch. 22, pp. 67–68, 70–71. Codronchi expressed milder views on this subject in an earlier vernacular publication, Condronchi, *Casi di conscienza* in *Viaggi spirituali, dell'huomo christiano al cielo,* discussed in Prosperi, *Infanticide, Secular Justice, and Religious Debate,* p. 259.

4. Mercurio, *De gli errori popolari*, bk. 2, ch. 26, f. 108r–v, and bk. 5, ch. 14, f. 251v–253v.

5. Hippocrates *Iusiurandum*, in Girolamo Mercuriale's edition of Hippocrates's works, *Hippocratis Coi Opera quae extant* (Venice, 1588), quarta class., p. 1.

6. Lucillo Filalteo, *Il Giuramento, e le sette parti de gli aforismi d'Hippocrate Coo* (Pavia: Francesco Moscheno, 1552), p. 2.

7. Tarduccio Salvi, *Il chirurgo, trattato breve* (Rome: Gio Battista Robletti, 1642), p. 3.

8. The *Oath* received considerable attention in the fifteenth and sixteenth centuries. See Thomas Rutten, "Receptions of the Hippocratic Oath in the Renaissance: The Prohibition of Abortion as a Case Study in Reception," *Journal of the History of Medicine and Allied Sciences* 51 (1996): pp. 456–483.

9. Hippocrates, *The Nature of the Child,* 13, in *The Hippocratic Treatises "On Generation", "The Nature of the Child", "Diseases IV,"* ed. and trans. Ian Lonie (Berlin: De Guyter, 1981), p. 7. For discussion of this passage, see Helen King, *Hippocrates' Women: Reading the Female Body in Ancient Greece* (London: Routledge, 1998), p. 136.

10. Girolamo Mercuriale, *De morbis muliebribus praelectiones* (Venice: Felicem Valgrisius, 1601), bk. 1, ch. 2, pp. 23–24.

11. Mercurio, *De gli errori popolari,* f. 109r.

12. Zacchia, *Quaestionum medico-legalium*, bk. 6, tit. 1, quest. 7, n. 13, p. 412.

13. The case is discussed in all its rich detail in Renée Baernstein and John Christopoulos, "Interpreting the Body in Early Modern Italy: Pregnancy, Abortion and Adulthood," *Past and Present* 223 (2014): pp. 41–75.

14. The medical practitioners examined here were born into a world were gynecology was a specialized medical subject. Late medieval and Renaissance physicians succeeded in reinventing "women's medicine" as a learned and masculine discipline, in concept if not necessarily in practice. Academic and popular interest in women's bodies led to a pan-European explosion of male-authored works on generation, pregnancy, and women's diseases in both Latin and the vernacular. See Monica Green, *Making Women's Medicine Masculine: The Rise of Male Authority in Pre-Modern Gynaecology* (New York: Oxford University Press, 2008), ch. 6, esp. pp. 275–287 and Green's appendix for a list of sixteenth century works of women's medicine published throughout Western Europe. Katharine Park has observed that Renaissance male medical authors sought to unveil and disseminate their discoveries and learning through publication in the service of "public interest and public good." Park, *Secrets of Women: Gender, Generation and the Origins of Dissection* (New York: Zone Books, 2006), pp. 116, 120. On similar developments in England, see Mary Fissell, *Vernacular Bodies: The Politics of Reproduction in Early Modern England* (Oxford: Oxford University Press, 2004); and Wendy Churchill, *Female Patients in Early Modern Britain* (Aldershot, UK: Ashgate, 2012). For France, Lianne McTavish, *Childbirth and the Display of Authority in Early Modern France* (London: Routledge, 2005).

15. On the importance of discovery coming from hands-on investigation, as opposed to scholastic educational traditions that emphasized textual understanding over empirical knowledge production, see Andrea Carlino, *Books of the Body: Anatomical Ritual and Renaissance Learning*, trans. John Tedeschi and Anne C. Tedeschi (Chicago: University of Chicago Press, 1999); Park, *Secrets of Women*; Gianna Pomata, "Observation Rising: Birth of an Epistemic Genre, 1500–1650," in *Histories of Scientific Observation*, ed. Lorraine Daston and Elizabeth Lunbeck (Chicago: University of Chicago Press, 2011), pp. 45–80; Gianna Pomata, "A World of Empirics: The Ancient Concept of Observation and Its Recovery in Early Modern Medicine," *Annals of Science* 68 (2011): pp. 1–25; Bradford Bouley, *Pious Postmortems: Anatomy, Sanctity, and the Catholic Church in Early Modern Europe* (Philadelphia: University of Pennsylvania Press, 2017).

16. Paolo Zacchia's important compendium *Quaestionum medico-legalium* (first published in Rome in 1621 and expanded until 1661) digested previous works into a handbook of forensic medicine used by physicians and jurists. Bernardino Cristini, *Pratica medicinale & osservationi*, bk. 2,

De mali particolari delle Donne (Venice: Bodio, 1681). This treatise was first published in Latin in 1676.

17. Jennifer F. Kosmin, *Authority, Gender and Midwifery in Early Modern Italy: Contested Deliveries* (London: Routledge, 2020).

18. See Barbara Duden, "The Fetus on the 'Farther Shore': Toward a History of the Unborn," in *Fetal Subjects, Feminist Positions*, ed. L. M. Morgan and M. W. Michaels (Philadelphia: University of Pennsylvania Press, 1999), pp. 13–25; Lynn M. Morgan, *Icons of Life: A Cultural History of Human Embryos* (Berkeley: University of California Press, 2009); Janelle S. Taylor, *The Public Life of the Fetal Sonogram: Technology, Consumption and the Politics of Reproduction* (New Brunswick, NJ: Rutgers University Press, 2008); Julie Roberts, *The Visualised Foetus. A Cultural and Political Analysis of Ultrasound Imagery* (Surrey, UK: Ashgate, 2012); Deborah Lupton, *The Social Worlds of the Unborn* (Basingstoke, UK: Palgrave, 2013).

19. Elena Cocchi: "Anzi, che quando io me cominciai a conoscer esser gravida, feci venire la mia solita mammana chiamata Dionora che me ha raccolto altri figlioli, alla quale dissi che dubitavo esser gravida et lei mi vidde et disse che io ero gravida che poi me si era cominciato ad ingrossare anco il corpo." ASR, TcG, Processi, 1634, b. 295, f. 1700v–1701r.

20. Gowing, "Secret Births and Infanticide," p. 114. See also Cathy McClive, "The Hidden Truths of the Belly: The Uncertainties of Pregnancy in Early Modern Europe," *Social History of Medicine* 15 (2002): pp. 209–227; Laura Gowing, *Common Bodies: Women, Touch and Power in Seventeenth-Century England* (New Haven: Yale University Press, 2003), ch. 4; Terpstra, *Lost Girls*, ch. 4.

21. Albertino Bottoni, *De morbis muliebribus libri tres* (Venice: Paulum Meietum, 1588), bk. 2, ch. 11, f. 9v–12r; Giovanni Marinello, *Le medicine partenenti alle infermita delle donne* (Venice: Giovanni Bonadio, 1563), bk. 3, ch. 2, f. 241r–242v; ch. 6, f. 253r–255v; ch. 7, f. 256r–258r; Zacchia, *Quaestionum medico-legalium*, bk. 1, tit. 3, quest. 1–2, pp. 50–57. For an earlier period, see Rudolph Bell, *How to Do It: Guides to Good Living for Renaissance Italians* (Chicago: University of Chicago Press, 1999).

22. For examples from the seventeenth century, see Marina D'Amelia, "Becoming a Mother in the Seventeenth Century: The Experience of a Roman Noblewoman," in *Time, Space, and Women's Lives in Early Modern Europe*, ed. Anne Jacobson Schutte, Thomas Kuehn, and Silvana Seidel Menchi (Kirksville: Truman State University Press, 2001), pp. 223–244; for early modern France, see Susan Broomhall, *Women's Medical Work in Early Modern France* (Manchester: Manchester University Press, 2004), ch. 8.

23. Evidently Christine was right, and Caterina was pregnant, but she suffered a miscarriage in July 1617. ASF, MDP, 6110, f. 343, letter from

Christine de Lorraine in Florence to Caterina de' Medici Gonzaga, in Mantua, 28 April 1617, digitized by the Medici Archive Project, BIA, accessed May 27, 2020, bia.medici.org, Doc ID# 7037.

24. Elena Cocchi: "Io so che ero gravida da detto tempo incirca perché non havevo havuto il mio tempo, come ero solita di havere, me si era seccato il latte che allattavo un figliolo, havevo havuto vomiti et non potevo magnare, che simili segni hanno le donne gravide et ho hauto sempre io l'altre volte che sono stata gravida." ASR, TcG, Processi, 1634, b. 295, f. 1700v–1701r.

25. ASB, Torrone, Atti e Processi, 1586, b. 1898, f. 225r–250v.

26. Astonida da Santo Jesi heard Livia dei Banchi say: "Fermati, non fare! Tu voi mostrar le spalle per Roma! Non vedi che costei è pregna?" ASR, TcG, Processi, 1603, b. 28bis, f. 773v–774r.

27. ASR, TcG, Registrazioni d'Atti, b. 148, f. 152v.

28. For similar and different perceptions of pregnant women, single and married, in early modern Germany and England, see Ulinka Rublack, "Pregnancy, Childbirth and the Female Body in Early Modern Germany," *Past and Present* 150 (1996): pp. 84–110; Gowing, *Common Bodies*, ch. 4.

29. Sperone Speroni, *Del Tempo del Partorire delle Donne* in *Dialogi di M. Speron. Speroni* (Venice: Comin da Trino di Monferrato, 1564), f. 45r.

30. ASF, MDP, 2951, unnumbered folio, letter from Alessandro Senesi in Mantua to Andrea di Giovanni Battista Cioli in Tuscany 8 September 1618, digitized by the Medici Archive Project, BIA, accessed May 27, 2020, bia.medici.org, Doc ID# 5535.

31. Girolamo Mercuriale, *Praelectiones Pisanae . . . De hominis generatione* (Venice: Giunta, 1597), ch. 18, pp. 26–27. Again following Hippocrates, Mercuriale and others held that the time required for a fetus to be viable or "perfect" was about triple the time taken for motion: if a male fetus was formed in 40 days and moved after its 80th day, it would be viable around the 240th day from conception.

32. Mercuriale, *De hominis generatione*, ch. 18, pp. 26–27; ch. 25, pp. 32–33; Bottoni, *De morbis muliebribus*, bk. 2, ch. 23 and 24, f. 21r–25v. See also Paolo Zacchia's thorough analysis of these issues, *Quaestionum medico-legalium*, bk. 1, tit. 2, quest. 7, pp. 43–45; quest. 10, pp. 48–49; bk. 9, tit. 1, pp. 1–26; and bk. 10, cons. 37, pp. 209–212.

33. Marinello, *Le medicine partenenti*, bk. 3, ch. 1, f. 237v; Juan Valverde de Amusco, *La anatomia del corpo umano* (Venice: Giunta, 1586), bk. 3, ch. 16, f. 91v.

34. D'Amelia, "Becoming a Mother," p. 231.

35. Bianca was not pregnant. ASF, MDP, 5042, unnumbered folio, letter from Bianca Cappello-de'Medici in Florence to Vincenzo di Andrea

Alamanni in Spain, February 27, 1586, digitized by the Medici Archive Project, BIA, accessed May 27, 2020, bia.medici.org, Doc ID# 15404.

36. Zacchia, *Questionum medico-legalium,* bk. 1, tit. 3, quest. 1 n. 7, p. 50; bk. 3, tit. 2, quest. 9, n. 2, p. 234.

37. The historical literature on menstruation has grown rapidly. Important recent studies containing ample bibliographies include King, *Hippocrates' Women*; Helen King, *Midwifery, Obstetrics and the Rise of Gynaecology: The Uses of a Sixteenth-Century Compendium* (Aldershot: Ashgate, 2007), pp. 52–59; Sara Read, *Menstruation and the Female Body in Early Modern England* (London: Palgrave, 2013); and Cathy McClive, *Menstruation and Procreation in Early Modern France* (London: Routledge, 2015). Sexual activity was thought to increase heat in the body and encourage regular purgation. See Helen King, *The Disease of Virgins: Green Sickness, Chlorosis, and the Problems of Puberty* (London: Routledge, 2004).

38. On oppilation, "the pathologic retention of humors inside the body," see Gianna Pomata, *Contracting a Cure: Patients, Healers, and the Law in Early Modern Bologna,* trans. R. Foy and A. Taraboletti-Segre (Baltimore: The Johns Hopkins University Press, 1998), pp. 133–134. For women, this mostly stemmed from menstrual suppression. Barbara Duden, *The Woman beneath the Skin: A Doctor's Patients in Eighteenth Century Germany* (Cambridge, MA: Harvard University Press 1991), ch. 4.

39. For the ambiguities of the male body, see Gianna Pomata, "Menstruating Men: Similarity and Difference of the Sexes in Early Modern Medicine," in *Generation and Degeneration: Tropes of Reproduction in Literature and History from Antiquity to Early Modern Europe,* ed. V. Finucci and K. Brownlee (Durham, NC: Duke University Press, 2001), pp. 109–152; Cathy McClive, "Masculinity on Trial: Penises, Hermaphrodites and the Uncertain Male Body in Early Modern France," *History Workshop Journal* 68 (2009): pp. 1–24; Lisa Wynne Smith, "The Body Embarrassed? Rethinking the Leaky Male Body in Eighteenth-Century England and France," *Gender and History* 23 (2010): pp. 26–46.

40. The Modenese Giovanni Marinello believed that "no woman may conceive who is not regularly purged by way of menstruation." Marinello, *Le medicine pertenenti,* ch. 16; ch. 18, f. 101v. In sixteenth-century France, menstruation was commonly referred to as women's *besongnes,* a term that can be translated as "needs." Broomhall, *Women's Medical Work,* p. 216.

41. Similarly, the onset of a period was not evidence that a woman was not with child. Some women menstruate throughout pregnancy, and others menstruate rarely or never at all and "yet they conceive," wrote Zacchia. *Quaestionum medico-legalium,* bk. 1, tit. 3, quest. 1, n. 28–29, p. 51.

42. Modern medical language labels this condition "ascites." Current understandings of causes include different types of cancer (ovaries, uterus,

pancreas, colon, liver) and other diseases of the liver, such as hepatitis B and C infection and alcohol abuse. "Ascites," *MedlinePlus Medical Encyclopedia*, 2018, National Library of Medicine, U.S, and U.S National Institutes of Health, accessed May 27, 2020, http://www.nlm.nih.gov /medlineplus/ency/article/000286.htm.

43. Marinello, *Le medicine partenenti*, bk. 2, ch. 25, f. 193v–196r.

44. Zacchia, *Quaestionum medico-legalium*, bk. 1, tit. 3, quest. 1, n. 36–40, p. 52.

45. Mercuriale, *De morbis muliebribus praelectiones*, bk. 4, ch. 17, pp. 202-204; Alessandro Massaria, *Praelectiones de morbis mulierum, conceptus & partus* (Leipzig: Abraham Lamberg, 1600), ch. 10, pp. 313–321; Scipione Mercurio, *La commare o ricoglitrice* (Venice: Gio Battista Ciotti, 1601), bk. 3, ch. 16, pp. 331-333; Giovanni Zecchi, *Consultationum Medicinalium* (Rome: Facciottus, 1599), cons. 39, pp. 224-228.

46. This Italian word is derived from the Latin and Greek word for millstone (*mola, molon*). The uterine growth mola supposedly resembled the shape of the said stone and hence its name. Today, a *molar pregnancy* refers to the generation of a tumorlike mass, called a hydatiform mole, in the uterus. It is generated when a nonviable egg (without chromosomes and genes) is fertilized by sperm. "Hydatiform Mole," *MedlinePlus Medical Encyclopedia*, 2018, National Library of Medicine, U.S, and U.S National Institutes of Health, accessed May 27, 2020, https://medlineplus.gov/ency /article/000909.htm.

47. Some authors believed that molae were common in lascivious women: too much intercourse renders a husband's seed weak and in short supply; a great desire in a woman could cause her to produce copious amounts of seed and menses and make her womb very hot and unfit for conception. Molae were also believed common in marriages where the wife was young and the husband much older. Some physicians also thought that a mola could be generated entirely by a woman without any contribution from a man. Though not fully convinced that a mola could be generated by a woman alone, Marinello stated that the most telling sign of a mola was if a truly chaste and holy woman who has never known a man shows all the accidents of pregnancy. Most physicians, however, thought that the only way that the womb could get hot enough to generate a mola would be if it was excited by sex. Marinello, *Le medicine partenenti,* bk. 2, ch. 26, f. 199r; Zacchia, *Quaestionum medico-legalium,* bk. 1, tit. 3, quest. 6, pp. 63–65. For a detailed analysis of all the possible causes, Sylvio Lanceano, *De Molae generatione & cura* (Rome: Lepidum Facium & Stephanum Paulinum, 1602), p. 12–64.

48. Marinello, *Le medicine partenenti,* bk. 2, ch. 26, f. 196r–v, 197r; Mercurio, *La commare,* bk. 2, ch. 41, pp. 268–276; Bottoni, *De morbis mulierbribus,* bk. 2, ch. 55-60; Mercuriale, *De morbis mulierbribus,* bk. 1, ch. 3, pp. 25–26, 31; Massaria, *Praelectiones de morbis mulierum,* ch. 8, pp. 298-299; Zacchia, *Questionum medico-legalium,* bk. 1, tit. 3, quest. 5, pp. 61–62.

49. *Vocabolario degli accademici della crusca*, p. 524.

50. Maria Conforti, *"Affirmare quid intus sit divinare est"*: Mole, Mostri e Vermi in un Caso di Falsa Gravidanza di Fine Seicento," *Quaderni Storici* 130 (2009): pp. 125-152; McClive, "Hidden Truths," pp. 219-223; Cathy McClive and Helen King, "When Is a Foetus Not a Foetus?" in *L'embryon humain à travers l'histoire: images, savoirs et rites,* ed. V. Dasen (Gollion: Infolio, 2007), p. 226.

51. Mercurio, *La commare*, bk. 2, ch. 41, pp. 272; Massaria, *Praelectiones de morbis mulierum,* ch. 8, pp. 289-290. For a similar conclusion, see Mercuriale, *De morbis muliebribus,* bk. 1, ch. 3, pp. 31-32; Bottoni, *De morbis muliebribus,* bk. 2, ch. 59; Lanceano, *De molae generatione & cura,* pp. 65-67; and Zacchia, *Questionum medico-legalium,* bk. 1, tit. 3, quest. 2, n. 39 40 and 43-44, p. 56.

52. Mercurio, *La commare*, bk. 2, ch. 41, pp. 272. In a similar story from Giovanni Marinello, a married woman who had experienced pregnancy three times was fooled, along with her physicians, by a moving mola into thinking that she was truly pregnant. Only after fourteen months of living with a swollen belly did her physician start to believe that she was not pregnant but was harboring a mola. Marinello, *Le medicine partenenti,* bk. 2, ch. 26, f. 199v-200v. See also Mercuriale, *De morbis muliebribus,* bk. 1, ch. 3, pp. 25-26; Massaria, *Praelectiones de morbis mulierum,* ch. 10, pp. 315-316.

53. Whether the object was a true mola or some other growth was debated. Conforti, "Affirmare quid intus sit divinare est," pp. 125-152.

54. Zacchia, *Questionum medico-legalium,* bk. 1, tit. 3, quest. 1, n. 17-19, pp. 50-51. Dianora Prosperi: "Non basta che il corpo di una donna sia grosso per poter conoscere che sia gravida, perché ce ne sono molte che l'hanno grosso et non sono gravida." ASR, TcG, Processi, 1634, b. 295, f. 1717r.

55. Mercurio, *La commare*, bk. 1, ch. 17, pp. 85-86.

56. ASF, MDP, 4027a, f. 377, Avviso, Rome to Florence, October 13, 1663, digitized by the Medici Archive Project, BIA, accessed May 27, 2020, bia.medici.org, Doc ID# 19844.

57. Cristini, *Pratica medicinale,* bk. 2, ch. 14, osservatione. xli, p. 98.

58. Zacchia, *Quaestiones medico-legalium,* bk. 10, cons. 39, pp. 214-217. Nevertheless, the case did not go away as the plaintiffs argued that the fleshy growth was a mola, which could only have been generated through sexual intercourse, thus proving her infidelity. Zacchia, however, questioned whether the expulsion was a true mola or some other kind of growth. Zacchia also entertained the possibility that the growth had been generated by her husband's seed, which Violente harbored in her womb from their last sexual encounter before he died and grew very slowly over a two-year period. Zacchia concluded that he could not

determine with certainty whether the expulsion meant that Violante had had sexual relations after her husband's death. See also Zacchia, *Quaestionum medico-legalium,* bk. 1, tit. 3, quest. 6, pp. 63–65, for discussion of molae generated by means of sexual activity.

59. Susan Broomhall has astutely observed that "[early modern women's] sensory perceptions were as socially coded by contemporary discourses as were those of the learned physicians of the medical faculty, even if the discourses themselves were different. It would be simplistic to suggest that physicians drew their notions on the female body, about its function and reactions, from medical texts, while women of all social levels drew theirs from 'authentic' observation of their own bodies." Broomhall, *Women's Medical Work,* p. 238.

60. Baernstein and Christopoulos, "Interpreting the Body." See the supplementary material for the translation of the primary source, accessed May 27, 2020, https://academic.oup.com/past/article/223/1/41/1426162.

61. Maria da Brescia: "Io non sappevo d'esser gravida, che io non ero mai piu stata gravida et non sappevo che cosa mi havessi nel corpo, che sebene bendassi una bolla nel corpo, ma per che spesso ho uno dolor di stomaco et cosi non cognoscevo d'essere gravida." ASB, Torrone, Atti e processi, 1577, 1165, f. 223r, 225r–v.

62. Mercuriale, *De morbis muliebribus,* bk. 1, ch. 2, p. 25.

63. Cristini, *Pratica medicinale,* bk. 2, ch. 2, p. 9.

64. ASR, TcG, Processi, 1613, b. 116, the trial begins on f. 831r and has its own internal foliation, f. 1r–194r.

65. Helen Rodnite Lemay, ed. and trans., *Women's Secrets: A Translation of Pseudo-Albertus Magnus's "De Secretis Mulierum" with Commentaries* (Albany: State University of New York Press, 1992), p. 103.

66. This has led John Riddle to erroneously argue that Renaissance men were ill informed in matters of herbal abortion and contraception, and also that this knowledge was suppressed during the early modern witch hunts of the sixteenth and seventeenth centuries. Riddle, *Contraception and Abortion*; Riddle, *Eve's Herbs.*

67. For examples of men organizing abortions for women they impregnated, see Ferraro, *Nefarious Crimes,* pp. 162–163, 194; Hardwick, *Sex in an Old Regime City,* ch. 4.

68. Marinello, *Le medicine partenenti,* bk. 2, ch. 26, f. 204v–205r; Mercurio, *La commare,* bk. 1, ch. 17, p. 87; and again in bk. 2, ch. 18, p. 177; Bottoni, *De morbis muliebribus,* bk. 2, ch. 61; Mercuriale, *De morbis muliebribus,* bk. 1, ch. 3, p. 33.

69. On the development of caesarean section in Italy, see Nadia Maria Filippini, *La nascita straordinaria: tra madre e figlio la rivoluzione del taglio cesareo, sec. XVII–XIX* (Milan: Franco Angeli, 1995); Park, *Secrets of Women,*

pp. 64–65, 134–135, 150–158, 239–248; Katharine Park, "The Death of Isabella Della Volpe: Four Eyewitness Accounts of a Postmortem Caesarean Section in 1545," *Bulletin of the History of Medicine* 82 (2008): pp. 169–187; Alessandra Foscati, "'Nonnatus dictus quod caeso defunctae matris utero prodiit.' Postmortem Caesarean Section in the Late Middle Ages and Early Modern Period," *Social History of Medicine* 32 (2018): pp. 465–480.

70. Pietro Paolo Magni, *Discorsi di Pietro Paolo Magni Piacentino intorno al sanguinare i corpi humani* (Rome: Bartolomeo Bonfadino, & Tito Diani, 1584), ch. 17, p. 63; Giovanni Andrea Della Croce, *Cirugia universale e perfetta di tutte le parti pertinenti all'ottimo chirurgo* (Venice: Giordano Ziletti, 1583), bk. 5, trat. 2, ch. 27, f. 16r v; Tarduccio Salvi, *Il ministro del medico, trattato breve* (Rome: Gio. Battista Robletti, 1643), pt. 1, ch. 10, pp. 6–7; ch. 12, p. 8; Cintio d'Amato, *Prattica nuova et utilissima di tutto quello, ch'al diligente Barbiero s'appartiene* (Venice: Gio. Battista Brigna, 1669), pp. 20–24. Vesalius called it the "matricis vena & virginalis," in *De humani corporis fabrica* (Venice: F. Franciscium and J. Criegher, 1568), bk. 3, ch. 10, p. 302; Realdo Colombo, *De re anatomica, libri XV* (Venice, 1559; reprint Brussels: Culture et Civilization, 1969), bk. 6, p. 174; Valverde, *Anatomia del Corpo,* f. 125v. On the "diseases of virgins," see King, *Diseases of Virgins.*

71. Marinello, *Le medicine partenenti,* bk. 2, ch. 18, f. 102r–103r. In a 1626 letter to Christine de Lorraine, a Medici envoy to Mantua informed her that her daughter Caterina de' Medici Gonzaga was recovering well from a recent illness and that Caterina's physicians wanted to bleed her from the foot to encourage a purge. Caterina wanted to delay a day or two perhaps because she did not feel strong enough yet. ASF, MDP, 2954, unnumbered folio, letter from Alessandro Bartolini Baldelli in Mantua to Christine de Lorraine in Florence, October 16, 1626, digitized by the Medici Archive Project, BIA, accessed May 27, 2020, bia.medici.org, Doc ID# 5784. See also Cristini, *Pratica medicinale,* bk. 2, ch. 2, pp. 15–22, for his cases of treating suppression with bleeding.

72. Gianna Pomata, "Barbieri e comari," in *Cultura popolare nell'Emilia Romagna. Medicine, erbe e magia* (Milan: Silvana Editoriale, 1981), p. 175.

73. Marinello, *Le medicine partenenti,* bk. 3, ch. 5, f. 251v, 259v; Massaria, *Praelectiones de morbis mulierum,* ch. 11, pp. 328–330; Mercurio, *La commare,* bk. 2, ch. 18, p. 177; Pietro Castelli, *De Abusu phlebotomiae* (Rome: Francesco Corbelletti, 1628), 63–64.

74. Zacchia, *Quaestionum medico-legalium,* bk. 6, tit. 1, quest. 7, n. 17, p. 413.

75. "Et particolarmente, non sia lecito ad alcuno cavar sangue alle donne dal piede, o d'altrove, per causa delle gravidanze, se non haveranno espressa commissione a bocca, o in scritto d alcun Medico Dottore approbato, sotto pena di viticinque lire per ciascuna volta, d applicarsi come di

sopra." ASB, Studio, Divers. riguardante il buon governo della citta, 1571-1769, b. 233, *Provisione sopra il grave abuso di quelli che senza licenza presumono medicare moderatione rinovata sopra li spetiali, e barbieri* (Bologna, 1581), p. 4; also in the *Liber pro recta administratione protomedicatus* (Bologna, 1666), p. 17, n. 30.

76. Salvi, *Il ministro del medico,* pt. 1, ch. 10, pp. 6-7.

77. For examples of the practice from Spain, England and France, see Renato Barahona, *Sex Crimes, Honor, and the Law in Early Modern Spain: Vizcaya, 1528–1735* (Toronto: University of Toronto Press, 2003), pp. 91–92, 106; Gowing, *Common Bodies,* pp. 47, 120; and Hardwick, *Sex in an Old Regime City,* ch. 4.

78. Baernstein and Christopoulos, "Interpreting the Body," pp. 58–59.

79. Girolamo Sertorelli, *Barchetta di penitenza* (Venice: Marco Guarisco, 1609), p. 328.

80. On Renaissance and early modern pharmacy, see James Shaw and Evelyn Welch, *Making and Marketing Medicines in Renaissance Florence* (Amsterdam: Rodopi, 2011); David Gentilcore, *Medical Charlatanism in Early Modern Italy* (Oxford: Oxford University Press, 2006), ch. 6; Sean David Parrish, "Marketing Nature: Apothecaries, Medicinal Retailing, and Scientific Culture in Early Modern Venice, 1565-1730" (PhD diss., Duke University, 2015); and Sharon Strocchia, *Forgotten Healers: Women and the Pursuit of Health in Late Renaissance Italy* (Cambridge, MA: Harvard University Press, 2019), ch. 3-4.

81. See discussions of menstrual retention, dropsy of the womb and similar blockages, remedies against sterility, and methods of encouraging childbirth and expelling afterbirth, dead fetuses, molae, and other growths in Bottoni, *De morbis muliebribus,* bk. 1, ch. 30-31; bk. 2, ch. 49, 53, 61, 74, 80-81; Mercurio, *La commare,* bk. 2, ch. 22-27, 30-31, 38; bk. 3, ch. 16; Marinello, *Le medicine partenenti,* bk. 2, ch. 18; bk. 3, ch. 5, 8, 11, 13; Massaria, *Praelectiones de morbis mulierum,* ch. 2, 7, 9-13; Mercuriale, *De morbis muliebribus,* bk. 1, ch. 2, 3; bk. 2, ch. 1, 3, 4; bk. 4, ch. 1; Lanceano, *De molae generatione & cura,* pp. 71-108; Cristini, *Pratica medicinale,* bk. 2, ch. 19, pp. 140-144.

82. Mercuriale, *De morbis muliebribus,* bk. 2, ch. 1, p. 44; Bottoni, *De morbis muliebribus,* bk. 2, ch. 41, f. 41r; ch. 62, f. 63v-64r; Massaria, *Praelectiones de morbis mulierum,* ch. 11, pp. 330-332.

83. The following works are surveyed here: Pietro Andrea Mattioli, *I discorsi di M. Pietro Andrea Matthioli . . . ne i sei libri di Pedacio Dioscoride Anazarbeo della materia Medicinale* (Venice: Vincenzo Valgrisi, 1563); Francesco Sansovino, *Della materia medicinale libri qvattro* (Venice: Gio. Andrea Valvassori, 1562); Prospero Borgarucci, *La fabrica degli spetiali* (Venice: Vincenzo Valgrisio, 1566); Girolamo Calestani, *Delle osservationi . . . Parte*

prima (Venice: Francesco de' Franceschi, 1580); Castore Durante, *Herbario nuovo* (Rome: Bartholomeo Bonfadino & Tito Diani, 1585); *De i semplici purgativi, et delle medicine composte* (Venice: Bibliotheca Aldina, 1589).

84. Mattioli, *I discorsi*: aristolochia—bk. 3, ch. 4, p. 360; artemesia and matricaria—bk. 3, ch. 121, pp. 457-458; ch. 149, pp. 479-480; savin—bk. 1, p. ch. 85, p. 102; calamint—bk. 3, ch. 38, p. 394; scammony—bk. 4, ch. 172, p. 627; bryony—bk. 4, ch. 183, p. 637; pennyroyal—bk. 3, ch. 31, pp. 387-388; rue—bk. 3, ch. 47, 48, pp. 400-403; myrrh—bk. 1, ch. 44, pp. 71-74; centaurea—bk. 3, ch. 6, pp. 363-364; colocynth—bk. 4, ch. 178, pp. 631-632; hellebore—bk. 4, pp. 152-153, 606-607; mandrake—bk. 4, ch. 78, pp. 549-551. See discussions of these in Sansovino, *Della materia medicinale*, f. 7v, 25v-26v, 207r, 69r-71r, 245r-v, 218r-219r, 178r-179r, 190r-191r, 74r-v, 141r-143r; Borgarucci, *La fabrica degli spetiali,* pp. 197, 175, 255-256, 518, 221, 116-117; Calestani, *Delle osservationi . . . Parte prima,* pp. 17-18, 19, 76, 28-29, 78, 27, 75, 65-66; 33-34, 40, 125-126; Durante, *Herbario nuovo,* pp. 43-44, 47-48, 405-407, 83, 417-418, 478-479, 381, 402-405, 295-296, 104-105, 142-143, 167-168; *De i semplici purgativi,* pp. 193, 128, 152, 139, 197.

85. Physicians sought to insert themselves into medical transactions by framing themselves as "protectors" of the consumers of health. On issues of medical authority, hierarchy, and the economics of healing, see Pomata, *Contracting a Cure,* pp. 67-69; David Gentilcore, *Healers and Healing in Early Modern Italy* (Manchester: Manchester University Press, 1998), pp. 78-81. Michele L. Clouse reports similar concerns and initiatives in early modern Spain. Clouse, *Medicine, Government and Public Health in Philip II's Spain: Shared interests, Competing Authorities* (Burlington, VT: Ashgate, 2011), ch. 4. On sixteenth- and seventeenth-century Italian antidotaries, see generally Alfonso Corradi, *Le prime farmacopee Italiane ed in particolare dei Ricettari Fiorentini* (Milan: Fratelli Rechiedei Editori, 1887).

86. Electuaries are confections in the form of pastes made of pulverized simples brought together with honey or sugar and consumed orally. *Antidotarium Bononiense* (Bologna: Joannem Rossium, 1574, the 1647 is cited here), pp. 3-4; the 1574 edition (p. 104-105) lists the drug but does not mention these properties; the *Ricettario Fiorentino* (Florence: Stamperia dei Giunti, 1574) lists this recipe but calls it "Lattouaro Iustino di Niccolao," p. 175.

87. *Antidotario Romano, Latino, e Volgare. Tradotto da Ippolito Ceccarelli . . . con le annotationi del Sig. Pietro Castelli* (Rome: Pietro Antonio Facciotti, 1639), pp. 29-30.

88. *Antidotario Romano,* pp. 72-74, at 74; *Antidotarium Bononiense,* pp. 119-120; *Ricetario Fiorentino,* p. 195; Giovanni Battista Cortesi, *Pharmacopoeia seu antidotarium Messanense* (Messina: Petri Breae, 1629), p. 169; Borgarucci, *La fabrica degli spetiali,* pp. 450-451; Calestani, *Delle osservationi . . .*

Parte seconda, pp. 134–135; Giorgio Melichio, *Avertimenti nelle compositioni de medicamenti per uso della spetiaria, Utilissimi a Medici, a Spetiali, & ad'ogni famiglia* (Venice: Nicolo Polo, 1596), f. 15v.

89. *Antidotarium Bononiense,* pp. 176–177, 179, 231–233; *Antidotario Romano,* pp. 136, 145–146, 169–170; *Ricetario Fiorentino,* pp. 156, 178, 225; Cortesi, *Pharmacopoeia seu antidotarium Messanense,* pp. 24–25, 145, 147; Borgarucci, *La fabrica degli spetiali,* pp. 196–197, 670–671; Calestani, *Delle osservationi . . . Parte seconda,* pp. 257–258; Melichio, *Avertimenti nelle compositioni,* f. 69rv, f. 112v.

90. The bandi of the Roman protomedicato are contained in ASR, Universita, Collegio Medico, b. 24 and ASV, Mis. Arm., IV–V, b. 68, *Bando concernente il buon reggimento della facolta di medicare, e dell'arti, che a lei seruono, e somministrano: da osseruarsi in Roma, e fuori in tutto lo Stato Ecclesiastico, cosi mediate, come immediate sottoposto alla Santa Sede Apostolica* (Rome, 1595), n. 12. In 1608, Lorenzo Rossi changed the wording of the prohibition from "far sconciar le donne gravide" to "provochino aborto." *Bando Del Protomedico per Roma* (Rome: 1608). Cagnati returned as protomedico in 1610 and used his own wording. The prohibition remained in the protomedicato's bandi into the nineteenth century.

91. ASB, Studio, Divers. riguardante il buon governo della citta, 1571–1769, b. 233, *Provisione sopra il grave abvso di qvelli che senza licenza presumono medicare moderatione rinovata sopra li spetiali, e barbieri* (Bologna, 1581), p. 4; repeated in the *Bando, et provisione, Sopra quelli che senza autorita & licenza dell'Eccellentiss. Collegio di Medicina di Bologna danno, ordinano, vendono, & applicano medicamenti in alcun modo, overo essercitano alcuna parte di medicina* (Bologna, 1594, 1604, 1617). This bando was also republished in the *Liber pro recta administratione protomedicato* (Bologna: Typographia Ferroniana, 1666), p. 16, n. 24.

92. ASR, Universita, Collegio Medico, b. 24, *Bando del Protomedico di Roma* (Rome, 1638 and 1653).

93. *Constitutiones, capitula, jurisdictiones, ac pandectae Regii protomedicatus offici* (Palermo: Nicolai Bua, 1657), p. 148, n. 7.

94. *Antidotario Romano,* pp. 72–74, at 74; *Antidotarium Bononiense,* pp. 119–120; *Ricetario Fiorentino,* p. 195; Cortesi, *Pharmacopoeia seu antidotarium Messanense,* p. 169; Borgarucci, *La fabrica degli spetiali,* pp. 450–451; Calestani, *Delle osservationi . . . Parte seconda,* pp. 134–135.

95. On the difficulties of reconstructing pharmacy clientele, women clients in particular, see Shaw and Welch, *Making and Marketing Medicines,* pp. 57–58, 84–85, 90–93, and Strocchia, *Forgotten Healers,* pp. 116–121.

96. ASR, Universita, Collegio Medico, b. 24, *Ordine del s. re Protomedico, [M. Cagnatus] per li Droghieri* (Rome: 1595).

97. Gentilcore, *Healers and Healing;* Pomata, *Contracting a Cure;* Sandra Cavallo, *Artisans of the Body in Early Modern Italy: Identities, Families, and Mascu-*

linities (Manchester: Manchester University Press, 2007); Strocchia, *Forgotten Healers*.

98. Fra Donato D'Eremita, *Antidotario . . . nel quale si discorre intorno all'osservanza, che deve tenere lo spetiale* . . . (Naples: Secondino Roncagliolo, 1639), p. 4, quoted in Gentilcore, *Healers and Healing*, p. 79.

99. Emphasis added, ASB, Studio, Divers. riguardante il buon governo della citta, 1571–1769, b. 233, *Avvertimenti, & Provisione intorno li Speciali, & quelli, che essercitano la Medicina* (Bologna: 1600), n. 7.

100. Filippo De Vivo, "Pharmacies as Centres of Communication in Early Modern Venice," *Renaissance Studies* 21 (2007): pp. 505–521; Shaw and Welch, *Making and Marketing Medicine*. Ch. 4; Strocchia, *Forgotten Healers*, ch. 3.

101. Giovanni Zecchi, one-time archiater of Sixtus V and protomedico of Rome, prescribed decoctions of savin, artemisia, and other purgative simples, as well as a trochisci of myrrh, to help a Marchesia Reani expel stubborn afterbirth. *Consultationum medicinalium*, cons. 68, pp 345–346. Following the delivery of her son, Pellegrina Venturi (daughter of Bianca Cappello and adopted daughter of Francesco I de' Medici) was given strong purgative medicines, which apparently made her feel quite ill and kept her off her feet for some days. ASF, MDP, 5928, f. 202, letter from Ulisse Bentivoglio in Florence to Bianca Cappello de' Medici in Florence, October 16, 1626, digitized by the Medici Archive Project, BIA, accessed May 27, 2020, bia.medici.org, Doc ID# 21649. For general medical discussion, see also Bottoni, *De morbis muliebribus*, bk. 2, ch. 81, f. 75r–77v; Massaria, *Praelectiones de morbis mulierum*, ch. 13, pp. 406–413; Mercuriale, *De morbis muliebribus*, bk. 2, ch. 3, pp. 63–69; ch. 4, pp. 69–70; Marinello, *Le medicine partenenti*, bk. 3, ch. 8, f. 265r–v; ch. 11, f. 285r; ch. 13, f. 290r–291r.

102. See note 1 above.

103. As reported by Emilio de Bonis: "era per una donna di buon parentado, et che haverebbe remediato alli scandali che potessero nascere, che però di gratia lo facesse." ASR, TcG, Processi, 1613, b. 116, f. 50r.

104. On midwives and midwifery in early modern Italy, see Claudia Pancino, *Il Bambino e l'acqua sporca: storia dell' assistenza al parto dalle mammane alle ostetriche (secoli XVI–XIX)* (Milan: Franco Angeli, 1984); Pomata, "Barbieri e comari"; Nadia Maria Filippini, "Levatrici e ostetricanti a Venezia tra sette e ottocento," *Quaderni storici* 58 (1985): pp. 149–180; Nadia Maria Filippini, "The Church, the State and Childbirth: The Midwife in Italy during the Eighteenth Century," in *The Art of Midwifery: Early Modern Midwives in Europe*, ed. Hilary Marland (London: Routledge, 1993), pp. 152–175; Gentilcore, *Healers and Healing*, pp. 81–86; Pomata, *Contracting a Cure*, pp. 77–80; Claudio Schiavoni, "L'attività delle levatrici o

'mammane' a Roma tra XVI e XVIII secolo: storia sociale di una professione," *Sociologia* 2 (2001): 41-61; Alessandro Pastore, *Il medico in tribunal: la perizia medica nella procedura penale d'antico regime (secoli XVI–XVIII)* (Bellinzona, Switzerland: Edizioni Casagrande, 2004), pp. 129-148; Kosmin, *Authority, Gender and Midwifery.*

105. Mercurio, *La commare,* bk. 1, ch. 18, pp. 87-90. See also his discussion in *De gli errori popolari,* bk. 6, ch. 2, p. 262.

106. Mercurio, *La commare,* bk. 2, ch. 24, p. 190; bk. 2, ch. 41, p. 276. See also remedies for encouraging a postpartum purge, for afterbirth, and for dropsy in bk. 2-3.

107. See Joanne Ferraro, *Marriage Wars in Late Renaissance Venice* (New York: Oxford University Press, 2001); and Daniela Hacke, *Women, Sex and Marriage in Early Modern Venice* (Aldershot: Ashgate 2004) for examples of how important midwives could be in assessing sexual difficulties among married couples.

108. Schiavoni, "L'attività delle levatrici o 'mammane' a Roma," 45; David Gentilcore, "'All that Pertains to Medicine': *Protomedici* and *Protomedicati* in Early Modern Italy," *Medical History,* 45 (1994): pp. 121-142, at 131-132; Pomata, *Contracting a Cure,* 64.

109. Pomata, *Contracting a Cure,* p. 77. Midwives were also known to let blood. Pomata, "Barbieri e comari," p. 175.

110. Dianora Prosperi: "Le mammane officio loro è di raccogliere le creature con quella debita diligenza che se rechiede et, per esser bona mammana, deve havere molti requisiti cioé: conoscere se una donna è gravida o no; se nelle gravidanze le donne se sentono qualche dolore, sapere conoscere dove ne procede et darci remedii opportuni; se qualche altra donna però suppone esser gravida, sapere conoscere se è gravida o no, se da quanto tempo; se venendole qualche accidente che dovesse sconciarsi, come sole avvenire, darli medicamenti o attaccarli ceroti acciò non se sconci; sapere anco conoscere se, venendoli qualche segno, se devono infantare a suo tempo o no, overo se tra un giorno, o dui, o più et meno; così anco se una donna si sconcia, o sia per sconciarsi, o che sia sconciata, conoscerlo et altri requisiti." ASR, TcG, Processi, 1634, b. 295, f. 1701v.

111. Marinello, *Le medicine partenenti,* bk. 3, ch. 13, f. 290r. See Green, *Making Women's Medicine Masculine,* for examples of physicians admitting to learning from midwives.

112. The term "agent of health" is Monica Green's. "Bodies, Gender, Health, Disease: Recent Work on Medieval Women's Medicine," *Studies in Medieval and Renaissance History* 2 (2005): pp. 1-49.

113. William Eamon, *Science and the Secrets of Nature: Books of Secrets in Medieval and Early Modern Culture* (Princeton, NJ: Princeton University Press, 1996); Gentilcore, *Medical Charlatanism.*

114. *La seconda parte de'secreti del reverendo donno Alessio Piemotese* (Pesaro: Bartolomeo Cesano, 1559), bk. 1, pt. 2, p. 26; Pietro Bairo, *Secreti medicinali* (Venice: Francesco Sansovino, 1562), f. 204rv (including five pages of recipes for cures of sterility [f. 193r–195v]); Benedetto Vitorri da Faenza, *Prattica d'esperienza* (Venice: Bolognino Zaltieri, 1570), ch. 33, f. 100r–103r; Leonardo Fioravanti, *La cirugia* (Venice: Michele Bonibelli, 1595), p. 173; Tommaso Tomai da Ravenna, *Idea del giardino del mondo* (Venice: Domenico Imberti, 1611), f. 36r–37r; Floriano Canale, *De secreti universali raccolti et esperimentati, . . . ne quali si hanno rimedii per tutte l'infermita de corpi Humani, come anco de Cavalli, Bovi, & cani* (Venice: Pietro Bertano, 1613), pp. 124–125; Timotheo Rossello, *Della summa de'Secreti universali . . . Si per huomini, & donne, di alto ingegno, come ancora per Medici, & ogni sorte di Artefici industriosi, & a ogni persona virtuosa accommodate* (Venice: Pietro Miloco, 1619), f. 17v–18r, 84r–85r.

115. Bairo, *Secreti medicinali*, f. 204r–v. He includes five pages of remedies for retained menstruation.

116. Bairo, *Secreti medicinali*, f. 200r–201r, at 200v; Vitorri da Faenza, *Prattica d'esperienza*, ch. 33, f. 100r–103r, at 101v; see also ch. 45, f. 126r.

117. *Secreti diversi & miracolosi. Raccolti da Falopia & approbati da altri Medici di gran fama* (Venice: Alessandro Gardano, 1578), pp. 62–63. The compiler was likely referring to Fallopia's *De simplicibus medicamentis purgantibus* (Venice: Giordani Ziletti, 1565).

118. Charlatans could acquire licenses to sell purgatives: for example, in 1620, the charlatan Dionigio Alberti was licensed to sell a purgative consisting of prepared *seme di ricino* (castor-bean seeds) in the Piazza Navona in Rome. Among other things, this remedy could heal dropsy. Gentilcore, *Medical Charlatanism*, p. 234. Paolo Zacchia prohibited the sale of seme di ricino without a physician's prescription (see note 92 above). Tommaso Garzoni lists a number of purgative herbs as sold by herbalists. *La piazza universale di tutte le professione del mondo* (1585), ed. P. Cerchi and B. Collina (Turin: Einaudi, 1996), vol. 1, disc. 23, pp. 332–335; vol. 2, disc. 89, pp. 1059–1065. In Naples grocers fell under the inspection of the protomedicato in 1581 after several deaths resulted from the selling of poisons by grocers; however, this oversight was revoked in 1604. The Roman protomedico could fine grocers for "misdemeanours," but it is unclear what exactly this meant and how often fines were imposed. Gentilcore, "All that Pertains," p. 137; Gentilcore, *Healers and Healing*, p. 44.

119. *Antidotario Romano*, p. 57.

120. Pietro de Crescenzi, *Trattato dell'agricoltura* (Florence: Cosimo Giunti, 1605), bk. 5, ch. 10, p. 330; see also the entry for rue—bk. 6, ch. 101, p. 359.

121. Carlo Ruini, *Anatomia del cavallo, Infermita et suoi rimedi* (Venice: Fioravante Prati, 1618), vol. 2, bk. 5, ch. 14, "Del far disgravidare le cavalle pregne," pp. 207–208.

122. On this connection, see Albano Biondi, "La signora delle erbe e la magia della vegetazione," in *Cultura popolare nell'Emilia Romagna*, pp. 183-205; Claudio Bondi, *Strix: Medichesse, streghe e fattucchiere nell'Italia del Rinascimento* (Rome: Lucarini, 1989); David Gentilcore, *From Bishop to Witch: The System of the Sacred in Early Modern Terra d'Otranto* (Manchester: Manchester University Press, 1992), ch. 5; Katharine Park, "Medicine and Magic: The Healing Arts," in *Gender and Society in Renaissance Italy,* ed. Judith Brown and Robert C. Davis (London: Longmans, 1997), pp. 129-149; Oscar Di Simplicio, *Inquisizione, stregoneria, medicina: Siena e il suo stato (1580–1721)* (Siena: Il Lecio, 2000); Jonathan Seitz, *Witchcraft and Inquisition in Early Modern Venice* (Cambridge: Cambridge University Press, 2011).

123. This important point has been emphatically made by Monica H. Green, "Gendering the History of Women's Healthcare," *Gender and History* 20 (2008): pp. 487-518; and Helen King, "When Is a Purge Not an Abortion," in *Hippocrates' Women,* pp. 145-146. See also their reviews of John Riddle's *Eve's Herbs,* in *Medical History* 48 (1998): pp. 412-414; and *Bulletin of the History of Medicine* 73 (1999): pp. 308-311, respectively.

124. January 21, 1629, *Letters to Father: Suor Maria Celeste to Galileo,* ed. and trans. Dava Sobel (New York: Penguin, 2001), pp. 100-105. Maria Celeste suffered from a similar obstruction one year later and again consumed purgative medicines to clear her womb. May 25, 1630, p. 115.

125. Zecchi, *Consultationum medicinalium*, cons. 39, pp. 226-228.

126. Zecchi, *Consultationum medicinalium,* cons. 67, pp. 341-334; cons. 86, pp. 418-419. See also Girolamo Mercuriale, *Responsa et consultationes medicinales,* vol. 1 (Venice: Gioliti, 1587), cons. 93, pp. 214-218, esp. p. 217. For discussions of sterility and its cures, see Mercuriale, *De morbis muliebribus,* bk. 1, ch. 2, esp. pp. 20-22; Bottoni, *De morbis muliebribus,* bk. 2, ch. 59, f. 47v-49r; Massaria, *Praelectiones de morbis mulierum,* ch. 6, pp. 254-262; Marinello, *Le medicine partenenti,* bk. 2, ch. 8, f. 71r-85r.

127. Calestani, *Delle osservationi . . . Parte seconda,* pp. 134-135; Borgarucci, *La fabrica degli spetiali,* p. 450; Melchiori, *Avvertimenti,* f. 15v.

128. Christine de Lorraine, however, warned her daughter against it, believing that a purge would trouble (*guasterete*) her general health and this would diminish her chances of conceiving. ASF, MDP, 6110, f. 44, letter from Christine de Lorraine in Florence to Caterina de' Medici Gonzaga in Mantua, 3 October 1617, digitized by the Medici Archive Project, BIA, accessed May 27, 2020, bia.medici.org, Doc ID# 6884.

129. Mennoca Liberatori: "Et sibene li dissi de non so che melo et scarpetta che io ho sentito dire che se adopra quando la donna e partorita et che non è venuta fuori la scapha per farla venire fuori." ASR, TcG, Processi, 1602, b. 1, f. 978r.

130. This important question has been a matter of controversy. For an optimistic account of efficacy, see Riddle, *Contraception and Abortion* and *Eve's Herbs*; for more balanced discussion, see Stefania Siedlecky, "Pharmacological Properties of Emmenagogues: A Biomedical View," in *Regulating Menstruation: Beliefs, Practices and Interpretations*, ed. Etienne van de Walle and Elisha Renne (Chicago, 2001), pp. 93-112; and Sara E. Nelson, "Persephone's Seeds: Abortifacients and Contraceptives in Ancient Greek Medicine and their Recent Scientific Appraisals," *Pharmacy in History* 51 (2009): pp. 57-69. For a synthesis of more recent ethnopharmacological research, see Tinde van Andel, Hugo de Boer, and Alexandra Towns, "Gynaecological, Andrological and Urological Problems: An Ethnopharcological Perspective," in *Ethnopharmacology*, ed. Michael Heinrich, Anna K. Jäger (Chichester, U.K.: Wiley and Sons, 2015), pp. 199-211.

131. Shaw and Welch, *Making and Marketing Medicines*, pp. 89-92.

132. Cristini, *Pratica medicinale*, bk. 2, ch. 18, osservatione, xcv, p. 132.

133. Discussing a case where a young boy died because his physician refused to bleed him, Paolo Zacchia discussed dangers that could arise from withholding therapies: he cited a case reported by Galen where a twenty-one-year-old woman was suffering from menstrual retention but her physician refused to draw blood; she developed difficulties breathing, eventually suffocated, and died, "much to [her doctor's] disgrace." Zacchia thought that such a "crime cannot go unpunished." Zacchia, *Quaestionum medico-legalium*, cons. XL, p. 218.

134. ASR, TcG, Processi, 1610, b. 89, f. 1376r-1384v.

135. Borelli however concluded that there were too many uncertainties in this case to find Calander guilty of having caused the abortion and killing Superna. Camillo Borelli, *Consiliorum sive controversiarum forensium* (Venice: Guerilium, 1598), cons. 60, 106v-108r, quotes from 106v and 107r.

136. Mercurio, *La commare*, bk. 2, ch. 18, pp. 176-177; Mercurio, *De gli errori popolari*, bk. 5, ch. 7, f. 239r-241r.

137. ASF, MDP, 6110, f. 16, letter from Christine de Lorraine in Pisa to Caterina de' Medici Gonzaga in Mantua, April 13, 1617, digitized by the Medici Archive Project, BIA, accessed May 27, 2020, bia.medici.org, Doc ID# 6874.

138. Lemay, *Women's Secrets*, pp. 102-103.

139. Bottoni, *De morbis muliebribus*, bk. 2, ch. 53, f. 52r.

140. Garzoni, *La piazza universale*, vol. 2, disc. 75, p. 974.

141. Rublack, "Pregnancy, Childbirth and the Female Body."

142. Marco Scarsella, *Giardino di sommisti nel quale si dichiarano dodicimila, e piu casi di conscienza* (Venice: Antonio Somasco, 1600) pt. 2, ch. 337, "Del spavento o far paura," f. 283v.

143. ASR, TcG, Processi, 1603, b. 28bis, f.785v–786r.

144. Paolo Zacchia acknowledged that the dietary restrictions imposed during Lent might be dangerous for pregnant women, *Il vitto quaresimale* (Rome: Pietro Antonio Facciotti, 1636), pp. 110–111, 225–226. In a 1576 letter to his pregnant daughter, Sperone Speroni warned her not to fast. Sperone Speroni, *Opere,* vol. 5, letter 322 (Rome: Vecchiarelli, 1989), pp. 228–229.

145. Mercuriale, *Responsa et consultationes medicinales,* vol. 1, cons. 101, pp. 131–134. It is unclear when this consilium was composed (the first edition of his consilia was published in 1587), but in 1577 Maria was diagnosed as suffering from a "malign tumor, that is a cancer of the womb." ASF, MDP, 695, f. 357, letter from Tommaso Cornacchini in Pisa to Francesco I de'Medici in Florence, March 7, 1576, digitized by the Medici Archive Project, BIA, accessed May 27, 2020, bia.medici.org, Doc ID# 12613.

146. Silvia De Renzi, "The Risks of Childbirth: Physicians, Finance, and Women's Deaths in the Law Courts of Seventeenth-Century Rome," *Bulletin of the History of Mediicne* 84 (2010): pp. 549–577.

147. Allessandro de Angelis, *In astrologos coniectores libri quinque* (Rome: Bartholomaei Zannetti, 1615), bk. 2, ch. 8–9, pp. 69–72, on particular planetary conjunctions that may cause fetal death and premature delivery. Giulia Calvi says that an especially high rate of miscarriages associated with plague "embodies an absolutely feminine aspect in the reading of contagion. For a great number of women, the bubo was a prelude to a stillbirth or miscarriage; the bubo's fantastic projection made it resemble a monstrous pregnancy from which one could, perhaps, be saved only by sacrificing the other pregnancy, the one that gives life." Giulia Calvi, *Histories of a Plague Year: The Social and the Imaginary in Baroque Florence,* trans. Dario Biocca and Bryant T. Ragan Jr. (Berkeley: University of California Press, 1989), p. 89. ASF, MDP, 3384, f. 262, letter from Torquato Montauto in Rome to Giovanni Battista di Alessandro Gondi in Florence, December 7, 1658, digitized by the Medici Archive Project, BIA, accessed May 27, 2020, bia.medici.org, Doc ID# 22577. On how a cough can induce an abortion, see Pietro Castelli, *Exercitationes medicinales* (Toulouse: R. Colomerium, 1616), p. 197.

148. Mercurio, *De gli errori popolari,* bk. 5, ch.7, f. 241r. On the internal and external causes of miscarriage, see Marinello, *Le medicine partenenti,* bk. 3, ch. 5, f. 250r–251r; ch. 6, f. 253r–255v; and ch. 8, f. 264v–265r; Mercurio, *La commare,* bk. 2, ch. 17–18, pp. 172–178; Bottoni, *De morbis muliebribus,* bk. 2, ch. 62, f. 62r–64r; Massaria, *Praelectiones de morbis mulieris,* ch. 11; Mercuriale, *De morbis muliebribus,* bk. 1, ch. 4, p. 35; bk. 2, ch.1, pp. 43–46; Zecchi, *Consultationes medicinales,* cons. 86, pp. 416–424; cons. 94, pp. 450–454.

149. Adlotia Pomponi: "o che habbia partorito, o che se sia sconcia, che io questo non lo posso sapere." ASR, TcG, Processi, 1613, b. 116, f. 21r.

150. Zacchia, *Questionum medico-legalium,* bk. 3, tit. 2, quest. 9, "Mulierem pe-perisse, aut abortum fecisse, ex quibus conjici possit," p. 234.

151. Mercurio, *Degli errori populari,* bk. 5, ch. 7, f. 241r.

152. Marsilia Tomasi: "Mi posso imaginar la caussa per che mi sono sconcia la prima fu la bevanda che mi diede d. Lauro, la seconda i stretii che mi faceva detta Isabetta mia cognata, et Isabetta mia cognata . . . et d. Lauro per farmi sconciare mi dete questi mi dica et Isabetta mi saltava con i piedi sopra la schiena et rene et io ce lo dissi perche mi sentevo gravida." ASR, TcG, Processi, 1606, b. 53, f. 480r–v.

153. Unfortunately, Zacchia did not include details surrounding this case. He did however conclude that the cleric was not responsible for the death of the woman because the beating took place three months before the hemorrhaging and miscarriage that led to her death. Zacchia, *Questionum medico-legalium,* bk. 10, cons. 47, pp. 234–236.

154. See De Renzi, "Risks of Childbirth," esp. pp. 559–562.

155. Girolamo Perlini, *De morte caussa graviditatis, abortus, et partus* (Rome: Aloysii Zannetti, 1607), pp. 8–10; De Renzi, "Risks of Childbirth." Paolo Zacchia gave counsel on a case where a six-months-pregnant woman developed dropsy, which may have led to her death; Zacchia was brought in as an expert witness to determine the causal relationship between her pregnancy, dropsy, and death, which had financial consequences for her husband. Zacchia, *Quaestionum medico-legalium,* bk. 10, cons. 56, pp. 261–263.

156. Marcello Donati, physician and counsellor to the Dukes of Mantua, claimed to have seen a mola, described as a round fleshy thing resembling the head of a child, that was attached to the afterbirth of a fetus. Donati, *De medica historia mirabili* (Venice: Fel. Valgrisium, 1588), ch. 25, "Molae admirabiles," f. 245v–250r.

157. De Renzi, "Risks of Childbirth"; Park, *Secrets of Women,* esp. pp. 97–103; King, *Midwifery, Obstetrics, and the Rise of Gynaecology;* Green, *Making Women's Medicine Masculine.*

158. Marinello, *Le medicine partenenti,* bk. 3, ch. 5, f. 250r–251r; ch. 6, f. 253r–255v; and ch. 8, f. 258v–260, 264v–265r; Bottoni, *De morbis muliebribus,* bk. 2, ch. 62, f. 62r–64r; Mercuriale, *De morbism muliebribus,* bk. 1, ch. 4, p. 35; bk. 2, ch.1, pp. 43–46; Massaria, *Praelectiones de morbis mulierum,* ch. 11; Zecchi, *Consultationes medicinales,* cons. 86, pp. 416–424; cons. 94, pp. 450–454.

159. Mercuriale, *De morbis muliebribus,* bk. 1, ch. 2, p. 24.

160. Ferraro, *Marriage Wars;* ch. 3; Hacke, *Women, Sex and Marriage,* ch. 7. For Spain, see Edward Behrend-Martínez, *Unfit for Marriage: Impotent Spouses on Trial in the Basque Region of Spain, 1650–1750* (Reno: University of Nevada Press, 2007).

161. For instance, see the physical examinations and surgical procedures Margherita Farnese endured before she was found to be incapable of sexual intercourse and of generation, which also meant the dissolution of her marriage (1583) to Vincenzo Gonzaga recounted in Valeria Finucci, "The Virgin's Body and Early Modern Surgeons," in *Masculinities, Violence, Childhood: Attending to Early Modern Women and Men,* ed. Amy Leonard and Karen Nelson (Lanham, MD: University of Delaware Press, 2010), pp. 195–221. More generally, see Ferraro, *Marriage Wars,* pp. 91–97; and Hacke, *Women, Sex and Marriage,* pp. 155–164. Further research may indicate whether such practices were more common.

162. Sansovino, *Della materia medicinale,* bk. 4, "prohibere la concettione," f. 323v–324r.

163. Codronchi, *De christiana ac tuta medendi ratione,* pp. 70–71.

164. Mercurio, *La commare,* bk. 2, ch. 20, p. 181. See also Mercurio, *De gli errori popolari,* bk. 2, ch. 26, f. 108v–109r.

165. Mercuriale, *De morbis muliebribus,* bk. 1, ch. 2, p. 25.

166. Bottoni, *De morbis muliebribus,* bk. 2, ch. 73 [err. 83], f. 68v.

167. Salvi, *Il ministro del medico,* pp. 6–7.

168. Zacchia, *Quaestionum medico-legalium,* bk. 6, tit. 1, quest. 7, n. 14, p. 413.

169. Zacchia, *Quaestionum medico-legalium,* bk. 6, tit. 1, quest. 7, n. 15, p. 413.

170. David A. Grimes, Janie Benson, Susheela Singh, Mariana Romero, Bela Ganatra, Friday E. Okonofua, Iqbal H. Shah, "Unsafe Abortion: The Preventable Pandemic," *The Lancet* 368, vol. 9550 (November 25–December 1, 2006): pp. 1908–1919; "Preventing Unsafe Abortion," World Health Organization, June 26, 2019, accessed May 27, 2020, https://www.who.int/news-room/fact-sheets/detail/preventing-unsafe-abortion.

171. Mercuriale, *De morbis muliebribus,* bk. 1, ch. 2, p. 24.

172. Bottoni, *De morbis muliebribus,* bk. 2, ch. 74, f. 70v.

173. Mercurio, *La commare,* bk. 1, ch. 17, p. 86.

174. Mercurio, *De gli errori popolari,* bk. 2, ch. 26, f. 110r.

175. Authors suggested milder medicines that pregnant women could consume for less grave illnesses: Mercurio, *La commare,* bk. 1, ch. 22, pp. 100–103; Marinello, *Le medicine partenenti,* bk. 3, ch. 5, f. 251v; ch. 8, f. 258v–259v; Bottoni, *De morbis muliebribus,* bk. 2, ch. 62, f. 63v–64r; Mercuriale, *De morbis muliebribus,* bk. 1, ch. 4, pp. 35–39; Massaria, *Praelectiones de morbis mulierum,* ch. 11, pp. 348–362; Giovanni Zecchi, *Consultationes medicinales,* cons. 86, pp. 420–421.

176. Zacchia, *Quaestionum medico-legalium,* bk. 6, tit. 1, quest. 7, n. 15, p. 413.

177. D'Amelia, "Becoming a Mother," p. 227. Similarly, Caroline Castiglione shows distrust of physicians among aristocratic women when it came to healing infants and children. Castiglione, *Accounting for Affection:*

Mothering and Politics in Early Modern Rome (London: Palgrave Macmillan, 2015), pp. 106–123.

178. ASF, MDP, 3467, f. 244, letter from Averardo di Antonio Serristori in Rome to Cosimo I de' Medici in Florence, May 22, 1551, digitized by the Medici Archive Project, BIA, accessed May 27, 2020, bia.medici.org, Doc ID# 24132.

179. ASF, MDP, 4027a, insert 1, f. 27, Avviso from Rome to Florence, October 2, 1649, digitized by the Medici Archive Project, BIA, accessed May 27, 2020, bia.medici.org, Doc ID# 19394. Available evidence suggests that she did miscarry (or in fact that she was not pregnant as was thought) as Olimpia birthed four children from her marriage to Camillo Pamphili and none in 1649–1650 when the event in question transpired.

180. See De Renzi, "Risks of Childbirth."

181. Marinello, *Le medicine partenenti*, bk. 3, ch. 12, f. 285r–289r; Mercuriale, *De morbis muliebribus*, bk. 2, cap. 3, pp. 66–69; Bottoni, *De morbis muliebribus*, ch. 73–74; Massaria, *Praelectiones de morbis mulierum*, ch. 11, p. 362, Cristini, *Pratica medicinale*, bk. 2, ch. 19, p. 141.

182. Elizabeth Cohen, "Miscarriages of Apothecary Justice: Un-separate Spaces for Work and Family in Early Modern Rome," *Renaissance Studies* 21 (2007): p. 501.

183. Bartolomeo Gittio, *Tractatus de casibus reservatis in quo praecipue explicantur reseruati in dioecesi Beneuentana* (Naples: Constantini Vitalis, 1621), pp. 142–143.

184. Marinello, *Le medicine partenenti*, bk. 3, ch. 12, f. 285r–289r; Mercuriale, *De morbis muliebribus*, bk. 2, ch. 3, p. 63; Bairo, *Secreti medicinali*, f. 200r–201r; Bottoni, *De morbis muliebribus*, ch. 71; Mercurio, *La commare*, bk. 2, ch. 19, pp. 178–179; Massaria, *Praelectiones de morbis mulierum*, ch. 11, pp. 347–348; Christini, *Pratica medicinale & osservationii*, bk. 2, ch. 19, pp. 140–141.

185. It is also important to note that Camotio's decision not to intervene was made in a specific legal context: Angela had denounced another woman for assaulting her and causing the death of her fetus. Had Camotio intervened and hastened the expulsion of the fetus, the case might have been contaminated. Timoteo Camotio: "Trattatoli il corpo la trovai fredda et tutto calato abbasso haveva l'umbelico fuora della natura, nero, senza moto et freddo, segni manifesti del feto morto, et questa mattina revisitandola l'ho trovata peggio di hier sera." ASR, TcG, Processi, 1603, b. 28bis, f. 771v.

186. Cristini, *Pratica medicinale*, bk. 2, ch. 18, oss. xcv, p. 132.

187. Giacomo Menochio, *De arbitrariis iudicum quaestionibus & causis, libri duo* (Venice: Antonium de Franciscis, 1624), bk. 2, casus 357, n. 20, p. 665.

ROSANA AND GIOVANNI

1. ASR, TcG, Processi, 1598, b. 310, f. 905r–910v. Hereafter, for all notes that cite this trial, I give only the folio number and the name of the witness. The small area known as the Borgo, stretching between Saint Peter's and Castel Sant'Angelo, had its own tribunal, which mostly served prelates and their entourage who lived in the area. It tried criminal issues, but, according to Fosi, its main purpose was "whisking a privileged population tied to the curia out from under the surveillance of Rome's other judges." Irene Fosi, *Papal Justice: Subjects and Courts in the Papal State, 1500–1750,* trans. T. V. Cohen (Washington, DC: Catholic University of America Press, 2011), pp. 29–31. From time to time, ordinary Romans who lived nearby, such as Giuseppe Ansaloni, used the court to settle their disputes.

2. Efforts have been made to retrieve information about the protagonists of this trial in parish records (Parrocchia di San Lazzaro fuori porta Angelica; Parrocchia di Santa Maria in Traspontina, Parrocchia di San Giacomo in Borgo) held in the Archivio Storico del Vicariato, but to date they remain elusive.

3. Giuseppe Ansaloni: "Nell'hora della mezza notte detto Giovanni si levò di letto di sua moglie et se ne callò a basso e per forza hebbe da fare con detta Rosana sua cognata ponendoli un suagiatore alla boccha acciò non gridasse e non facesse rumore alcuno. Nondimeno donna Fantilla sua matre che dormeva con lei se ne acorse et volle gridare, ma detto Giovanni con belle parole vedendosi così scoperto che le quietò promettendoli di fare et di dire, et se ne partì e retornò a dormire con Pelegrina sua moglie." f. 906v.

4. Bartering virginity for a dowry and the promise of a husband was not uncommon in early modern Italy. In a 1605 case studied by Claudio Povolo, the Friulan nobleman Paolo Orgiano, among numerous transgressions, promised Menega Caponata to find her fifteen-year-old daughter a husband if she allowed him to have sex with her first. Menega initially refused, but Paolo persisted and eventually raped the fifteen-year-old Caterina. Claudio Povolo, *Il processo di Paolo Orgiano (1605–1607)* (Rome: Viella, 2003), pp. 132–137. See also Cohen, *Love and Death*, ch. 4, esp. pp. 142–143.

5. Giuseppe Ansaloni: Rosana "non voleva pigliare detta medicina o bevanda detto Giovanni . . . dicendoli che le pigliasse, che serebbe la ventura sua et che non seria svergognata." f. 907r.

6. In his testimony, the barber Giacomo referred to Giovanni as being his "grande amico" up until the time that he realized that Giovanni had impregnated Rosana, had tricked him into bleeding her and possibly

causing her to abort, and had falsely married her off to Giuseppe as a virgin. f. 910r.

7. Giovanni reportedly gave Rosana a syrup of Sant'Onofrio. I have been unable to find this product in early modern pharmacological or medical literature.

8. Giuseppe Ansaloni: "Rosana mi ha detto che li diedero a bevere una bevanda facendola sedere sopra al cantaro, cioè sopra il necessario et lei lì si infantò et fece una creatura che andò giù pel necessario. . . . Che come ho detto la pigliò e poco doppo se infantò facendola sedere sopra il necessario che ce la teneva per forza la Pelegrina sua sorella, et infantata che fu mezza morta la misero in letto, dove stette circa a doi mesi. Et detto Giovanni vedendo poi questo che lei s'era infantata volendosi acertare e vedere se che fosse callò a basso dove respendeva il necessario, levò via certa poca che stava sopra **** a certe tavole, e trovò che era una creatura morta quella che detta Rosana haveva partorito, il che poi vedendo detto Giovanni gettò quella creatura che haveva trovato et levato dal necessario et la gettò nel pozzo che sta lì propª a muro della casa in un cortile di casa dove ancora si può vedere che ci sta et ci habita. Et gettata che hebbe detta creatura nel pozzo fece nettare il cantaro dicendo che era pieno et all'hora non fu altro et la cosa se ne stava così che quando lei partorì non ci fu nessuno presente se non la sorella, la matre e lui. **** giorno dopo essendosi poi guarita la detta Rosana fece il bagno dal basso e chiamò con lei acciò l'aiutasse donna Cleria che non so di chi, ma è Romanesca et habita al Arco di S. Angelo e mentre dico tutte doi cavavano l'acqua con il secchio detta Rosana e Cleria tirorno su dove nel secchio detta creatura e vedendo queste donne questo la firmorno sopra la vascha e chiamorno detto Giovanni, Fantilla matre di Rosana et Pelegrina et le mostrorno quella creatura dicendoli, ecco la creatura che me ha fatto facere il cognato Giovanni! Et all'hora donna Fantilla matre predetta prese la creatura et la sepelì nel cortile et la copersero et così passò el fatto quanto mi ha confessato la detta Rosana, che chiamandola lei trovarà che così è la verità." f. 907r–v. On drains and waste disposal in early modern Rome, see Katherine Wentworth Rinne, *The Waters of Rome: Aqueducts, Fountains, and the Birth of a Baroque City* (New Haven, CT: Yale University Press, 2010), ch. 9.

9. Both brothers reported this. Giuseppe Ansaloni: "Et Giovanni vedendosi cosi afrontato disse, io no ne so niente, ma che volete a peccatori! Penitenza, pecchò San Pietro ancora, e per questo volete voi che io lasci li mei figlioli et la mia moglie? Ma vedete se si può remediare." f. 908r. Giacomo Ansaloni: "E lui mi confessò et me disse che le cose erono fatte, et che diavolo fa fare gran cose, che voi che facci acciò che io vada via? Peccò San Pietro e simile parole." f. 910r.

10. Giuseppe Ansaloni: "Partiti che furno io mi sono consigliato et mi sono resoluto di farli questa questa [*sic*] querela come le faccio et adimando che sia castigato conforme alle giustitia. Ma vostra signoria accerta che quando detto Giovanni se acorse che io mi ero accorto di questo fatto et che Rosana mi haveva detto ogni cosa detto Giovanni chiamò Rosana e Pelegrina sua moglie e le disse che stesse quieta et che non confessasse niente et che lasciasse fare a lui, che haverebbe trovato doi testimoni **** et mi haverebbaro aperto, che io fossi un furbo et che me haverebbe fatto mandare in una galera, promettendoli di darli et trovarli un altro marito, et Rosana me lo disse a me e così è passato tutto il fatto con questo **** ce ne dò querela et adimando che sia castigato conforme alla giustizia." f. 908rv.

CHAPTER TWO ∾ ABORTION AND THE CHURCH

1. Sixtus V, *Contra Procurantes, consulentes, & consentientes, quocumque modo Abortum, CONSTITUTIO* (Rome: Antonio Blado, 1588).

2. ASV, Cong. Vescovi e Regolari, "Positiones," 1590, D–M, Il Vescovo di Lodi . . . alla S. d. N. S. Papa Sisto Quinto, April 1590.

3. ASV, Congr. Vescovi e Regolari, "Registra Episcoporum," 19 (1590), May 4, 1590, f. 149r–v.

4. Mercurio, *De gli errori popolari*, bk. 2, ch. 26, f. 107v–110r.

5. Alongside Prosperi's recent and rich discussion, *Infanticide, Secular Justice, and Religious Debate*, pp. 187–230, see the foundational work of Noonan, "An Almost Absolute Value in History," pp. 1–59; Sardi, *Aborto ieri e oggi*; Connery, S. J., *Abortion*.

6. In his oration at the 1569 Synod of Florence, the Vicar General Guido Serguidi stated that "the ignorance of the faithful was a consequence of the inadequacies of the clergy in its pastoral mission." Quoted in Arnaldo D'Addario, *Aspetti della controriforma a Firenze* (Rome, 1972), p. 199, and Kathleen Comerford, "'The Care of Souls Is a Very Grave Burden for [the Pastor]': Professionalization of Clergy in Early Modern Florence, Lucca, and Arezzo," in *The Formation of Clerical and Confessional Identities in Early Modern Europe*, ed. Wim Janse and Barbara Pitkin (Leiden: Brill, 2005), pp. 349–368.

7. The 1517 Synod of Florence characterized confessors as "ignorant, greedy, without charity, without zeal, and inclined to examine their penitents' purses more than their consciences." *Statuta Concili Florentini* (Florence: Giunti, 1518), f. 18v. For Catholic criticisms of the practice of confession, see Wietse De Boer, *The Conquest of the Soul: Confession, Discipline and Public Order in Counter-Reformation Milan* (Leiden: Brill, 2001), ch. 1.

8. Carlo Borromeo, *Avvertenze . . . a i Confessori nella Citta, e Diocese,* in *Acta ecclesiae mediolanensis* (Milan, 1583), f. 231v; De Boer, *Conquest of the Soul,* p. 53.

9. For instance, Simona Negruzzo has found more positive results in Lombardy, where seminaries and religious houses (such as those of Jesuits, Barnabites, and Somaschans) appear to have been more successful in the overall training of secular clergy than their neighbors to the south. This relative success was no doubt owed, at least in part, to the involvement of Carlo Borromeo. Negruzzo, *Collegij a forma di Seminario. Il sistema di formazione teologica nello Stato di Milano in eta spagnola* (Brescia: Editrice La Scuola, 2001). For the success of Jesuit educational institutions, see John W. O'Malley, *The First Jesuits* (Cambridge, MA: Harvard University Press, 1993).

10. The literature on clerical professionalization is vast: see Luciano Allegra, "Il parroco: un mediatore fra alta e bassa cultura," in *Intellettuali e potere,* ed. Corrado Vivanti (Turin: Einaudi, 1981), pp. 895-947; Gaetano Greco, "Fra disciplina e sacerdozio: il clero secolare nella societa italiana dalcinquecento al settecento," in *Clero e societa nell'Italia moderna,* ed. Mario Rosa (Bari: Laterza, 1992), pp. 45-113, esp. p. 94; Angelo Turchini, "La nascita del sacerdozio come professione," in *Disciplina dell'anima, disciplina del corpo e disciplina della societa tra medioevo ed eta moderna,* ed. Paolo Prodi (Bologna: Il Mulino, 1994), pp. 225-256; Kathleen Comerford, *Reforming Priests and Parishes: Tuscan Dioceses in the First Century of Seminary Education* (Leiden: Brill, 2006); Celeste McNamara, *The Bishop's Burden: Reforming The Catholic Church in Early Modern Italy* (Washington, DC: The Catholic University of America Press, 2020), ch. 4. See generally Black, *Church, Religion and Society,* pp. 62-129.

11. Adriano Prosperi, *Tribunale della coscienza. Inquisitori, confessori, missionari,* (Turin: Einaudi, 1996); Giovanni Romeo, *Ricerche su confessione dei peccati e inquisizione nell'Italia del Cinquecento* (Naples: La Città del sole, 1997); Michele Mancino, *Licentia confitendi: Selezione e controllo dei confessori a Napoli in eta moderna* (Rome: Edizioni di storia e letteratura, 2000); De Boer, *Conquest of the Soul*; Vincenzo Lavenia, *L'infamia e il perdono: Tributi, pene e confessione nella teologia morale della primaeta moderna* (Bologna: Il Mulino, 2004); Elena Brambila, *La giustizia intollerante. Inquisizione e tribunali confessionali in Europa (secoli IV–XVIII)* (Rome: Carocci, 2006).

12. *Catechismo, cioe istruttione secondo il Decreto del Concilio di Trento, a' parochi . . . tradotto poi per ordine di S. Santita in ligua uolgare dal reuerendo Padre frate Alessio Figliucci* (Venice: Aldo Manuzio, 1567), p. 301. Following the theologians and canonists, the *Cathecism* reaffirmed that marriage is also a good in that it satisfies desire and eliminates the risk of fornication; however, couples should abstain from the conjugal debt to devote them-

selves to prayer and then return together "lest Satan tempt you by your incontinence." *Catechismo,* p. 295.

13. *Catechismo,* p. 365.

14. Carlo Borromeo, *Acta ecclesiae mediolanensis* (Milan: Pacifici Pontii, 1599), pp. 182, 761.

15. Quoted in Lorenzo Paliotto, *Giovanni Fontana Vescovo di Ferrara (1590–1611)* (Ferrara: Edizioni Cartografica: 2002), p. 642.

16. Angelo Carletti [da Chiavasso], *Summa angelica de casibus conscientialibus . . . cumadditionibus quam commodis R.P.F. Iacobi Ungarelli* (Venice: Regazola, 1578); Sylvestro Mazzolini [da Prierio], *Summae Sylvestrinae, quae summa summarum merito nuncupatur,* 2 vols. (Venice: Franciscum Zilettum, 1587); Cajetan [Tomasso de Vio], *Peccatorum summula* (Venice: Dominicum Farreum, 1575); Bartolomeo Fumi, *Summa, aurea armilla nuncupata, casus omnes ad animarum curamattinentes, breuiter complectens,* (Venice: Giovanni Battista Somasco, 1572).

17. On this genre, Miriam Turrini, *La coscienza e le leggi. Morale e diritto nei testi per la confessione della prima eta moderna* (Bologna: Il Mulino, 1991). For the development of this genre pre-Trent, see Thomas Tentler, *Sin and Confession on the Eve of the Reformation* (Princeton, NJ: Princeton University Press, 1975), pp. 28-53. Tentler speculates that these Latin works would have been purchased by educated clerics who had a desire to keep up with recent developments in moral theology, perhaps indicating an attitude of reform.

18. Carletti's *Angelica* saw twenty-four editions; Mazzolini's *Summa,* ten; Cajetan's *Summula,* eleven; Fumi's *Armilla* saw twenty-seven Latin and vernacular editions from 1549 to 1602. See Turrini, *La coscienza e le leggi,* "Censimento."

19. Carletti, *Summa angelica,* vol. 1, p. 5, "Aborsum"; Mazzolini, *Summae Sylvestrinae,* vol. 1, f. 3r-v; Cajetan, *Peccatorum summula,* p. 1, "Aborsus"; Fumi, *Summa, aurea armilla,* p. 6, "De Aborsu." See also entries for *Homo/Homine, Homicidium,* and *Si occides* in these works.

20. Carletti, *Summa angelica,* vol. 1, pp. 282–289, "Debitum coniugale"; Mazzolini, *Summae Sylvestrinae,* vol. 1, p. 230, "Debitum coniugale"; Cajetan, *Peccatorum summula,* p. 318, "matrimonium."

21. Mazzolini, *Summae Sylvestrinae,* vol. 2, f. 171r, "De medico et infirmis,"; Fumi, *Summa, aurea armilla,* p. 6, "De Aborsu." See also Carletti, *Summa angelica,* vol. 2, pp. 125-127; "Medicus"; and Cajetan, *Peccatorum summula,* pp. 322-323, "Medici peccata."

22. The first Spanish edition, from which the Italian was translated, was published in 1554. The Latin editions were the most frequently printed, and the work would largely be known through its Latin title: *Enchiridion, sive manuale confessariorum et poenitentium.* The version used here is the

Italian translation, *Manuale de' Confessori et Penitenti* (Venice: Gabriel Giolito di Ferrara, 1569), which went through at least twenty-nine Italian editions between 1564 and 1600 from all the major printing centers of Italy. See Turrini, *La coscienza e le leggi,* "Censimento." For Azpilcueta's life and work, see Vincenzo Lavenia, "Martin Azpilcueta: un profilo," *Archivio italiano per la storia della pieta* 16 (2003): pp. 14-148.

23. This genre peaked between 1570 and 1610: 147 titles published in the 1580s alone. Sixteenth-century readers demanded them and, as Anne Jacobson Schutte has remarked, we should not assume that they were purchased to adorn bookcases or to impress visitors. Anne Jacobson Schutte, "Consiglio spirituale e controllo sociale: Manuali per la confessione stampati in volgare prima della Controriforma," in *Citta italiane del '500 tra Riforma e Controriforma: Atti del Convegno Internazionale di Studi Lucca* (Lucca: M. Pacini Fazzi, 1988), pp. 45-59. Generally, see Turrini, *La coscienza e le leggi,* "Tabelle e grafici."

24. Fumi, *Summa, aurea armilla,* pp. 6-7; Azpilcueta, *Manuale de' Confessori,* p. 166; Pietro Filomuso, *Breue trattato di confessione* (Florence: Bartolomeo Sermartelli, 1580), no. 4 (unpaginated); Paolo Morigia, *Il gioiello de christiani* (Venice: Girolamo Polo, 1581), f. 108r-v; Antonio Pagani, *La Breve somma delle essamine de confitenti, per la necessaria riforma del huomo interiore* (Venice: Giovanni Battista Somasco, 1587), p. 34, 43, 85-86 (erroneously printed as "76"); Fabio Incarnato, *Scrutinio sacerdotale, overo modo di essaminare tanto nelle visite de' Vescovi, quanto nel pigliare gli Ordini Sacri* (Venice: Domenico Nicolini da Sabbio, 1588), f. 200v-201r.

25. Pagani, *Breve Somma,* p. 34; Morigia, *Il gioiello,* f. 108r; Incarnato, *Scrutinio,* f. 200v-201r; Filomuso, *Breue trattato,* no. 4. Giovanni Molisso da Sarno, *Accorgimento de fideli intorno la sacramentale confessione* (Naples, 1589), p. 320.

26. "Io non velo consiglio, ma se tal cosa facesse, sanarebbe." Azpilcueta, *Manuale de' Confessori,* p. 630. Fumi, *Summa, aurea armilla,* p. 6; Pagani, *Breve somma,* pp. 110, 111-112; Molisso da Sarno, *Accorgimento de fideli,* pp. 428, 430, 442-443, for apothecaries.

27. *The Canons and Decress of the Council of Trent,* trans. Reverend H. J. Schroeder (Rockford, IL: Tan Books and Publishers, 1978), pp. 91-92.

28. *Canons and Decrees of the Council of Trent,* session 14, ch. 7, p. 96. See generally Henry Charles Lea, *A History of Auricular Confession and Indulgences in the Latin Church* (Philadelphia: Lea Brothers & Co., 1896), vol. 1, pp. 312-342; Elena Brambilla, "Confessione, casi riservati e giustizia 'spirituale' dal XV secolo al concilio di Trento: i reati di fede e di morale," in *Fonti ecclesiastiche per la storia sociale e religiosa d'Europa: XV–XVIII secolo,* ed. Cecilia Nubola and Angelo Turchini (Bologna: Il Mulino, 1999), pp. 491-540; Elena Brambilla, "Casi riservati," in *Dizionario storico dell'Inquisizione,*

ed. Adriano Prosperi, Vincenzo Lavenia, and John Tedeschi (Pisa: Edizioni della Normale, 2010), vol. 1, pp. 290-291.

29. Reserving abortion was not unique to the Tridentine episcopate: several
bishops in the fifteenth and early sixteenth centuries reserved it to their
offices. Nonetheless, it seems that after Trent many more bishops were
inclined to do so, most likely in emulation of Borromeo. For reserved
cases before Trent, see Lea, *History of Auricular Confession*; Brambilla,
"Confessione, casi riservati" and "Casi riservati."

30. Borromeo included "Qui abortum procurarint" among sins and crimes
of sexual violence, such as the rape of virgins and incest; the crime of
voluntary homicide, including the exposure of infants; heresy, magic,
and superstition; and "polluting the church": Borromeo, *Acta ecclesiae mediolanensis*, pp. 11, 339, 992.

31. *Constitutiones editae, et promulgatae in synodo dioecesana Placentina quam illustrissimus et reuerendissimus D. D. Paulus De Aretio, . . . anno MDLXX die
XXVI Augusti* (Piacenza: Franciscum Comitem, 1570), p. 220; *De Casibus
reservatis Illustrissimo, et Reverendiss. Domino Paulo Aretio Card. Et Archiepiscopo Neapolitano*, in Gian Battista Antonucci, *Catechesis, seu Instructio
civitatis ac dioecesis Neapolitanae* (Naples: Horatium Salvianum, 1577),
p. 354.

32. *Constitutiones et decreta provincialis synodi Neapolitanae, sub Illustriss. et Reverendiss. D. D. Mario Carrafa Archiepiscopo, Anno Domini MDLXXVI . . . e mandato Illustrissimi ac reverendissimi D. D. Annibalis a Capua* (Naples: Ex Officina Salviana, 1580), p. 27; and *Casus reservati Illustriss. et Reverendiss.
D. Ann. Cap.* in *Catechesis seu institutio civitatis ac dioecesis Neapolitanae* (Naples: Matthiae Cancer, 1587), p. 342.

33. *Constitutiones et Decreta condita in synodo dioecesana Ravennatensi, quam illustrissimus, &reverendissimus dominus D. Christophorus Boncompagnus
Dei, . . . anno domini MDLXXX die quinta Maij* (Ravenna: Franciscum Thebaldinum, 1580), f. 55v.

34. *Constitutiones, et decreta Dioecesanae Synodi Viterben per admodu Illustrem, et
Reuerendiss D. D. Carolum Archiepiscopu Motiliu(m) Episcopum Viterben* (Viterbo: Augustinum Colaldum, 1584), p. 110.

35. *Synodo Dioecesana camerinensi quam illvstris, et reverensissimvs Dominus Hieronymvs de Bobus . . . MDLXXXVII. die XXIIII. Mensis Septembris* (Camerino: Franciscum Gioiosum, 1588), p. 58.

36. Carlo Borromeo, Paulo Burali d'Arezzo, and Giovanni Fontana were
particularly fond of the reservation of cases. See discussions in Ottavio Pasquinelli, "Peccati riservati a Milano dopo San Carlo (1586-
1592)," *La Scuola Cattolica* 121 (1993): pp. 679-721; De Boer, *Conquest of
the Soul*; Franco Molinari, *Il cardinale teatino beato Paolo Burali e la riforma tridentina a Piacenza (1568–1576)* (Rome: Universitatis Gregori-

anae, 1957) p. 143; Mancino, *Licentia confitendi*; Paliotto, *Giovanni Fontana,* pp. 257–260.

37. Mancino, *Licentia confitendi,* pp. 37, 71.

38. De Boer, *Conquest of the Soul,* pp. 63–64, 228–233. The reservation of cases was also particularly difficult to enforce during Lent, when confessors heard many confessions due to its annual obligation. The system of reservation had to be significantly relaxed during this time. See De Boer, *Conquest of the Soul,* pp. 228–229.

39. *Statuta Concili Florentini* (Florence: Bartholomaeum Sermartellium, 1564), pp. 125–126; *Decreta provinciales synodi Florentinae . . . Antonio Altovita, Archiepiscopo* (Florence: Barholomaeum Sermartellium, 1574); *Constitutiones et decreta condita in provinciali Synodo Consentina sub. Reuerendiss. Domino D. Fantino Petrignano Dei & Apostolicae Sedis gratia Archiepiscopo Consentiae, anno MDLXXIX* (Rome: Franciscum Zanetium, 1580), p. 112. Sega reserved cases of infant suffocation, incest in the second degree or higher, and sex with beasts, but not abortion. *Sinodo Diocesana di Mons. Rever. Philippo Sega vescovo della Ripatransona . . . publicati i treprimi giorni di maggio 1576* (Macerata: Sebastiano Martellini, 1577), 34v.

40. Tommaso Zerola, *Praxis sacramenti poenitentiae* (Venice: Georgium Variscum, 1599), ch. 24, question 16, f. 114r–115v; Azpilcueta, *Manuale de' confessori,* ch. 26, p. 688; Lea, *History of Auricular Confession,* p. 339.

41. On the misdeeds of clergy and responses by the Church and the laity, see Oscar Di Simplicio, *Peccato penitenza perdono, Siena 1575–1800. La formazione della coscienza nell'Italia moderna* (Milan: Franco Angeli 1994); De Boer, *Conquest of the Soul*; Giovanni Romeo, *Amori proibiti. I concubini tra Chiesa e Inquisizione* (Bari: Laterza, 2008); Fosi, *Papal Justice,* ch. 9; Joanne Ferraro, *Nefarious Crimes,* pp. 158–199; Thomas Deutscher, *Punishment and Penance: Two Phases in the History of the Bishop's Tribunal of Novara* (Toronto: University of Toronto Press, 2012), pp. 60–69; Michele Mancino and Giovanni Romeo, *Clero Criminale. L'onore della Chiesa e i delitti degli ecclesiastici nell'Italia della Controriforma* (Bari: Laterza, 2013); Prosperi, *Infanticide, Secular Justice and Religious Debate,* pp. 93–103; McNamara, *The Bishop's Burden,* pp. 64–71. For a later period, Marco Cavarzere, *La giustizia del Vescovo. I tribunali ecclesiastici della Liguria Orientale* (Pisa: Pisa University Press, 2012).

42. G. B. Intra, "Di Ippolito Capilupi e del suo tempo," *Archivio storico Lombardo* 20 (1893): pp. 76–142, at pp. 102–107 (letter from Ippolito Capilupi to Carlo Borromeo, November 9, 1561). The case is recounted in Mary Laven, *Virgins of Venice: Enclosed Lives and Broken Vows in the Renaissance Convent* (New York: Viking, 2002), pp. 161–166.

43. The case was brought to court by Violante's husband, who sought a marital separation on the grounds of adultery. Laura Turchi, "Adulterio,

onere della prova e testimonianza. In margine a un processo Correggese di eta tridentina," in *Trasgressioni. Seduzione, concubinato, adulterio, bigamia (XIV–XVIII secolo),* ed. Silvana Seidel Menchi and Diego Quaglioni (Bologna: Il Mulino, 2004), pp. 305–350.

44. The vicar, however, wondered whether these allegations against the bishop were more reflections of the community's distaste for their bishop than truthful retellings of his actual behaviors. ASV, *Congregazione dell'Immunita ecclesiastica. Acta, 1517–1598.* The letter is transcribed in the online primary source documents companion to Mancino and Romeo's *Clero Criminale,* available for download from the digital archive of the Universita degli Studi Federico II, pp. 74–77, accessed May 27, 2020, http://www.fedoabooks.unina.it/index.php/fedoapress/catalog /view/15/12/68-1.

45. Giovanni Rossi, *Catalago de Vescovi di Telese* (Naples: Stamperia della Società tipografica, 1827), pp. 144–145.

46. The Apostolic Penitentiary heard and decided on numerous issues involving ecclesiastical censures and restrictions pertaining to both clergy and laity. The Cardinal Penitentiary, acting on behalf of the pope, granted dispensations from some of the requirements of canon law and absolutions for those who violated certain ecclesiastical canons. It also made decisions pertaining to the external forum and mostly regarding marriage—whether people who were closely related could get married—and illegitimacy; for the clergy, the penitentiary was mostly concerned with issues of irregularity. See Fillipo Tamburini, "Per la storia dei cardinali penitenzieri maggiori e dell'archivio del Penitenzieria apostolic," *Rivista di storia della Chiesa in Italia* 36 (1982): pp. 332–380; Fillipo Tamburini, *Santi e peccatori: Confessioni e suppliche dai Registri della Penitenzieria dell'Archivio Segreto Vaticano (1451–1586)* (Milan: Istituto di propaganda libraria, 1995); Kirsi Salonen and Ludwig Schmugge, *A Sip from the "Well of Grace": Medieval Texts from the Apostolic Penitentiary* (Washington, DC: Catholic University of America Press, 2009); Elena Brambilla, "Penitenzieria Apostolica," in *Dizionario storico dell'Inquisizione,* vol. 3, pp. 1183–1185.

47. Martin de Azpilcueta, *Consiliorum sive responsorum,* bk. 5 (Rome: Aloysii Zannetti, 1595). For Azpilcueta's career at the penitentiary, see Lavenia, "Martin Azpilcueta: un profilo." Azpilcueta served several major penitentiaries over his long career in Rome, these included Carlo Borromeo (1565–1572), Filippo Boncompagni (1579–1586), and Ippolito Aldobrandini (later Pope Clement VIII [1586–1592]).

48. Azpilcueta, *Consiliorum*, bk. 5, cons. 47, p. 455.

49. Azpilcueta, *Consiliorum*, bk. 5, cons. 47, p. 455.

50. Azpilcueta, *Consiliorum*, bk. 5, cons. 49, p. 457.

51. Azpilcueta, *Consiliorum*, bk. 5, cons. 49, p. 457.

52. Gaetano Moroni, *Dizionario di erudizione storico-ecclesiastica*, vol. 5 (Venice: Tipografia Emiliana, 1840), pp. 276–287.

53. Sixtus V, *Contra Procurantes . . . Abortum. Constitutio*. Sixtus's bulls are reprinted in most modern collections of papal bulls. See *Bullarium diplomatum et privilegiorum Sanctorum Romanum Pontificum*, vol. 8 and 9 (Turin: Sebastiano Franco et Filiis, 1863 and 1865).

54. For an overview of the bull, see Noonan, "An Almost Absolute Value," p. 33; Prosperi, *Infanticide, Secular Justice, and Religious Debate*, pp. 260–262; Terpstra, *Lost Girls*, pp. 91–93.

55. Sixtus V, *Contra Procurantes, . . . Abortum. Constitutio*, f. 1r.

56. Sixtus V, *Contra Procurantes, . . . Abortum. Constitutio*, f. 1r.

57. The decree Sixtus referenced was issued at what has come to be referred to as the Council in Trullo, which met in 691 or 692, a decade after the Third Synod of Constantinople (680–681), which is referred to as the Sixth Ecumenical Church Council. The Council in Trullo (named after the domed hall of the Imperial Palace of Constantinople, where the council met) discussed matters of Church discipline whereas the previous meeting discussed issues of faith and doctrine. The early modern Catholic church held the Council in Trullo to have been an addendum or a second and concluding session to the Third Synod of Constantinople and not as an ecumenical council in its own right. (On the complicated history of the Council in Trullo, see George Nedungatt and Michael Featherstone, eds., *The Council in Trullo Revisited* (Rome: Pontificio Istituto Orientale, 1995.) Accordingly, in the bull, Sixtus situates the proclamation within the decrees of the "Sixth [Ecumenical Council, the Third] Synod of Constantinople." The decrees of this council were published in 1585 as part of a massive five-volume edition of the acts of Church councils, both general and provincial, which Sixtus V approved. The documents pertaining to the Third Council of Constantinople appear in volume 3 and are on pp. 234–374; the decrees of the Council in Trullo are on pp. 391–406. The decree on abortion reads: "Eas quae dant abortionem cientia medicamenta, & quae foetus necatia venena accipiunt, homicidae poenis subijcimus." *Conciliorum omnium, tam Generalium quam Provincialium*, vol. 3 (Venice: Dominicum Nicolinum, 1585), "Sextae Synodi Constantinopolinae Canones," canon 91, p. 404.

58. On the abortion ruling of the Council of Lleida (Lerida), see Mistry, Abortion in the Early Middle Ages, pp. 94–97.

59. Sixtus V, *Contra Procurantes, . . . Abortum. Constitutio*, f. 1rv.

60. Sixtus V, *Contra Procurantes, . . . Abortum. Constitutio*, f. 1r.

61. Sixtus V, *Contra Procurantes, . . . Abortum. Constitutio*, f. 1r.

62. Sixtus V, *Contra Procurantes, . . . Abortum. Constitutio*, f. 1v.

63. If a penitent is near death, all priests may absolve them from all sins and censures, including reserved cases. See *Canons and Decrees of the Council of Trent,* session 14, ch. 7, p. 96.

64. Sixtus V, *Contra Procurantes, . . . Abortum. Constitutio,* f. 1v.

65. Sixtus V, *Contra Procurantes, . . . Abortum. Constitutio,* f. 1r.

66. Sixtus V, *Contra Procurantes, . . . Abortum. Constitutio,* f. 1rv.

67. Sixtus V, *Contra Procurantes, . . . Abortum. Constitutio,* f. 1v.

68. Sixtus V, *Contra Procurantes, . . . Abortum. Constitutio,* f. 1rv.

69. On Sixtus's "draconian politics" and penal laws, see Ludwig von Pastor, *The History of the Popes from the Close of the Middle Ages,* vol. 21, *Sixtus V (1585–1590)* (London: Kegan Paul, 1932), pp. 89–95; Jean Delumeau, *Vie économique et sociale de Rome dans la seconde moitié du XVIe siècle* (Paris: E. de Boccard, 1959), vol. 1, p. 430. Ombretta Fumagalli, "Sisto V e la 'questione criminale,'" in *Sisto V. Roma e il Lazio,* ed. Marcello Fagiolo and Maria Luisa Madonna (Rome: Istituto Poligrafico e Zecca dello Stato, 1992), vol. 1, pp. 85–94; Irene Fosi, "Justice and Its Image: Political Propaganda and Judicial Reality in the Pontificate of Sixtus V," *Sixteenth Century Journal* 24 (1993): pp. 75–95.

70. Sixtus V, *Super de temeraria tori separatione, ac publicis adulteriis, stupris et lenociniis in quibusdam casibus severius coercendis* (Rome: Antonio Blado, 1586); Sixtus V, *Constitutio contra Incestuosos* (Rome: Antonio Blado, 1587).

71. Fosi, *Papal Justice,* pp. 234–236. Alongside various mentions of punishments meted out for adultery in the avvisi reports (BAV. Urb. Lat. 1053–1058), many *giustizie* stories recounted the fates of adulterers, seducers, and rapists. See BAV. Vat. Lat. 7439 and 8891; Capponi, 189 and Urb. Lat. 1644.

72. Avviso, June 7, 1586, BAV. Urb. Lat., 1054, f. 215r; Pastor, *History of the Popes,* p. 92, although he mispaginates the archival document as f. 205.

73. Santori reported this in his diary, which has been transcribed and published by Giorgio Cugnoni, "Autobiografia di monsignor G. Antonio Santori cardinale di S. Severina," *Archivio della R. Società Romana di Storia Patria* 13 (1890): pp. 151–207, at p. 179.

74. *Constitutio Contra illegitimos, legitimatos, criminosos, & reddendis rationibus obnoxios ad aliquam Religionem transire volentes, Et contra Regulares absque Superiorum licentia de Provincia in Provinciam euntes, seu transmigrantes* (Rome: Antonio Blado, 1587), and *Declaratio, circa promotionem Fratrum illegitimorum ad sui ordinis dignitates, & officia* (Rome: Antonio Blado, 1588).

75. *Editto che li Regolari non possino tenere, ne andare per Roma in Cocchio o Carrozza* (Rome: Antonio Blado, October 1588). On carriage riding in Rome, see John M. Hunt, "Carriages, Violence, and Masculinity in Early Modern Rome," *I Tatti Studies in the Italian Renaissance* 17 (2014): pp. 175–196.

76. *Canons and Decrees of the Council of Trent,* pp. 110–111.

77. Avviso, June 14, 1586, BAV. Urb. Lat. 1054, f. 231r–v.

78. Pastor, *History of the Popes,* p. 130.

79. Pastor, *History of the Popes,* pp. 33–34; Prosperi, *Tribunali della conscienza,* p. 98.

80. Sixtus chose Cesare Bellochio, son of a prominent family from Fano with intimate ties to Sixtus and the curia. Among his first orders of episcopal business was the establishment of a seminary for training priests. Rossi, *Catalago de Vescovi di Telese,* pp. 145–146.

81. Emphasis added. Cugnoni, "Autobiografia," pp. 183–184.

82. See Paolo Prodi, *Papal Prince* and *Una storia della giustizia: Dal pluralismo dei fori al moderno dualismo tra coscienza e diritto* (Bologna: Il Mulino, 2000); Fosi, *Papal Justice,* ch. 7.

83. In Bologna, printed by Alessandro Benacci in 1589 and 1590; in Florence, printed by Giorgio Marescotti in 1588; in Venice, printed by Calle dale Rase in 1588; and in Naples, printed by Orazio Saviani in 1589.

84. "Nunc vero Papalis iuxta Constit. Sixti Quinti, q. incipit Effrenatam." *Decreta et constitutiones editae a Frabricio Gallo, Neapolitano Episcopo Nolano in Synodo dioecesana celebrat Nolae sub die sexto Mensis Novembris, Anno MDLXXXVIII* (Naples: Horatium Salvianum, 1590), p. 56.

85. *Constitutiones editae per Reverendiss in Christo Patrem D. Io. Matthaeum Gibertum, Episcopum Veronae, . . . ab Illustrissimo, ac Reveredendiss. D. D. Augustino Valerio* (Verona: Hieronymum Discipulum impressorem Episcopalem, 1589), p. 173.

86. *Synodus dioecesana sub admodum ill. et reverendiss.mo Domino Philippo Sega episcopo Placentiae & Comite, Primo habita, anno do. MDLXXXIX. V. No. Maii* (Piacenza: Ioannis Bazachii, 1589), p. 133.

87. Biblioteca Marciana, BNM 65.C.98. *Sommario di tre Bolle de Sommi Pontefici, cioe di Pio V, sopra i censi, di Sisto V sopra gl'aborti, et l'altrae de gli patti reprobati nelle Compagnie che salvano il Capitale, e in nome di guadagno, pongono certa riposta* (Ancona: Francesco Salvioni, March 15, 1590). I thank Silvia Manzi for drawing my attention to this document. For vernacular translations and summaries, and often interpretations, of papal orders for clergy and laity, see Manzi, "*Nella lingua di ciascuno*: Church Communication between Latin and Vernacular during the Counter-Reformation," *Studies in Church History* 53 (2017): 196–209.

88. My thanks to Vincenzo Lavenia for alerting me to the holdings of the Congregation of Bishops and Regulars. See Lavenia, "'D'animal fante': teologia, medicina legale e identita umana: secoli XVI–XVII," in *Salvezza delle anime e disciplina dei corpi: un seminario sulla storia del battesimo,* ed. Adriano Prosperi (Pisa: Edizione della Normale, 2006), pp. 483–526.

89. ASV, Congr. Vescovi e Regolari, "Positiones," 1589, unpaginated, Larino [Ill. Vic. Apost.] a D. V.S., June 17, 1589.

90. ASV, Cong. Vescovi e Regolari, "Positiones," 1590, D–M, Il Vescovo di Lodi alla S. d. N. S. Papa Sisto Quinto, April 1590.

91. ASV, Cong. Vescovi e Regolari, "Positiones," 1590, A–B, Stefano Campanari al Cardinale di Sens, April 14, 1590.

92. ASV, Cong. Vescovi e Regolari, "Positiones," 1590, M–P, Archiv. di Milano alla Sacra Cogr; and "Positiones," 1590, R–V Siena alla Sacra Congr. I was not able to find an original letter or copy from Potenza or from Trani in the "Positiones" of 1590. The contents of these letters can, however, be discerned from the congregation's responses.

93. "Avvertendo il popolo nei sermoni et prediche che li saran fatte, la gravita del peccato et la difficulta ch'haveranno quei chi vi incorrerano per consequire l'assolutione." ASV, Congr. Vescovi e Regolari, "Registra Episcoporum," 17 (1589), to Isernia, August 22, 1589, f. 245r.

94. ASV, Congr. Vescovi e Regolari, "Registra Episcoporum," 19 (1590), May 4, 1590, to Lodi, Siena, Aversa, Potenza and Trani, f. 140r–v.

95. Sixtus V, *Contra prucurantes . . . Abortum,* 1r.

96. Natalie Zemon Davis, *Fiction in the Archives: Pardon Tales and Their Tellers in Sixteenth-Century France* (Stanford, CA: Stanford University Press, 1987); Cecilia Nubola, "Supplications between Politics and Social Conflicts in Early Modern Europe," *International Review of Social History* 46 (2001): pp. 35–56; Cecilia Nubola and Andreas Würgler, eds., *Suppliche e "gravamina". Politica, amministrazione e giustizia in Europa (secoli XIV–XVIII)* (Bologna: Il Mulino, 2004); Ottavia Niccoli, *Perdonare: Idee, pratiche, rituali in Italia tra Cinque e Seicento* (Bari: Laterza, 2007); Fosi, *Papal Justice,* pp. 207–223.

97. Santori reported this in his diary. Cugnoni, "Autobiografia," pp. 186–187. Santori was apparently also skeptical about Sixtus V's bull on adultery. Cugnoni, "Autobiografia," p. 177.

98. ASV, Cong. Vescovi e Regolari, "Registra Episcoporum," 19, 1591, to Trani, May 7, 1591, f. 311.

99. ASV, Cong. Vescovi e Regolari, "Positiones," 1591, A–C, L'archiprete di Altamura, Giangiacomo de Mansi al Cardinale di Sens, May 22, 1591.

100. ASV, Cong. Vescovi e Regolari, "Registra Episcoporum," 19, 1591, to Altamura, June 18, 1591, f. 331v.

101. "Habita super hoc cum venerabilibus fratribus nostris S. R. E. cardinalibus, super negociis et consultationibus episcoporum deputatis, matura deliberatione, de eorum consilio, constitutionem praeditam sic duximus moderandam." Gregory XIV, *Constitutio moderatoria bullae fel. rec. Sixti PP. Contra Abortum quovis modo procurantes* (Rome: Paolo Blado, 1591), f. 1v; reprinted in *Bullarium diplomatum et privilegiorum Sanctorum*

Romanum Pontificum, vol. 9, pp. 430–431. Drafts of the bull with slightly different wording are contained in ASV, Fondo Borghese, Serie I, b. 652, f. 115r-119v.

102. Gregory XIV, *Costitutio moderatoria,* f. 1r.
103. These will be explored in the next chapter.
104. *Canons and Decrees of the Council of Trent,* session 24, "Reform," ch. 6.
105. Gregory XIV, *Costitutio moderatoria,* f. 1v.
106. Gregory XIV, *Costitutio moderatoria,* f. 1v.
107. Avviso of June 12, 1591: "La Bolla mandata fuori la settimana passata da NS.re sopr gli abhorti riformatoria di quella di Sisto V contiene che S.Sta leva dalla detta bolla la scomica et l'assoluttione che lo detto Sisto haveva riservato al Pontefice in questi casi et finalmente la S.Bne la reduce ad viam iuris." BAV, Urb. Lat. B. 1059 p. 2, f. 63v.
108. Biblioteca Archiginnasio, 16. Q. V. 39 op 09, *Sommario della constitutione di N. S. Papa Gregorio XIIII Moderativa della Bolla della felice mem. di Papa Sisto V Contro quegli che in qual si voglia modo danno opera al misfatto dello aborto* (Bologna: Vittorio Benacci, 1591).
109. As the following have shown: Connery, *Abortion,* pp. 168–188; Prosperi, *Infanticide, Secular Justice, and Religious Debate,* pp. 269–298; Stefania Tutino, *Uncertainty in Post-Reformation Catholicism: A History of Probabilism* (Oxford: Oxford University Press, 2017), ch. 11.
110. Tutino, *Uncertainty in Post-Reformation Catholicism,* p. 329.
111. Zacchia, *Quaestionum medico-legalium,* bk. 9, tit. 1, quest. 1, pp. 1–4. For discussion, see Antonio Lanza, *La questione del momento in cui l'anima razionale e infusa nel corpo* (Rome: Pontificio Ateneo Lateranense, 1939), pp. 155–159; Prosperi, *Infanticide, Secular Justice, and Religious Debate,* pp. 269–279; and Tutino, *Uncertainty in Post-Reformation Catholicism,* pp. 328–330.
112. Antonino Diana, *Resolutionum moralium, pars septima* (Lyons: Gabriel Boissat & Laurent Anisson, 1645), tract. 5, "De abortu iuxta bullas Sixti V et Gregorii XIV," pp. 168–191.
113. Diana, *Resolutionum moralium,* resol. 2, p. 168.
114. Diana, *Resolutionum moralium* resol. 11, p. 173
115. Diana, *Resolutionum moralium,* resol. 7, pp. 170–171.
116. Diana, *Resolutionum moralium,* resol. 39, p. 190.
117. Diana, *Resolutionum moralium,* resol. 39, p. 190.
118. For instance, to justify her attempted abortion, in 1603, Mennocca Liberatori from the small town of Filettino told a judge that she feared that her brothers might kill her in an act of vengeful violence should they learn that she was pregnant from an adulterous rape. Similarly, in 1577, Maria da Brescia from Bologna told a judge that she tried to hide her dead fetus in a latrine so that her brothers would not find out that she had been pregnant and kill her. Both these cases will be discussed in the next chapter.

119. Albert R. Jonsen and Stephen Toulmin, *The Abuse of Casuistry: A History of Moral Reasoning* (Berkeley: University of California Press, 1988), pp. 231–249; Wiesner-Hanks, *Christianity and Sexuality*, pp. 138–139; Jean-Louis Quantin, *Le Rigorisme Chrétien* (Paris: Cerf, 2001); Jean-Pascal Gay, *Morales en conflit. Théologie et polémique au Grand Siècle (1640–1700)* (Paris: Cerf, 2011).

120. *Decreta edita et promulgata in synodo dioecesana laudensi, Quam per Illustris, & Reuerendiss.D. Ludovicus Taberna* (Milan: Pacificum Pontium, 1591), p. 33.

121. *Decreta edita et promulgata in synodo dioecesana laudensi,* pp. 77–80.

122. *Decreta et constitutiones editae a Fabricio Gallo Neapolitano Episcopo Nolano, In prima et secunda Synodo Dioecesana, Celebratis Nolae die sexto mensis Novembris anno MDLXXXVIII, Una, vigesimo quinto Aprilis MDLXXXXIIII, Altera* (Rome: Gulielmum Facciottum, 1600), p. 52.

123. Gabriele Paleotti, *Archiepiscopale Bononiense siue de Bononiensis Ecclesiae administratione* (Rome: Giulio Ruffinelli Burchioni and Luigi Giovanni Angelo Zanetti, 1594), pt. 3, no. 8, p. 112; *Constitutiones editae in diocesana synodo barensi,* bk. 2, tit. 8, no. 15, "De casibus reservatis," in Giovanni Pinto, *Riforma tridentina in Puglia* (Bari: Editoriale Universitaria, 1968), vol. 2, p. 72; *Decreta edita et promulgata in Synodo Dioecesana Ferrariensi habita anno a Christi Natiuit MDXCIX a Reuerendissimo D. Domino Ioanne Fontana* (Ferrara: Victorium Baldinum, 1599), p. 130; *Decreta et monita Synodalia Ecclesiae Perusinae iussu admodum illis. ac. R. mi. D. Neapolionis Comitoli Perusiae Episcopi, edita* (Perugia: Petrum Jacobum Petrutium, 1600), pp. 29–30; *Constitutiones, et decreta condita in synodo dioecesana Placentina* (Piacenza: Ioannem Bazacchium, 1600), p. 345; *Decreta Dioecesanae Synodi Ravennatis primae ab Illustriss.mo et Reverendiss.mo D. Petro Aldobrandino, Anno MDCVII Die III Maij* (Venice: Iuntas, 1607), p. 83; *Acta ecclesiae Brixiensis, ab Illustriss et Reverendiss D. D. Dominico Bollano eius Episcopo, Promulgata, Anno Domini MDLXXIIII* (Venice: Georgius Variscus, 1608), p. 230; *Constitutiones Dioecesanae synodi Faventinae ab Illustrissimo, & Reverendissimo Domino Herminio [Valenti] . . . Anno MDCXV Die 15 Mensis Octobris* (Faenza: Ioannem Symbenium, 1615), p. 111; *Constitutiones et decreta, . . . D. Laurentii Castruccii, Episcopi Spoletani, habita in Synodo Dioecesana Anno Domini MDCXXI* (Perugia: Aloysii, 1622), p. 26; *Constitutiones et decreta illustriss. & Reverendiss. D. D. Marci Cornelii Patavini Episcopi . . . in septima Dioecesana Aynodo promulgata, die 17 & 18 Aprilis 1624* (Padua: Typis Pasquati, 1624), p. 99; *Constitutiones et decreta Em. & Rev. D. D. Marci Antonii . . . Episcopi Vicentini, . . . de anno 1647 in synodo dioecesana promulgata* (Vincenza: Heredes Francisci Grossi, 1647), pp. 63–64.

124. Clement VIII, *Super casuum reservatione ab omnibus Regularium Superioribus observandum* issued on May 26, 1593, and reconfirmed by Urban VIII on September 21, 1624, in *Bullarium diplomatum et privilegiorum Sanctorum*

Romanum Pontificum, vol. 13 (Turin: Sebastiano Franco et Filiis, 1868), p. 212

125. See, for example, those of Luca Pinelli, *Del sacramento della penitenza* (Venice: Ciotti, 1604), pp. 320, 336; Girolamo Sertorelli, *Barchetta di penitenza* (Venice: Ciotti, 1609), pp. 156, 327–328, 343; Agostino Gotutio, *Cinque giornate della penitenza fatte tra uno penitente et il suo padre confessore* (Venice: Fioravante Prati, 1611), p. 244; Bartolomeo da Saluthio, *Porta della Salute* (Brescia: Bartolomeo Fontana, 1622), p. 293.

126. Such as Marco Scarsella, *Giardino di sommisti nel qule si compredono sette mila, e piu casi di conscienza* (Venice: Gio. Battista Somascho, 1600), f. 4r–5v; Niccodemo di Firenze, *Pratica de casi di coscienza overo specchio de confessori* (Florence: I Giunti, 1619), pp. 179–181.

127. Emilio de Bonis: "Superio gli soggiunse che se ne poteva confessare, perché era per una donna di buon parentado, et che haverebbe remediato alli scandali che potessero nascere, che però di gratia lo facesse," ASR, TcG, Processi, 1613, b. 116, f. 48v.

128. Archivo Histórico Nacional, Madrid, *Inquisición*, lib. 898, f. 538r-v. I thank Mauricio Drelichman for sharing his research and reproductions of materials from the Sicilian Inquisition.

129. On the Sicilian Inquisition, see Maria Sofia Messana, *Il Santo Ufficio dell'Inquisizione. Sicilia 1500–1782* (Palermo: Institutio Poligrafico Europeo, 2012).

130. ASDN, Processus criminalis, 1625, Pro Reverendo Domino Fisco contra Clericum Antonium d'Avosso Neapolitanum. The trial started on August 4, 1625; Antonio d'Avosso was found innocent, and the case was closed on June 18, 1627. I thank Michele Mancino for helping me navigate this archival fond, which, at the time of consultation, was in the process of being catalogued.

131. ASDN, Processus criminalis, 1627, Pro Reverendo Domino Fisco contra Clericum Mattia de Fusco de Neap, f. 1r-36r

132. ASDN, Processus criminalis, 1627, Pro Reverendo Domino Fisco contra Clericum Mattia de Fusco de Neap, f. 2r-4r.

133. ASDN, Processus criminalis, 1627, Pro Reverendo Domino Fisco contra Clericum Mattia de Fusco de Neap. The judge asked several witnesses: "Cuius esset etatis et an pulcra vet turpis" f. 32r.

134. Giulio della Starita: "Io sono venuto qua per sgravarme la coscienza, atteso io feci querela contro d. Mattio de Fusco sotto pretesto ch'esso havesse stuprato mia figlia. Et detta querela io la feci per detto della medesima mia figlia, quale me disse che detto d. Mattio l'haveva stuprata et perche hoggi di io sono chiamato di questa verità dalla medesima mia figlia, quale mi ha chiarito che non è stato esso altrimente ma che è stato mio genero, nomine Gio. Bernardino Castellano, quale al presente è morto che fu amazzato che haverà un ano per quale io sono venuto a fagli escolpatione à

detto d. Mattio." ASDN, Processus criminalis, 1627, Pro Reverendo Domino Fisco contra Clericum Mattia de Fusco de Neap, f. 35r.

135. Archivio storico della Penitenzieria Apostolica, Valentino Mangiono, *Methodus expedita Supplicandi in Sacra Poenitentiaria*, manuscript volume (ca. 1634–1660), p. 9.

136. Marco Paolo Leone, *Praxis ad litteras maioris poenitentiarii et officii Sacrae Poenitentiariae apostolicae* (Rome: Grignani, 1644), pp. 466–469.

137. Leone, *Praxis,* p. 466.

138. Leone, *Praxis,* p. 467.

139. Leone, *Praxis,* p. 466.

140. Most of the historiographical attention on seventeenth- and eighteenth-century anticlericalism has focused on Venice. See Federico Barbierato, *Politici e ateisti. Percorsi della miscredenza a Venezia tra Sei e Settecento* (Milan: Edizioni Unicopli, 2006); and Edward Muir, *Culture Wars in Later Renaissance Venice: Skeptics, Libertines, and Opera* (Cambridge, MA: Harvard University Press, 2007). For an earlier period, see Silvana Seidel Menchi, "Characteristics of Italian Anticlericalism," in *Anticlericalism in Late Medieval and Early Modern Europe*, ed. Peter A. Dykema and Heiko A. Oberman (Leiden: Brill, 1993), pp. 271–281; Ottavia Niccoli, *Rinascimento anticlericale: Infamia, propaganda and satira tra quattro e cinquecento* (Bari: Laterza, 2005). On Clerical immunity, J. E. Downs, *The Concept of Clerical Immunity* (Washington, DC: Catholic University of America Press, 1941).

141. For instance, see Wikipedia, s.v. "Catholic Church and Abortion," accessed May 27, 2020, https://en.wikipedia.org/wiki/Catholic_Church _and_abortion.

142. Of course, a systematic study of ecclesiastical tribunals is needed to further confirm whether procurers of abortion, lay and clerical, were brought before ecclesiastical authorities, with what frequency, and whether they received the harsh penalties that in theory were to be meted out. The current state of research, however, suggests that this was not the case.

143. Prosperi, *Tribunali della coscienza;* Black, *Church, Religion, and Society;* Christopher Black, *The Italian Inquisition* (New Haven, CT: Yale University Press, 2009).

FEMIA AND ANTINO

1. ASR., TcG., Processi, 1595, b. 269, f. 572r–738r. Hereafter, for all notes that cite this trial I give only the folio number and the name of the witness. Andreozza Battaglione: "Io non marito dette miei figliole perché non si trova, essendo io poveretta." f. 692r.

2. We do not yet have a specific study of food shortages in this area north of Rome. For a more general study, see Guido Alfani, "The Famine of the

1590s in Northern Italy: An Analysis of the Greatest 'System Shock' of the Sixteenth Century," *Histoire et Mésure* 26 (2011): 17–50; Guido Alfani, Luca Mocarelli, and Donatella Strangio, "Italy," in *Famine in European History*, ed. Guido Alfani (Cambridge: Cambridge University Press, 2017), pp. 25–47.

3. Ettore Girifalco, f. 577v–578r. Although no one stated so, the priest may have been a familiar or even Antino's father.

4. *Consitutioni et regole della Congregatione de padre della Dottrina Christiana di Roma fatte di nuovo, stabilite di ordine de suoi Fratelli* (Rome, 1604), "Dell'Offitio del Sacristano," ch. 14, f. 19v–20r; *Caeremoniale Episcoporum Iussu Clementis VIII* (Rome, 1600), "De Offcio Sacristae," ch. 6, pp. 19–20.

5. Giuseppe de Fabbio, f. 615r; Andreana Farfa, f. 703v; Desiderio de Baccholini de Prato, f. 659v; Michele Filicis, f. 721v; Agostino del Nero, f. 715r-v.

6. Giovanni Casciotti: "a me non mi pare che habbi mai tenuto vita da prete." f. 732v.

7. Archpriest Giacomo Filici, f. 729r-v; Belardino Ziano, f. 719r-720r.

8. Desideri Bacholini, f. 660vbis. Antonio Cola also testified that he stole bells but from the Churches of San Belardino and Santa Catterina and sold one in Rome. f. 658r.

9. Antonio Cola, f. 658r; Giuseppe Fabbi, f. 616v; Giovanni Casciotti, f. 733r.

10. Giuseppe Fabbi, f. 616v; Desiderio Baccholini, f. 660vbis.

11. Bartolomea Dominici, f. 606v; Luca Farfa, f. 699–701r; Andriana Farfa, f. 702v–703v.

12. Michele Filici, f. 722v–723r.

13. Christiana Zizze: "tutti questi di questo castello parlano per una lingua." f. 666v; Antonio Cola: "si vede giornalmente dar da esso mali esempii." f. 657r; Desiderio de Baccholini: "comettendo molte sceleragine et dando continuamente mal esempio a tutto il populo." f. 659v.

14. Agostino Paris, f. 726r–727v; Archpriest Giacomo Filici f. 727v–728v.

15. Femia de Andreozza: "detto Antino praticava in casa mia perche non havea nissuno, et mia madre li lavava li panni et me faceva la cucina. Et non ce praticava per mal nissuno." f. 632v.

16. Although men often expected sexual favors from their servants, and servants often knew this could be part of the "job," even when it was consensual, it was in the context of unequal power. When sex was denied, men often resorted to physical force and violence. In the same year that Antino and Femia were being investigated, a priest named Jean Chardon was arrested in Dijon for having a sexual relationship with his married servant: he justified his behavior by stating that "it was commonplace for servants to sleep with their masters." James Farr, *Authority and Sexuality*

in Early Modern Burgundy (New York: Oxford University Press, 1995), p. 72. See also Terpstra, *Lost Girls*, pp. 102-104.

17. Femia de Andreozza: "per il tempo passato sonno stata amica del dicto Bernardino [i.e., Antino], et con lui ce ho hauto da fare carnalmente, et molte volte io non volevo consentire al desiderio del dicto Antino, et lui mi dava delle botte et mi bravava." f. 595r; and "Sonno da quattro anni che io ho amicitia et ho havuto che fare carnalmente con detto prete Antino, ma credo che ci praticasse un anno incira havanti che mi potesse havere, che mi sforzò et non volsi aconsentire altrimente. . . . Sonno doi anni incircha che prete Antino mi ha goduto pacificamente, ma per prima sempre mi ha hauto contra mia voglia." f. 707r–v.

18. Christiana Zizzi, f. 666v; Catterina Venanti, f. 731v; Vittorio Guidi, f. 737r.

19. On the categorization of such relationships, see Oscar Di Simplicio, "Perpetuas: The Women Who Kept Priests," in *History from Crime: Selections from Quaderni Storici,* ed. Edward Muir and Guido Ruggiero (Baltimore: Johns Hopkins University Press, 1994), pp. 32–64.

20. Letter from the *popolo* of Trevignano, f. 663r; Carissima de Nocera, f. 671r; Petruccia da Milano, f. 675v; Vittorio Guidi, f. 736v–737r. According to the slipper and shoemaker, Giovanni de Tolentino, Antino brought Femia to his bottega many times to be fitted for several pairs of slippers and shoes. f. 659r.

21. Antonio di Cola: "si dice publicamente per la terra di Trivignano ne ha hauto duoi figlioli, uno delli quali per quanto si dice publicamente la fece sconciare, et la sconciatura la fece buttare nel lago di Bracciano et Trevignano. Et un'altra volta ancora la fece sconciare similmente, et quella chriatura la buttò nello stabbio nel casalino che ha vicino a casa di Fenia quale di fatto. Et ciò publicamente si è detto per la terra di Trivignano. Et detta chriatura fu scavata da certi cani che se la mangiavano." f. 657r–v.

22. Antonio Montanaro characterized Francesco's feelings for Femia as love: "Francesco sapeva che il prete ci haveva che fare et d'ogni modo l'ha voleva per l'amor che li portava." f. 647v–675r. Femia also characterized his feelings towards her as love: "Antino ha braccato con questo Francesco che non voleva che mi pigliasse et lui, per il ben che mi voleva, sempre disse di volerme et fece ogni opra perché mi haveva preso già amore et se ne piangeva." f. 706v

23. Marina de Nocera: "essendo io vicina a casa di detta Fenia sula porta don Antino disse a Fenia: Hai pigliato il bel marito, hai preso Francescaccio, et lei rispondeva: Francesco è huomo da bene et lo voglio et non voglio più bazzicharti et non me venire più inanzi et prete Antino respondeva dandoli la burlata: Porti la centerella et hai preso un bel marito che è

Francescaccio, ma non passaranno tre dì che non la porterai più et poi detto Antino entrò dentro in casa di Fenia et si repigliò un matarazzo et certe altre robbe che gli haveva dato et di li a doi e tre giorni fu posto un editto nella chiesa che non si potesse pigliar moglie né marito se non si haveva la fede di huomo dal suo paese che non haveva altra moglie et si non si provava che fusse morto il primo marito et che si fusse visto sepelire et fu detto publicamante da ognuno che prete Antino per essere amico del vicario di Sutri li haveva ottenuto da lui il sudetto bando et in quel dì proprio che venne quel bando, venendo Antino in casa di Fenia, io sentetti quando . . . lei disse ad Antino: 'Tu sei quello che hai fatto venire quel bando et ai impedito che io non pigli questo Francesco accusì si mi fai! Ah! Io volevo levarmi dal peccato et non haver più bazzechate et tu m'ai impedito!' et queste parole le replicò più e più volte et prete Antino gli rispose Sta queta, sta queta, sta queta! et non sentetti che gli dicesse più altro et poi lui entrò in casa di Fenia et io non sentette et né viddi più altro." f. 682v–683r. See also Christiana Zizzi, f. 666v; Lucia Ricci, f. 679v, for similar reports.

24. Femia de Andreozza, f. 706r–v. See also Antonio Montanaro's testimony, f. 674r–675r.

25. Femia de Andreozza: "se ne pianse alcune volte con me, dolendosi che questo prete Antino l'impedisse et che gli havesse braccato et ultimamente, dolendosi et piangendo, se partì da me partendosi da questa terra et andò a star a Sutri, dicendo che lui si partiva disperato." "Io dico che è cosa chiarissima che prete Antino è stato quello che ha impedito detto matrimonio et quattro o cinque mesi che durò questa pratica del parentado sera e mattina a cercato di braccarmi et braccarmi et opporsi quanto poteva che e stato la ruina mia, perché io me sei stata con il mio partito et non havrei appensare ad altro. . . . Prete Antino non ha impedito questo matrimonio per altra causa se non per potere continuare la praticha con me come haveva per prima." f. 705r–707r.

26. Copy of a letter written by Antonio di Cola, Bastiano Bachinello, Giovanni Bastianello et Bastiano Corpino, in the presence of the Governor of Trevignano Giulio Galganetti, and signed by Bernardino Tiano, Vangelista Pasqualino, Vittorio Guido, Pietro Cascello, Mutio Morgita, Sebastiano Parisci, Tiano Tiani, Simone di Meo, Virgilio Parisci, Silvestro Silvestri, Tomao Parisci, mastro Oliveri Zoppa, Iovani Caciotto, et Anetinio Magistris, tutti consiglieri delli Dodici, tutti in casa della Communità, dated August 31, 1594. f. 574r–v.

27. Christiana Zizze: "Signore, sopra di queste cose son stata esaminata anco dal vescovo di Nepe che venne qui e scrisse un pocho di quel che dicevo et non volse più scrivere, dicendo che non mi credeva." f. 668v. Christiana says that it was the bishop of Nepe who conducted the interview, but this seems to be a mistake.

28. Vittorio Guidi: "Contro detto Antino sonno state date più querele dalla comunità di Trivignano avanti il vescovo di Sutri et, appena doppoi molta et molta instantia, fu ottenuto dal detto vicario che venisse un notaro a esaminar qua contra detto prete Antino qual venuto, esaminava et scriveva solamente quel che li pareva, per quanto si dice per la terra et io l'o provato 'ché, essendo io esaminato da detto notaro e deponendo quanto io ho detto a vostra signoria, credo che non scrivesse niente di queste cose, perché mi disse che: 'Io non ricercho di questo!'" f. 737r.

29. "La communità e populo del castello di Trivignano sotto la diocesi di Nepe, fa sapere alle signorie vostre illustrissime come in detto castello si ritrova un certo Antino de Benedictis, chierico in minoribus, sacrestano della chiesa parrochiale et beneficiato in altre il quale, havendo per molti anni tenuto et continuamente tenendo pessima et scandalosa vita, né curandosi il suo ordinario procederli per essere da lui favorito, ne vengono i semplici di quello popolo a patire assai et a pigliare esempii perniciosissimi all'anime loro, perciò detta comunità ricorre dalle signorie vostre illustrissime per opportuno remedio conforme al'importanza dello scandalo publico et enormità de' delitti de' quali alcuni qui sotto se annoterano. . . . Et perché li delitti et sacrileggi di questo pessimo huomo sono infiniti comessi nelli quali tuttavia persevera et ne commette ogni giorno, deche ne nascono grandissime mormorationi et scandali grandissimi in tutto quello populo et, desiderando essa comunità che di essi delitti et publico scandalo ne siano le signorie vostre illustrissime benissimo certificate con provedere a tal radice infetta et all'edificatione di quello populo, però le supplica humilmente si degnino mandare in quello castello un commissario per vedere, sentire et chiarirsi della verità del fatto che oltre sarà cosa conforme alla giustitia essa comunità lo riceverà per gratia singolarissima per salute di quelle anime etc." f. 663r.

30. Femia De Andreozza: "Essendo io sola in casa, venne prete Antino et, volendo detto Antino far con me, sapendo io che mia matre era per tornar presto, non volevo et fece resistentia assai et, perché prete Antino è un huomo stizzoso assai, cominciò a scorecciarsi con me et a darmi delli calci et pugni per la vita et strapazzandomi et mi buttò anco doi o tre volte per terra che tutta mi pistò et in quello arrivò mia matre et, prima che si partisse, mi prohibì che non dicesse niente a nisuno et la dimane venendo, sibene mi sentivo tutta pista, per bisogno andai a mondar il lino et la sera avanti che calasse il sole, sentendomi male, me ne tornai a casa et mi messi in letto et, in capo di otto giorni, mi calò et cursi fuora per lo stomaco una gran quantità di sangue et allhora mi sconciai che mi scappò per la stomaca una cosa come un pezzo di carne. . . . Io tengo di essermi sconciata per quelle botte che mi dette prete Antino, come ho detto, perché mi pistò tutta et mi dette tanto et

sfraccassò di maniera che io mi misi nel letto et mi sconciai, come ho detto, et non so di haver hauto altro che mi habbia fatto sconciare se non questo." f. 708r-709r.

31. Femia de De Andreozza: "Signore la verità la voglio dire che è questa: che quando io ero gravida, come ho detto di sopra, prete Antino mi portò un bichiero una sera entrando in casa mia qual era quasi pieno di una certa cosa gialla come il vino et mi disse che bevesse quella cosa et, domandandoli io che cosa era lui mi disse: 'Che ne voi tu sapere? Beve qui!' et io dicevo che io non ne volevo bevere si non me lo diceva che cosa era quello et lui sempre mi tenne detto: 'Beve qua, beve qua 'ché è una cosa buona per te et non cercar altro che cosa sia!' et così, come per forza, ne bevetti un pocho di quella robba de quel becchiero et, per essere amara, io non la potei bever tutta et, subbito bevuta, mi cominciò a conturbarmi tutto lo stomaco et poi cominciai a gomittare et io ero sola in casa et prete Antino, subbito che mi hebbe dato da bere, se ne partì et si portò via il sudetto bechiere con quella robba che ci era restata dentro et il stomaco mi si conturbò di tal maniera che cominciai gomittare assai con gran affanno et dolore et la mattina prete Antino se ne tornò in casa quando mia madre fu andata alla messa et riportò quel bechiere con quella robba et medemamente mi fu adosso et volse che io gli pigliasse il restante della robba che era rimansta nel becchiero et io disse non volerlo, facendo gran resistenza di non volerlo, dicendo, Perché voi che lo piglia? Da che è buono? Perché me lo voi dare, io non ho male nisuno et lui rispose, Pigliala, pigliala che si fussi gravida, come me dici, ti farà sconciare, et io non lo volevo pigliare, ma esso Antino melo fece pigliare per forza 'ché me ce dette sino delle botte et mi pistò tutta acciò la pigliasse, come ho detto nel altre miei esamine, et detta bevanda per allhora non mi fe' altro se non che mi sconturbò il stomaco et non gomittai come l'altra volta et non so si in quel giorno, o il giorno seguente fu che io andai fuora et tornai amalata et mi misi nel letto et mi sconciai come ho detto nel altro mio esamine. . . . La mia sconciatura non può essere venuta da altro se non per quel bichiero di robba che mi dette da bevere don Antino che mi disse esser buon per questo et da quelle battiture che mi dette detto Antino." f. 717r-718r.

32. Femia De Andreozza: "Io dissi nel altre esamine che mi ero sconcia per le botte che mi haveva dato prete Antino et non vi dissi che havesse preso quel bechiero pieno di quella cosa che mi dette detto prete Antino per paura che non mi gastigasse et facesse qualche male perché io havevo bevuto quella roba. . . . E che signor quella cosa io la bevetti perché me la fece detto Antino bevere per forza et così è la verità et non l'ho voluto bere, nemeno l'haverei bevuta si non mi havesse sforzata detto prete Antino." f. 718r-v.

33. Indeed, there was reason to doubt Femia's depiction of herself as completely passive. Judge Pelingotti had heard from the witness Carissima de Nocero that, just before she had the abortion, Femia asked Carissima "for something to cause an abortion" to which Carissima responded, "I do not know these things." f. 670v–671r.

34. Femia de Andreozza: "Signor no che io non ho mai detto niente a mia matre, nemeno ad altro che prete Antino mi desse le botte, come ho detto, et che per quella causa io mi sconciasse. . . . Signor sì che mia matre mi ha adomandato da che poteva esser venuto che mi ero sconciata et che mi era venuto tanto sangue, ma gli dissi di non saper la causa. . . . Io non lo disse con mia matre la causa perché io mi ero sconcia perché lei mi gridava et non si contentava che io havesse che far con detto Antino et, acciò che non mi braccasse, non gli volse dire che prete Antino mi haveva dato et pisto et questo mi haveva fatto sconciare come ho detto." f. 709r–v.

35. Femia de Andreozza: "mi calo et cursi fuora per lo stomaco una gran quantità di sangue et all hora mi sconciai che mi scappò per la stomaca una cosa come un pezzo di carne quale io non viddi, ma me l'ho disse mia matre 'ché lei l'haveva presa et messa fra li lenzoli et che lei li portò allavare al lago." f. 708r.

36. Femia de Andreozza: "[io] fece gran quantità di sangue di sotto et feci la criatura, per quanto mi disse mia matre, 'ché io non me ne acorsi perché stavo tanto male che non mi acorgevo quasi di niente se non del gran sangue che io feci et la malatia fu di tal sorte che ne stette mal più di cinque mesi amalata 'ché mi ero avedutta che non potevo il fiato et questo è la verita." f. 718r.

37. Andreozza Battaglione: "Signore io vi voglio dire la verità: in la prima volta che io andai a lavare i lenzoli bagnati di sangue per la malatia di Fenia mia figliola, quando fui al fiume et che apperse detti lenzoli tutti insanguinati et molto più le camice sue, trovai in detti panni un modeletto di carne longo et largho quanto questa lettera qui piegata . . . et era alta circa un dito et secondo me quella carne era una chriatura che Fenia mia figliola si era sconcia et io bottai nel lago detta carne et sconciatura con l'altre tristitie che erano dentro a detti panni. . . . Detto pezzo di carne non si muoveva et non guardai si havesse segno niuno di chriatura humana. . . . Signore si che mentre Fenia stava in letto gli disse d'haver trovato questo pezzo di carne che era secondo me la criatura che lei si era sconcia et lei rispose che non si era mai acorta di esser gravida et non mi dette troppa fantasia perché lei stava male assai. . . . Io tengo che detto Antino l'habbia fatto sconciar Fenia perché lui è un tristo." f. 696v–697r.

38. Femia de Andreozza: "Signor no, che io non ho detto la verità in quel mio esamine, che feci nanzi il detto commissario in Trivignano, perché

quello che io disse me lo fecero dire per forza, che me lusingavano quello
che scrivea et lo commissario medesimo, dicendome tutte dui che io dicesse male de patre Antino, perché me volevano maritare, et me volevano
far la dote et io me lo credevo.... Io dirrò a vostra signoria la verità d'ogni
cosa. Io so che il detto commissario esaminò prima mia madre et dopo
un giorno esaminò me. Et nel esaminare me domandò se prete Antino
praticava in casa mia, et se havea hauto da fare carnalmente con me, et
nel primo esamine mio io disse di no, come è la verità. Et me domandò si
dicto Antino m'havea impedito che io non pigliase marito, et io rispose
che ciò non lo sapevo, che non lo possevo dire. Et nel dicto primo esamine non me domandò altro, che io me ricordi, si non che me bavava, et
me diceva villania, perché io non dicevo a modo suo. Et cossì poi, finito
detto esamine, me fece mettere prigione in una stanza dela medema os-
teria. . . . Il giorno seguente me esaminò un'altra volta detto commissario, et me domandò se io ero mai ingravidata da Antino, et si io m'ero
sconciata. Et io li respose che non era vero cosa alcuna. Et doppo che io
negai un pezzo nel esaminarme me mandorno, il detto commissario et il
detto cancelliero, nela medema camera, dove ci venne mia madre, quale
me disse, figlia mia, è meglio che tu lo dichi, che Antino te ha ingravidato, et che t'ha fatto sconciare, perché essi te l'appongono. Et io le rispose, non so come me fare a dirlo se non è vero. Et lei me disse che c'era
stato Antoniello de Cola con il cancelliero dello commissario a parlarli
in casa mia, et che l'haveva detto, che mia madre me esortasse che io lo
dicesse. Et cossì mia madre me venne a parlare in detta camera dove io
stavo prigione, et me disse queste parole, figlia mia, è meglio che tu lo
dichi, che prete Antino te ha ingravidato et te ha fatto sconciare, et dichi
ala peggio, perché se tu non dici cossì, lui non capitarà male, et costoro
vogliono che capiti male, et tu non patirai niente se lo dici; et beata te: te
vogliono maritare, te vogliono far la dote, et non haverai mal nissuno, et
starai in casa tua, et detto Antino andrà in malhora. Et me ****
detta mia madre, che lei ancor havea detto il medemo, perché l'havean
facto dire per forza, che l'havean tenuta a esaminare tucto dì integro. Et
cossì io rispose a mia madre che cosa volesse che io dicha, se non è vero, et
che l'appropii quello che non è, et lei me rispose, pensace un poco, io non
so quello che me te dire altro se non che bisogna che tu lo dichi, che
questi voglion dare tanto **** che bisogna che tu lo dichi per forza.
Et cossì lei se partì. Come lei uscita de camera, venne lo birro et me menò
a ba[sso] avanti al detto commissario, quale me domandò se io haveo
pensato ancor quello che havea da dire, et io li disse che haveo pensato
pure, et lui me disse, che hai pensato? È pur vero che detto Antino te ha
ingravidato et te ha fatto sconciare? Et io le rispose, io non saccio d'esser
stata mai gravida, se non che una volta stette un mese che non hebbi il

mio tempo, ma non cognoscevo si ero gravida. Et lui me disse, che te
dette detto Antino a bevere, che te fece sconciare? Et io li rispose . . . io
non lo so, se non che me dette una cosa nel bicchiero, et disse che io la
bibbe. Ma che se fosse io non lo sapevo. Et disse che quella cosa non mi
havea fatto niente. Se non che io diesse d'haverla rebuttata. Et detto commissario me replicò et disse, che te fece detta bevanda, et si m'havea fatto
sangue da le parte nante de sotto, et io li rispose che io non l'ò visto,
perché stavo nel letto ammalata, dove stette cinque mesi. Et io non so che
cosa se fosse. Et disse che la malatia fu causata che andai fuora a mundar
lo lino, et tornai a casa con la febre . . . quello che ho detto hora a vostra
signoria è vero, et quello che io disse avanti al commissario nel 2° mio
constituto non è vero. Et particolarmente che detto Antino mi habbi
dato a bere cosa alcuna per farme sconciare." f. 626r–627r.

39. Andreozza Battaglione: "tutto quello che io dissi in quella mia examina
contra detto sagrestano et mia figliola, che dissi io a mia filiola che lo
dicessi, io non lo dissi che fusse la verità, ma per quelle parole che mi
disse detto Antonio et il notario, havendo desiderio che mia figliola si
maritasse. . . . quello che io dissi ad Eufemia mia figliola, che dicesse che
s'era sconcia, io dissi la bugia, ma lo dissi come ho detto di sopra, per
desiderio che mia figliola si maritasse, et per le parole del sopradetto Antonio, et promissioni che mi fece quel notario." f. 631v.

40. Letter from Bishop Orazio Morone to Vicar Francesco Mezzaroma: "ho
visto quanto me scrivete con la costra delle 13 circha la causa d'Antino et
Eufemia. Mi pare necessario tormentare Eufemia per saper in qual detto
persiste. Pertanto procedete a questo atto, se in detta Eufemia non è alcuno impedimento d'infirmità o gravidanza. Et nostro signore Dio ve
guardi da male. De Nepe, ale 16 d'ottobre 1595." Unpaginated, after f.
636v.

41. Femia de Andreozza: "io ho detta la verità adesso, nelli miei esamine ul-
time. Et si io disse all'hora che Antino m'haveva ingravidato, et mi
havesse sconcia a posta, io disse la bugia, et la disse perché li medesimi
homini che ho nominati di sopra mi dicevano che io dicesse come ho
detto di sopra, con mettermi su a dire male tanto, che trista a me. . . . Et
si ho detto altrimente io l'ho detto perché me l'hanno fatto dir loro per
forza. . . . O matre mia, ohimé, ohimé, ohimé, Dio, o matre mia, o Dio . . .
ohimé matre, io l'ho detta la verità! Ohimé ohimé." f. 637v–638r.

42. Femia de Andreozza: "Sig. che è la verità, che la mattina di Pasqua grande
essendo io andata alla chiesa di Santa Maria di Trevignano a comuni-
carmi et a fare le mie oratione, et mentre dico che io stavo alla banca del
Santissimo Sacramento et che mi ero comunicata, Prete Antino Bene-
detti, sacrestano di detta Chiesa, quale portava il beufieri dov da levare
doppo che si d preso il Santissimo Sacramento vedendomi in compagni

delli altri mi cominciò a dire Vaccha poltiera tu ti vergogni venire a bevere da me, ma che quadraccio tu non ti vergogni portarli et queste parole le disse con voce alta che tutte le donne che erono presso me lo sen-
tirno." ASR, TcG, Processi, 1598, b. 309, f. 878v–879r.

CHAPTER THREE ∞ ABORTION AND THE LAW

1. Die secunda Januarii 1578

> Ad aures et notitiam illustrissimi et excellentissimi Domini Audi-
> toris Tursoni et eius curie devenit in domo M. Domini Eminentis
> de Deseideriis Bononiensis quamdam ancillam in dicta domo in-
> servientem et commorantem peperisse partumque in quadam
> clavica seu necessitario proiecisse timore divino minime servato
> etc.
>
> Quare in continentia ordinavit mihi notario inferiori ut una
> cum birruarios me personaliter conferrem ad domum M' Domini
> antedicti causa et occasione super premissis capiendi quascumque
> necessarias intentiones nec non reperta dicta ancilla domi seu alibi
> per supradictos birruarios ad Carceres Turronitianas mitterem
> una cum cadavero pueri.
>
> Quapropter in executione commissionis mihi iniuncti me per-
> sonaliter contuli ad domum M' domini eminentis de Deseideriis
> antedicti sictam in capella sancti thome et primum una cum M'lo
> Domino predicto et birruariis seu cum Lana altero ex cursoribus
> accessi ad stantias inferiores domus ut dicitur *nella stantia delle bo-
> cate* in qua quidam erectus in presentia mei cum nec non supra-
> dictis in quadam porticella fuit de m'lo serviente M' Domini mei
> qui transmissus in quadam clavica necessarii ad effectum re-
> periendi puerum seu cadaver ipsius et reperto recognoscendi et alia
> faciendi necessaria quo demum per supradictum Jaco[b]um bac-
> ulum reperto et sursum evecto fimo ac stercore affecto lavare feci
> quo lavato et sic mortuum dictum cadaver ad carceres turroniana
> cum domina Maria ancilla reperta in quodam cubili transmissi et
> demum visitavi locum precisum acceptis tamen prius infrascriptis
> informationibus et vidi locum precisum ubi adest necessarium in
> quodam stantiolino prope cameram in qua fuit reperta superdicta
> domina Maria ancilla etc.

ASB, Torrone, Atti e Processi, 1577, b. 1165, f. 220r–220v.

2. "Ill. molto R. S. com. Frello, se bene quella Maria serva del s. Enea
Desiderii che ritorna caut. p[er] la causa che l'ho intenderà dal Auditore
del Torr. fusse degna della pena della morta. Tuttavia considerando la

fragilita del sesso si è pensato di commutarli la pena della vita in quale si altra pure che sia tale che non possi render infamia a parenti pro a V.S. si remette il castigo che si gli havera da dare, e me le offero di Roma." ASB, Torrone, Atti e Processi, 1577, b. 1165, f. 220r-v, unpaginated, last page in the dossier.

3. For a sampling of exemplary early modern studies that balance legislation, jurisprudence, and trial records, and situate these documentary genres within varied social, political and intellectual contexts, see Leslie Peirce, *Morality Tales: Law and Gender in the Ottoman Court of Aintab* (Berkeley: University of California Press, 2003); Tamar Herzog, *Upholding Justice: Society, State, and the Penal System in Quito (1650–1750)* (Ann Arbor: University of Michigan Press, 2004); Matthew Gerber, *Bastards: Politics, Family, and Law in Early Modern France* (Oxford: Oxford University Press, 2012); Michelle A. McKinley, *Fractional Freedoms: Slavery, Intimacy and Legal Mobilization in Colonial Lima, 1600–1700* (Cambridge: Cambridge University Press, 2018). For Italy, see Thomas Kuehn, *Law, Family, and Women: Toward a Legal Anthropology of Renaissance Italy* (Chicago: Univeristy of Chicago Press 1991); Thomas Kuehn, *Family and Gender in Renaissance Italy, 1300–1600* (Cambridge: Cambridge University Press, 2017); Trevor Dean, *Crime and Justice in Late Medieval Italy* (Cambridge: Cambridge University Press, 2007); Marco Bellabarba, *La giustizia nell"Italia moderna. XVI–XVIII secolo* (Rome: Laterza, 2008); Fosi, *Papal Justice*.

4. Mercurio, *De gli errori popolari,* p. 109.

5. On Italian statute law and statutes as historical documents, see Dean, *Crime and Justice,* pp. 84–94 passim.

6. Early modern statutes have not been as extensively studied as medieval ones. Nevertheless, there is clearly continuity between the two. As Trevor Dean notes, statutes were rarely completely overhauled; legislators mostly modified and added to existing laws; sometimes laws remained identical for over a century. The most comprehensive list of Italian statutes is the *Catalogo della raccolta di statute, consuetudini, leggi, decreti, ordini e privilege dei comuni, delle associazioni e degli enti locali italiani dal Medioevo alla fine del secolo XVIII,* 8 volumes (Rome, 1943–1999), available in a digital format at the Biblioteca del Senato della Republica, Rome.

7. The following statutes are surveyed here: Perugia, 1523, *Statutorum Auguste Perusiae* (Perugia, 1523); Senigalia, 1537, *Statutorum & Reformationu[m] magnifice ciuitatis Senigalie* (Pessaro, 1537); Sezze, 1547, *Statuta, sive constitutiones Civitatis Setie* (Rome, 1547); Macerata, 1553, *Volumen statutorum civitatis Maceratae* (Macerata, 1553); Monterubbiano, 1574, *Statuta seu leges municipales magnificae terrae, et hominum Montis Rubiani* (Ancona, 1574); Fermo, 1589, *Statuta Firmanorum* (Fermo, 1589); Genoa, 1573 and 1590, *Criminalium iurium civitatis Genuensis* (Genoa, 1573) and *Delli statuti*

criminali di Genova (Genoa, 1590); Benevento, 1603, *Statuta civitatis Beneventi acthoritate Apostolica condita, & a Sixto V. Pontifice Maximo confirmata* (Rome, 1603); Milan, 1552, 1574, and 1617, *Constitutiones Domini Mediolanensis* (Milan, 1562), *Constitutiones Domini Mediolanensis* (Milan, 1574), and *Constitutiones provinciae Mediolanensis cum decretis ordinibus et declarationibus Senatvs hac novissima editione ampliatis et illustratis* (Milan, 1617). These and other statutes were consulted in Rome at the Biblioteca del Senato della Repubblica and Archivio di Stato di Roma.

8. Milan, *Constitutiones*, bk. 4, f. 74v; and in the 1617 *Constitutiones*, p. 140. Genoa, *Criminalium iurium*, bk. 2, ch. 8, pp. 37–38; and *Delli statute*, bk. 2, ch. 8, p. 39. Benevento, *Statuta*, bk. 3, pp. 95–96.

9. Perugia, *Statutorum*, bk. 3, rub. 14, De pena homicidii, f. 11r.

10. Senigalia, *Statutorum*, bk. 3, rub. 35, f. 10v; Monterubbiano, *Statuta*, bk. 5, rub. 118, p. 212.

11. Sezze, *Statuta*, bk. 3, ch. 13, p. 34.

12. Senigalia, *Statutorum*, bk. 3, rub. 35, f. 10v; Macerata, *Volumen statutorum*, rub. 50, f. 31v. If, however, beverages and foodstuffs were given to either a man or a woman in order to harm them (i.e., their fertility or as poisons) or to kill them, the culprit would be executed. If the victim did not die, the aggressors would be fined two hundred *libri denariorum* in Senigalia and one hundred in Macerata. The authorities in Monterrubiano were apparently not willing to inflict corporal punishment on offenders, preferring to fine them (women and men) four hundred lire. Monterubbiano, *Statuta*, bk. 5, rub. 118, p. 212.

13. Benevento, *Statuta*, bk. 3, pp. 95–96.

14. Genoa, *Delli statuti*, bk. 2, p. 39.

15. Rome, *Statuta Almae Urbis Romae* (Rome, 1580 and 1590). Abortion is mentioned once in the Roman statutes as a *casibvs per inquisitonem*, specifically the abortion of a viable fetus (*foetu iam vivificato*), but no penalty is stated. *Statuta Almae Urbis Romae*, 1580, bk. 2, ch. 5, p. 86. For glosses and annotations to these and later statutes, see *Statuta Almae Urbis Roma . . . cum glossis Leandri Galganetti* (Rome, 1611); and Giovanni Battista Fenzonio, *Annotationes in Statuta sive ius municipal romanae urbis* (Rome: Andreae Phaei, 1636).

16. For legal discussion on how jurists were to interpret statute law, see Mario Sbriccoli, *L'interpretazione dello statuto: contributo allo studio della funzione dei giurista nell'eta comunale* (Milan: Giuffrè 1969).

17. Marzia Lucchesi, *Si quis occidit occidetur. L'omicidio doloso nelle fonti consiliarie (secoli XIV–XVI)* (Padua: Cedam, 1999); Dean, *Crime and Justice*, p. 86.

18. Annibale Monterenzi, *Ad statuta tam Civilia, quam etiam Criminalia inalitae Civitatis Bononiae* (Bologna: Caesarem Salvietum, 1582), bk. 5, rub. 18, "De poena homicidae," p. 107, marginal note E. See also rub. 20, "De pena venenantis aliquem," p. 117.

19. *Statuta Almae Urbis Roma . . . cum glossis Leandri Galganetti,* bk. 2, ch. 17, gloss, p. 564; Fenzonio, *Annotationes in Statuta sive ius municipal romanae urbis,* bk. 2, ch.. 17, p. 583.

20. In Bologna bandi were issued by the city's legates and vice-legates (papal representatives in the Ecclesiastical States) in collaboration with the Senate; in Rome they were issued by the governor, who was a bishop and the pope's vice-chancellor. For registers of the many bylaws and regulations issued, see for Bologna *Bononia Manifesta: Catalogo dei bandi, editti, costituzioni e provvedimenti diversi, stampati nel XVI secolo per Bologna e il suo territorio,* ed. Zita Zanardi (Florence: Olschki, 1996); and for Rome *Registi di bandi, editti, notificazioni, e provvedimenti diversi relative alla citta di Roma e dello Stato Pontificio* (Rome: Commune di Roma 1928-1950), vols. 1-3. The bandi examined here were consulted at the ASR, Statuti, b. 303 and 410; ASV, Mis. Arm, IV-V, b. 47 and b. 68; Biblioteca Casanatense, CC. N.V 137; VOL MISC. 3001, PER est 18.3.

21. For Roman bandi, see Alfredo Cirinei, "Bandi e giustizia criminale a Roma nel cinque e seicento," *Roma moderna e contemporanea* 5 (1997): pp. 81-95. On the visibility of the printed bando on Roman streets, see Rose Marie San Juan, *Rome: A City Out of Print* (Minneapolis: University of Minnesota Press, 2001), ch. 1.

22. Before Dandino's 1588 prohibition, abortion had not appeared in Bolognese bandi since the 1536 bando of Cardinal Legate Henrico Caetani, which stated that the abortion of an animated fetus by poisoning was a capital offence. Such a statement was not repeated in the bandi issued in 1557, 1559, 1560, 1566, 1567, 1573, 1580, and 1586. *Bandi generali del molt'illustre & Reuerendiss. Monsig. Anselmo Dandino Prothonotario Apostolico di Bologna Vicelegato* (Bologna, 1588), p. 19. Dandino issued the exact same decree in 1586 while he was governor for Perugia and Umbria, and this law remained intact and was repeated in successive bandi until the end of the century. *Bandi Generali del molto Illustre et Reverendissimo Mons.re Anselmo Dandino, Prothonotario Apostolico, di Perugia, & Vmbria General Gouernatore* (Perugia, 1586), p. 27; and *Bandi generali dell'Illustriss. e Reverendiss. Sig. Cardinale Silvio Savelli* (Perugia, 1598), p. 39. This decree was reissued verbatim in Bologna by Vice-Legate Antonio Gianotti in 1596. *Bandi Generali dell'Illustrissimo & Reuerendiss. Monsig. Antonio Gianotti, Archivescovo d'Urbino, & di Bologna Uicelegato* (Bologna, 1596).

23. *Bando generale Dell'Illustrissimo, & Reverendissimo Sig. Benedetto Card. Giustiniano, Legato di Bologna* (Bologna, 1608), ch. 10, p. 18.

24. *Bando generale Dell'Illustrissimo, & Reverendissimo Sig. Benedetto Card. Giustiniano, Legato di Bologna* (Bologna, 1610), ch. 6, p. 16.

25. *Bando Generale,* 1608, ch. 18, p. 42; and *Bando Generale,* 1610, pp. 64-65.

26. *Bando circa il governo di Roma . . . Gulielmus Bastonus Gubernator,* (Rome, November 9, 1591).

27. *Bando Generale concernente il Governo di Roma,* (Rome, September 16, 1595), "Dar veneno."

28. *Bandi Generali publicati di commissione di Nostro Sig* (Rome, 1599), pp. 3–4. On the plurality of laws and confusion of jurisdiction in the Papal States, see Fosi, *Papal Justice.*

29. *Bandi Generali publicati di commissione di Nostro Sig,* n. 66, p. 21.

30. Giovanni Battista De Luca, *Il dottor volgare, overo il compendio di tutta la legge, civile, canonica, feudale, e municipale, nelle cose piu ricevute in pratica* (Rome: Giuseppe Corvo, 1673) bk. 14, pt. 2, ch. 5, p. 111.

31. The law practiced in cities across the peninsula was shaped by Roman law and the ius commune. Lawyers and judges were trained in a similar way in universities and often worked in various tribunals throughout the peninsula. See Mario Ascheri, *Tribunali, giuristi e istituzioni. Dal Medioevo all'eta moderna* (Bologna: Il Mulino, 1989); Manlio Bellomo, *The Common Legal Past of Europe, 1000–1800,* trans. Lydia G. Cochrane (Washington, DC: Catholic University of America Press, 1995); Aldo Mazzacane, "Law and Jurists in the Formation of the Modern State in Italy," in *The Origins of the State in Italy, 1300–1600,* ed. Julius Kirshner (Chicago: University of Chicago Press, 1996), pp. 62–67; and Dean, *Crime and Justice.*

32. Marc'Antonio Savelli, *Pratica universale . . . estratto in compendio per alfabeto dalle principali Leggi, Bandi, Statuti, Ordini, e Consuetudini, massime Criminali, e miste, che vegliano nelli Stati del Serenessimo Gran Duca di Toscana* (Florence: Giuseppe Cocchini, 1665), "Aborto," pp. 20–22; "Adulterio," p. 23; "Incesto," p. 223; "Sodomia," pp. 369–371; "Stupro," p. 383.

33. Farinacci's *Praxis* was one of the most influential works of criminal jurisprudence. Farinacci the man had a somewhat polarizing reputation: he was favored by several cardinals and popes and held various positions in the papal government; in 1585 he tried to defend Cardinal Marco Sittico d'Altemps's nephew against charges of rape; he also defended Beatrice Cenci in her trial for killing her father; both Altemps and Cenci were executed. Farinacci himself was charged in 1595 for sodomizing a sixteen-year-old boy; he was accused of corruption and abusing his papal office; he was once arrested for carrying an arquebus and throwing it in the Ponte Sisto so that it would not be found on his person. His published works were, however, very well respected. See Aldo Mazzacane, "Farinacci, Prospero," *Dizionario Biografico degli Italiani,* vol. 45 (Rome: Istituto della Enciclopedia Italiana, 1995), pp. 1–5, accessed May 27, 2020, http://www.treccani.it/enciclopedia/prospero-farinacci _%28Dizionario-Biografico%29/.

34. The historiography on Italian jurisprudence is vast and specialized. Here I cite the works that most influenced my reading of the primary

sources: Ascheri, *Tribunali, giuristi e istituzioni*; Bellabarba, *La giustizia nell'Italia moderna*; Mario Sbriccoli, *Storia del diritto penale e della giustizia. Scriti editi e inediti (1972–2007)* (Milan: Giuffrè, 2009); Mario Sbriccoli and Antonella Bettoni, eds., *I Grandi tribunali e Rote nell'Italia di antico regime* (Milan: Giuffre, 1993); Michele Pifferi, "Criminalistica in antico regime," in *Il contributo italiano alla sotria del pensioro,* ed. P. Cappellini, P. Costa, M. Fioravant, and B. Sordi (Rome: Istituto della Enciclopedia Italiana, 2012), pp. 141–148; Rodolfo Savelli, "Tribunali, 'Decisiones' e giuristi. Una proposta di ritorno alle fonti," in *Origini dello Stato. Processi di Formazione statale in Italia fra medioevo ed eta moderna,* ed. C. Chittolini, A. Molho, and P. Schiera (Bologna: Il Mulino, 1994), pp. 397–421.

35. The three Roman laws most cited in discussions of abortion were the *Lex cornelia* on murderers and assassins, the *Lex Divus Severus et Antoninus,* and the *Qui abortionis,* in *The Digest of Justinian,* ed. and trans. Theodor Mommsen, Paul Krueger, and Alan Watson (Philadelphia: University of Pennsylvania Press, 1985), vol. 1, 1.5.7, p. 15; vol. 4, 47.11.4, p. 784; 48.8.1, nu. 1, 3, and 8, p. 820; and 48.19.38, n. 5, p. 853. Significantly, abortion was not mentioned in the *Lex Pompeia* on parricide, 48.9, pp. 821–822. On abortion in the Greco-Roman world, see Enzo Nardi, *Procurato aborto nel mondo Greco romano* (Milan: Giuffrè, 1971); and Konstantinos Kapparis, *Abortion in the Ancient World* (London: Duckworth, 2003).

36. For interpretations of Roman law on abortion and the development of its criminalization in the medieval west, see Müller, *The Criminalization of Abortion.*

37. Prospero Farinacci, *Praxis, et theoricae criminalis* (Lyon: Horatii Cardon, 1610), pt. 4, quest. 122, n. 139–143, p. 172. Farinacci wondered whether the question of animation was better left "to the philosophers."

38. Zacchia, *Quaestionum medico-legalium,* bk. 1, tit. 2, quest. 9, n. 24, p. 48; and bk. 9, tit. 1, pp. 1–32.

39. Giacomo Menochio, *De arbitrariis iudicum quaestionibus & causis, libri duo* (Venice: Antonium de Franciscis, 1624), bk. 2, case 357, n. 12–14, p. 666. Chiara Valsecchi, "Menochio, Giacomo," *Dizionario Biografico degli Italiani,* vol. 73 (Rome: Istituto della Enciclopedia Italiana, 2009), pp. 521–524, accessed May 27, 2020, http://www.treccani.it/enciclopedia/giacomo-menochio_(Dizionario-Biografico)/.

40. De Luca, *Il dottore volgare,* bk. 14, pt. 2, ch. 5, p. 110.

41. Menochio, *De arbitrariis iudicum,* bk. 2, case 357, n. 10–11, p. 666. See also his discussion in the section "Ages of Man," *De arbitrariis iudicum,* bk. 2, case 57, n. 8, p. 203. Paolo Zacchia agreed, even as he noted that some call it a child "once it is complete in the uterus, with all its members formed." Zacchia, *Quaestionum medico-legalium,* bk. 1, tit. 1, quest. 3, n. 10, p. 4.

42. Antonino Tesauro, *Novae decisiones sacri senatus Pedemontani* (Turin: Ioannem Dominicum, 1609), decision 12, n. 6–8, f. 21v–22r. On these grounds, Tesauro and Farinacci both thought that infanticide was undoubtedly a capital offense, though it too was difficult to investigate and there could be mitigating factors, as will be examined below. Tesauro, *Novae decisiones,* decision 13; Farinaci, *Praxis, et theoricae criminalis,* quest. 122, n. 156, p. 173.

43. Zacchia was asked to give his expert opinion on a case where a woman named Lucretia claimed the estate of her dead husband through their son, who was born premature and died after eight days. Lucretia's husband's family argued against her claim on the grounds that the son could not inherit because it was a six-months gestated fetus and was therefore aborted, not born. *Quaestionum medico-legalium,* bk. 10, cons. 37, pp. 209–212. See also Zacchia, *Quaestionum medico-legalium,* bk. 1, tit. 2, quest. 7, pp. 43–45 and quest. 10, pp. 48–49. The Rota Romana heard a similar case in 1596 that rested on the gestational age of the fetus: Francisco Peña, *Sacrae rotae Decani Recollectae Decisiones* (Lyon: Petri Prost, Philippi Borde, & Laurentii Arnaud, 1648), decis. 521, pp. 370–372.

44. See Park, "The Death of Isabella della Volpe," pp. 169–187, for a case where the question of whether the infant had survived the mother, even if only by a few moments, had large financial consequences for the heirs. Giovanni Battista De Luca gave this matter careful attention in his *Theatrum veritatis, et justitiae,* bk. 11 (Venice: Paulum Balleonium, 1698), pars. 2, "De successionibus ab intestato," disc. xlvi, pp. 89–91.

45. De Luca, *Il dotto volgare,* bk. 14, pt. 2, ch. 5, pp. 110–111.

46. Antonio Maria Cospi, *Il giudice criminalista* (Florence: Zanobi Pignoni, 1643), ch. 32, p. 496.

47. Vincenzo de Franchis, *Decisiones sacri regii consilii Neapolitani* (Venice: Andrea Pellegrini, 1608), pt. 4, decision 592, f. 67r–68r.

48. Cospi, *Il giudice criminalista,* ch. 34, n. 13, pp. 499, 502–503.

49. Farinacci, *Praxis, et theoricae criminalis,* quest. 122, n. 144, p. 172.

50. Cospi, *Il giudice criminalista,* p. 502

51. De Luca, *Il dottor volgare,* bk. 14, pt. 2, ch. 5, p. 110.

52. Marina Graziosi, "'Fragilitas sexus.' Alle origini della costruzione giuridica dell'inferiorita delle donne," in *Corpi e storia. Donne e uomini dal mondo antico all'eta contemporanea,* ed. Nadia Maria Filippini, Tiziana Plebani, and Anna Scattigno (Rome: Viella, 2002), pp. 19–38.

53. Tesauro, *Novae decisiones,* dec. 12, n. 12, f. 22v; Menochio, *De arbitrariis iudicum,* bk. 2, case 357, n. 22, p. 666; de Franchis, *Decisiones sacri regii consilii,* dec. 592, n. 2, f. 67v–68r; Farinacci, *Praxis, et theoricae criminalis,* quest. 122, n. 156 and 158, p. 173; see also pt. 3, quest. 92, n. 41, p. 127–128 and n. 136, p. 137, for a discussion of age as a factor mitigating pen-

alties; Savelli, *Prattica universale,* "Aborto," pp. 21-22. According to De Luca there was no consensus of what "eta minore" meant across Italy: in the Kingdoms of Naples and of Sicily, in Milan, Florence, and Lucca, it meant eighteen years old; in Rome, twenty; in other parts, twenty-five. De Luca, *Il dottor volgare,* bk. 14, pt. 2, ch. 7, n. 5-7, p. 344-350.

54. De Luca, *Il dottor volgare,* bk. 14, pt. 2, ch. 5, pp. 112-113.

55. ASR, TcG, Processi, 1602, b. 1, f. 922r-990v.

56. Mennoca Liberatori: "dicesse che non volevo, et che li facesse resistenza un gran pezzo, al fine, per essere io ignuda et haver esso più forza di me, me saltò sopra et me cognobbe carnalmente. Et questo è il peccato che io voglio dire, con ché me ritrovo gravida per detto peccato che ho fatto con il detto don Cinthio." ASR, TcG, Processi, 1602, b. 1, f. 928r.

57. The legal requirements and trial narratives for defloration were similar throughout Italy. While adulterous rape has been less studied, its narratives were often similar to those of defloration. For Rome, see Cohen, "No Longer Virgins," pp. 169-191; and Elizabeth Cohen, "The Trials of Artemisia Gentileschi: A Rape as History," *Sixteenth Century Journal* 31 (2000): pp. 47-75; for Venice, Guido Ruggiero, *Boundaries of Eros,* pp. 89-107; for Bologna, Cesarina Casanova, *Crimini nascosti,* pp. 148-167; for Florence, Giorgia Arrivo, "Raccontare lo stupro: Strategie narrative e modelli gudiziari nei processi fiorentini di fine Settecento," in *Corpi e storia. Donne e uomini dal mondo antico all'eta contemporanea,* ed. Nadia Maria Filippini, Tiziana Plebani, and Anna Scattigno (Rome: Viella, 2002), pp. 69-86; on the differences between ecclesiastical and secular courts, Daniella Lombardi, "Il reato di stupro tra foro ecclesiastico e foro secolare," in *Trasgressioni. Seduzione, concubinato, adulterio, bigamia (XIV–XVIII secolo),* ed. Silvana Seidel Menchi and Diego Quaglioni (Bologna: Il Mulino, 2004), pp. 351-382.

58. Mennoca Liberatori: "io voglio inferire et dire per quelle parole dette di sopra che era andata in casa del mio compare per il peccato che ho che me ritrovo gravida da gennaro," ASR, TcG, Processi, 1602, b. 1, f. 927r; "questo peccato che io voglio dire che mi ritrovo pregna da gennaro in qua è che io ho fatto male" f. 927r; "questo peccato che io voglio dire che mi ritrovo pregna da gennaro in qua è che io ho fatto male," f. 927r; "ho fatto male con altro homo che con mio marito," f. 927v; "io ho fatto male una volta solamente con don Cinthio," f. 927v; "questo e il peccato che io voglio dire, con che me ritrovo gravida per detto peccato che ho fatto con il detto don Cinthio," f. 928r; "Antonio mio marito a quel hora che io feci questo peccato con don Cinthio et per il quale me ritrovo pregna da gennaro in qua non stava in questi paesi," f. 928r.

59. As reported by Maria Christophoro, Mennoca's sister: "Mennocca mi disse 'o, per l'amor d'Iddio, che io lo voglio recuperare al meglio che

posso, che mi voglio mangiare un melo scricto, che forsi mi si verrà il ventre", et anco mi disse che voleva buttare per farse sgravidare quando haveva magnato detto melo scricto." ASR, TcG, Processi, 1602, b. 1, f. 932v.

60. ASR, TcG, Processi, 1602, b. 1, f. 926r; f. 927r and 932r.

61. ASR, TcG, Processi, 1602, b. 1, f. 935r.

62. Mennoca's mother, Angela, told the judge that she yelled at her daughter when she found out that she tried to abort and made her promise not to try again. ASR, TcG, Processi, 1602, b. 1, f. 935r.

63. ASB, Torrone, Atti e Processi, 1586, b. 1898, f. 225r–250v.

64. ASB, Torrone, Atti e Processi, 1586, b. 1898, f. 230v–2231r.

65. Aorelia di Battista: "Son doi tre anni che un Pietro di Lazzaro . . . comincio a far l'amor me et dirme se io volevo dargli da chiavare et io gli risposi di no più volte, et questo Pietro cominciò ad aiutarmi à lavorare con li bovi un poco di poss.ne che ho de miei figli et darmi anco qualche tira di pane et aiutarmi in quello che potevo con il quale aiuto si contentaria li sopradetti miei figlioli et continuamente me stimolava che io gli desse da chiavare che me haveria aiutato in quello che havesse possuto si sostentare la mia figliola io vedendomi povera et che non potevo constatar la sopradetta mia fameglia, accio che il sopradetto Pietro me aiutasse et sovvenesse di quello che poteva per poter allevar più facilmente li sopradetti miei figlioli come ho detto, et cosi andassemo dietro circa un anno che il sopradetto Pietro venne ad aiutarme senza che io volesse lassarmi chiamare da esso, se bene mi molestava spesse volte. Finalmente circa doi anni sono stretta dal bisogno et dal desiderio d'essere aiutata dal detto Pietro venendo in casa mia una sera dormette con me et me chiamo, et cosi continuato questi doi anni, che è venuto in casa mia à magnare et bevere pubblicamente che non si guardava da nessuno come fusse stato mio marito et dorminomo insieme insieme." ASB, Torrone, Atti e Processi, 1586, b. 1898, f. 228v–229r.

66. ASB, Torrone, Atti e Processi, 1586, b. 1898, f. 244v–245r.

67. Pietro di Lazzaro: "io sono andato in casa della sopraddetta Aorelia di giorno et di notte come pareva et piaceva a me, et ho dormito seco, et l'ho chiavata a mio commodo et li ho dati delli denari, per modo gli ho havuti et io lo chiavata come puttana che e che la chiamano degli altri ancora, ma io non saprei dire chi l'havesse chiamata, ma l'ho sentito dire pubblicamente che questa donna si faceva chiavare a diverse persone." ASB, Torrone, Atti e Processi, 1586, b. 1898, f. 246v.

68. As no sentence has been found for this case, we cannot know how Aorelia's legal ordeal ended. ASB, Torrone, Atti e Processi, 1586, b. 1898, f. 248r–250r.

69. Lucia Pivinelli: "detto Sabbatino incomincio a che io li volessi dare da negotiare che lui mi haverebbe dato delli quatrini et agiutatami dicen-

domi: 'Tu sei poveretta, io ti agiutaro o ti trarro per moglie.' Et veneva qui a casa mia a stimularme in questa maniera, et io mai li volsi acconsentire serialmente. Una sera che non mi ricordo de che mese si fusse, ma credo fusse di novembre o di settembre, venne qui in casa che dovevano essere da due hore di notte et busso alla porta et io li apersi, et lui venne di sopra dove io ero à canto al fuoco et mi comincio di nuovo a ricercare che io li volessi acconsentire. Et doppo havermi pregato un pezzo, essendo io poveretta, et per il bisogno sperando mi desse qualche cosa li acconsentii et mi stratai li in terra et lui mi venne à dosso et mi alzo li panni denanzi, et mi mise il suo membro nella mia natura che mi fece molto male. Et doppo havere fatto il fatto suo si levo su, et io nettandomi la natura et coscie con la camiscia veddi che mi era uscito del sangue dalla natura et la camiscia resto insanguinata. Et detto Sabbatino doppo essersi fermato li un pezzolo mi diede una chiappa, depone et poi se ne ando via et non me diede altro, et vi torno poi parecchie volte la sera. Et haveva che fare meno carnalemnte et mai mi ha dato altro che alle volte delle chiappe." ASB, Torrone, Atti e Processi, 1610, b. 4266, f. 318v–319r.

70. For similar dynamics at play in other jurisdictions and contexts, see Gowing, *Domestic Danger*; Peirce, *Morality Tales*; and Hardwick, *Sex in an Old Regime City*. For methodological discussion of legal narratives more broadly, see the foundational work of Davis, *Fiction in the Archives*, and more recent treatments of Frances Dolan, *True Relations: Reading, Literature, and Evidence in Seventeenth-Century England* (Philadelphia: University of Pennsylvania Press, 2013), pp. 111–153; and Tim Stretton, "Women, Legal Records, and the Problems of the Lawyer's Hand," *Journal of British Studies* 58 (2019): pp. 684–700.

71. Antonella Bettoni, "Voci malevole: Fama, notizia del crimine, e azione del giudice nel processo criminale (secc. XVI–XVII)," *Quaderni Storici* 121 (2006): pp. 13–38; Giorgia Alessi Palazzola, *Prova legale e pena: La crisi del sistema tra evo medio e moderna* (Naples: Jovene, 1979), esp. pp. 61–66, 79–81.

72. De Luca, *Il dottor volgare*, bk. 14, pt. 2, ch. 5, p. 109.

73. Pastore, *Il medico in tribunale*; Silvia de Renzi, "Medico-Legal Cases in Seventeenth-Century Rome," *Studies in the History and Philosophy of Science* 33 (2002): pp. 229–232; Silvia de Renzi, "Medical Expertise, Bodies and the Law in Early Modern Courts," *Isis* 98 (2007): pp. 315–322; Seitz, *Witchcraft and Inquisition*, ch. 9; Elizabeth Mellyn, *Mad Tuscans and Their Families: A History of Mental Disorder in Early Modern Italy* (Philadelphia: University of Pennsylvania Press, 2014); Bouley, *Pious Postmortems*.

74. Angela Ferranta: "Signor sì che io sono stata chiamata più et più volte a vedere sconciature in diversi tempi et più et diverse donne, anzi che alle volte di tre mesi gli ho dato l'anima ancorché fossero sconciature. . . . Io sono stata sempre pagata mentre sono andata a vedere le sconciature et

chi me ha dato cinqui giulii, et chi più et chi meno et, quando andai a vedere quella donna nel vicolo della Vaccha, me fu dato minestrone." ASR, TcG, Processi, 1634, b. 295, f. 1723r.

75. Cospi, *Il giudice criminalista,* ch. 33, pp. 493–494; Savelli, *Prattica universale,* "corpo di delitto," n. 15 and 17, p. 111. Recall that evidence of Femia's alleged abortion was disposed of in Lake Bracciano and Rosana's was allegedly buried in the courtyard of her apartment building.

76. Angela Ferranta: "La sconciatura che non hanno anima se buttano per il necessario, et così io uso quando non li battizzo et che non siano vivi." ASR, TcG, Processi, 1634, b. 295, f. 1723r.

77. Anastasia Fanensi called the *beccamorto* Giacamo to collect her six-months-developed female fetus, which she miscarried following an altercation with a fruit vendor. ASR, TcG, Processi, 1630, b. 257, f. 1871r.

78. Sandra de Lanciallini: "et io gli dissi pigliandoli il corpo che cosa hai fatto del tuo corpone che l'havevi cosi grosso, et hora non l'hai piu." ASB, Torrone, Atti e Processi, 1574, b. 980, f. 25r.

79. One witness confirmed that she saw Pellegrina twice in the last few years with a swollen belly but did not say whether she believed Pellegrina to have been pregnant or sick. ASB, Torrone, Atti e Processi, 1574, b. 980, f. 28r.

80. Cospi, *Il giudice criminalista,* ch. 34, pp. 499–502; Savelli, *Pratica Universale,* "Corpo di delitto," p. 112.

81. Zacchia, *Quaestionum medico-legalium,* bk. 3, tit. 2, quest. 9, n. 4, 18–19, pp. 234–235; and bk. 10, cons. 69, pp. 298–300; Cospi, *Il giudice criminalista,* ch. 40, pp. 530–533; Savelli, *Prattica universale,* "Donne," n. 29, p. 148.

82. Zacchia, *Quaestionum medico-legalium,* bk. 10, cons. 69, pp. 298–300, at n. 6, p. 300. These issues are also discussed in a section on "simulation," bk. 3, tit. 2, quest. 9, pp. 234–235. The case is discussed by De Renzi, "Medico-Legal Cases," pp. 229–232.

83. Zacchia, *Quaestionum medico-legalium,* bk. 10, cons. 69, p. 298.

84. Zacchia, *Quaestionum medico-legalium,* bk. 3, tit. 2, quest. 9, n. 8–11, pp. 234–235; Savelli, *Pratica universale,* "Aborto," p. 21, n. 3.

85. Zacchia, *Quaestionum medico-legalium,* bk. 3, tit. 2, quest. 9, n. 14, p. 235.

86. Cospi, *Il giudice criminalista,* ch. 38 (Della recognizione del corpo del delitto nello stupro), p. 525.

87. Cospi, p. 527. Zacchia, *Quaestionum medico-legalium,* bk. 3, tit. 2, quest. 9, n. 6 and 13, pp. 234–235.

88. Zacchia, *Quaestionum medico-legalium,* bk. 3, tit. 2, quest. 9, n. 14, p. 235.

89. On the laws of evidence, see Jean-Philippe Lévy, "L'évolution de la preuve, des origines à nos jours," *Recueils de la societe Jean Bodin* 17, no. 2 (1965): pp. 9–70, 137–167; Alessi, *Prova legale e pena;* Isabella Rosoni, *Quae singula non prosunt collecta iuvant. La teoria della prova indiziaria nell'età medievale e moderna* (Milan: Giuffrè, 1995).

90. Cospi, *Il giudice criminalista,* ch. 41, pp. 534–535.

91. For the use of similar defenses in England, Germany, and Venice, see Gowing, "Secret Births and Infanticide," pp. 87–115; Rublack, "The Public Body," pp. 59–61; Rublack, *The Crimes of Women,* pp. 170, 174–175; Ferraro, *Nefarious Crimes,* p. 141.

92. Farinacci, *Praxis, et theoricae criminalis,* pt. 4, quest. 122, n. 156, p. 173.

93. Maria da Brescia: "io non sappevo d'esser gravida che io non ero mai poi stata gravida et non sappevo che cosa m'havevo in mio corpo che sebene . . . una bolla nel corpo ma per che spesso ho uno dolore di stomaco, et cosi non cognoscevo d'essere gravida" and "lo gettai nel . . . necissario per paura di mio fratello che si chiama Francesco che non mi dasse." ASB, Torrone, Atti e Processi, 1577, b. 1165, f. 223r and 224v.

94. Francesco Vivio, *Decisiones regni Neapolitani* (Venice: Damino Zenari, 1592), n. 13, p. 140. See also Cospi, *Il giudice criminalista,* ch. 35, p. 504.

95. Zacchia, *Quaestionum medico-legalium,* tomus prior, bk. 3, tit. 2, quest. 9, pp. 234–235.

96. Aorelia di Battista: "Il giorno poi me sentetti il corpo greve ma per questo non cessai fare quello che bisognava per casa ultimamente la sera che era notte andai per serrare la porta di casa mia dove stavan dentro tutti li miei figli et mentre serravo bussero me sentetti cascare la creatura dal corpo senza che me facesse fastidio alcuno." ASB, Torrone, Atti e Processi, 1586, b. 1898, f. 229v.

97. Ferraro, *Nefarious Crimes,* p. 56.

98. Cospi, *Il giudice criminalista,* ch. 33, n. 3, p. 494, and seqq.; Savelli, *Prattica universale,* "corpo di delitto," n. 16, p. 111.

99. For examples, see Pastore, *Il medico in tribunale;* Casanova, *Crimine nascosti.*

100. Lucrezia Capillori: "Io vi dico per l'esperientia che ne ho che questo cadavero di questo putto maschio l'è compito qui stando che si conosce benissimo ma quanto poi al dare giuditio che lo sia nato morto ò vivo io ve dico vi è piu dubio et tengo poi questo che lo sia nato morto che altrimente perche questa ma che l'ha partorito se l'ha non ha hauto agiuto facile cosa è che l'habbia afogato nel partore forsi per il timore che la non gridi et non sia inteso da persona, et questo facilmente puo stare, et questo è quanto vi posso dire di questo putto morto." ASB, Torrone, Atti e Processi, 1577, b. 1165, f. 227r.

101. Veronica Gartolai: "Io quanto al mio giuditio do giuditio fermo che questo putto morto quando l'è stato partorito s'era di tempo compito, ma però non so dar giuditio fermo se sia nato morto o vivo, ma più tosto giudico che lo sia nato morto perche ho facile cosa e che per sospetto di sua madre non volendo esser scoverta ne che si sappia nel partorire lo può havere afogato che mi trovo con l'experientia che oltra aggiuto che hanno le pover donne gravide tutta volta fanno delle creature morte che

noi com. con il nostro studio glie rendono il fiato da ogni bando di modo che si termine d'un 'hora et tale volta più tornano vivi che questo è quanto vi posso diri ritorno a ciò in causa sciente." ASB, Torrone, Atti e Processi, 1577, b. 1165, 227v–228r.

102. ASB, Torrone, Atti e Processi, 1610, b. 4266, f. 346r–v.

103. ASB, Torrone, Atti e Processi, 1610, b. 4266, f. 300v–302r, 346r–348v.

104. Virginia Vigorisi: "Quando una donna partorisce una creatura morta senza puro assai perche la creatura non ha fiato da uscir fuori et e senza che la donna da se stessa a forza di fiato la maddi fuora che si stenta al doppio di quando si fanno vivi, che quando si fanno delle creature morte se vi stenta un di due di mezzo di una notte et più et meno secondo che piace poi à Iddio, basta che si stenta più che quando si fatto vivi, et quella che partorisce sente magior dolore che a farli vivi. . . . Quando una creatura nasce morta esce fuori dal corpo della madre fredda fredda, et non ha fodezza in se che pare un panno lavato bianco bianco, et difficilmente una donna puol partorire una creatura morta senza aiuto di commone ò d'altre donne de simil mistero." ASB, Torrone, Atti e Processi, 1610, b. 4266, f. 347r–v.

Elizabetta Jacobi: "Ma creatura subito nata si puol far morire senza che ne apparisce segno alcuno con lasciarli l'ombellicolo sciolto, perche de li li escie il fiato et campano che poche hore chi due, chi tre hore et chi più chi meno secondo che ha fiato la creatura et che ha patito nel nascere. . . . Quando una donna partorisce una creatura morta ci stenta piu assai che seu stà delli giorni intieri avanti li cavi fuora, perche la creatura non ha fiato et bisogna che la donna di sua forza la butti fuora, et quando escie fuora è fredda fredda et bianca come un panno lavato et la donna che la partorisce sente grandissimo dolore et magiore che quando la partorisce viva, et vi stenta più al doppio." ASB, Torrone, Atti e Processi, 1610, b. 4266, 348r–v.

105. Lucia Pivinelli: "Signore la creatura era morta quando io la partorii, et so ch'io non li ho fatto mal nesuno è che volete voi li legasse l'ombellicolo se era morta quando io la partorii." ASB, Torrone, Atti e Processi, 1610, b. 4266, f. 515v.

106. Lucia Pivinelli: "Non era vivo signore et non potrò mai dire perche non era, et non ci posso fare altro supra a questo che non posso essere sopra à quello ch'è padrone de tutto il mondo, è piaciuto a Dio che si nata morta, io non so che meii fare." ASB, Torrone, Atti e Processi, 1610, b. 4266, f. 514v.

107. Lucia Pivinelli: "Et m. Domeniddio mi perdoni tutti l'altri peccati ma questo non mel perdoni mai. . . . Sig.re questa non è la verità ch'io habbi fatto male nesuno à qualle creatura, ma era morta quando io la partorii et perciò non pretendo essere incorsa in alcuna pena." ASB, Torrone, Atti e Processi, 1610, b. 4266, f. 516v–517r.

108. See Jackson, *New-Born Child Murder*; Povolo, "L'imputata accusa," p. 568; Ferraro, *Nefarious Crimes*, p. 126.

109. Savelli, *Pratica universale*, "Aborto," n. 9, p. 21. Most jurists were in agreement: see Tesauro, *Novae Decisiones*, dec. 13, f. 23r; Menochio, *De arbitrariis iudicum*, bk. 2, case 357, n. 22–24, p. 667; de Franchis, *Decisionum Sacri Regii Consilii Neapolitani*, f. 68r; Farinacci, *Praxis, et theoricae criminalis*, pt. 4, quest. 122, n. 156, p. 173.

110. Ferraro, *Marriage Wars*, ch. 5; for France, see Hardwick, "Early Modern Perspectives on the Long History of Domestic Violence: The Case of Seventeenth-Century France," *Journal of Modern History* 78 (2006): pp. 1–36.

111. For legal discussion of miscarriage caused by assault during the middle ages, see Butler, "Abortion by Assault," and Müller, *The Criminalization of Abortion*.

112. ASR, TcG, Processi, 1608, b. 74, f. 138–179, discussed by Cohen, "Miscarriages of Apothecary Justice," pp. 496–497.

113. Farinacci, *Praxis, et theoricae criminalis*, p. 4, quest. 122, n. 153, p. 173; Savelli, *Prattica universale*, "Aborto," p. 21.

114. On the difficulties of processing blood as evidence in early modern criminal trials, see McClive, "Blood and Expertise."

115. Domenico Cocchi, ASR, TcG, Processi, 1634, b. 295, f. 1695r–1696r.

116. While there is no way of knowing whether Elena suffered a miscarriage or faked it, what is clear is that she was seeking justice against her very abusive husband. For similar uses of miscarriage as a resource against violence and as grounds for claiming better treatment, see Rublack, "Pregnancy, Childbirth and the Female Body"; Ferarro, *Marriage Wars*, ch. 5.

117. Cospi, *Il giudice criminalista*, ch. 36, n. 1–3, pp. 505–506; see also ch. 33, n. 8, pp. 495–496 and ch. 35, n. 4, pp. 504–505.

118. Venere da Bologna, ASR., TcG., Processi, 1603, b. 28bis, f. 777v–778r.

119. Chiara Tibaldi: "Io non posso giudicare che la creatura di detta Angela sia morta per le percosse che lei dice esserli state date, perché può anco esser causato che lei si habbia fatto negoziare, et perché anco lei ha male abbasso, ma io non so che male se sia, et per questo io non posso giudicare che detta creatura sia morta per dette percosse, ma il medico forsi ve lo saprà dire." ASR., TcG., Processi, 1603, b. 28bis, f. 779v–780r; Timoteo Camotio, f. 772v.

120. ASB, *Cronace delle giustizie eseguite in Bologna era del 1030–1750*.

121. On the concepts of poena extraordinaria and arbitrium iudicis, see Rosoni, *Quae singula non prosunt collecta iuvant*, pp. 125–126; and Massimo Meccarelli, *Arbitrium. Un aspetto sistematico degli ordinamenti giuridici in età di diritto comune* (Milan: Giuffrè, 1998), pp. 250–254.

122. De Luca, *Il dottor volgare*, bk. 14, pt. 2, ch. 5, p. 112.

123. ASB, Torrone, Atti e Processi, 1574, b. 980, f. 21r.
124. Tesauro, *Novae decisiones,* decis. 13, n. 3–4, f. 23r.
125. Tesauro, *Novae decisiones,* decis. 13, n. 6–7, f. 23r.
126. de Franchis, *Decisionum Sacri Regii Consilii Neapolitani,* f. 68r.
127. Girolamo Basilico, *Decisiones criminalis magnae Regiae curiae Regni Siciliae* (Florence: Joannis Philippi Cecchi, 1669), decis. 7, p. 94.
128. Savelli, *Pratica universale,* "Aborto," pp. 111–112.
129. Nicholas Terpstra, "Theory into Practice: Executions, Comforting, and Comforters in Renaissance Italy," in *The Art of Executing Well: Rituals of Execution in Renaissance Italy* (Kirksville, MO: Truman State University, 2008), pp. 152–153.
130. "Et Dominis quod ad ipsa respondere nesciat ad rationes add.tas per predictos peritos concludenter videtur quod ipsa necaverit predictam puellam presertim stantibus aliis inditiis coniecturis et presumptionibus de quibus supra fuit facta mentio et ideo aufugere non potest poenas impositas contra huiusmodi delinquentes.

    Die 23 octobris 1610.

    Congregaverunt illustres domini Iohannes Baptista de Sancto Petro senator et rector et Marcus Antonius Malvatricus prior battutororum et magnificus dominus Laurentius Guerrierus Cam[erari?]us ac Ginus Segatius sindicus et prior venerabilis archiconfraternitatis Sancte Marie de Vita Bononie et presentaverunt breve apostolicum gratie concessum per illustrissimum dominum nostrum Clementem decimum felicis recordationis Pontificem Maximum Datum Rome die 13 Januarii 1602 liberandi unum condemnatum ad mortem quemcumque dicti domini officiales petiverunt et insteterunt in vim et in executionem dicti brevis et gratie in honorem solemnitatis beati Rainerii que celebratur die crastina sibi concedi Luciam Antonii Piccinelli de Communi Montagu, Ragazza nuncupato carceratam pro infanticidio que licet condemnata non sit in poenam ultimi suplicii nichil ut credaverunt condemnanda esset et hoc etiam in vim gratie concesse per illustrissimum dominum legatum prout in memoriali quod presentaverunt subscripto ab eodem Illustrissimo domino cardinali legato et relaxum commicti in formam eamque relaxari et liberari et ultra promisserunt accusatore non molestari et pro omni meliori modo.

    Qui Illustrissimus et excellentissimus dominus Auditor Turroni visis habito verbo cum Illustrissimo et Reverendissimo domino cardinali legato et de eius ordine mandato in vim dicte gratie et privilegii inherendo etiam rescripto dicti Illustrissimi domini legati supra memoriale supra exibito sub his verbis *Si concedi la gratia ancor che non sia condannata* dictam Luciam ut supra carceratam dicte archiconfraternitati illiusque officialibus condonari et propterea mandatum quodcumque necessarium in

forma relaxavit et dictis offitialibus consignari mandavit omnis et amp-
lius occasione presentis infanticidii non molestari.

    Iul. Casb. Ant."

    ASB, Torrone, Atti e Processi, 1610, b. 4266, f. 516v–518r.

131. ASR, TcG, Registrazioni d'Atti, b. 148, f. 152v.

132. Tesauro, *Novae decisiones,* decis. 12, "additiones," f. 22v.

MARIA AND SUPERIO

1. ASR, TcG, Processi, 1613, b. 116: the trial begins on f. 831r and has its
own internal foliation, f. 1v–194r. The latter is cited here. Hereafter, for
all notes that cite this trial, I give only the folio number and the name of
the witness.

2. Maria de Vecchis: "io non sono maritata, che non mi sono voluta mai
maritare per essere stroppiata come mi vedete, che ho tocca che me si è
uscita fuora della schiena, ho il mal tisico, il mal attico et ogni male."
f. 22v.

3. It is possible that Superio was related to Pomponio de Magistris, who
occupied several ecclesiastical offices in Rome under the papacies of
Sixtus V, Innocent IX, Gregory XIV, Clement VIII, and Paul V and died in
1614 as the bishop of Terracina, Sezze, and Priverno. The de Magistris
family would continue to occupy positions in the curia and the bishopric
of Terracina, Sezze, and Priverno from the seventeenth to the nineteenth
centuries. See Teodoro Valle da Piperno, *La regia et Antica Piperno* (Naples,
1637), pt. 2, p. 13; and Gaetano Moroni, *Dizionario di erudizione storico-ecclesiastica,* vol. 65 (Venice, 1854), p. 58.

4. Superio's son Simone was periodically also accused of having sex with
Maria, but almost no attention was given to him in this investigation.

5. Lisa Antonii saw Maria pregnant through a window. f. 54v. Antonia Catuti specified that Maria was pregnant during Lent. f. 56v. Pasquale de
Tantis reported "Pasquale de Tantis reported that Maria stayed in her
home for about six months." f. 8r.

6. According to Giovanni Battista Colasanti, "procurato di far andare via
la creatura." f. 58r. Antonia Catuti used the phrase "farci andare il
ventre." f. 56v.

7. Pietro Normesino: "Et tutto questo fatto . . . l'ho inteso dire publicamente da tutta Sezze, come l'ho detto di sopra, che per la terra di Sezze lo
sanno sino alle galline, tanto il fatto è noto." f. 32v. The following testimonies are the most helpful for reconstructing the main allegations
under investigation: Angelo Cima's summary of the allegations, f. 7v–8v;
Pietro Normesino, f. 31r–33r; Giuseppe Contuggi, f. 35r–37r; Giovanni
Ranucci, f. 43r–46r; Tommaso Ciammaricone, f. 46v–47v, 56r–57r; and

Giovanni Battista Colasanti, f. 58r–59r. The women who testified in this case all appear to be Maria's neighbors: Orsidea de Tantis, f. 53v–54v; Lisa Antoni, f. 54v–55r; Alessandra da Citta di Castello, f. 55r–56r; Antonia Catuti, f. 56v–57v.

8. *Statuta, sive constitutiones Civitatis Setie* (Rome, 1547), bk. 3, cap. 13, p. 34.

9. Angelo Cima, f. 6r.

10. Superio de Magistris called Cima "my enemy." f. 140r.

11. The documentation created during the two phases of the investigation is long and varied, comprising many witness testimonies, subpoenas, and letters between various authorities regarding the organization of the investigation. However, neither judge pursued the alleged bribery of the Sezze magistrates.

12. Maria de Vecchis: "io non sono stata mai conosciuta carnalmente né da Superio de Magistris, né da Simone suo figliolo. Questi sono miei parenti et non c'è tal cosa." f. 126v; "io sia stata mai conosciuta carnalmente da persona alcuna, et non mai sono stata gravida, né meno mi sono sconcia, né ho cercato di commettere aborto né di farmi sgravidare con remedio alcuno." f. 126r. Maria made similar statements several times in the trial.

13. Superio said that, had Cornelia de Vecchis not asked him to talk with a physician or a surgeon about her daughter, "I would not have meddled." f. 65v.

14. Perhaps realizing that she would not be forthcoming, Judge Giandi never asked Cornelia about her daughter's sexual history, the alleged incest, or the abortion. Rather, he asked about Maria's health and who generally treated her. f. 67v–68r. In Rome, Judge Lunte did not question Cornelia at all.

15. Ortensio Simeoni, f. 91v–92r, 177r–178v, 180v.

16. Maria de Vecchis, f. 126v–133v, 145v–147v; Superio de Magistris, f. 139v–145r, 149r–152r.

17. Giulia Colienda from Ceccano: "Io ho vista benissimo questa giovane gobba con la quale Vostra Signoria mi ha fatto versare nella stanza, et l'ho vista particolarmente nella parte da basso et nella natura, et anco nel ventre et nelle zinne ho trovato che lei è sverginata et che è stata gravida et bisogna che di fresco se sia sconcia o che habbia partorito, perché si vede che la natura è larga, et il ventre pare un zaino muscio, che questi sono segni che sia stata sverginata et che sia stata gravida. Et il più evidente segnio poi che lei è stata gravida è che havendogli viste le zinne e sprizzatele c'esce ancora del latte, che si vede chiaramente, che se Vostra Signoria lo vuol vedere, lo potrà vedere. Et è cosa sicurissima che una che è vergine et che non sia stata gravida non haverà mai il latte così nelle zinne come l'ha costei." f. 19v–20r.

Adlotia Pompei from Roccagorga: "Io ho vista questa giovane gobba che dice chiamarsi Maria, che sta in una camera qua del palazzo, dove

Vostra Signoria mi ha fatta condurre. Et havendola vista nella natura ho trovato et visto che lei non è vergine, et ho visto ancora che ha del latte bianco come neve nelle zinne, che questo è un segnio manifestissimo che lei è stata gravida, et è necessario o che habbia partorito, o che se sia sconcia, che io questo non lo posso sapere. Et ha il ventre ancora tutto greppposo, che dà a conoscere et ad intendere che lei è stata gravida." f. 20r–21r.

Beatissima Amadei from Roccagorga: "Io ho visto benissimo questa giovane che chiamasi Maria, che sta in una stanza qua del Palazzo dove Vostra Signoria mi ha fatto condurre. Et havendola vista nella natura ho trovato et visto che lei non è vergine, . . . tanto più che havendoli io visto il petto n'esce il latte come Vostra Signoria lo potrà anco vedere evidentemente, che ciò dimostra non solo non esser vergine, ma che sia stata gravida, et si conosce anco dal corpo che sta vacante, che quando una è zitella et non ha partorito tiene il ventre tirato, et io al mio giudizio tengo o che habbia partorito, o che se sia sconcia. Et questo è quanto posso dire per la verità." f. 21v–22r.

18. Maria de Vecchis: "io mi trovo svergianta dal anno santo in qua prossimo passato, et racontaro a V.S. come mi successe questa disgratia: l'anno santo mio fratello chiamato Tolomeo studiava in Roma e nel tornare qua al paese vicino a Sezze una donna chiamata Silvia che haveva un figlio che non me ricordo come se dimandasse, ch'era una donna grossa grossa grande et bella, et essendo andati assieme a spasso in una nostra possessione posta in contrada del Gioco, che credo fosse del mese di ottobre, se ben me ricordo, et cominciaro a commettere assieme et essendoci li un fossatello che era largo da doi o tre palmi, volendolo io saltare, et essendo piccola mi sborsai li et mi cominciai a sentire gran calore nelle parti dabbasso, cioè nella natura, et mi cominciò a gocciolare il sangue in gran quantità, che veramente fu assai; et quella donna havendomi visto così gocciolare il sangue mi volse vedere da basso et mi disse che io mi ero sverginata, et concorse lì a quel rumore mio fratello dicendo, che cosa è?! che cosa è?!, et detta Silvia gli disse che mi ero sverginata a saltare quel fosso, et mio fratello mi cominciò a gridare che io ero una fiasca et che mi ero arrovinata senza proposito, et mi disse che se io ero donna da marito bisognava che denuntiassi questo fatto alla Corte, ma perch'ero così stroppiata non occorreva di far altro. Che detto mio fratello morse in quell'istesso anno che a me venne questa disgratia." f. 22v–23v.

Early modern Europeans were fascinated by stories of bizarre and terrible things happening to women who ran too fast or jumped over obstacles. Almost two decades before Maria told the judge about her accident, Michel de Montaigne famously reported the story of Germain from Vitry-le-François, "who was a girl up to the age of twenty-two" known as Marie. "One day when she made an effort in jumping, her virile instruments came out," and from that day forward she was a man. Germain's experience became a warning: "In this town there is still a song commonly in the girls' mouths, in which they warn one another not to stretch their legs too wide for fear of becoming males, like Marie Germain." Michel de Montaigne, *The Complete Works: Essays, Travel Journal, Letters*, trans. Donald M. Frame (New York: Alfred A. Knopf, 2003), "Travel Journal," pp. 1059-1060. Many scholars have studied the story in relation to early modern notions of "hermaphroditism" and to the one-sex model of Thomas Laqueur, *Making Sex: The Body and Gender from the Greeks to Freud* (Cambridge, MA: Harvard University Press, 1990), pp. 126-128.

19. Maria de Vecchis: "E vero che le mammane me hanno visto le zinne et che hanno cavato del latte, ma questo latte me lo puole haver causato le purghe, perché quando mi vengono le purghe è solito di venirmi il latte nelle zinne, ma ce ne vene poco. . . . Il mio ventre non sta tirato come e solito delle giovane che non si sono mai ingravidate perché io sono stata sempre male da piccola, et il male mi ha accocinato come mi vedete." f. 24r. This sentence was underlined, and there is a marker next to it in the margins, perhaps reminding Giandi to investigate this claim further later on.

20. Adlotia Pompei: "figlia mia, e quel latte vuol essere venuto dal cielo?" f. 26v. Giulia Colienda: "figlia mia, una giovane che non sia stata gravida et che non habbia partorito non ha il latte come havete voi." f. 25v.

21. Giulia Colienda said: "Mostra qua le zinne che voglio che il signor auditore qui presente veda il latte!" Maria replied: "Non vi basta di haverlo visto una volta[?] Già gli l'ho confermato ancora io che mi esce il latte dalle zinne, non occorre che il signor commissario me lo veda altrimente." f. 25r.

22. Maria de Vecchis: "esser vero tutto quello che costei dice, solo gli asserisco non esser vero ch'io sia stata gravida, perché non ho conosciuto huomo nessuno." f. 27v.

23. Pasquale de Tantis, 51r-v. Domenico Pellegrini, another customer in Pasquale's shop at the time, confirmed the warning that Cola should not give Maria anything to be consumed orally without a prescription from a physician. f. 73r.

24. Notarial description and Paquale de Tantis, f. 74r-75r.

25. Ortensio testified to treating Maria off and on over the last few years, most recently a few weeks before the start of the investigation on account of a fever stemming from her liver. f. 90r-92r. Giuseppe Contuggio, f. 36r; Giovanni Battista Colasanti, f. 58r.

26. Emilio de Bonis: "io dissi che Tomeo Ciolli di Bassiano spetiale qui nella terra di Sezze alcuni giorni prima me haveva detto che era stato ricercato

da detto Superio de Magistris che gli desse qualche remedio per fare sgravidare una donna, come veramente me lo disse, che essendo io andato una volta nella sua spetiaria, stando io assentato nella loggia me disse, non sai quello che non ti voglio manco dire. Et io gli risposi che se era una cosa segreta non me l'havesse manco detto. Et stando un poco sopra di sé disse, horsù, te lo voglio pur dire, perché io so che tu non dirai niente. Et esso disse, Superio de Magistris mi ha recercato che io gli voglia dare qualche remedio per fare sgravidare una donna, et che gli haveva risposto che era peccato et che non lo poteva fare, et che detto Superio gli soggiunse che se ne poteva confessare, perché era per una donna di buon parentado, et che haverebbe remediato alli scandali che potessero nascere, che però di gratia lo facesse; et io gli dissi che avvertisse bene che non lo facesse in nessuna maniera. Lui mi replicò che non lo voleva fare resolutamente." f. 48v. Other witnesses who named Tomeo include Pietro Normesino, f. 33r; Giovanni Ranucci, f. 45r; Antonio Senemici, f. 65r.

27. Pietro Normesino, f. 32r; Giuseppe Contuggio, f. 36r; Tommaso Ciammaricone, f. 46v–47r; Tranquillo Pacifici, f. 50v; Antonio Senemici, f. 65r.

28. Ortensio Simeoni, f. 61v–62r, 90r–92r, 176r–181r. Commissary Giandi falsely told the physician that one witness, Giuseppe Contugi, testified that Ortensio had told him Superio's request to have Maria bled was explicitly for abortion. Contugi did not say this in any of his recorded testimonies, so Commissary Giandi was clearly trying to trick Ortensio into saying something more damning about Superio, but the physician did not bite.

29. Tomeo Ciolli, f. 181v–183r.

30. Tomeo Ciolli, f. 184v–185r.

31. Fra Maccabeo: "detto Superio me disse che haveva fatta sanguinare la donna gravida dal piede, et che haveva anco adoprato la Sabina et la Zaffarana, ma che non haveva giovato." f. 163rv.

32. In theory, this vendor could have been fined twenty-five ducats; see Chapter 1. On the goods available in the Piazza Navona, see Anna Modigliani, *Mercati, botteghe e spazi di commercio a Roma tra Medioevo ed eta Moderna* (Rome: Roma nel Rinascimento, 1998).

33. Here is fra Maccabeo's uninterupted testimony: "questo gennaro prossimo passato in Sezze per alcuni servigi del convento, mi trovò in piazza messer Superio de Magistris et disse che haveva bisogno di parlarmi, et così andassimo nel suo fondico di panni che lui tiene in detto luogho, dove mi tirò da parte et mi cominciò a dire che haveria voluto ch'io gli avessi fatto un servigio grande et che haveva bisogno di me, che non gli fosse mancato in modo alcuno, et così mi cominciò a conferire che lui si trovava havere sverginata una zitella et insieme anco ingravidata et che

già di doi o tre mesi in circa era gravida,et che per tanto io gli volesse in-
segnare qualche remedio per farla spregnare, dicendomi inoltre che
haveva adoprato certi altri remedii, et che non havevano fatto effetto alcuno. Io alla prima gli dissi che non havevo remedio alcuno. Finalmente
lui mi stette tanto a torno et mi pregò con tanta instanza che bisognò gli
promettesse ritornare fra tre o quattro giorni et di portargli remedii di
far fare questo aborto. Et detto messer Superio mi promise, se la cosa
havesse effetto, di farmi un habito novo, sebene io gli resposi et dissi che
facesse quello che gli piacesse, perché io non mi curavo di niente. Passato
che fu questo ragionamento tra me e lui nel suo fondico come ho detto di
sopra io uscetti fuora et me ne andai per il fatto mio, et dissi che la matina seguente mi sarei partito per Terracina. Così la matina, mentre ero
nel partire veddi che messer Superio mi stava aspettando lì, fuora del
nostro convento, et di nuovo se abboccò con me, et con molta instanza
mi pregò che di grazia non gli volessi mancare in questo suo bisogno
come io gli promessi di fare. Hora io me ne andai poi a Terracina, non
ritornai a Sezze nel tempo determinato tra di noi, onde mi accorsi che
una matina di buon hora comparse lì da me detto Superio, che disse che
non essendo io andato a Sezze era lui venuto di persona a pigliare quel
servigio. Io mi scusai con dirgli che non mi ero sentito troppo bene, ma
che però il servigio gli l'havessi portato presto a Sezze, et così se ne tornò.
[Maccabeo returned to Sezze], e portai con me un fiaschetto con infusione di cola quintida che havevo accommodato et preparato a Terracina,
et lo diedi al detto Superio de Magistris e gli imparai il modo come si
haveva da adoprare, dicendoli che la donna havesse bevuto di quella infusione che era nel fiaschetto la matina, che senza altro si sarebbe spreg-
nata. Et io mi fermai a Sezze un giorno o doi, salvo la verità, et fù ado-
prata detta infusione dalla donna gravida per quanto mi disse Superio,
ma che non haveva fatto effetto, solamente l'haveva fatta andare del
corpo assai. Onde, essendo io in viaggio per venire a Roma per alcuni
miei servigi, detto Superio mi ricercò a volergli abuscare et trovare un
poco di herba di Sabina fresca, che è cosa pur atta a fare spregnare, dicendomi che l'haveva adoperata questa ancora, ma che per essere secca non
haveva fatto operatione, et così me ne venni verso Roma, dove ancora me
disse Superio che sarebbe venuto ancor lui, et che ce saressimo reveduti
all'hostaria del Paradiso in Campo di Fiore. Et a Sermoneta mi accompa-
gniai con un fra' Pietro franzese laico dell'ordine nostro che all'hora era
romito, et di compagnia venissimo fino a Roma, . . . et nel resto me ne
stetti sempre all'hostaria del Paradiso in Campo di Fiore, dove capitò
anco detto Superio de Magistris; et in detta hostaria ci stassimo due
notti, et la sera pagava da cena per me et per il mio compagno il detto
Superio, perché la matina né noi né lui magniavamo in detta hostaria.

Hora mentre mi trattenni quei doi giorni a Roma trovai in piazza Navona un poco di Sabina fresca, che la comprai da quelli herbaroli, che spesi un grosso, et la diedi al detto Superio. Io poi mi ritornai a Terracina con detto fra' Pietro et lasciai in Roma detto Superio, et dal'hora in qua io non sono stato più a Sezze, né più ho veduto detto Superio, solamente che questa quadragesima prossima passata essendo andato fra' Pietro sudetto a Sezze, Superio mi mandò a dire per esso che quella cosa non haveva fatto alcuna operatione et che havessi trovato qualche altra cosa et che glie l'havessi mandata. Che è quanto è passato tra me et detto messer Superio sopra quello che Vostra Signoria mi ha dimandato." f. 160v–163r

34. Fra Maccabeo: "io credo che Superio si movesse a parlarmi di questo servigio perché me ha veduto più et più volte guarire le fatture a Sezze et a Terracina, che a Terracina io ne ho guarite molte donne che erano state affatturate, et per questo credo che me ne parlasse." f. 163r.

35. Historical records show that consumers desired the blending of spiritual with natural remedies, whose effects they could see and feel more acutely. The boundaries between supernatural and natural illness were fluid, overlapping and often difficult to separate or even distinguish. If their studies of the cause of illnesses were necessarily different, the maladies' manifestations on the body and their cures were often the same. See Gentilcore, *Healers and Healing,* pp. 16, 162–165, 195; Di Simpliccio, *Inquisizione, stregoneria, medicina,* pp. 106–109; Seitz, *Witchcraft and Inquisition,* ch. 4 and 5.

36. Fra Maccabeo: "Et quanto alla colaquintida io giudicai che fosse a proposito, perché io so che move gagliardamente il corpo, et non essendo la donna gravida più di doi o tre mesi, per quanto me diceva Superio, giudicai che questa infusione havesse possuto far l'effetto che desiderava." f. 163r.

37. Superio de Magistris: "se questo frate vuol dire queste cose, lui dice centomilia bugie, sfratato poltrone fattochiero! Io non gli ho dimandato mai tal cosa, né lui mi ha dato mai tal cosa. . . . Io non so che detto frate habbia dette queste cose, ma se l'ha dette sarà stato subornato dalli miei inemici." f. 169rv. And again: "io dico che questo frate se ne mente per la gola di quanto dice, et che è un tristo, un fattochiero, et è bugia tutto quello che dice." f. 170v–171r.

38. Fra Maccabeo: "io a questo settembre finisco ottantanove anni, et vedete che io non ho se non quattro denti in bocca adesso, che tutti li altri mi sono cascati per l'età" prout ego notarius vidi et hic pro veritate adnotavi." f. 171r.

39. "Tunc dominus ad tollendam omnem dubietatem que possit oriri circa personam vel dicta ipsius adducti, ex quo fecit se socium criminis, et

ad tollendam omnem maculam si qua exinde orta fuisset contra
ipsum adductum, et ad magis coadiuvandum et fortificandum eius
depositionem et afficiendum magis personam ipsius ac aliorum nominatorum in eius examine, et ad omnem alium bonum finem et ef-
fectum etc., decrevit et mandavit dictum adductum existentem in loco
torturarum, ex quo propter etatem torqueri non potest supponi per
custodes carcerum tormento taxillorum in caput et faciem ipsius presentis et aliorum nominatorum in dicto eius examine et dum tibialis
pedis dexteri exueretur et in ordine poneretur ad dictum tormentum
fuit pluries per dominum benigne monitus et hortatus ut caveat ne
aliquem seu aliquos indebite inculpet, quia rationem reddere tene-
retur non solum in hoc mundo sed etiam in alio, et ×××× quia ipse
adductus est sacerdos et religiosus ordinis Sancti Francisci, ideo bene
advertat ad dicendum veram veritatem, que sola ab ipso requiritur."
f. 171rv

40. Fra Maccabeo: "Sig[nore], vedete, quel ch'io ho detto nel mio essame e
l'istessa verità, e se n[on] fusse la verita come volete mai che sono sacer-
dote e religioso sono venuto qua a dirlo et a fare una testimonianza tale
che fosse in pregiudizio del'anima mia." f. 171v.

41. Antonia Agnelli: "sono venuta qui per ordine di vostra signoria et ho
veduta et visitata una donna forastiera ... Maria da Sezze per vedere et
conoscere se lei haveva mai fatti figlioli sì o de no; et havendola io veduta benissimo et tocchata dove faceva bisogno dico che questa donna
securamente ha partorito et fatti figlioli, per li segni che ho veduti alla
natura, al ventre, et alle zinne: prima perché ho trovato la carne della
natura scorata oscura, et ho trovato spartito quel pezzo che sta dentro
la natura, quale si spartisce nel parturire che fa la donna, et ancora
spartita la pellicella da basso verso il cesso; et il ventre l'ho trovato
segnato et crepato sopra il pettignone, più dal canto manco che dal
dritto; et alle zinne ci ho trovato il latte et trovato anco il capitello
stacchato, come l'hanno quelle donne che hanno partorito et dato la
zinna. Et però io concludo per tutti questi segnali che ho detto, per
l'esperienza che ne ho, che detta Maria ha partorito, come chiaramente ogni mammana che la vedrà per li sopradetti segni che ve si
trovano dirà il medesimo. Et tanto dico et affermo per la verita."
f. 192rv.

Ginevra Marioti: "Io ho visto benissimo una donna che dice chiamarsi madonna Maria de Vecchis da Sezze, che è qui in Tor di Nona prigione, alla quale havendoli visto benissimo il corpo, la natura et le zinne,
per l'esperienza che io ho di avere esercitato da 30 o 40 anni in qua la
mammana, dico liberamente che questa Maria è stata gravida, et ha
fatto figlioli, et li segni sono tanto evidenti che un cieco lo conoscerà,

perche ha il ventre tagliato et affettato et la sua natura anco lo dimostra, et si conosce anco alle zinne, che si vede essere state adoprate per havere li capitelli stacchati, et cosi io dico et giudico per l'esperienza che ho come detto di sopra." f. 192v–193r.

Lucia de Balconi: "havendoli visto il corpo et le zinne o, per dire, il ventre, quale ho trovato che è tagliato, overo crepato, come interviene alle donne che hanno partorito et anco le zinne hanno il latte cioè colastria, et per detti segni io per l'esperienza che io ho di mammana da sette overo otto anni in qua dico resolutamente che lei ha partorito et fatto figli, che questo ogni mammana che la vedrà lo conoscerà, che lei ha partorito." f. 193r.

42. Vincenzo Pastore: "havendo io havuto ordine dall'illus[trissim]o et emin[entissim]o sig[nore] Girolamo Felice Lunte di visitare una certa madonna Maria de Vecchis da Sezze carcerata in Tor di Nona, et havendo io visto et considerato il piede destro nella vena che volgarmente detto della madre, dove io ho visto essere un segno di cicatrice nella detta vena; io dico et affermo che quello è segno fatto da lancetta per sanguinarla et cavarli il sangue da detta vena; et tanto, per la verità et per l'esperienza che ho, dico et referisco." f. 193v.

43. Pietro Normesino: "Et tutto questo fatto . . . l'ho inteso dire publicamente da tutta Sezze, come l'ho detto di sopra, che per la terra di Sezze lo sanno sino alle galline, tanto il fatto è noto." f. 32v.

44. ASR, TcG, Registrazioni d'Atti, b. 170, f. 60v. On court-brokered peace agreements, see Fosi, *Papal Justice*, pp. 39–45.

CONCLUSION

1. Derek Massarella, ed., *Japanese Travellers in Sixteenth-Century Europe. A Dialogue Concerning the Mission of the Japanese Ambassadors to the Roman Curia (1590)*, trans. J. F. Moran (London: Ashgate, Hakluyt Society, 2012), "Colloquium XV,—Of the size of the cities, the splendour of the churches and the magnificence of other buildings," pp. 194–195.

2. For the development of Catholic theology and canon law on abortion from the eighteenth century onward, see Connery, *Abortion* and Sardi, *Aborto ieri e oggi*. For a nuanced study of nineteenth-century positions in the context of medical development, see Emmanuel Betta, *Animare la vita. Disciplina della nascita tra medicina e morale nell'Ottocento* (Bologna: Il Mulino, 2006).

3. See the important studies of Alessandra Gissi, "L'aborto procurato. 'Questione sociale' e paradigmi giuridici nell'Italia liberale (1860–1911)," *Genesis* 14 (2015): pp. 141-161; Alessandra Gissi, "'Io non dovevo avere nessun rimorso.' Il procurato aborto tra reato e cura (1889–1943)," *Me-*

dicina nei secoli. Giornale di Storia della Medicina 28 (2016): pp. 39–52; Alessandra Gissi, "Reproduction," in *The Politics of Everyday Life in Fascist Italy: Outside the State?*, ed. Joshua Arthurs, Michael Ebner, and Kate Ferris (New York: Palgrave Macmillan, 2017), pp. 99–122.

4. Elena Caruso, "Abortion in Italy: Forty Years On," *Feminist Legal Studies* 28 (2020): pp. 87–96.

BIBLIOGRAPHY

ARCHIVAL MATERIALS

Archivo Histórico Nacional, Madrid

Inquisición, lib. 898

Archivio Segreto Vaticano (ASV)

Fondo Borghese, Serie I, b. 652
Mis. Arm., IV–V, b. 47 and b. 68
Positiones, (1589) D-M; (1590) A–B, D-M, M-P, R-V; (1591) A-C
Registra Episcoporum b. 17 (1589); b. 19 (1590); b. 19 (1591)

Archivio di Stato di Bologna (ASB)

Sala di Consultazione
· Cronace delle giustizie eseguite in Bologna era del 1030–1750.
Tribunale del Torrone (Torrone)
· Atti e Processi, 1574, b. 980; 1577, b. 1165; 1586, b. 1898; 1610, b. 4266
Assunteria dello Studio (Studio)
· Divers. riguardante il buon governo della citta, 1571–1769, b. 233

Archivio di Stato di Firenze (ASF)

Mediceo del Principato (MdP), 695, 2951, 4027a, 5042, 5928, 6110 (accessed
through the Medici Archive Project BIA)

Archivio di Stato di Roma (ASR)

Statuti, b. 303, 410
Tribunale Criminale del Governatore (TcG)
· Processi, 1595, b. 269; 1598, b. 309; 1598, b. 310; 1602, b. 1; 1603, b. 28bis;
  1606, b. 53; 1610, b. 89; 1613, b. 116; 1630, b. 257; 1634, b. 295
· Processi, Registrazioni d'Atti, b. 148; b. 170
Universita, Collegio Medico, b. 24

Archivio Storico Diocesano di Napoli

Processus criminalis, 1625 and 1627

Archivio storico della Penitenzieria Apostolica

Valentino Mangiono, *Methodus expedita Supplicandi in Sacra Poenitentiaria,* manuscript volume, ca. 1634–1660.

Biblioteca Apostolica Vaticana (BAV)

Capponi, b. 189
Urb. Lat. b. 1054; b. 1059 p. 2; b. 1644
Vat. Lat. b. 7439; b. 8891

Biblioteca Archiginnasio

Coll. 16. Q. V. 39 op. 09

Biblioteca Casanatense

Coll. CC. N.V 137; VOL MISC. 3001, PER est 18.3

Biblioteca Marciana

Coll. BNM 65.C.98.

PRINTED PRIMARY SOURCES

Acta ecclesiae Brixiensis, ab Illustriss et Reverendiss D. D. Dominico Bollano eius Episcopo, Promulgata, Anno Domini MDLXXIIII. Venice: Georgius Variscus, 1608.

Antidotario Romano, Latino, e Volgare. Tradotto da Ippolito Ceccarelli . . . con le annotationi del Sig. Pietro Castelli. Rome: Pietro Antonio Facciotti, 1639.

Antidotarium Bononiense. Bologna: Joannem Rossium, 1574. Reprint, Bologna, 1647.

Antonucci, Gian Battista. *Catechesis, seu Instructio civitatis ac dioecesis Neapolitanae.* Naples: Horatium Salvianum, 1577.

———. *Catechesis seu Institutio civitatis ac dioecesis Neapolitanae.* Naples: Matthiae Cancer, 1587.

Aretino, Pietro. *Dialogues.* Edited and translated by Raymond and Margaret Rosenthal. Toronto: University of Toronto Press, 2005.

———. *Sei giornate.* Edited by Giovanni Aquilecchia. Bari: Laterza, 1980.

Auuertimenti, & Prouisione intorno li Speciali, & quelli, che essercitano la Medicina. Bologna: Vittorio Benacci, 1600.

Azpilcueta, Martino de. *Consiliorum sive responsorum.* Rome: Aloysii Zannetti, 1595.

——. *Manuale de confessori et penitenti . . . tradotto dalla linguia Latina nella nostra Italiana da Camillo Camilli.* Venice: Giorgio Angelieri, 1584.

——. *Manuale de' confessori et penitenti . . . tradotto di Spagnuolo in Italiano dal R. P. Fra Cola di Guglinisi.* Venice: Gabriel Giolito di Ferrara, 1569.

——. *Manuale de confessori . . . tradotto di Spagnuolo in Italiano dal R. P. Fra Cola di Guglinisi.* Venice: I Gioliti, 1584.

——. *Manuale del Navarro, ridotto in compendio da Pietro Giuvara theologo e tradotto dal Latino nella lingua Toscana da Camillo Camilli.* Turin: Gio. Dominico Tarino, 1591.

Bairo, Pietro. *Secreti medicinali.* Venice: Francesco Sansovino, 1562.

Bandi generali dell'Illustriss. e Reverendiss. Sig. Cardinale Silvio Savelli. Perugia, 1598.

Bandi Generali dell'Illustrissimo & Reuerendiss. Monsig. Antonio Gianotti, Archivescovo d'Urbino, & di Bologna Vicelegato. Bologna, 1596.

Bandi generali del molt'illvstre & Reuerendiss. Monsig. Anselmo Dandino Prothonotario Apostolico di Bologna Vicelegato. Bologna, 1588.

Bandi Generali del molto Illvstre et Reverendissimo Mons.re Anselmo Dandino, Prothonotario Apostolico, di Perugia, & Umbria General Governatore. Perugia, 1586.

Bandi Generali publicati di commissione di Nostro Sig. Rome, 1599.

Bando circa il governo di Roma . . . Gulielmus Bastonus Gubernator. Rome, November 9, 1591.

Bando concernente il buon reggimento della facolta di medicare, e dell'arti, che a lei servono, e somministrano: da osservarsi in Roma, e fuori in tutto lo Stato Ecclesiastico, cosi mediate, come immediate sottoposto alla Santa Sede Apostolica. Rome, 1595.

Bando Del Protomedico per Roma. Rome, 1608.

Bando, et provisione, Sopra quelli che senza autorita & licenza dell'Eccellentiss. Collegio di Medicina di Bologna danno, ordinano, vendono, & applicano medicamenti in alcun modo, overo essercitano alcuna parte di medicina. Bologna, 1594. Reprinted in 1604 and 1617.

Bando Generale concernente il Governo di Roma. Rome: Stampatori Camerali, 1595.

Bando generale Dell'Illustrissimo, & Reverendissimo Sig. Benedetto Card. Giustiniano, Legato di Bologna. Bologna, 1608.

Bando generale Dell'Illustrissimo, & Reverendissimo Sig. Benedetto Card. Giustiniano, Legato di Bologna. Bologna: 1610.

Bartoli, Daniello. *Dell'Istoria della Compagnia di Giesu. L'Asia. . . . Parte Prima.* Rome: Stamperia del Varese, 1667.

Basilico, Girolamo. *Decisiones criminalis magnae Regiae curiae Regni Siciliae.* Florence: Joannis Philippi Cecchi, 1669.

Bevilacqua, Antonio. *Vocabulario volgare, et latino.* Venice: Aldo Manuzio, 1573.

Boccaccio, Giovanni. *Il Decamerone di Messer Giovanni Boccaccio Cittadin Fiorentino. Di nuovo riformato da Luigi Groto Cieco d'Adria con permissione de' superiori.*

Et con le Dichiarationi Avertimenti, et un vocabolario fatto da Girolamo Ruscelli. Venice: Fabio & Agostin Zoppini, 1590.

Bononia Manifesta: Catalogo dei bandi, editti, costituzioni e provvedimenti diversi, stampati nel XVI secolo per Bologna e il suo territorio, ed. Zita Zanardi. Florence: Olschki, 1996.

Borelli, Camillo. *Consiliorum sive controversiarum forensium.* Venice: Guerilium, 1598.

Borgarucci, Prospero. *La fabrica degli spetiali.* Venice: Vincenzo Valgrisio, 1566.

Borromeo, Carlo. *Acta ecclesiae mediolanensis.* Milan: Pacifici Pontii, 1599.

Bottoni, Albertino. *De morbis muliebribus libri tres.* Venice: Paulum Meietum, 1588.

Bullarium diplomatum et privilegiorum Sanctorum Romanum Pontificum. 25 Vols. Turin: Sebastiano Franco et Filiis, 1857–1872.

Caeremoniale Episcoporum Iussu Clementis VIII. Rome: Ex Typographia linguarum externarum, 1600.

Cajetan [Tomasso de Vio]. *Peccatorum summula.* Venice: Dominicum Farreum, 1575.

Calestani, Girolamo. *Delle osservationi . . . Parte seconda.* Venice: Francesco de' Franceschi, 1575.

Canale, Floriano. *De secreti universali raccolti et esperimentati, . . . ne quali si hanno rimedii per tutte l'infermita de corpi Humani, come anco de Cavalli, Bovi, & cani.* Venice: Pietro Bertano, 1613.

The Canons and Decrees of the Council of Trent. Translated by Reverend H. J. Schroeder. Rockford, IL: Tan Books and Publishers, 1978.

Carletti [da Chiavasso], Angelo. *Summa angelica de casibus conscientialibus . . . cum additionibus quam commodis R.P.F. Iacobi Ungarelli.* Venice: Regazola, 1578.

Castelli, Pietro. *De abusu phlebotomiae.* Rome: Francesco Corbelletti, 1628.

——. *Exercitationes medicinales.* Toulouse: R. Colomerium, 1616.

Catalogo della raccolta di statute, consuetudini, leggi, decreti, ordini e privilege dei comuni, delle associazioni e degli enti locali italiani dal Medioevo alla fine del secolo XVIII. 8 vols. Rome: Biblioteca del Senato della Repubblica, 1943–1999.

Catechismo, cioe istruttione secondo il Decreto del Concilio di Trento, a' parochi . . . tradottopoi per ordine di S. Santita in ligua uolgare dal reuerendo Padre frate Alessio Figliucci. Venice: Aldo Manuzio, 1567.

Codronchi, Giovan Battista. *De christiana ac tuta medendi ratione: libri duo varia doctrina referti.* Ferrara, Italy: Mammarellum, 1591.

Colombo, Realdo. *De re anatomica, libri XV.* Venice: Nicolò Bevilacqua, 1559. Reprint, Brussels: Culture et Civilization, 1969.

Conciliorum omnium, tam Generalium quam Provincialium. Venice: Dominicum Nicolinum, 1585.

Constitutiones, capitula, jurisdictiones, ac pandectae Regii protomedicatus officii. Palermo: Nicolai Bua, 1657.

Constitutiones Dioecesanae synodi Faventinae ab Illustrissimo, & Reverendissimo Domino Herminio [Valenti] . . . Anno MDCXV Die 15 Mensis Octobris. Faenza: Ioannem Symbenium, 1615.

Constitutiones Domini Mediolanensis. Milan, 1562. Reprint, 1574.

Constitutiones editae, et promulgatae in synodo dioecesana Placentina quam illustrissimus et reuerendissimus D. D. Paulus De Aretio, . . . anno MDLXX die XXVI Augusti. Piacenza: Franciscum Comitem, 1570.

Constitutiones editae in diocesana synodo barensi. In Giovanni Pinto, *Riforma tridentina in Puglia.* 4 vols. Bari: Editoriale universitaria, 1968–1975.

Constitutiones editae per Reverendiss in Christo Patrem D. Io. Matthaeum Gibertum, Episcopum Veronae, . . . ab Illustrissimo, ac Reveredendiss. D. D. Augustino Valerio. Verona: Hieronymum Discipulum impressorem Episcopalem, 1589.

Constitutiones et decreta condita in provinciali Synodo Consentina sub. Reuerendiss. Domino D. Fantino Petrignano Dei & Apostolicae Sedis gratia Archiepiscopo Consentiae, anno MDLXXIX. Rome: Franciscum Zanetium, 1580.

Constitutiones, et decreta condita in synodo dioecesana Placentina. Piacenza: Ioannem Bazacchium, 1600.

Constitutiones et decreta condita in synodo dioecesana Ravennatensi, quam illustrissimus, &reuerendissimus dominus D. Christophorus Boncompagnus Dei, . . . anno domini MDLXXX die quinta Maij. Ravenna: Franciscum Thebaldinum, 1580.

Constitutiones, et decreta Dioecesanae Synodi Viterben. per admodu Illustrem, et Reuerendiss D. D. Carolum Archiepiscopu Motiliu(m) Episcopum Viterben. Viterbo: Augustinum Colaldum, 1584.

Constitutiones et decreta, . . . D. Laurentii Castruccii, Episcopi Spoletani, habita in Synodo Dioecesana Anno Domini MDCXXI. Perugia: Aloysii, 1622.

Constitutiones et decreta Em. & Rev. D. D. Marci Antonii . . . Episcopi Vicentini, . . . de anno 1647 in synodo dioecesana promulgata. Vincenza: Heredes Francisci Grossi, 1647.

Constitutiones et decreta illustriss. & Reverendiss. D. D. Marci Cornelii Patavini Episcopi . . . in septima Dioecesana Aynodo promulgata, die 17 & 18 Aprilis 1624. Padua: Typis Pasquati, 1624.

Constitutiones et decreta provincialis synodi Neapolitanae, sub Illustriss. et Reverendiss. D. D. Mario Carrafa Archiepiscopo, Anno Domini MDLXXVI . . . e mandato Illustrissimi ac reverendissimi D. D. Annibalis a Capua. Naples: Ex Officina Salviana, 1580.

Constitutiones provinciae Mediolanensis cvm decretis ordinibvs et declarationibvs Senatvs hac novissima editione ampliatis et illustrates. Milan, 1617.

Constitutiones Reverendissimi in Christo Patris & Domini Simplicii Caffarelli sacri monsterii Casiniensis abbatis et eiusdem diocesis, ac Iurisdictionis ordinarii. In Synodo dioecesana promulgata. Rome: 1626.

Constitutioni et regole della Congregatione de padre della Dottrina Christiana di Roma fatte di nuovo, stabilite di ordine de suoi Fratelli. Rome: Stampatori Camerali, 1604.

Cortesi, Giovanni Battista. *Pharmacopoeia seu antidotarium Messanense*. Messina: Petri Breæ, 1629.

Cospi, Antonio Maria. *Il giudice criminalista*. Florence: Zanobi Pignoni, 1643.

Criminalium iurium civitatis Genuensis. Genoa, 1573.

Cristini, Bernardino. *Pratica medicinale & osservationi: divisa in tre libri. 2. De mali particolari delle Donne*. Venice: Bodio, 1681. Originally published in Latin in 1676.

Cugnoni, Giorgio. "Autobiografia di monsignor G. Antonio Santori cardinale di S. Severina." *Archivio della R. Società Romana di Storia Patria* 13 (1890): pp. 151–207.

Da Cortona, Filippo Venuti. *Dittionario volgare et latino*. Turin: Gio. Dominico Tarino, 1590.

Da Faenza, Benedetto Vitorri. *Prattica d'esperienza*. Venice: Bolognino Zaltieri, 1570.

D'Amato, Cintio. *Prattica nuova et utilissima di tutto quello, ch'al diligente Barbiero s'appartiene*. Venice: Gio. Battista Brigna, 1669.

De Angelis, Allessandro. *In astrologos coniectores libri quinque*. Rome: Bartholomaei Zannetti, 1615.

De Crescenzi, Pietro. *Trattato dell'agricoltura*. Florence: Giunti, 1605.

Decreta Dioecesanae Synodi Ravennatis primae ab Illustriss.mo et Reverendiss.mo D. Petro Aldobrandino, Anno MDCVII Die III Maij. Venice: Giunta, 1607.

Decreta edita et promulgata in Synodo Dioecesana Ferrariensi habita anno a Christi Natiuit MDXCIX a Reuerendissimo D. Domino Ioanne Fontana. Ferrara: Victorium Baldinum, 1599.

Decreta edita et promulgata in synodo dioecesana laudensi, Quam per Illustris, & Reuerendiss.D. Ludovicus Taberna. Milan: Pacificum Pontium, 1591.

Decreta et constitutions editae a Fabricio Gallo Neapolitano Episcopo Nolano, In prima et secunda Synodo Dioecesana, Celebratis Nolae die sexto mensis Novembris anno MDLXXXVIII, Una, vigesimo quinto Aprilis MDLXXXXIIII, Altera. Rome: Gulielmum Facciottum, 1600.

Decreta et constitutiones editae a Frabricio Gallo, Neapolitano Episcopo Nolano in Synodo dioecesana celebrat Nolae sub die sexto Mensis Novembris, Anno MDLXXXVIII. Naples: Horatium Salvianum, 1590.

Decreta et monita Synodalia Ecclesia Perusinae iussu admodum illis. ac. R. mi. D. Neapolionis Comitoli Perusiae Episcopi, edita. Perugia: Petrum Jacobum Petrutium, 1600.

Decreta provinciales synodi Florentinae . . . Antonio Altovita, Archiepiscopo. Florence: Barholomaeum Sermartellium, 1574.

De Franchis, Vincenzo. *Decisiones sacri regii consilii Neapolitani*. Venice: Andrea Pellegrini, 1608.

De i semplici purgativi, et delle medicine composte. Venice: Bibliotheca Aldina, 1589.

Della Croce, Giovanni Andrea. *Cirugia universale e perfetta di tutte le parti pertinenti all'ottimo chirurgo*. Venice: Giordano Ziletti, 1583.

Delli statuti criminali di Genova. Genoa, 1590.

De Luca, Giovanni Battista. *Il dottor volgare, overo il compendio di tutta la legge, civile, canonica, feudale, e municipale, nelle cose piu ricevute in pratica*. 10 Vols. Rome: Giuseppe Corvo, 1673.

———. *Theatrum veritatis, et justitiae*. Book 11. Venice: Paulum Balleonium, 1698.

D'Eremita, Fra Donato. *Antidotario . . . nel quale si discorre intorno all'osservanza, che deve tenere lo spetiale*. Naples: Secondino Roncagliolo, 1639.

Diana, Antonino. *Resolutionum moralium, pars septima*. Lyon: Gabriel Boissat & Laurent Anisson, 1645.

Di Firenze, Niccodemo. *Pratica de casi di coscienza overo specchio de confessori*. Florence: Giunti, 1619.

Donati, Marcello. *De medica historia mirabili*. Venice: Fel. Valgrisium, 1588.

Dotti, Bartolomeo. *Per un aborto conservato in un'ampolla d'acque artificiali dal signor Giacopo Grandis fisico anatomico eccellentissimo*. In *Delle rime di Bartolomeo Dotti. i sonetti*. Venice, 1689.

Durante, Castore. *Herbario nuovo*. Rome: Bartholomeo Bonfadino & Tito Diani, 1585.

Editto che li Regolari non possino tenere, ne andare per Roma in Cocchio o Carrozza. Rome, October 1588.

Farinacci, Prospero. *Praxis, et theoricae criminalis*. Lyon: Horatii Cardon, 1610.

Fenzonio, Giovanni Battista. *Annotationes in Statuta sive ius municipal romanae urbis*. Rome: Andreae Phaei, 1636.

Filalteo, Lucillo. *Il Giuramento, e le sette parti de gli aforismi d'Hippocrate Coo*. Pavia: Francesco Moscheno, 1552.

Filomuso, Pietro. *Breue trattato di confessione*. Florence: Bartolomeo Sermartelli, 1580.

Fioravanti, Leonardo. *La cirugia*. Venice: Michele Bonibelli, 1595.

Florio, John. *A Worlde of Wordes: A Critical Edition*. Edited by Hermann W. Haller. Toronto: University of Toronto Press, 2013.

Folco, Giulio. *Effetti mirabili de la limosina et sentenze degne di memoria*. Venice, 1608.

Fumi, Bartolomeo. *Somma armilla del rev. padre Bartolomeo Fumo . . . Gia tradotta in lingua volgare dal Rever. P. Maestro Remigio dell'istesso Ordine, & dal R. M. Gio. Maria Tarsia, Fiorentini*. Venice: Domenico Nicolini, 1588.

———. *Summa, aurea armilla nuncupata, casus omnes ad animarum curamattinentes, breuiter complectens*. Venice: Giovanni Battista Somascho, 1572.

Galilei, Maria Celeste. *Letters to Father: Suor Maria Celeste to Galileo*. Edited and translated by Dava Sobel. New York: Walker, 2001.

Garzoni, Tommaso. *La piazza universale di tutte le professione del mondo* (1585). Vol. 1. Edited by P. Cerchi and B. Collina. Turin: Einaudi, 1996.

Giannetti, Laura, and Guido Ruggiero, ed. and trans. *Five Comedies of the Italian Renaissance*. Baltimore: Johns Hopkins University Press, 2003.

Gittio, Bartolomeo. *Tractatus de casibus reservatis in quo praecipue explicantur reservati in dioecesi Beneventana.* Naples: Constantini Vitalis, 1621.

Gotutio, Agostino. *Cinque giornate della penitenza fatte tra uno penitente et il suo padre confessore.* Venice: Fioravante Prati, 1611.

Gregory XIV. *Constitutio moderatoria bullae fel. rec. Sixti PP. V, contra Abortum quovis modo procurantes.* Rome: Paolo Blado, 1591.

———. *Sommario della constitutione di N. S. Papa Gregorio XIIII Moderativa della Bolla della felice mem. di Papa Sisto V Contro quegli che in qual si voglia modo danno opera al misfatto dello aborto.* Bologna: Vittorio Benacci, 1591.

Hippocrates. *The Hippocratic Treatises "On Generation," "The Nature of the Child," "Diseases IV."* Edited and translated by Iain Malcolm Lonie. Berlin: De Gruyter, 1981.

———. *Hippocratis Coi Opera quae extant Graece et Latine veterum codicum collatione restituta.* Edited by Girolamo Mercuriale. Venice: Industria ac sumptibus Iutarum, 1588.

Incarnato, Fabio. *Scrutinio sacerdotale, overo modo di essaminare tanto nelle visite de' Vescovi, quanto nel pigliare gli Ordini Sacri.* Venice: Domenico Nicolini da Sabbio, 1588.

Lanceano, Sylvio. *De Molae generatione & cura.* Rome: Lepidum Facium & Stephanum Paulinum, 1602.

Lemay, Helen Rodnite, ed. and trans. *Women's Secrets: A Translation of Pseudo-Albertus Magnus's De Secretis Mulierum with Commentaries.* Albany: State University of New York Press, 1992.

Leone, Marco Paolo. *Praxis ad litteras maioris poenitentiarii et officii Sacrae Poenitentiariae apostolicae.* Rome: Grignani, 1644.

Liber pro recta administratione protomedicatus, in quo plura notanda subjiciuntur, & offeruntur excellentissimis DD. prioribus Colllegii Medicinae, et ejus protomedicis pro tempore futuris, ut statuta praecipue. A multis summis pontificibus confirmata observentur, & secundum justitiam clare jus reddatur. Bologna: Typographia Ferroniana, 1666.

Magni, Pietro Paolo. *Discorsi di Pietro Paolo Magni piacentino intorno al sanguinar i corpi humani.* Rome: Bartolomeo Bonfadino, & Tito Diani, 1584.

Marinello, Giovanni. *Le medicine partenenti alle infermita delle donne.* Venice: Giovanni Bonadio, 1563.

Marino, Giovan Battista. "Nella sconciatura della Signora Veronica Spinola." In *La lira,* edited by Maurice Slawinski, p. 274. Turin: Edizioni RES, 2007.

Massarella, Derek, ed. *Japanese Travellers in Sixteenth-Century Europe: A Dialogue Concerning the Mission of the Japanese Ambassadors to the Roman Curia (1590).* Translated by J. F. Moran. London: Ashgate, Hakluyt Society, 2012.

Massaria, Alessandro. *Praelectiones de morbis mulierum, conceptus & partus.* Leipzig: Abraham Lamberg, 1600.

Mattioli, Pietro Andrea. *I discorsi di M. Pietro Andrea Matthioli . . . ne i sei libri di Pedacio Dioscoride Anazarbeo della materia Medicinale.* Venice: Vincenzo Valgrisi, 1563.

Mazzolini [da Prierio], Sylvestro. *Summae Sylvestrinae, quae summa summarum merito nuncupatur.* 2 Vols. Venice: Franciscum Zilettum, 1587.

Melichio, Giorgio. *Avvertimenti nelle compositioni de' Medicamenti per uso della Speciaria.* Venice: Nicolo Polo, 1596.

Menochio, Giacomo. *De arbitrariis iudicum quaestionibus & causis, libri duo.* Venice: Antonium de Franciscis, 1624.

Mercuriale, Girolamo. *De morbis muliebribus praelectiones.* Venice: Felicem Valgrisius, 1601.

——. *Praelectiones Pisanae Hieronymi Mercurialis Foroliviensis . . . tractatus primo, De hominis generatione. secundo, De Balneis Pisanis. tertio, de vino & aqua.* Venice: Giunta, 1597.

——. *Responsa et consultationes medicinales.* Vol. 1. Venice: Gioliti, 1587.

Mercurio, Scipione. *De gli errori popolari d'Italia.* Venice: Gio. Battista Ciotti, 1603.

——. *La commare o raccoglitrice dell'eccellentissimo signor Scipion Mercurio Divisa in tre libri.* Venice: Gio. Battista Ciotti, 1601.

Molisso da Sarno, Giovanni. *Accorgimento de fideli intorno la sacramentale conessione.* Naples: 1589.

Mommsen, Theodor, Paul Krueger, and Alan Watson, ed. *The Digest of Justinian.* 4 Vols. Philadelphia: University of Pennsylvania Press, 1985.

Monterenzi, Annibale. *Ad statuta tam Civilia, quam etiam Criminalia inalitae Civitatis Bononiae.* Bologna: Caesarem Salvietum, 1582.

Morigia, Paolo. *Il gioiello de christiani.* Venice: Girolamo Polo, 1586.

Ordine del s. re Protomedico, [M. Cagnatus] per li Droghieri. Rome: 1595.

Ottonelli, Domenico. *Alcuni buoni avvisi, e casi di coscienza intorno alla pericolosa Conversatione, Da proporsi a chi conversa poco medestamente.* Florence: Franceschini & Logi, 1646.

Pagani, Antonio. *La Breve somma delle essamine de confitenti, per la necessaria riforma del huomo interiore.* Venice: Giovanni Battista Somasco, 1587.

Paleotti, Gabriele. *Archiepiscopale Bononiense siue de Bononiensis Ecclesiae administratione.* Rome: Giulio Ruffinelli Burchioni and Luigi Giovanni Angelo Zanetti, 1594.

——. *Episcopale Bononensis civitatis et diocesis. Raccolte di varie cose, che in diversi tempi sono state ordinate.* Bologna: Alessandro Benacci, 1582.

Peña, Francisco. *Sacrae Rotae Decani Recollectae Decisiones.* Lyon: Petri Prost, Philippi Borde,& Laurentii Arnaud, 1648.

Perlini, Girolamo. *De morte caussa graviditatis, abortus, et partus.* Rome: Aloysii Zannetti, 1607.

Piemontese, Alessio. *La seconda parte de'secreti del reverendo donno Alessio Piemontese.* Pesaro: Bartolomeo Cesano, 1559.

Pinelli, Luca. *Del sacramento della penitenza*. Venice: Ciotti, 1604.

Porcacchi, Tommaso. *Vocabolario nuovo di M. Tomaso Porcacchi* published alongside Francesco Alunno, *Della fabbrica del mondo*. Venice: Gio. Battista Uscio, 1588.

Provisione sopra il grave abuso di quelli che senza licenza presumono medicare moderatione rinovata sopra li spetiali, e barbieri. Bologna, 1581.

Ravenna, Tommaso Tomai da. *Idea del giardino del mondo*. Venice: Domenico Imberti, 1611.

Registi di bandi, editti, notificazioni, e provvedimenti diversi relative alla citta di Roma e dello Stato Pontificio. 3 Vols. Rome: Commune di Roma, 1928–1950.

Ricettario Fiorentino. Florence: Giunti, 1574.

Rossello, Timotheo. *Della summa de'Secreti universali . . . Si per huomini, & donne, di alto ingegno, come ancora per Medici, & ogni sorte di Artefici industriosi, & a ogni persona virtuosa accommodate*. Venice: Pietro Miloco, 1619.

Ruini, Carlo. *Anatomia del cavallo, Infermita et suoi rimedi*. Venice: Fioravante Prati, 1618.

Ruscelli, Girolamo. *Vocabolario delle voci Latine dichiarate con l'Italiane*. Venice: Valerio Bonello, 1588.

Salvi, Tarduccio. *Il chirurgo, trattato breve*. Rome: Gio. Battista Robletti, 1642.

———. *Il ministro del medico, trattato breve*. Rome: G. B. Robletti, 1643.

Sansovino, Francesco. *Della materia medicinale*. Venice: Gio. Andrea Valvassori, 1561.

Savelli, Marc' Antonio. *Pratica universale . . . estratto in compendio per alfabeto dalle principali Leggi, Bandi, Statuti, Ordini, e Consuetudini, massime Criminali, e miste, che vegliano nelli Stati del Serenessimo Gran Duca di Toscana*. Florence: Giuseppe Cocchini, 1665.

Scarsella, Marco. *Giardino di sommisti nel quale si dichiarano dodicimila, e piu casi di conscienza*. Venice: Antonio Somasco, 1600.

Secreti diversi & miracolosi. Raccolti da Falopia & approbati da altri Medici di gran fama. Venice: Alessandro Gardano, 1578.

Sertorelli, Girolamo. *Barchetta di penitenza*. Venice: Marco Guarisco, 1609.

Sinodo Diocesana di Mons. Rever. Philippo Sega vescovo della Ripatransona . . . publicati i treprimi giorni di maggio. 1576. Macerata: Sebastiano Martellini, 1577.

Sixtus V. *Constitutio Contra illegitimos, legitimatos, criminosos, & reddendis rationibus obnoxios ad aliquam Religionem transire volentes, Et contra Regulares absque Superiorum licentia de Provincia in Provinciam euntes, seu transmigrantes*. Rome: Antonio Blado, 1587.

———. *Constitutio contra Incestuosos*. Rome: Antonio Blado, 1587.

———. *Contra Procurantes, consulentes, & consentientes, quocumque modo Abortum, CONSTITUTIO*. Rome: Antonio Blado, 1588.

———. *Declaratio, circa promotionem Fratrum illegitimorum ad sui ordinis dignitates, & officia*. Rome: Antonio Blado, 1588.

———. *Super temeraria tori separatione, ac publicis adulteriis, stupris et lenociniis in quibusdam casibus severius coercendis.* Rome: Antonio Blado, 1586.

Sommario di tre Bolle de Sommi Pontefici, cioe di Pio V, sopra i censi, di Sisto V sopra gl'aborti, et l'altrae de gli patti reprobati nelle Compagnie che salvano il Capitale, e in nome di guadagno, pongono certa riposta. Ancona: Francesco Salvioni, March 15, 1590.

Speroni, Sperone. *Del Tempo del Partorire delle Donne.* In *Dialogi di M. Speron. Speroni.* Venice: Comin da Trino di Monferrato, 1564.

———. *Orazione contra le cortigiane* in *Orationi del sig. Speron Speroni dottor et cavalier Padovano.* Venice: Ruberto Meietti, 1596.

———. *Opere,* vol. 5. Rome: Vecchiarelli, 1989.

Statuta Almae Urbis Roma . . . cum glossis Leandri Galganetti. Rome, 1611.

Statuta Almae Urbis Romae. Rome, 1580. Reprint, Rome, 1590.

Statuta civitatis Beneventi acthoritate Apostolica condita, & a Sixto V. Pontifice Maximo confirmata. Rome, 1603.

Statuta Concili Florentini. Florence: Giunti, 1518.

Statuta Concili Florentini. Florence: Bartholomæum Sermartellium, 1564.

Statuta Firmanorum. Fermo, 1589.

Statuta seu leges municipales magnificae terrae, et hominum Montis Rubiani. Ancona, 1574.

Statuta, sive constitutiones Civitatis Setie. Rome, 1547.

Statutorum & Reformationum magnifice ciuitatis Senigallie. Pessaro, 1537.

Statutorum Auguste Perusiae. Perugia, 1523.

Stoppelli, Pasquale. *La Mandragola: storia e filologia. Con l'edizione critica del testo secondo il Laurenziano Redi 129.* Rome: Bulzoni editore, 2005.

Synodo Dioecesana camerinensi quam illustris, et reverensissimvs Dominus Hieronymvs de Bobus . . . MDLXXXVII. die XXIIII. Mensis Septembris. Camerino: Franciscum Gioiosum, 1588.

Synodus dioecesana sub admodum ill. et reverendiss.mo Domino Philippo Sega episcopo Placentiae & Comite, Primo habita, anno do. MDLXXXIX. V. No. Maii. Piacenza: Ioannis Bazachii, 1589.

Tesauro, Antonino. *Novae decisiones sacri senatus Pedemontani.* Turin: Ioannem Dominicum, 1609.

Valverde de Amusco, Juan. *La anatomia del corpo umano.* Venice: Giunta, 1586.

Venusti, Antonio Maria. *Discorso generale di Antonio Maria Venusti: intorno alla generatione, al nascimento, de gli huomini, al breue corso della uita humana et al tempo.* Venice: Gio. Battista Somasco, 1562.

Vesalius, Andreas. *De humani corporis fabrica.* Venice: F. Franciscium and J. Criegher, 1568.

Vivio, Francesco. *Decisiones regni Neapolitani.* Venice: Damino Zenari, 1592.

Vocabolario degli accademici della crusca . . . seconda impressione. Venice: Jacopo Sarzina, 1623.

Volumen statutorum civitatis Maceratae. Macerata, 1553.

Zacchia, Paolo. *Il vitto quaresimale.* Rome: Pietro Antonio Facciotti, 1636.

——. *Quaestionum medico-legalium.* Lyon: Joannis-Antonii Huguetan and Marci-Antonii Ravaud, 1661.

Zecchi, Giovanni. *Consultationum medicinalium.* Rome: Facciottus, 1599.

Zerola, Tommaso. *Praxis sacramenti poenitentiae.* Venice: Georgium Variscum, 1599.

ACKNOWLEDGMENTS

I have been inspired by, learned from, and depended on so many people during the course of researching and writing this book. It is a pleasure to acknowledge and thank you here.

First off, this project would not have been possible without the generous support of numerous funding agencies and institutions. I am grateful for support from the Social Sciences and Humanities Research Council of Canada; graduate student grants and awards from the University of Toronto; a postdoctoral fellowship at York University; and research grants from the University of British Columbia. A glorious year at Villa I Tatti, the Harvard University Center for Italian Renaissance Studies as the Deborah Loeb Brice Fellow, provided an idyllic setting and an inspiring group of scholars that pushed me in intellectual directions I may never have taken. Thank you Alina Payne for fostering such a dynamic community and thank you Michael Rocke and your team for the incredible library and resources you make available to researchers. Of course, I am very grateful for the help and guidance offered by the staffs at the archives and libraries that I worked in.

I am grateful to Kate Lowe (series editor), and Andrew Kinney and Mihaela-Andreea Pacurar (Harvard University Press), for their enthusiasm and support for this project. HUP's reviewers' comments and suggestions were very helpful and appreciated. This book would be impoverished were it not for Lynda Guthrie, editor and critic extraordinaire—Lynda's presence is on every page, on every line of this book, and I am forever in her debt. I am grateful to Chelsea Shriver and the University of British Columbia's Rare Books and Special Collections Library, and Saint Michael's College and the Thomas Fisher Rare Book Library at the University of Toronto for providing digital copies of images that appear in this book.

Of the many, many people to whom I owe thanks, my first and most profound debt is to Elizabeth Cohen and Nick Terpstra. Libby and Nick, you have provided years of superlative mentorship, intellectual exchange, and friendship; you have constantly offered your wisdom, attention, and patience. Role models in every way, you have been vital sources of inspiration and of unyielding support. Thank you for showing the way.

Many scholars, colleagues, mentors, and friends have listened to half-baked ideas over coffee and at conferences, offered advice, shared their work and expertise, given me materials, and caught my mistakes. Thank you Victoria Addona, Sarah Amato, Monica Azzolini, Sara Beam, Alexandra Bamji, Chiara Bariviera, Andrew Berns, Christopher Black, Brad Bouley, Montserrat Cabré, Eleonora Canepari, Brendan Cook, Erin Corber, Ivano Dal Prete, Natalie Zemon Davis, Wietse de Boer, Jennifer DeSilva, Michele di Sivo, Mauricio Drelichman, Holly Flora, Irene Fosi, Diletta Gamberini, Alexis Gauvin, Allen Grieco, Tristan Grunow, Bert Hall, Julia Hairston, Tamar Herzig, Katharine Huemoeller, John Hunt, Daniel Jamison, Peter Jones, Chrisian Kleinbub, Pamela Long, Sarah Loose, Luigi Marsili, Vanessa McCarthy, Celeste McNamara, Christia Mercer, Emily Michelson, Ingrid Houssaye Michienzi, James Novoa, Natalie Oeltjen, Katharine Park, Diego Pirillo, Allyson Poska, Courtney Quaintance, Julia Rombough, Colin Rose, David Rosenthal, Nancy Siraisi, Luka Špoljarić, Sharon Strocchia, and Cristina Vasta. I am especially grateful to Renée Baernstein, Tom Cohen, Lucia Dacome, Konrad Eisenbichler, Paula Findlen, David Gentilcore, Julie Hardwick, and Natalie Rothman for reading drafts of my work at different stages, discussing its ideas, and providing invaluable critique and indispensable advice. You each deserve detailed and specific gratitude and I hope you can forgive my jumbling you all together. I am grateful for our exchanges, for your generosity, and for your labor.

This book has profited immensely from the intellectual riches provided by the University of British Columbia. I could not have asked for smarter and more generous colleagues. Thank you Chris Friedrichs, Leo Shin, Arlene Sindelar, Richard Unger, and the late Bob McDonald and Danny Vickers for offering sound advice on life and our vocation. Thank you Tim Brook, Kelly Midori McCormick, Richard Menkis, Tamara Myers, Sebastian Prange, Coll Thrush, Pheroze

Unwalla, and Jessica Wang for thought-provoking conversations and support. Thank you Janet Mui, Tuya Ochir, and Jocelyn Smith for your tireless work. Thank you to the undergraduate and graduate students I have been fortunate to have had: you have allowed me to test-run some of the ideas in this book in our classes—you have challenged me with your excellent questions and inspired me with your interest and insight.

As this project reached its final stages, I had the extraordinary gift of a manuscript workshop where colleagues helped me better articulate what this book is about and why it matters. Thank you Bob Brain for suggesting and organizing the workshop, and thank you Tim Cheek, Michel Ducharme, Joy Dixon, Chris Friedrichs, Eagle Glassheim, Jessica Hanser, Michael Lanthier, Tina Loo, Brad Miller, David Morton, Leslie Paris, John Roosa, Heidi Tworek, Richard Unger, and especially Courtney Booker, Paula Findlen, and Bill French for taking the time to read the manuscript and for helping me make it better. A very sincere thanks to Brad Miller, David Morton, and Heidi Tworek for always being available to listen to my complaints and worries and for never saying "no" when I asked "Can you read something for me?" I am grateful to all of you for your generosity, sharp critiques, and encouragement.

As a man writing a history of abortion and of women's bodies and the violent powers that were often exerted on them, I am reminded constantly of my privilege and the limitations of my experience. This awareness has been heightened and made more meaningful to me as colleagues and friends have shared their experiences of fertility, pregnancy, miscarriage, and abortion. Thank you for sharing your stories, for challenging me to think about my positionality, and for giving me an opportunity to listen and learn. I hope I have engaged with this history in a way that is both academic and empathetic.

Words cannot express my gratitude to my family. My grandparents, Panagiota and the late John Sellas; my parents, Litsa Sellas and Peter Christopoulos; and my brother Chris Christopoulos have provided unconditional love and have sacrificed more than I will ever know to support me. Thank you to Lynda and Randy Guthrie for encouragement and support. Thank you Erin Corber for helping me make perhaps the most important decision of my life and for your unflinching support ever since.

My greatest debt is to my best friend, sharpest critic, and fiercest ally, Avery Guthrie. You were there at the very beginning of this journey and you invested in it as much as I have. Thank you for your love and your patience. Thank you for challenging me, pushing and pulling me forward, and reminding me that history matters. Lastly, thank you to sweet Sam, love of my life, for always making me smile.

INDEX

abortifacient, 35, 84–87, 96, 123, 135, 180, 231. *See also* purgatives

abortion: ambiguity of, 12, 43, 52–68, 106–107, 153–154, 187, 212–229, 238–240, 253; and class/social status, 14–16, 60, 62, 97–98, 167, 172, 185–188, 202–212; as crime, 78–79, 94, 133–134, 138, 176, 178–179, 185–236; as sin, 107–171, 205–207; as therapy, 26, 91–100, 195; caused by violence, 26–27, 87–88, 91, 104–105, 123, 179–180; coerced, 15, 18, 154, 166, 182; definition of, 31–42; medical regulation of, 12–13, 49–52, 71, 77–81, 86–88; procured by clergy, 122–127, 135–138, 148, 159–168, 172–184; prosecution of, 27–31, 46–47, 103–106, 133–134, 172–188, 202–229, 236–246; punishment for, 78, 82, 183–184, 192–203, 229–233, 237–238, 246. *See also* infanticide and neonaticide; miscarriage

d'Acquapendente, Girolamo Fabrici, 54, 57

adultery, 6, 7, 19, 21, 29, 104, 118, 123, 130, 136, 192, 193, 197, 202

Aetius of Amida, 95, 96

Against those who Procure, Counsel and Consent in any way to Abortion (1588). *See* papal bulls: Sixtus V

Aldobrandini Pamphili, Olimpia, 97

Altoviti, Antonio, 121

Ambrose of Milan, 131

Amusco, Juan Valverde de, 54, 62, 71

anatomists, 38–40, 43, 54–55, 57, 62, 71, 84

Andreozza, Femia de, 44, 172–184

d'Angelo, Pellegrina, 215, 219, 230

animation, 8–11, 51, 132, 150–152, 165, 168–169, 199–201, 256. *See also* conception; pregnancy

Ansaloni, Rosana, 103–106

anticlericalism, 29, 166, 167

apothecaries, 46–49, 51, 69, 71, 74–75, 77–81, 86–88, 118, 159, 241–242. *See also* pharmacopoeia; pharmacy; purgatives

Aquinas, Thomas, 93

Aranzio, Giulio Cesare, 54

Aretino, Pietro, 35

d'Arezzo, Paolo Burali, 119, 121

Aristolochia (birthwort), 12, 69, 75–77, 80, 84–86, 99, 101, 241. *See also* pharmacy; purgatives

Augustine of Hippo, 9, 19

Avicenna (Ibn Sina), 95, 96

Azpilcueta, Martin de, 25, 33, 115, 124–126

baptism, 39, 145, 174, 200, 222

barber. *See* surgeons

Barberini, Antonio, 165

Barnaba, Sebastiano, 141

Basilico, Girolamo, 231

Bastoni, Gugliemo, 195

Battista, Aorelia di, 60, 207, 221, 230

Bello, Mattia de, 216–218

Benedictis, Antino de, 34, 172–184, 255